State and National Boundaries
of the United States

To my wife Carol,
sons Gary, Michael, and Jeffery,
and grandchildren
Melissa, Stephanie, Dorian,
Brittany, and Kelsey—
all whom I love dearly

State and National Boundaries of the United States

Gary Alden Smith

McFarland & Company, Inc., Publishers
Jefferson, North Carolina, and London

Library of Congress Cataloguing-in-Publication Data

Smith, Gary Alden, 1940–
State and national boundaries of the United States /
Gary Alden Smith.
p.   cm.
Includes bibliographical references and index.

ISBN 0-7864-1861-3 (illustrated case binding : 50# alkaline paper)

1. United States—Boundaries.
2. United States—Historical geography.
3. Boundaries, State.   4. U.S. states.   I. Title.
E179.5.S647   2004
911'.73 — dc22   2004007080

British Library cataloguing data are available

On the cover: 4 Corners, courtesy Library of Congress. Sky–Photospin ©2004

Manufactured in the United States of America

*McFarland & Company, Inc., Publishers
Box 611, Jefferson, North Carolina 28640
www.mcfarlandpub.com*

CONTENTS

Map List

PREFACE

Looking at a map of the United States, one can wonder why our state and national boundaries are such a curious collection of straight, sinuous, and jagged lines resulting in states with a wide variety of shapes and sizes. This book hopes to answer that question and many others by explaining how the boundaries came to be. Why does West Virginia have two panhandles? Why does a part of Minnesota rise above the 49th parallel? Why does Michigan have an Upper Peninsula? Why do Mississippi and Alabama have such narrow coastlines along the Gulf of Mexico? Why are states so large, and boundary lines so straight, in the land west of the Mississippi? These are among the many questions answered in this book.

We will see how international relationships between England and other countries shaped early colonial boundaries and how boundaries were affected by relationships of the United States with other nations. We will see that occasionally citizens on the frontier influenced boundaries; that Congress determined many of our state boundaries; and that in some cases the U.S. Supreme Court has resolved boundary disagreements between states. Additionally we will see instances where slavery and party politics have affected boundaries.

A boundary is an artificial, man-made line that divides the land into administrative units. They can be small, like a school or utility district, or large, like a nation. The United States is one nation of many on the globe. It is divided into states which are further divided into counties (in Alaska they are called boroughs and in Louisiana, parishes) which are further divided into a variety of smaller units. This book deals only with boundaries between states and the two national boundaries.

Chapter 1 offers an overview of the growth of the United States from Atlantic to Pacific and the establishment of some early boundaries. The remainder of the book is organized by region, with each of ten regions divided into states. Most boundaries are considered twice — once within the discussion of each state. While this arrangement results in some duplication of material, it offers the best understanding of a boundary by placing it in the context of the land on either side. The discussion of each state's boundary begins with brief general comments, followed by detailed comments on that state's boundaries with each of its neighboring states.

Historical context is important in understanding boundaries, but to keep from straying too far from the main theme, this book includes only enough historical information to provide background. The book does not go into surveying detail; the size, shape, or other features of monuments marking state and national boundaries; or extensive history of regions or states.

This text often refers to areas by state names before the areas became states; this is to assist the reader in identifying the area being discussed. So as not to encumber the text with redundancies, all references to latitude are north latitude, and all references to longitude are west of Greenwich or the District of Columbia as indicated in the text. All references to kings are to kings of England unless otherwise indicated. Distances in miles are always land miles unless otherwise noted. Instead of using the terms Revolutionary War and Civil War, the author has preferred using War for American Independence and War Between the States.

Most of the research for this book was done at the University of Oregon Knight Library. The author consulted numerous books and scholarly journals dealing principally with history and geography. The Congressional Globe (precursor of the Congressional Record) and the Serial Set (the documentation of the activities of Congress) also provided useful information. The author corresponded with staff at state libraries, state historical associations, and county historical associations and with individuals not associated with any of the above organizations. Newspaper articles also provided helpful information on boundary changes and resolution of boundary disputes.

The breadth of the subject dictated limited depth and also the reliance on secondary, rather than primary, sources. The goal was not to record minutiae, but to provide a general understanding of why boundaries are where they are. Additional detail, when the reader wants it, and when it is available, can be found in the sources cited in the bibliography. The bibliography is organized like the body of the book — into regions and states. Boundary information the author received via correspondence is not included in the bibliography.

The author especially thanks the staff of the Interlibrary Loan and Government Documents departments of the University of Oregon Knight Library for their generous assistance. This project also has been greatly enriched by the many people with whom he has corresponded.

1

INTRODUCTION

With the possible exception of oceans, boundaries are artificial, man-made divisions of geography. Many times their placement seems to make little sense and sometimes no sense at all. While boundary placement has produced some unusual configurations, it has nonetheless taken place with some basic principles in the minds of the decision makers. Boundaries in the United States are usually placed in reference to four major elements: watercourses, mountains, latitude, and longitude. River boundaries can be referenced to one of several different parts of the river. In some cases no part of a river is specified, and the watercourse is merely named. Byram Brook between New York and Connecticut is an example. A boundary can be in the middle of various parts of a watercourse, but the most common place designated for a boundary is the middle of the channel, as in the case of the Mississippi River. A river bank is another place for a boundary. For example, the New Hampshire-Vermont boundary is the west bank of the Connecticut River. A designation along a bank can be the high- or low-water line. A river can also be used as a reference. For example, a part of the Massachusetts–New Hampshire boundary is established as three miles north of the Merrimac River. The advantage of river boundaries is that they usually need no surveying. A disadvantage is that rivers don't always stay in the same place due to natural meandering and catastrophic events that alter the channel. Meandering is especially common in broad flood plains, with the Mississippi River and the lower Rio Grande being only two examples. Another disadvantage of rivers is that they tend to divide people who might have more in common with each other than with people on opposite sides of a mountain range, such as in Vermont and New Hampshire.

This book mentions middle of the river as a boundary for several different state boundaries. The context of the sources was not always clear whether middle of the channel or the physical middle of the river was the actual boundary.

Boundaries in lakes are usually along the center or deepest channel. The Great Lakes are good examples as the boundary follows the middle course of the lakes except for part of Lake Superior. Other water boundaries are made in sounds, such as the Long Island Sound, or in bays, such as the Bay of Fundy. A boundary in a bay is often referenced to certain features, such as the channel. The Maryland-Virginia boundary in the Chesapeake Bay which has an irregular course is marked by orange and white buoys. Bays are often used as harbors and are thus places of concentrated activity, making precise boundary placement important in the application of quarantine or health laws and laws pertaining to navigation, passengers, and fishing. Delaware and New Jersey have overcome these problems by allowing each state to exercise concurrent jurisdiction over the Delaware River and Bay.

Boundaries along a divide are where a boundary runs along land that separates river drainages, such as the northern boundary of Maine. A crest boundary, on the other hand, generally follows the highest parts or summits or a range of hills or mountains, such as the North Carolina–Tennessee border. A crest line is not the same as a divide, as some rivers will erode the valleys far beyond the general crest line. Both crest and divide lines are very irregular. Crest and divide lines usually form good boundaries as they are usually located far from areas of concentrated human activity.

Latitude and longitude play major parts in United States boundaries as most states have at least a part of a boundary that is either a numbered parallel of latitude or meridian of longitude or one of these lines referenced to a local geographic feature, such as the confluence of the Owyhee and Snake Rivers which was used as a reference point for part of the Oregon-Idaho border. Latitude and longitude played a prominent part in boundaries of western states as Congress did not have a good understanding of natural features of the area, so placing boundaries along artificial lines was a convenient substitute. Three states—Colorado, Utah, and Wyoming — have borders consisting entirely of latitude and longitude lines. New Mexico has only a few miles of border along the Rio Grande is not a latitude or longitude line. Numbered meridians can be based on the Greenwich Meridian, such as the California-Nevada border, or on the Washington (D.C.) Meridian, such as the Kansas-Colorado border.

Colonial Boundaries

United States boundaries have come into being through several mechanisms. The boundaries of most eastern states stem from charters, patents, and grants from English kings. All three of these documents usually defined boundaries, although often very vaguely, and established rights and privileges, including in some cases the right to form a government and to grant land. When the English kings were granting land in the New World, they had a very imperfect understanding of the geography of that area. Some of the grants referred to features that did not exist, and some grants overlapped each other.

Some of the early colonial charters were from sea to sea. Only six colonies claimed no western lands: Rhode Island, Maryland, New Hampshire, Delaware, Pennsylvania, and New Jersey. It was easy for English kings to grant land they did not own and had never seen. After 1763 the English colonies with sea-to-sea charters were limited in the west by the Mississippi River. The claim of Virginia was extensive, including the present states of Kentucky, West Virginia, Ohio, Indiana, Illinois, Michigan, Wisconsin, and part of Minnesota. In the Treaty of 1783 Britain recognized the independence of the United States with its western boundary as the Mississippi River, the northern boundary roughly where it is today, and the southern boundary at the 31st parallel from the Mississippi River to the Chattahoochee River, then down that river to its confluence with the Flint River, then east to the head of St. Marys River, and then along that river to the Atlantic Ocean.

Treaty Boundaries

International treaties established boundaries with adjacent nations. They are the Treaty of 1763, Treaty of 1783,* 1795 Pinck-

---

The names used for the treaties of 1763 and 1783 are inconsistent in the sources. To avoid confusion the two, treaty names have been simplified to their dates.

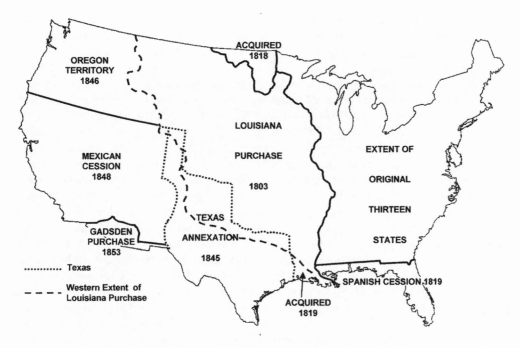

Map 1.1. Acquisitions of the United States

ney's Treaty, 1814 Treaty of Ghent, 1819 Adams-Onís Treaty, 1842 Webster-Ashburton Treaty, 1846 Oregon Treaty, and 1848 Treaty of Guadalupe Hidalgo. These treaties created international boundaries, some of which remain today as boundaries between states after the United States acquired previously foreign soil. The treaties were frequently based on faulty maps and included wording that was unclear, facts that caused conflict necessitating careful negotiations to adequately define boundaries.

Purchase Boundaries

Some boundaries have been established by purchase, for example the Louisiana Purchase, Gadsden Purchase, and Alaska Purchase. The boundaries of the Louisiana Purchase were vaguely defined but were roughly the drainage basin of the Mississippi River and its tributaries west of the Mississippi River. The Alaska Purchase and Gadsden Purchase were more carefully defined, but the working out of those definitions and placing of lines

on the ground, especially in the case of Alaska, took some time.

Growth of the U.S.

After the colonial era the new nation was not long satisfied with its vast expanse of land and acquired major chunks of new territory. In 1803 the United States bought the Louisiana Purchase from France, in 1818 it acquired a parcel north of the Louisiana Purchase, in 1819 it received Florida from Spain, in 1845 it annexed the independent Republic of Texas, in 1846 it established title to the Oregon Country, in 1848 it acquired the Mexican Cession by conquest and treaty, and in 1853 it acquired the Gadsden Purchase. (See map 1.1.) This completed the continental, conterminous states. Additional United States accretions of land that became states were the 1867 purchase of Alaska from Russia and annexation of Hawaii in 1898.

The Louisiana Purchase doubled the size of the United States. René-Robert Cavelier, Sieur de La Salle, explored the Mississippi

River in 1682 and claimed the entire drainage basin for France. In the Treaty of 1763 France ceded the land west of the river to Spain and the land east of the river to Great Britain, thus ending France's presence in North America for a while. Spain re-ceded its part of Louisiana, except for the area around New Orleans, to France in the 1800 Treaty of San Ildefonso. Part of this agreement was that France would never allow the area to fall into the hands of an English-speaking government. Napoleon, who needed cash to support his European conquests, broke the agreement and sold Louisiana to the United States in 1803 for $15 million. When asked about the boundaries of Louisiana, Charles Maurice de Talleyrand-Périgord, the French foreign minister, would say only "You have made a noble bargain for yourselves, and I suppose you will make the most of it."[*]

A question might be asked as to what claim to possession France had of the area called Louisiana? Discovering nations have generally assumed that they have the right to ownership of land they discover. France claimed the drainage of the Mississippi River by right of discovery; the United States bought this right. The United States and Great Britain reached an agreement in 1818 to extend their border from Lake of the Woods along the 49th parallel to the Rocky Mountains. This brought into U.S. possession a tract of land north of the Louisiana Purchase that was not a part of that purchase because it drains to Hudson Bay and not the Mississippi River.

The next major acquisition of land was the Floridas. The area called Florida was originally bordered on the north generally by the 31st parallel, on the east by the Atlantic Ocean, on the west by the Mississippi River, and on the south by the Gulf of Mexico. The area was initially settled by Spaniards. In 1763 it was ceded by Spain to Great Britain which created the provinces of East and West Florida. (See map 5.3.) While it still had possession of the area, Great Britain extended the boundary of West Florida to a parallel drawn from the confluence of the Yazoo and Mississippi rivers. (See map 5.3.) However, a 1782 treaty between the U.S. and Great Britain specified the 31st parallel as their boundary in West Florida. In 1783 Great Britain retroceded the Floridas to Spain. The United States and Spain disputed whether the West Florida boundary should be at the 31st parallel or the parallel from the Yazoo River. A treaty negotiated by Thomas Pinckney of the United States and Manuel de Godoy of Spain settled the boundary matter in 1795 at the 31st parallel from the Mississippi to the Chattahoochee River, down that river to its confluence with the Flint River, then east to the head of St. Marys River, and down that river to the Atlantic Ocean. This treaty is variously called Pinckney's Treaty and the Treaty of San Lorenzo. Spain ceded the Floridas to the United States in 1819. (See map 1.1.)

The Republic of Texas became a part of the United States in 1845 due to U.S. citizens, mostly from the South, settling in the area and eventually becoming dissatisfied with Mexican government. (See map 8.15.) The Texans declared their independence from Mexico in 1835 and set up an independent government the following year. At first neither the United States nor Texas was in favor of annexation. People from the northern states feared that if Texas were admitted to the Union that it would become a slave state. Sectionalism was a hot topic in Congress during the late 1830s and 1840s. In the early 1840s, when the idea of annexation gained momentum, considerable negotiation took place to determine the boundaries of Texas. Texans wanted the state boundaries to be the same as those of the Republic, but U.S. officials would not agree to those boundaries. The federal government finally got Texas to agree to its current boundaries by buying the land it finally agreed to cede.

The Oregon Country was loosely defined as north of the 42nd parallel, south of 54 degrees 40 minutes (the southern tip of the

*Edward S. Barnard, ed., Story of the Great American West (New York, 1977) p. 34.

Alaskan Panhandle), and between the Rocky Mountains and Pacific Ocean. (See map 10.12.) Spain, Russia, Great Britain, and the United States all had some claim to the area during its history. Spain relinquished its claim in a 1790 agreement with Great Britain and with the United States in 1819. Russia abandoned its claim in separate agreements with the United States and Great Britain in 1824 and 1825. These latter two countries had earlier agreed to jointly occupy the area in 1818. By the 1840s joint occupancy was not as feasible, and the boundary issue became more poignant. The United States made a tenuous claim to the entire area, and Great Britain wanted a boundary along the 49th parallel and the Columbia River. The two countries settled the boundary in the 1846 Oregon Treaty at the 49th parallel from the Rocky Mountains to the Strait of Georgia east of Vancouver Island.

The Mexican Cession resulted from a war lasting from 1846 to 1848 that began because of a dispute over whether Texas ended at the Nueces River, as the Mexicans contended, or approximately 110 miles further west at the Rio Grande, as the U.S. contended. (See map 8.15.) U.S. forces provoked a war and consistently defeated the Mexicans in battle. The war was concluded by the Treaty of Guadalupe Hidalgo which resulted in the United States gaining more than 500,000 square miles and placing the boundary along the Rio Grande and the line shown in map 1.1, excluding the Gadsden Purchase. The cession included the future states of Utah, Arizona, Nevada, and California and parts of Colorado, New Mexico, and Wyoming.

The 1853 Gadsden Purchase was necessitated because the border with Mexico negotiated in the Treaty of Guadalupe Hidalgo was based on a faulty map and the United States did not get land as far south as it had expected. The purchase was needed to provide a suitable railroad route from the east to the west coast. The purchase consisted of 29,640 square miles of mostly scrubby dessert. Mexico was willing to sell the land only because it needed the $10 million the United States paid for it.

The annexation of Hawaii and the purchase of Alaska are explained in chapter 11 and need no further comment here.

Territorial Process

After the formation of the thirteen colonies most states added to the United States came through a territorial stage. Exceptions to this rule were Vermont, Texas, and California, who all laid some claim, real or imagined, to being independent republics upon entering the Union. Hawaii was also an independent republic at one point in its history, but it went through territorial status before entering the Union. With the possible exception of Texas, none of the republics formed by Europeans were constructed with the goal of permanent independence.

Congress passed the Northwest Ordinance in 1787, a document that established the procedures for bringing new areas into the Union. Territorial governments were set up at both the initiative of Congress and frontier settlers after the population in an area became at least 5,000 free inhabitants. Often agitation existed in the frontier areas to establish a government, and the Congress simply responded. These governments established a modicum of law and order to newly acquired areas. The federal government paid for all costs of a territorial government and appointed its officials except for a popularly elected legislature. After a territory met the population minimum of 60,000 free inhabitants, sometimes less, it became eligible for statehood. Whether or not an eligible area might enter the Union depended on national politics often surrounding the slavery issue and the tug of war between Democrats and Republicans because each party did not want to admit states which might send congressmen of the opposite party to the national capital. Another factor affecting statehood was that when an area entered the Union it assumed the responsibility for paying its own officials and other costs of governing itself. Territorial officials frequently did not want to levy taxes to enable them to assume these costs. The upside of statehood, however, was that a state operated under its own constitution and had the right to elect and appoint its own officials.

Territories were temporary governments, and their area was often reduced in size, sometimes by the creation of a new territory and sometimes by the creation of a state. A few territories, Montana, Wyoming, and Colorado being examples, entered the Union with the same boundaries they had as territories. No definite time period existed for territorial status; Minnesota was a territory for only nine years, whereas Dakota was a territory for twenty-eight years.

The U.S. Congress had the sole authority to determine territorial boundaries, and it did this without having a lot of information about the terrain it was partitioning. Once an area became a state Congress could no longer alter its boundaries unless it had the state's consent. A boundary question between a territory and a state was negotiated by the state and Congress. Boundaries between states are arbitrated by the U.S. Supreme Court, which has the final say. Two states can agree to adjust a boundary between them, but only with the consent of Congress. A few states have received sizeable chunks of land after becoming states: Ohio received the Toledo Strip, Nevada received land in the east and south, and Missouri received a triangle of land in its northwest.

Surveying

There are no lines on the ground to denote boundaries until someone marks them, and this is the domain of surveyors and their crews. Colonial-era surveyors had very rudimentary training, usually an apprenticeship under an experienced surveyor, and had little understanding of math and crude instruments. The Jacob's staff was commonly used for early surveys. This was a compass mounted on a one-legged staff that could be tilted as necessary to balance the compass needle.

Sightings were made through thin wires mounted in dual forks. Surveyors used astrolabes for measuring celestial angles. Circumferentors were used for measuring vertical and horizontal angles. Handbooks supplied relevant geometrical and astronomical information. Land measuring was done with 66-foot chains consisting of 100 links with every tenth link being specially marked.

As time marched on, the education of surveyors became more sophisticated, and the quality and variety of instruments became much more refined with such instruments as the transit, better theodolites, and much more accurate compasses coming into use. The magnetic compass and chain were mainstays throughout the 17th, 18th, and 19th centuries when most state boundaries were being surveyed and marked. Steel measuring tapes were not used until around 1900.

Documents often are very clear as to where a boundary is to be located, as on a parallel or meridian for example, but determining where that line is on the ground is difficult. Surveyors calculated latitude by measuring the angle from the horizon of a specific star and calculating the observer's position from values in published tables. They determined longitude by measuring the time needed for Earth to rotate from Greenwich, England (or Washington, D.C., in some cases) to the observer's position — one hour equals 15 minutes of longitude. The need for accurate time was paramount for this calculation, and this was enhanced by the availability of the telegraph after the East and West Coasts were connected by telegraph lines in October 1861. Before the telegraph, chronometers were used but were unreliable especially after the rigors encountered in inclement weather and the rough use associated with a survey expedition. Before chronometers, longitude was determined by making lunar observations and their angular distance from specific stars and comparing this figure with published tables. The possibility for discrepancies is apparent in determining both latitude and longitude, and this accounts for many of the deviations of

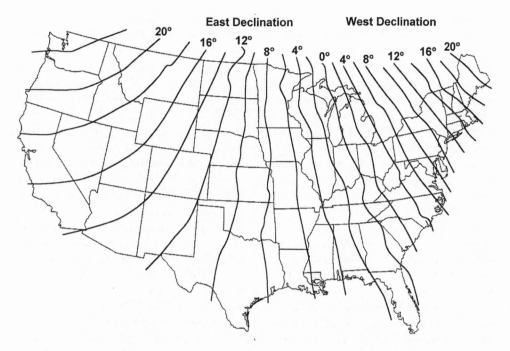

Map 1.2. Compass Deviation from Magnetic North. (In the western United States, the declination is east of true north; in the east, the declination is west of true north.)

boundaries from what they were meant to be and also for the fact that most boundary lines are not straight. Discrepancies could occur due to faulty equipment, faulty techniques, and even inaccurate tables.

Surveys using the compass caused many boundary inaccuracies. The compass needle was affected slightly by such things as daily, annual, and lunar variations and even by variations due to magnetic storms and static electricity in the compass glass. These, however, were minor compared to variation of the needle due to local deposits of iron ore that could greatly affect the needle. Another major problem stemming from compass use was due to the surveyor not knowing or not calculating properly the deviation of true north from magnetic north. (See map 1.2.) As the map indicates, this variation changes as one moves across the United States. For early surveys the deviation from magnetic north was not known at all for North America.

The use of the chain for measuring distances was another source of inaccuracies.

The links in a chain would become worn over time from being dragged along rough ground. Some surveyors kept an unused chain with which to compare chains in use to ensure accuracy, but this was not always done. Another problem with chains was that their proper use meant that the chain should be kept horizontal when making a measurement. Some surveyors did not do this when making measurements along slopes, thus inducing inaccuracies that would be increased with steeper hills. Some surveyors used 33-foot half-chains in rugged terrain to assist in making accurate measurements.

Another problem was calculating a distance across a chasm, river, or lake. This had to be done using mathematical means, and not all surveyors, especially the early ones, were skilled in mathematics.

It must also be kept in mind that surveys were often done under very demanding conditions. Steep mountains, deep ravines, thick forests, extreme cold and heat, rain, snow, fog, clouds, downed logs, brush, thickets, swamps, rivers, lakes, snakes, mosquitoes, ticks, horseflies, bees, chiggers, and vermin of all types that would test the patience of the most careful surveyor and wreak havoc with the accuracy of instruments and the legibility of field notes and astronomical tables. Surveying parties, which were sometimes quite large, could consist of any number of several workers from the following list: astronomer, engineer, axeman, transit man, topographer, barometrician, clerk, chainman, flagman, teamster, guide, hunter, packer, and cook.

Native Americans often resented the intrusion of surveying parties, whose purpose was unknown to them, and could be very hostile; consequently, a few survey crews were accompanied by military escort. Protection was frequently not available, and surveyors worked with haste due to fear of Indians. To add to surveying sloppiness, crews were often paid by the mile, so distance was frequently more important than accuracy.

Some boundary lines were marked with cut stones a few feet high with the name of the states indicated on the proper sides. But often boundaries were marked with less-enduring marks such as mounds of dirt or stones, sometimes with a wooden pole protruding from the top, or blaze marks on trees. The reader can readily recognize how ephemeral some of the boundary markings were as fire, heavy rains, and floods could easily and quickly obliterate the markings. Boundary markings were usually placed every mile or every five miles. Frequently, when a crew went to the field to continue a survey a few years later, they could not find the marks left by the previous crew and would simply have to begin at a place they figured was close to where the previous crew ended their work. To indicate just how indefinite some descriptions could be, one of the important state boundary references in the Cumberland Gap refers to "seven pines and two black oaks."

When we think of longitude we usually think of degrees west or east of the Greenwich Meridian in England. In 1850, however, the U.S. Congress passed an act that provided that a meridian passing through the dome of

the old Naval Observatory in Washington, D.C., would be the 0 meridian for the United States. When a meridian west of Washington is mentioned in this book, this is the reference point. The Washington Meridian was first used to denote the western boundary of Kansas but was later used also in the boundary definitions of the territories and states of Arizona, Colorado, Dakota, Idaho, Montana, Nevada, and Wyoming and the states of Nebraska, New Mexico, and Utah. The 0 Washington Meridian is 77 degrees 3 minutes 2.3 seconds west of Greenwich. By adding 77 to any longitude reference west of Washington one can get the approximate longitude west of Greenwich. Thus, the 102nd meridian west of Greenwich is close to the 25th meridian west of Washington, with the latter being slightly further west. The 3 minutes 2.3 seconds difference amounts to 2.3 miles difference in northern Montana and 3 miles in southern New Mexico. Congress repealed the act establishing the Washington Meridian in 1912.

The text mentions many "jogs" in state boundaries, but many more exist that are not mentioned that show up only on detailed maps. Most jogs are due to surveyors realizing they are no longer on the intended line, and not wanting to resurvey what they have already done, they simply move to what they deem the correct line and continue from there. Some jogs are due to surveyors beginning at a point with the intention of joining up with a previously surveyed line. Then when they encounter the existing line, they discover an adjustment is necessary to join the lines. Other causes of jogs are mentioned in the text.

Supreme Court Rulings

Knowing a few basic rulings of the U.S. Supreme Court will help in understanding boundary placement. The court has consistently ruled that it will not alter a boundary if "long acquiescence" by a state in its placement can be determined. The court in

Louisiana v. *Mississippi*, 202 U.S. 1, 53 (1906), stated,

> The question is one of boundary, and this court has many times held that, as between the states of the Union, long acquiescence in the assertion of a particular boundary and the exercise of dominion and sovereignty over the territory within it should be accepted as conclusive.

This case cites other examples in which the rule is stated. This is the ruling even when plaintiffs can demonstrate conclusively that a boundary was placed incorrectly. It is really a commonsensical ruling because altering a state boundary also affects the boundaries of counties; cities, in some cases; voting precincts; civil and criminal jurisdictions; and school, election, land, and water districts. The ripple effect of changing a state boundary is considerable, as is the potential for litigation.

The court has also ruled in *Iowa* v. *Illinois*, 147 U.S. 1 (1893), that for navigable rivers such as the Mississippi River any references to middle of the river means the middle of the main channel of the river. This is a much different understanding than a mathematical middle because the main channel can wander from side to side throughout the course of a river.

The court has also been consistent in ruling that sudden changes in river courses (avulsion) do not alter boundaries, but that gradual changes in the course of a river (accretion) do alter boundaries. The court stated in *Oklahoma* v. *Texas*, 260 U.S. 606 (1923),

> It is settled beyond the possibility of dispute that, where running streams are the boundaries between states, the same rule applies as between private proprietors, namely, that when the bed and channel are changed by the natural and gradual processes known as erosion and accretion, the boundary follows the varying course of the stream; while if the stream from any cause, natural or artificial, suddenly leaves its old bed and forms a new one, by the process known as an avulsion, the resulting change of channel works no change of boundary, which remains in the middle of the old channel.

Some meandering rivers are the Mississippi, Missouri, Sabine, Red, and Rio Grande. Any changes in the course of a river that are man made do not alter a boundary. Although the law is clear on the distinction of avulsion and accretion, distinguishing between the two in practice is not always easy.

Some exceptions are made to the accretion and avulsion rule. In *Ohio* v. *Kentucky*, 444 U.S. 335 (1980), the court ruled that the general rule did not apply in a case between these two states because it was the north bank of the river and not the river itself that was named as the boundary between them. The applicable comment from that case: "The Court suggests that the Ohio-Kentucky boundary should not be determined by reference to previous river boundary decisions because the border in this case is not 'the river itself, but … its northerly bank.'"

Native Americans

Humans have been in North America for at least 10,000 to 12,000 years, possibly longer. They are usually called "Indians" because early Europeans thought they had reached India when they landed in the New World, and the natives would therefore be Indians. Natives do not figure directly in the formation of most U.S. boundaries. There are a few exceptions, such as in the Arkansas-Oklahoma border where the boundary of Indian lands became a boundary between states. The author feels, however, that Native Americans figure into this study in the sense that they occupied the land and had to be dealt with by the Europeans before settlement could occur and boundaries could be drawn.

The major European presences in the New World were by the Spanish, French, Dutch, and English, and they each dealt with the natives differently. All wanted to Christianize them because the newcomers considered the natives heathens based on their apparent backward lifestyle and the fact that they were not Christian. The Spanish, who treated the natives very harshly, also wanted to change native culture to be more Europeanlike. The Spanish used the natives essentially as settlers by requiring them to do the work of maintaining the Spanish presence in the New World. The French treated the Indians a lot better than other nations and had the least impact on native culture. With the exception of Christianization, the French treated the Indians as allies and accepted them as they were. Nonetheless, the French did enslave some Indians in the southern portion of the United States. The English and Dutch tried to change the culture of the Indians in their Christianizing efforts but were not dependent upon them to do the menial work of establishing settlements and extracting a living from the land as was the case of the Spaniards. The English and Dutch also expected the Indians to conform to European law, unlike the French who did not.

All of the newcomers depended on the natives as a workforce in the sense that the Indians were the principle source of furs that were an integral part of the English-Dutch-French colonial economy because the furs were in demand in Europe. The natives came to be dependent upon the Europeans for guns, shot, powder, pots, pans, blankets, and many other items introduced by the newcomers.

When the term "Native Americans" or "Indians" is used, it often implies a sameness. In fact the variety of the natives was extensive. A full range of body types was evident as well as skin color, with some being light and others being dark, and they spoke hundreds of different languages. Some lived a very nomadic lifestyle, moving from place to place as the seasons changed in search of new food and firewood sources. Some lived in well-established, year-round communities with an agricultural economy supplemented by the meat brought in by hunting parties. Some groups had complex social, economic, religious, and political institutions, and some had very few formal tribal institutions and little organization. Some were very aggressive and warlike; others thought fight-

ing was anathema and were docile and gentle people. Some were bound into large confederations, such as the Iroquois, and some lived as discrete bands with little interaction with other groups.

Natives did not see themselves as a single people any more than the Europeans saw themselves as a homogeneous people. They saw themselves as Choctaws or Sioux and frequently didn't have any more use for other natives than they did for Europeans. In fact the natives often aligned themselves with the Europeans to fight their traditional enemies. Some Indian groups enslaved other Indians.

Many Europeans were conscientious about paying the natives for land; others had no uneasiness about displacing natives and taking their land. Many Europeans considered the Indians heathens, and since the natives used their land mostly for hunting, fishing, and food gathering, the newcomers figured the natives didn't utilize the land properly and therefore had no right to it. Other Europeans took Indian land feeling they had already compensated them by giving them Christianity and civilization and could therefore take the land with impunity.

When Indians sold land to the Europeans, they had a very different idea in mind than did those who were buying the land. Natives did not have a concept of exclusive personal land use. Land was an area all members of a group could use; no one person "owned" any land. The community of natives had use of it only so long as they could defend it and keep other groups out. Much movement of native communities occurred because one group would displace another. When natives sold land to Europeans, the natives thought they were simply giving the newcomers the right to jointly use the land. Many native groups sold land to the newcomers because they wanted to make friends and have good relations with them. One reason for having good relations with the Europeans was to avoid conflict; another was the fact that natives came to rely on European goods.

Natives were sometimes given rum or

whiskey in an effort to convince them to sell their land. Land speculators or traders would get the Indians drunk and then, when the natives' inhibitions were lowered, the Europeans would frequently get them to agree to give up or sell their land. The whiskey used in trading with Indians was devastating in its effects and simple in its manufacture. Two authors spoke of it this way:

> Particularly disastrous to the Indian was the trader's "firewater" for which they had as little tolerance as they did to the diseases brought by whites. And trade whiskey was far worse than the liquors consumed by most whites. The trader's basic recipe called for one gallon of grain alcohol, three gallons of water, and a pound of chewing tobacco. To this might be added a variety of other ingredients such as red pepper, ginger, and black molasses, depending on their availability.*

The U.S. government in its treaties frequently included a provision that involved payment for land taken. Sometimes this was in the form of other land to which the Indians would be moved and sometimes in material goods or foodstuffs. The goods and foods did not always get to the Indians because agents would appropriate the goods for themselves for resale. Sometimes the goods the natives received would be defective or poorly manufactured or spoiled.

Europeans gave some items that the Indians did not need — such as disease. Diseases introduced unknowingly by Europeans killed thousands of natives who had no natural immunity to them. Sometimes entire communities were killed, and often without the victims ever having seen a European. Smallpox was the big killer, but other deadly diseases were measles, malaria, typhus, and influenza. Stories exist of whites purposefully infecting blankets given to Indians with smallpox.

King George III issued a proclamation in 1763 setting a boundary generally along the Allegheny Mountains in an attempt to limit the westward expansion of the colonies and lessen the impact of the newcomers on native residents. This didn't work, as settlement soon expanded beyond the mountains. After American independence the U.S. government tried to deal with the natives by negotiating treaties with them and resettling them continually westward, trying to keep them away from the advancing Americans. This didn't work either, and the history of this country is one of encroachment by white settlers, conflict with the natives, negotiation between the Indians and the federal government, and a resettlement of the natives into another area. This process always favored the whites over the natives. The federal government broke one treaty after another in its dealings with the natives.

---

*James C. Olson and Ronald C. Naugle, History of Nebraska (Lincoln: University of Nebraska Press, 1997), p. 49.

2

NEW ENGLAND REGION

Map is not to scale; boundaries are roughly drawn.

Connecticut

With the blessing of Massachusetts Bay, Puritans left that colony for Connecticut in 1634. This was not easily granted because the Puritans liked to keep their people near one another and under close scrutiny. The Connecticut settlers did not receive a charter until King Charles II granted one in 1662. That charter loosely defined the colony's boundaries as the Narragansett Bay on the east, the Atlantic Ocean on the south, the South Sea (Pacific Ocean) on the west, and Massachusetts Bay on the north. (See map 2.1.)

Map 2.2. Connecticut

We now know Connecticut as the third smallest state, behind Rhode Island and Delaware, but its earliest history was one of trying to become larger than it is now and of having a fear of being reduced in size. In an attempt to become larger it tried unsuccessfully to extend its eastern boundary to Narragansett Bay as stipulated in its charter. The boundary issues with Rhode Island took 65 years to resolve. The boundary problems with Massachusetts, which went on for 185 years, did not affect large amounts of land as did the east and west boundaries. Connecticut's most serious, and potentially most damaging, boundary issue was with New York, a struggle that went on for 200 years.

With New York. Two years after receiving its charter Connecticut was contending with New York concerning their common border. The Duke of York's 1664 charter, issued by his brother Charles II, gave him a grant of land extending from the Delaware River to the Connecticut River. (See map 3.1.) Since Connecticut claimed and had settled land nearly to the Hudson River (map 2.2), this created considerable disagreement between New York and Connecticut. New York Governor Richard Nicolls and his fellow

commissioners acknowledged Connecticut's right to land west of the Connecticut River in 1667 without defining a boundary. Connecticut encroached further on what New York considered its territory, and in May 1675, New York governor Edmund Andros demanded that Connecticut give up all claim to land west of the Connecticut River. Two months later he appeared in the town of Saybrook to reinforce his claim, but a show of force by the Connecticut militia convinced him to back down. By 1683 the two colonies had worked out an agreement that placed Connecticut's western border approximately 20 miles east of the Hudson River. This might have worked out satisfactorily except that Connecticut had already granted lands that fell within this 20-mile area. Part of this protruding area was the former colony of New Haven that combined with Connecticut in 1665. This is the somewhat rectangular extension in southwest Connecticut as seen in map 2.2.

The negotiated boundary with New York begins at the mouth of Byram Brook (or river), a very small stream entering the Atlantic Ocean, and proceeds upstream to the "wading place," then 8 miles northwest, then 12 miles northeast paralleling Long

Island Sound, then turning northwest again to a point where it is approximately 20 miles east of the Hudson River, then roughly paralleling that river to the Massachusetts border. Since the southwest corner of Connecticut (the former New Haven Colony) was closer to the Hudson River than 20 miles, New York received an equivalent tract of land often called the Oblong (shown in map 3.12), in 1731. This moved the border 1¾ miles to the east beginning at the Massachusetts border and continuing down that line and the first turn to the southeast ending 8 miles from Long Island Sound, where the border turns sharply to the southwest. The Oblong consists of 61,440 acres.

For many years the boundary and the jurisdiction of the Oblong were unclear; consequently, it was a haven for those eluding sheriffs and tax gatherers, establishing a need by both colonies to officially fix the boundary. Surveyors in 1725–1731 had trouble with their magnetic compasses due to mineral deposits in the area, so their line was not straight. Connecticut lobbied for a straight line in 1855, a line that would have given them an additional 2,800 acres. New York, however, found the 100-year-old markers and argued that they should be the official boundary. The line was finally settled in 1881 in New York's favor, thus making the line that had been finished in 1731 the official boundary. At this same time Connecticut was allowed to extend its southern boundary into Long Island Sound.

Long Island is another area New York and Connecticut squabbled over. In 1635 Charles I granted a patent to William Alexander Stirling for Long Island. The inhabitants of the island were Dutch in the western part and English in the center and east. The English towns sought, and received, jurisdiction under Connecticut. By 1664 Connecticut claimed all of the island partly because the towns sought Connecticut jurisdiction and because the 1662 Connecticut charter included all islands and a good deal of Long Island is directly offshore from Connecticut. (See map 2.2.)

When Stirling died, his grant went to men from the towns of New Haven and Saybrook, none of whom ever bothered to pay off the mortgage to establish ownership. Saybrook and New Haven later united with Connecticut. Connecticut eventually lost the island because the Duke of York bought the patent for the island from Stirling's heirs, and that charter granted him the island. The fact that the duke was the brother of the king didn't harm his case either.

Fishers Island in Long Island Sound is another strange story. This island lies 2½ miles from the southeastern Connecticut shore and seemingly would belong to that state due to its charter provision including offshore islands. In fact, Connecticut apparently had control of the island until near the end of the War for American Independence. At that time New York began to assume control of the island based on the interpretation of the Duke of York's 1664 charter, the same interpretation that gave New York control of eastern Long Island. A joint New York–Connecticut committee met in 1878–79 to resolve the ownership of the island. While maintaining their right to possession of the island, Connecticut reluctantly ceded all claims in 1880 acknowledging that New York should have the title since it had actual possession of the island for about a century.

With Massachusetts. Connecticut's boundary with Massachusetts is based on the 1629 Massachusetts charter specifying its southern boundary as 3 miles south of the most southern part of the Charles River. (See map 2.8 later in this chapter.) Massachusetts had this line surveyed in 1642 by Nathaniel Woodward and Solomon Saffery, two men of questionable surveying skills. They determined the point that was 3 miles south of the Charles River. Then, instead of surveying west, they boarded a ship and sailed around Cape Cod and up the Connecticut River to a point they thought was on the same parallel as the point they had determined to be 3 miles south of the Charles River. They were in error, as the point they selected on the

Connecticut River was 7 to 8 miles too far to the south, thus cutting into land that was rightfully Connecticut's. Massachusetts established at least four towns in this area — Suffield, Enfield, Somers, and Woodstock.

Connecticut suspected the line was in error and ordered a survey run in 1695 to determine a true east-west line from the point Woodward and Saffery earlier determined as 3 miles south of the Charles River. This survey confirmed the suspicions of Connecticut that the Woodward-Saffery survey was inaccurate. In 1702 representatives of both colonies made additional surveys further demonstrating that the 1642 line was too far south. Massachusetts maintained that even if the line was not according to its charter, it was still valid as it had been made before Connecticut's charter was granted in 1662. Massachusetts did not prevail in its argument, and the line as re-run in 1695 was ultimately accepted as the true boundary in 1713 but not finally resolved until 1826. Unfortunately, it is not an accurate east-west line either. The point where this line meets the New York boundary is about 2 miles north of the point where it meets the Rhode Island boundary. The reason for this error is most likely due to errors in reading the compass, local magnetic interference, or error in determining proper deviation of the compass from true north (as shown in map 1.2). Part of the dispute was created because the towns of Suffield, Enfield, Somers, and Woodstock, in the contested area, wanted to be under the aegis of Connecticut because that colony had lower taxes than Massachusetts.

The Connecticut-Massachusetts line has a southerly deflection just east of the Connecticut River where the Massachusetts town of Longmeadow juts into Connecticut. This irregularity dates from the 1600s when the towns of Enfield and Longmeadow were both part of Massachusetts. Part of the bound-

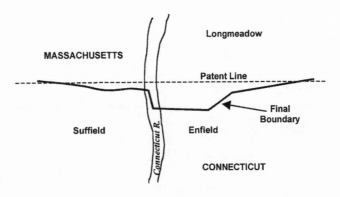

Map 2.3. Suffield and Enfield

ary between the two towns was apparently the Longmeadow River. When Enfield became a part of Connecticut, no effort was made by either Enfield or Connecticut to correct the line. The accepted boundary line between the towns thus became the boundary between the Connecticut and Massachusetts for about 3 miles. (See map 2.3.) The current line does not follow the present course of the river, but rather the approximate course where the river was when it was a boundary between the two towns when originally established.

Immediately west of the Connecticut River is a another small deflection in the line. It can be seen on map 2.3 that part of the boundary of the town of Suffield is below the patent line. This deflection can be explained by the boundary of the town becoming a state boundary, just as in the case of Enfield and Longmeadow.

A larger protrusion below the patent line further west of the Connecticut River is called the Southwick Jog. The Massachusetts town of Southwick had been settled before the boundary between the colonies had been determined. When the boundary was defined, Southwick protruded into Connecticut. In the 1790s commissioners from both states met to determine the line from the Connecticut River to the New York border. They decided the Southwick Jog should be given to Massachusetts in compensation for towns Connecticut held that Massachusetts protested. Connecticut officials, of course, adamantly

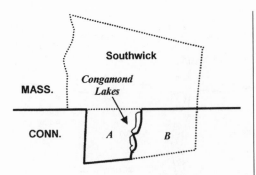

Map 2.4. Southwick Jog

disagreed with the commissioners' determination, but in 1804 the states reached a compromise. The disputed area was nearly bisected by the Congamond Lakes. The compromise was for Massachusetts to get the western part ("A" on map 2.4) and Connecticut the eastern part ("B" on map 2.4), about three-eighths of the total area. Congress approved the boundary in 1914.

With Rhode Island. Connecticut's eastern boundary with Rhode Island also created a bitter dispute. Connecticut was settled by strict Puritans from Massachusetts Bay. Rhode Island was settled by people who were very religious but did not adhere to conventional Puritan principles and had been banished from Massachusetts Bay. This established the initial point of Connecticut's contention with Rhode Island, a contention shared by Massachusetts Bay and Plymouth. Connecticut had also participated with Massachusetts in conquering Indians west of Narragansett Bay and felt that gave them rights to the area. Another point was the fact that Connecticut's 1662 charter gave them the land as far east as Narragansett Bay and Narrangansett River. Roger Williams had received a patent for land in 1644, but it was defined on the west only vaguely as bordering on the land of the Narragansett Indians. This was generally understood, however, to be the Pawcatuck River. (See map 2.5.)

Connecticut obtained its 1662 charter before Rhode Island realized this was happening. When the Rhode Island agent in

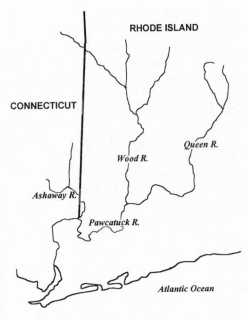

Map 2.5. Pawcatuck and Ashaway Rivers

London got wind of it, he was able to get the charter recalled and then negotiated successfully with the Connecticut agent to define Narragansett Bay as the Pawcatuck River. Thus Rhode Island was able to maintain its western boundary as what it interpreted its charter to be. Connecticut officials, however, maintained that their London agent's official status ended after he obtained the charter, and he therefore had no authority to subsequently negotiate with the Rhode Island agent. Connecticut officials refused to accept the agreement the two agents had made.

A royal commission went to New England to consider several problems, the Connecticut–Rhode Island border being one of them. The British Board of Trade, disgusted with both areas, had recommended that both colonies lose their charters and be annexed to New Hampshire, a shocking suggestion that prodded both colonies to resolve their differences. Connecticut feared its intransigence in the border matter might cause an unwanted reexamination of its entire charter and so in 1664 entered into negotiations with Rhode Island to settle the issue. Negotiations continued sporadically until agreement was finally reached in 1703 to accept a boundary up the middle of the Pawcatuck River to the confluence with the Ashaway River, then to a point 20 miles due west of Warwick Neck on Narragansett Bay, then on to the Massachusetts border, making a slight deflection to the west. (See map 2.10 later in this chapter.) If Connecticut had been able to enforce its claim to Narragansett Bay, Rhode Island would have been reduced to almost nothing.

The original 1663 agreement between the agents placed the boundary in the Pawcatuck River to its source and then north to the Massachusetts border. This agreement would have deprived Rhode Island of a strip of land several miles wide, depending on which feeder stream had been considered the head of the Pawcatuck River. (See map 2.5.)

A question arises as to why the northern borders of Connecticut and Rhode Island do not share a common straight line with Massachusetts since the southern boundary of Massachusetts is supposed to be a line drawn from 3 miles south of the Charles River. The best answer seems to be that Connecticut fought hard to get its line with Massachusetts adjusted, and Rhode Island was content to let matters stand as they were, since both colonies had made grants along the border. The northeast corner of Rhode Island's boundary is very close to a parallel 3 miles south of the Charles River. The fact that it isn't at the western end of the line may simply be due to improper determination of deviation of the compass from true north or perhaps due to local conditions affecting a compass reading. The northern Rhode Island border might also be the original line surveyed by Woodward and Saffery.

And New Haven. Ultra conservative Puritans bought land from the Indians on the north side of Long Island Sound, Long Island, and near the Delaware River. These settlers ultimately established villages on the north side of the sound and on Long Island beginning in 1638, although they never had a royal charter defining boundaries or author-

ity to establish a government. They fiercely maintained independence from all nearby jurisdictions, but by the summer of 1664 New Haven's treasury was nearly bankrupt, and with the salaries of officers reduced, it had great difficulty in finding people willing to hold colonial offices.

Some officials suggested moving away from English jurisdiction altogether and joining with the Dutch in New Netherland (New York). When the Duke of York took over New Netherland, this was no longer a viable option. New Haven had to do something, however, and as offensive as union with the liberal Congregationalists of Connecticut was, union with the Anglicans of New York was even worse. Consequently, in 1664 New Haven undertook negotiations with Connecticut to join with them. Connecticut had previously offered New Haveners autonomy for their churches, considerable religious freedom, and political representation if New Haven would unite with Connecticut. By January 1665 the union had been accomplished, although about 100 families eventually left and settled in New Jersey. The former New Haven area is in the extreme southwest part of Connecticut. (See map 2.2.)

With Atlantic Ocean. Most of Connecticut's southern boundary is in Long Island Sound and Block Island Sound. Only the extreme southeastern part abuts the Atlantic Ocean. The U.S. Geological Survey says that, generally speaking, the individual states recognize an offshore boundary of 3 nautical miles. The United States territorial sea limit contiguous zone has been set at 12 nautical miles but is expected to be extended to 24 nautical miles. The exclusive economic zone boundary is 200 nautical miles. (A nautical mile equals 1.15 land miles.)

Maine

Maine was originally included in the grants for both Plymouth and Massachusetts Bay Colonies. Then in 1622 it was included in a grant to Ferdinando Gorges and John Mason for land between the Merrimack and Kennebec Rivers. This grant was divided in 1629 at the Piscataqua River with Mason taking the southwestern part that he named New Hampshire and Gorges retaining the northeastern part which became Maine.

In 1652 seven Maine towns voted to unite with Massachusetts. Maine was restored to the original grant holder by royal order in 1664. In 1677 Massachusetts bought Maine outright from the heirs of the holder of the original grant. The Massachusetts charter of 1691 included Maine as part of its jurisdiction. From then until 1820, Maine was a part of Massachusetts. The two areas were very diverse; Massachusetts was an economically rich and sophisticated colony whose citizens were interested in Maine only for land speculation and other opportunities to make money. Maine was populated by people who were neither rich nor sophisticated and who wanted to settle there to farm the land and to log the forests.

Since the two areas were separated culturally, economically, and physically, political separation soon became an issue. Although some sentiment for separation from Massachusetts existed in Maine in the early eighteenth century, agitation for independence began most prominently during the War for American Independence. It became more acute during the War of 1812 when Maine officials realized that Massachusetts would quickly sacrifice Maine's interests to save or serve its own. Debate was hot as contending parties argued their respective sides. Shippers and merchants in Maine especially did not want separation from Massachusetts because they thought it would retard trade and thus their profits. Nonetheless, separation seemed inevitable. First of all, the two areas were divided by New Hampshire so thus were not contiguous.

Furthermore, some officials in Massachusetts feared that the growing population of Maine, which is four times the area of Massachusetts, would soon have too great a voice in the Massachusetts legislature. Massachusetts was predominantly Federalist, and Maine was predominantly Democratic-Republican. The Federalists feared the Democratic-Republicans would gain the upper hand in the legislative assembly. The Bay Colony citizens feared their political, literary, and religious institutions were in danger from the northern rustics.

As is usually the case, not everyone in either area was in favor of separation. Nonetheless, Maine voted overwhelmingly for separation in 1819; a convention wrote a constitution, and Maine was admitted to the Union as a separate state in 1820.

With Canada. The Treaty of 1783 ended the War for American Independence and defined the boundaries between Britain and the United States in the northeast. With regard to Maine, this treaty defined the boundary as north from the mouth of the St. Croix River, then to the highlands, along those highlands which divide the rivers that drain into the St. Lawrence from those that drain into the Atlantic Ocean, and then to the most northwestern head of the Connecticut River.

After the Treaty of 1783 Britain and the United States maintained an uneasy peace that eventually broke out in the War of 1812. After this conflict, a troubled peace was again maintained that came close to armed conflict a number of times over boundary issues. The need for both sides to solve the northeast boundary issue was paramount.

The seemingly workable boundary definition of 1783 was written by men whose knowledge of the area was minimal and based on unreliable and inaccurate maps and surveys; it posed a number of major problems. One was that no one river existed in North America that was named the St. Croix; several rivers were apparently known by that name. Another problem was the meaning of the term "highlands." Did it mean mountains, or merely a watershed? Another problem was that the location of the northwestern head of the Connecticut River was not firmly established.

Delegates from England and the United

States met in Paris and proposed two rivers as candidates for matching the description of the St. Croix. With biases obviously aimed at establishing control over the most land, the British favored the most western called the Schoodic, while the Americans favored the most eastern called the Magaguadavic, which was about 20 miles to the east. A commission of U.S. and British delegates in 1796 officially proclaimed the Schoodic as meeting the boundary description. They were influenced by comparing maps made by Frenchman Samuel de Champlain in the early 1600s with maps their own surveyors had made.

The problem of the definition and location of the highlands was one that would not be finally resolved until the Webster-Ashburton Treaty in 1842. In the meantime, settlers from both countries settled in the disputed area, and troops and militia postured without armed conflict being waged. The Americans drew a boundary line well to the north, whereas the British drew a line well to

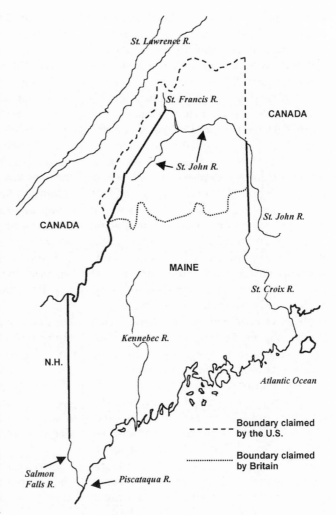

Map 2.6. Disputed Maine Boundaries

the south. The contested area consisted of about 12,000 square miles. (See map 2.6.) This conflict came to a head in the so-called Aroostook War in 1839. It was not much of a war, as the troops fired no shots and spilled no blood. However, it did consist of a lot of flag waving, finger pointing, parading, and posturing by both countries.

The two nations tried several times before 1842 to settle the border issue, but without success. They agreed to an arbitrator to settle the matter in 1831, and the king of the Netherlands accepted the challenge to determine the boundary. Each of the participants submitted their version of the boundary, the

king was to decide which of the two best matched the 1783 treaty. Instead, the king felt that neither version matched the treaty, and he drew a third line that nearly split the difference of the contested area. His resolution would have given a little more than half of the disputed 12,000 square miles to the United States.

U.S. officials, including President Andrew Jackson, privately would have accepted this plan, even Great Britain was reported willing to accept it. Maine and Massachusetts (Massachusetts still had financial interests in Maine), however, were incensed and would not hear of it. Officially both the United States and Britain denounced the king's plan because he had chosen a third boundary option instead of following his instructions to decide between the versions put forth by the two countries.

Both nations saw the need to settle the matter to avoid a major conflict that neither wanted. Britain sent Lord Ashburton (Alexander Baring) as a special minister to the United States in 1842. He and U.S. secretary of state Daniel Webster met for several months with the object not only to establish the northeastern boundary but also to establish or affirm existing treaties dealing with the northern boundary as far west as the Rocky Mountains. The U.S. position in the negotiations was greatly complicated by the issue of states' rights and state sovereignty as the federal government could not unilaterally make a decision that involved a state. Maine officials, holding out for the most northern boundary, were not inclined to cede any land to a country for which they had a great dislike.

Maine officials were eventually brought into the negotiations between Ashburton and Webster with the hope that they would be more conciliatory than they had been previously. Britain had a strong need for a military road to connect their maritime provinces to the lower Canadian provinces. The United States realized this and was willing to be flexible. Webster and Ashburton finally put together a proposal that gave the United States a little more than half of the disputed area, although not the same line as proposed by the king of the Netherlands in 1831. Maine and Massachusetts were still unwilling to cede land, but the federal government cleverly offered Maine $300,000 for lost land if the two states would agree to accept the deal, and they did. Although Maine did not get all the land it wanted, it is still larger than the other five New England states added together.

The Webster-Ashburton Treaty gives the following boundary for Maine. Beginning at the mouth of the St. Croix River and proceeding north along this river to its headwaters, then due north to its intersection with the St. John River. Then up this river to the mouth of the St. Francis River. Continuing up this river to the outlet of Lake Pohenagamook. Then southwesterly, in a straight line, to a point opposite the northwest branch of the St. John River, 10 miles distant from the main branch of the St. John River. This point is on the crest of highlands separating watersheds of the St. Lawrence River and the St. John River. Then in a straight line to where latitude 46 degrees 25 minutes intersects the Southwest Branch of the St. John River. Then south on this branch to its source in the highlands, then along the highlands which divide the drainages of the St. Lawrence from the Atlantic Ocean. This boundary then intersects with the Maine–New Hampshire boundary. River boundaries are in the middle of the rivers.

The ownership of islands in the St. Croix River was determined by commissioners from the two countries in 1913.

The Webster-Ashburton negotiations also resolved the issue of the most northwestern head of the Connecticut River, but since this is part of the New Hampshire border, it is discussed there.

With New Hampshire. Maine (at the time a part of Massachusetts) and New Hampshire tried several times to establish their common border, but they were unable to do so. Both agreed the boundary ascended the Piscataqua and Salmon Falls rivers, but here the agreement ceased. New Hampshire claimed it should run due north, whereas Maine claimed the line should run northwest from the headwaters of Salmon Falls River. They finally submitted the issue to the English king for settlement. In 1739 King George II determined that the line between New Hampshire and Maine was to begin in the Atlantic Ocean, ascend the Piscataqua Bay and River, then to the head of Salmon Falls River. From there it was to go due north in a straight line for 120 miles. The boundary is two degrees west of due north, an error most likely due to surveyors not knowing the variation of true north from magnetic north or not making the proper calculations for the deviation. (See map 1.2.) After the Webster-Ashburton Treaty, this line ended in the highlands as defined by that treaty.

In recent years Maine and New Hampshire have disputed ownership of the Portsmouth Naval Shipyard that is on a 297-acre island in the Piscataqua River. In May 2001 the U.S. Supreme Court settled the dispute ruling that the shipyard belongs to Maine.

With Atlantic Ocean. Ownership of islands in the Passamaquoddy Bay were determined by a joint commission set up by the 1814 Treaty of Ghent. Determining the ownership of these islands did not come easily, however. The Treaty of 1783 defined the boundary as along the St. Croix River from its mouth in the Bay of Fundy and including all islands within 20 leagues of the shore except those islands already within the limits of Nova Scotia. Nova Scotia included New Brunswick at the time the Treaty of 1783 was drawn up. One problem was that the mouth of the St. Croix was in Passamaquoddy Bay and not the Bay of Fundy. Another was that Nova Scotia had exercised jurisdiction over all the major islands for years. Commissioners finally awarded Moose, Dudley, and Frederick islands to the United States and all others to Great Britain.

The U.S. Geological survey says that generally the individual states recognize an offshore boundary of 3 nautical miles. The United States territorial sea limit contiguous zone has been set at 12 nautical miles but is expected to be extended to 24 nautical miles. The exclusive economic zone boundary is 200 nautical miles. (A nautical mile equals 1.15 land miles.)

Massachusetts

The area that eventually became Massachusetts was one of the earliest areas to be settled by the English in the New World and was the subject of many boundary disputes. Charters issued in 1606 and 1620 by King James I specified settlement somewhere between the 37th and 48th parallels. The specific parallels vary depending on which history one is reading.

The most important Massachusetts charter for boundary purposes, however, was issued in 1629 and gave the Massachusetts Bay Colony the land from 3 miles south of the Charles River to 3 miles north of the Merrimack River and from the Atlantic Ocean to the Pacific Ocean. This charter obviously established some real problems unless those two rivers ran east-west, which they didn't. So, did this mean that the boundaries were from 3 miles from the mouths of the rivers, from the most southerly and northerly tributaries, or from some other point relative to the 3-mile designation? These questions were to plague boundary settlement for about 200 years.

Another potential conflict was with the Pilgrims who settled Plymouth Colony in 1620, ten years before the Puritans settled Massachusetts Bay. (See map 2.7.) The map indicates the approximate boundaries of Plymouth Colony, but in fact the boundaries of the colony were never established with any certainty. Why should they have been? After all, America was big and unsettled. The fact

Map 2.7. Plymouth Colony

that the new land was occupied by Native Americans didn't mean much to most Englishmen, as the natives didn't properly utilize the land so their rights didn't count for much in the eyes of the Europeans. This fact notwithstanding, some settlers did take native rights into account and negotiated with them to purchase land and treat them in an equitable manner. To the English settlers, the French, Spanish, and Dutch were not important either because they were either weak, such as the Dutch or far to the south in Florida, such as the Spanish, or to the north in Canada, such as the French.

English grants were also vague and often overlapping. In New Hampshire a grant conflicted with Massachusetts in that the New Hampshire grant was from the middle of the Merrimack River (map 2.9), whereas the Massachusetts grant was from 3 miles north of the Merrimack. In Maine the Duke of York claimed land from the Kennebec River north to the St. Croix River, and the French claimed all land north of the Kennebec (map 2.6). Rhode Island received a grant in 1644 that gave it land only vaguely defined. Connecticut received a grant in 1662 that did not clearly define boundaries. Based on its 1664 charter, New York claimed land all the way to the Connecticut River and the islands of Martha's Vineyard and Nantucket in addition to part of Maine. Plymouth's boundaries were never clear on any side except that of the ocean.

Massachusetts Bay managed to extend its boundaries several times during its early years. New Hampshire, unable to form a government of its own and raise sustainable taxes, petitioned Massachusetts for protection under its government in 1641. This arrangement endured until 1679, when the king decreed New Hampshire as a separate jurisdiction. New Hampshire returned under the aegis of Massachusetts for a brief time until 1691, when the English sovereigns William and Mary designated New Hampshire a separate royal colony. In 1652 seven Maine towns voted to unite with Massachusetts because they were economically untenable and unable to form a government. The Duke of York gave up his claim to Maine and the islands of Martha's Vineyard and Nantucket in 1691. Maine officially became a part of Massachusetts in the latter's 1691 charter. The unsteady relationship between Maine and Massachusetts would last until 1820, when Maine became a separate state.

Massachusetts lost some of its boundary disputes because of the displeasure of the crown. This was because the Bay Colony did not grant its people the same freedoms as Englishmen in England, permitted only Congregational Church members (Puritans) the right to vote, persecuted all other religious groups, were arbitrary in assessment of taxes, and would not make an accounting of taxes collected. The colony further antagonized the crown by claiming lands belonging to Rhode Island, Plymouth, Connecticut, and New York and had usurped Captain Mason's (New Hampshire) and Sir Ferdinando's (Maine) patents. Massachusetts Bay also administered itself under its own law without regard to English law and unwisely ignored the monarchy.

With New Hampshire. The boundary disputes between Massachusetts and New Hampshire are as tortuous as the general history of the area. The 3-mile designation north of the Merrimack River was a point that obviously needed clarification. Massachusetts, in an understandable attempt to push its borders as far north as possible, tried to establish that its charter meant its northern border began at the Atlantic Ocean 3 miles north of the Merrimack, then followed that river to its head 3 miles distant on the north and east sides, then headed due west. Such an interpretation would have placed its northern border well into the center of New Hampshire. (See map 2.9 later in this chapter.) Massachusetts was never able to establish this interpretation. The king finally settled the boundary issue between Massachusetts and New Hampshire in 1740 when he decreed that the northern border of Massachusetts was to begin at the Atlantic Ocean and run from 3 miles north of the mouth of the Merrimack River and nearly paralleling that river 3 miles to the north until that line reached a point 3 miles north of Lowell, Massachusetts (some sources say 3 miles north of Pentucket Falls). From that point the line was to run due west until it "met his majesty's other governments."

When it came time to survey this line, Massachusetts refused to participate, but New Hampshire surveyors, who were supposed to run the line only to the Connecticut River, ran the line to within 20 miles of the Hudson River, thinking that was the extent of their jurisdiction. The line as run is slightly north of due west. The reason the line is north of west is that Richard Hazen, when surveying the line in 1741, improperly calculated the correct deviation from magnetic north. Massachusetts gained a nice chunk of land at the expense of both New Hampshire and Vermont.

With Vermont. Although the history of Vermont is complicated, with New York and New Hampshire contending for the area, the Massachusetts border with Vermont was easily established as it is a continuation of the Massachusetts–New Hampshire border. It also runs north of west for the same reason stated in the previous paragraph.

With New York. Massachusetts's border with New York was the focus of several years of minor warfare and violence. Mobs of rioters burned crops, forests, barns, and houses; settlers robbed and beat up each other; and sheriffs jailed those assumed to violate the law as they interpreted it. A few were killed, but most of the destruction was to property. Based on its charter, New York felt it had a solid claim over land to the Connecticut River. (See map 2.8.) Massachusetts

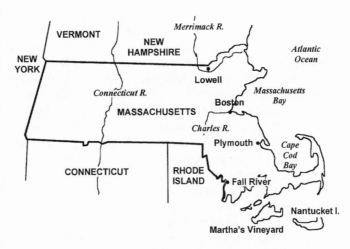

Map 2.8. Massachusetts

based its argument for possessing land west of the Connecticut River on three elements: Its settlers were already in the area; New York had, in 1683, settled with Connecticut on a boundary roughly 20 miles east of the Hudson River; and the original Massachusetts charter extended all the way to the South Sea (Pacific Ocean). (Massachusetts officials likely wanted to ignore the king's 1740 decree concerning the Massachusetts–New Hampshire boundary that stated it ran west until it met other English governments, not the Pacific Ocean.) None of these elements formed a strong argument, but the location of the New York–Connecticut border was probably the most cogent.

Disgusted with the strife between the two colonies, the English Board of Trade in 1757 established a "line of peace" drawn 20 miles east of the Hudson River. Prodded by continuing disorder in the area, the English government in 1766 ordered the two colonies to settle the border dispute along the "line of peace." By the next year they had gotten the disputed area down to 14,000 acres. Influential men from both colonies met in 1771 and by 1773 had worked out most of the problems with the boundary. It was not finally settled until 1787.

The Massachusetts–New York boundary created an anomaly in the very extreme southwest corner of Massachusetts. An area called Boston Corners was virtually cut off from its home state of Massachusetts due to a small range of hills. (See map 3.11.) Because of its remoteness, it became a haven for criminals and others fleeing the law. Inhabitants were also inconvenienced by the need to travel through both Connecticut and New York to get to a Massachusetts town to conduct official business. In 1848 Boston Corners inhabitants petitioned Massachusetts for their area to be ceded to New York, which agreed to accept it. Massachusetts was willing, and a few years later Congress approved the transfer of a little over a thousand acres to New York. This action created the sharp southeasterly change in direction of the extreme southern part of Massachusetts's western border.

With Connecticut. The interpretation of the southern boundary of Massachusetts based on its 1629 charter is that it was 3 miles south of the mostly southern part of the Charles River. The boundary with Connecticut, established in 1713 and reestablished in 1822–26, is generally based on this interpretation. The line runs slightly north of due west rather than due west, as the charter states, probably due to errors in actually being able to maintain a true west bearing using a compass. It has a southerly deflection just east of the Connecticut River where the Massachusetts town of Longmeadow juts into Connecticut. The line as it exists today is the boundary between Longmeadow, Massachusetts, and Enfield, Connecticut, that was established in the 1600s. (See map 2.3.) When the boundary was drawn between the colonies in 1713, the boundary of the two towns became the boundary between the colonies for this segment of the line. Connecticut did not contend this boundary in the 1826 boundary agreement.

Another deflection in the line occurs immediately west of the Connecticut River. This is the northern border of the Connecticut town of Suffield that became the boundary for about 4 miles. (See map 2.3.)

A larger border deflection into Con-

necticut west of the Connecticut River is called the Southwick Jog. (See map 2.4.) The Massachusetts town of Southwick was settled before a boundary between the colonies was an issue. Once the boundary was defined, however, Southwick protruded into Connecticut. Commissioners from both states met in 1790 to resolve the issue. They decided the Southwick Jog should be given to Massachusetts for towns Connecticut held that Massachusetts thought belonged to it. Connecticut disagreed, and in 1804 they reached a compromise that nearly bisected the area along the Congamond Lakes. Massachusetts got the western part, about five-eighths of the total area, and Connecticut got the eastern part.

A strict interpretation of the southern Massachusetts charter would have the boundary with Connecticut and Rhode Island continuing in a straight line. The eastern part of Rhode Island's northern border is on the same parallel as the eastern part of Connecticut's northern border, but it runs south of west before striking Connecticut's eastern border. This line looks suspiciously like the original incorrect line run by Nathaniel Woodward and Solomon Saffery in 1642 that was discussed earlier in the Massachusetts paragraphs of the Connecticut section, or it may be due to an incorrect determination of the deviation of the compass from true north for that longitude. See map 1.2 for information on the deviation of the compass from true north for various longitudes in the United States.

With Rhode Island. Roger Williams and some associates settled Rhode Island in 1636. They had been kicked out of Puritan Massachusetts Bay because of their unconventional and nonconforming religious beliefs. The Rhode Islanders were considered heretics by their Puritan neighbors in Massachusetts and Connecticut and by the Pilgrims in Plymouth. The result was that Rhode Island was constantly being squeezed, and despised, by its neighbors.

As mentioned earlier, the southern border of Massachusetts was established as 3 miles south of the Charles River; this, in effect, established Rhode Island's northern border. This line begins in the west at the border with Connecticut and ends in Burnt Swamp in the east. The line is straight but runs south of west running from the east. The location of this line was contested by the two states for about 200 years and, when finally settled in 1883, was just about where Rhode Island thought it should have been all along.

In the 1630s Massachusetts laid claim to land between the Pawcatuck River (the current western boundary of Rhode Island) and Narragansett Bay based on its claim of conquering the Pequot Indians in that area. (See map 2.10 later in this chapter.) Connecticut participated with Massachusetts in conquering the Pequots and also claimed part of the area. Neither colony was successful in pursuing its claims which, if sustained, would have effectively removed Rhode Island from the map.

Rhode Island's charter of 1663 gave it land 3 miles to the east side of Narragansett Bay. Massachusetts and Plymouth consistently ignored this boundary, and Rhode Island was powerless to insist on its rights. Plymouth was reasonably content with its vague borders until it came under the influence of Massachusetts Bay Colony; then it began to be more aggressive in regard to its western neighbor, Rhode Island. Even though Rhode Island's charter gave it land 3 miles to the east of Narragansett Bay, Plymouth insisted on claiming land all the way to the edge of the bay. When Massachusetts absorbed Plymouth in 1691, it, of course, continued to pursue hegemony over land to the edge of the bay.

The boundary dispute went to the Supreme Court in 1846, but Massachusetts and Rhode Island could not agree on the court's judicial interpretation. It went to the Supreme Court again in 1861 for further interpretation. The boundary line was finally run in 1861 following the high-water lines of named ponds and rivers. This was an obviously impractical way to mark a border, so in 1897 the border was reestablished using a series of straight lines, following as closely as possible the 1861 boundary. Other adjustments occurred in 1861 or 1862, sources vary, when Rhode Island gained the towns of East Providence and Pawtucket from Massachusetts and ceded the town of Fall River to Massachusetts. The northern part of this north-south boundary was delineated in the 1663 charter as directly north from Pawtucket Falls to the Massachusetts border.

With Atlantic Ocean. The laws of Massachusetts state that "the territorial limits of the commonwealth shall extend seaward to the outer limits of the territorial sea of the United States." Since the territorial sea limit of the United States is 12 nautical miles, this would put the boundary at 13.8 land miles. This is in spite of a communication to the author from the U.S. Geological Survey saying that, generally speaking, the individual states recognize an offshore boundary of 3 nautical miles. The United States territorial sea limit contiguous zone is expected to be extended to 24 nautical miles. The exclusive economic zone boundary is 200 nautical miles. (A nautical mile equals 1.15 land miles.)

New Hampshire

New Hampshire was included in a large grant given by King James I in 1622 to Ferdinando Gorges and John Mason that included land between the Merrimack and Kennebec rivers. (See map 2.1.) In 1629 Mason made a deal with Gorges to divide this area, with Mason receiving the area between the Merrimack and Piscataqua Rivers (New Hampshire). The eastern portion retained the name Maine, while Mason renamed the western portion New Hampshire in honor of his home county of Hampshire in England. New Hampshire was originally to run no more than 60 miles inland.

Due partly to economic problems, the residents of New Hampshire's four towns, Dover, Exeter, Hampton, and Portsmouth, had difficulty agreeing on a government. In 1641 they sought, and received, protection under the government of Massachusetts. Charles II made New Hampshire a royal colony separate from Massachusetts in 1679. The vague boundaries at that time were Massachusetts on the south and Maine on the east; no western or northern boundaries were mentioned. This worked for a while, but the colony again sought protection under Massachusetts laws briefly before being declared a royal province by William and Mary in 1691.

With Vermont. New Hampshire sought to extend its boundary west of the Connecticut River in the 1700s, notwithstanding the fact that New York's charter gave it jurisdiction over land to that river. New Hampshire considered the New York charter invalid, and relying on New York's earlier cessions of land to both Connecticut and Massachusetts to within 20 miles east of the Hudson River (map 3.1), it also claimed jurisdiction that far west.

Acting on this interpretation, New Hampshire's royal governor, Benning Wentworth, made 138 township grants in what would become southwest Vermont. New York, thinking it controlled land all the way to the Connecticut River, also granted land in this area. Some of these grants overlapped those of New Hampshire. This conflict resulted in jailings, beatings, burning of houses and crops, and some bloodletting. The English Board of Trade finally issued a decree in 1764, confirmed by the king, that placed New Hampshire's western border at the low-water mark on the west side of the Connecticut River. This ended the boundary issue as far as English officials were concerned, but New Hampshire officials continued to eye the area in the hope of controlling it. New York also continued its attempt to control Vermont, but Vermont would declare independence from all jurisdictions and eventually become the 14th state in 1791.

An unusual boundary anomaly exists between New Hampshire and Vermont due to inaccurate surveying of the 45th parallel by Valentine and Collins, who placed their line slightly north of the parallel. Since the boundary between New Hampshire and Vermont was the west bank of the Connecticut River, the Valentine-Collins Line did not strike the river until it passed Halls Stream. (See map 2.12 later in this chapter.) Therefore, the border between the two states extends along the Connecticut River past the 45th parallel, then east and slightly south before it continues northward again to where it intersects the Valentine-Collins Line. Then the boundary runs west to where it intersects Halls Stream, which is the boundary between Canada and New Hampshire. This unusual area called the "Gore" is approximately 1¾ by 1 mile.

With Canada. The north border of New Hampshire is with Canada. The Treaty of 1783, ending the War for American Independence, sought to fix the northeastern boundary between the United States and England. The geography of the area was so poorly understood and the wording of the treaty so imprecise that the exact location of this boundary was unknown until determined by the Webster-Ashburton Treaty in 1842.

Very little of the 1783 treaty affected the New Hampshire boundary, but two points were important. The first was the location of the most northwestern head of the Connecticut River. The wording of the treaty specified that the most northwestern head of the Connecticut River would form part of the boundary. Unfortunately the two countries could not agree on which of two streams fit the description. With each side trying to gain the most territory out of the interpretation, the British argued for the most easterly stream, called Indian Stream. (See map 2.12.) The United States argued for the most westerly, called Halls Stream. The U.S. argument eventually prevailed, and it gained a slight amount more land than if the British position had succeeded. Before settlement of the issue, inhabitants in the disputed area were beset by both countries. They were so frustrated in not knowing to which county they belonged that in the early 1830s they voted 56–3 to form an independent jurisdiction called the United Inhabitants of Indian Stream Territory. New Hampshire took control of the area in 1835.

The other important point of the treaty regarding New Hampshire was the location of the highlands. Did this term mean mountains or merely a watershed? The two countries made attempts to settle the boundary, most notably in 1814, but were unable to do so until the Webster-Ashburton Treaty in 1842 defined the highlands as the watershed separating rivers that drain to the St. Lawrence from those that drain to the Atlantic Ocean.

With Maine. Representatives from New Hampshire and Maine met several times to resolve their boundary conflicts. They were unsuccessful, and in 1730 King George II ordered a settlement that ran the boundary from the Atlantic Ocean, up the Piscataqua Bay and River, and continuing up Salmon Falls River to its headwaters. Then the course was intended to run due north for 120 miles. The actual boundary is about 2 degrees west of north, an error probably due to surveyors not fully understanding the variations between true north and magnetic north for that area. This boundary now ends in the highlands between Canada and the United States as defined in the Webster-Ashburton Treaty.

In May 2001 the U.S. Supreme Court settled a long-standing dispute between New Hampshire and Maine over ownership of an island in the Piscataqua River that contained the Portsmouth Naval Shipyard. The court ruled that the island belonged to Maine.

With Atlantic Ocean. Part of the eastern border of New Hampshire is approximately 16 miles of coastline on the Atlantic Ocean. The U.S. Geological Survey says that generally the individual states recognize an offshore boundary of 3 nautical miles. The United States territorial sea limit contiguous zone has been set at 12 nautical miles but is expected to be extended to 24 nautical miles. The exclusive economic zone boundary is 200 nautical miles. (A nautical mile equals 1.15 land miles.)

With Massachusetts. New Hampshire had much difficulty establishing its borders with Massachusetts; keep in mind that Maine was also a part of Massachusetts as this time. Based on its charter, Massachusetts claimed jurisdiction 3 miles to the north side of the Merrimack River all the way to its headwaters, then west. Such an interpretation, if upheld, would have stripped a considerable amount of land from New Hampshire as the Merrimack runs north into the central part of the state. (See map 2.9.) For a time New Hampshire argued that the boundary should

Map 2.9. New Hampshire

begin 3 miles north of the Merrimack River and then run due west to New York. The two colonies could not agree on exactly where the point 3 miles north of the Merrimack was to begin.

Since New Hampshire and Massachusetts could not settle their border dispute, King George II ordered a settlement in 1740. The resulting agreement specified that the northern border of Massachusetts was to run from 3 miles north of the mouth of the Merrimack River and nearly paralleling that river 3 miles to the north until that line reached a point 3 miles north of Lowell, Massachusetts (some sources say 3 miles north of Pentucket Falls). From that point the line was to run due west until it "met his majesty's other governments."

Massachusetts refused to participate in the survey, but New Hampshire surveyors ran the line. Instead of stopping at the Connecticut River, as the king's order stipulated, they continued to within 20 miles of the Hudson River, expecting that their territory would eventually extend that far west. The line as run is slightly north of west because the 1741 survey by Richard Hazen allowed for an incorrect variation of the compass from magnetic north. This error cost New Hampshire 59,873 acres.

Rhode Island

Rhode Island's early history was one of strikingly undefined boundaries as the settlers bought land from the local Indians with vague boundary descriptions; the boundaries of neighboring colonies were nearly as indefinite. The boundaries were so confusing that Rufus Choate, counsel for Massachusetts in comments before the U.S. Supreme Court in 1851, declared that "the boundaries of Rhode Island might as well have been marked on the north by a bramblebush, on the south by a bluejay, on the west by a hive of bees in swarming time, and on the east by five hundred foxes with firebrands tied to their tails."*

Rhode Island was settled in 1636 by Roger Williams, who had been banished from Massachusetts because he refused to believe and adhere to the strict Puritan doctrine demanded there. Where many other Englishmen considered the Indians savages, Williams respected them. He learned their language, probably the dialect of the Narragansetts, and insisted on buying, rather than just taking, land from them. He bought land around the north end of Narragansett Bay. Additionally, Williams helped Anne Hutchinson, also banished from Massachusetts for heretical religious beliefs, purchase Aquidneck Island from the Indians. Williams also served as interpreter as other settlers bought land from the natives.

For the first several years the area had only four settlements, Providence and Warwick on the mainland, and Portsmouth and Newport on Aquidneck Island. None of these settlements had a British charter to form a government or to own land, so in 1644 Williams went to England and obtained a charter. The charter gave no clear boundaries other than specifying the lands purchased from the Indians and bounded by Connecticut, Plymouth, and Massachusetts. (See maps 2.2, 2.7, and 2.8.) This created problems because Plymouth Colony's 1629 charter gave them the land as far west as Narragansett Bay, and Connecticut's 1662 charter gave them land as far east as Narragansett Bay. The overlapping of charters was a common problem among the colonies.

Because Rhode Island had been settled by people who had very different and distinct ideas, they could not get along with each other any more than they could get along with the communities from which they were banished. They squabbled over religion, government, and even whether or not they should unite with each other or with a neighboring colony. Rhode Island was often called by its

*Federal Writers' Project, Rhode Island: A Guide to the Smallest State (Boston: Houghton Mifflin Company, 1937), p. 36.

neighbors "Rogue's Island." This was due not only to the area being seen as a cesspool of heresy, and a place where people thought differently, but also to the fact that Rhode Islanders drove extremely hard deals in business, and it was a haven for smugglers and privateering. The one thing Rhode Islanders did agree on, however, was that religious toleration was important and that toleration needed to be put into practice. Rhode Islanders continued to be seen as mavericks by other colonists. Even into the 1770s and 1780s they continued to curry ill will because of their reluctance to pay their part of the debt for the War for American Independence. They also refused thirteen different times to join the federal union and were the last of the original thirteen colonies to do so.

In 1663 Rhode Island received a charter that, in most respects, gave them the boundaries that exist today, although it took about 200 years and a lot of animosity and ill will before its neighbors agreed to those borders. This charter specified a western border as the Pawcatuck River to the mouth of the Ashaway River then north to the Massachusetts border. On the east the boundary was specified as 3 miles east of Narragansett Bay to Pawtucket Falls then north to the Massachusetts border. The Atlantic Ocean was specified as the southern boundary, with Block Island included as a part of Rhode Island. Rhode Island's northern boundary was the southern boundary of Massachusetts as stated in that colony's 1629 charter.

With Connecticut. Rhode Island's charter borders, however, were not agreed to by any of its neighbors. Connecticut, in 1662, had received a charter giving it land all the way to Narragansett Bay and River. This would have left Rhode Island with only the towns of Providence, Warwick, and the island towns of Portsmouth and Newport, in reality almost nothing and certainly not enough to sustain a colony. The Rhode Island agent was able to negotiate with the Connecticut agent in London to define the meaning of Narragansett Bay as the Paw-

catuck River. Consequently, the Rhode Island charter of 1663 specified that river as the beginning point of the boundary.

Officials in Connecticut refused to acknowledge the Pawcatuck River as a boundary, and the two colonies haggled over the area for years. Part of Connecticut's claim to land all the way to the bay was based on their charter; another part was based on their participation, along with Massachusetts, in conquering Indians immediately west of Narragansett Bay in the Pequot War in 1637, an action in which Rhode Island's participation was very meager. Finally, in 1703, a commission agreed on a line, adjusted later but not finally settled until 1887. The final line begins in the Atlantic, ascends the middle of the Pawcatuck River to its confluence with the Ashaway River, then goes slightly east of north to a point 20 miles due west of Warwick Neck on Narragansett Bay, then heads slightly west of north to the Massachusetts border. The northern point of this line is on a meridian with the point on the Pawcatuck where the line turns north. The slight deflection in this line, only about a half mile, to the east is likely due to the fact that in 1720 Rhode Island, without the cooperation of Connecticut, ran the line from the Pawcatuck to a spot 20 miles west of Warwick Point, possibly thinking this was on a true north-south bearing from the confluence of the Ashaway River, and then claimed this as the western limit of the colony. Then when the line was continued north to the Massachusetts border, it was not straight. (See map 2.10.)

With Massachusetts. Rhode Island's northern border should have been easy to determine. Massachusetts's 1629 and 1691 charters specified that its southern border should be 3 miles south of the southernmost part of the Charles River. This point was determined by Nathaniel Woodward and Solomon Saffery in 1642. In 1710 officials from Massachusetts and Rhode Island agreed to run their common east-west boundary from the point 3 miles south of the Charles River to the west. The line run is not due west but instead would

Map 2.10. Rhode Island

that the crown, which was displeased with Massachusetts Bay on several accounts, would grant their request just to humble the increasingly important and powerful Massachusetts Bay. They were correct. A royal commission established Rhode Island's rights to the east side of the bay in 1741, and this was confirmed by royal decree in 1746. The border continued to be disputed and reached the U.S. Supreme Court in 1846. The two states still could not agree on the judicial interpretation of the line, and the issue ended in the Supreme Court again in 1861.

One of the interpretations of the line was named rivers and ponds on the east side of the bay, to Pawtucket Falls on the Seekonk River, then due north to the Massachusetts border. This was an unworkable line in a flat, marshy area with many watercourses, so in 1897 surveyors established a series of straight lines following as closely as possible the line of ponds and rivers. The southern part of this north-south line was not redefined as straight line because the citizens there wanted the line to remain as it always had been.

The middle part of the north-south line is heavily industrialized in some areas and densely settled in others. In some instances it cuts through barns and houses. No one pays much attention to this, but some farmers do have to register deeds and pay taxes in both Rhode Island and Massachusetts. This part of the line also creates some cumbersome problems relating to gas and electricity distribution, and sewerage. Since the states have different laws concerning taxation and development, industries have occasionally moved a short distance east or west to gain an economic advantage.

In 1859 commissioners met to consider the Fall River, Massachusetts, situation. (See

have met the Connecticut River a few miles south of a due-west line had it been run that far. The line is south of west most likely due to surveyors not knowing the proper deviation of the compass needle from true north for that area. (See map 1.2.)

Although Rhode Island's 1663 charter gave it land 3 miles to the east of Narragansett Bay, Massachusetts and Plymouth consistently ignored the charter provisions not only because they wanted the land but because they despised the heretical Rhode Islanders. Plymouth claimed land to the shore of the bay based on its charter, and it claimed Aquidneck Island as well. The Plymouth settlers were lenient concerning the border placement in the early years, but later, especially under the influence of Massachusetts Bay, they became more strident in pushing their rights to the edge of the bay. Rhode Island was powerless to enforce its rights, and people from Massachusetts and Plymouth settled the east side of the bay.

Rhode Island decided to force its right to the east side of the bay in 1741, thinking

map 2.8.) This city was growing rapidly and needed more land, especially in the south. Providence, Rhode Island, was also growing and had spilled into Massachusetts. The commissioners put together a land trade whereby Rhode Island gained land east of Providence, and Massachusetts gained land south and west of Fall River. At first Rhode Island found this exchange unacceptable, as did some people from Massachusetts claiming Rhode Island was getting much the better deal. Both sides later came to agreement in 1861. The U.S. Supreme Court confirmed the exchange in 1862.

With Atlantic Ocean. Rhode Island's laws claim jurisdiction over territorial waters and submerged lands 3 nautical miles, about 3.45 land miles, into the sea from the mean low-water mark. This conforms with the generally accepted offshore boundary of individual states of 3 nautical miles, according to the U.S. Geological Survey. The United States territorial sea limit contiguous zone has been set at 12 nautical miles but is expected to be extended to 24 nautical miles. The exclusive economic zone boundary is 200 nautical miles. (A nautical mile equals 1.15 land miles.)

Vermont

Comfortably situated in New England, one would think that Vermont was one of the original thirteen colonies; it wasn't. Through much of the colonial period Vermont was fought over principally by New York and New Hampshire, but Massachusetts also laid a weak claim to the southern part. While others were jockeying to control their area, Vermonters were fiercely maintaining independence from all of the contenders.

Representatives from towns in the New Hampshire Grants (township grants made in southern Vermont mostly by New Hampshire governor Benning Wentworth) met in July 1777, adopted a constitution, and declared their independence from both New York and New Hampshire, thereby creating the independent Republic of Vermont. After much political turmoil, Vermont subsequently joined the Union in 1791 as the fourteenth state. It was one of only a few areas claiming to be an independent republic before entering the Union; Texas, Tennessee (not really claiming to be an independent republic but having set up an autonomous state, the State of Franklin), Hawaii, and California were others. The name "Vermont" comes from Frenchman Samuel de Champlain, who reportedly looked at Vermont's mountains and exclaimed *les verts monts*— the green mountains. A range of mountains called the Green Mountains bisects the state north to south.

With Massachusetts. Vermont's border with Massachusetts was essentially fought and settled by New Hampshire, which was also contending with Massachusetts to settle their common boundary. Vermont's southern border is thus an extension of New Hampshire's southern border. To understand this boundary, a discussion of New Hampshire's struggles with Massachusetts is needed.

Massachusetts's claim to part of Vermont was without much basis. Massachusetts Bay's 1629 charter put its northern border 3 miles north of the Merrimack River. (See map 2.8.) Massachusetts interpreted this as running from 3 miles north of where the Merrimack entered the sea, then roughly paralleling the river, 3 miles north and east of it, to its headwaters well into the center of New Hampshire (map 2.9), then due west to where it met New York. New Hampshire did not agree with this interpretation and asked King George II to settle the matter. He did in 1740 when he determined the line to follow a course 3 miles north of the Merrimack River to a point 3 miles north of Lowell, Massachusetts, then due west.

New Hampshire appointed a commission to run the line, but Massachusetts refused to participate. New Hampshire had the line surveyed and marked, but instead of stopping at the Connecticut River, the limit set by the king, they continued to within 20

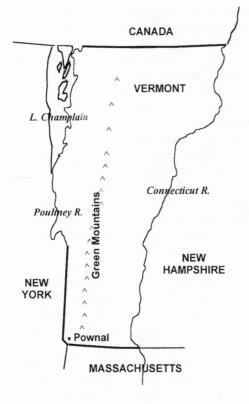

Map 2.11. Vermont

tually became the state of Vermont. (See map 2.11.)

New Hampshire also claimed the land west of the Connecticut River, and the resulting New York–New Hampshire conflict caused some bloodshed, but most of the violence was directed at the destruction of property, filing of lawsuits, and threats of bodily injury. Some settlers were forced to pay taxes and declare allegiance to both colonies. The Green Mountain Boys of Vermont were especially good at using threats, intimidation, and other scare tactics to get rid of New York surveyors and settlers. Finally, in 1777, frustrated and belligerent representatives from towns in the disputed area met and declared themselves an independent republic. The ensuing fourteen years of independence was not recognized by the Continental Congress, New Hampshire, nor New York.

Between 1750 and 1764 New Hampshire governor Benning Wentworth made 138 grants of land to settlers in the area west of the Connecticut River and to within 30 miles of the Hudson River. This area was referred to as the "New Hampshire Grants." His position was that since New York had ceded land west of the Connecticut River to Connecticut and Massachusetts, New Hampshire expected the same treatment. George III ruled against Wentworth and New Hampshire, but settlers were already on land they thought was theirs.

New Hampshire lost its claim to the land west of the Connecticut River in 1764 when the king established this colony's western border at the Connecticut River. New York saw an opportunity to establish hegemony over the Vermont area but blundered badly in its attempt. New York was effective in governing the area west of the Green Mountains, a north-south range of mountains in about the center of Vermont, but failed miserably to establish courts or other provincial authority east of the mountains, an area that became a law unto itself. Then, when New York did try to establish authority, the settlers did not take kindly to its effort. New York further blundered in that it insisted that

miles east of the Hudson River. The actual boundary runs slightly north of due west because the 1741 surveyor of the line did not properly calculate the proper deviation of the compass needle from true north, and so the line runs north of west. This error cost Vermont 133,897 acres.

With New York. Before Vermont declared its independence, New York and New Hampshire fought bitterly over this land. New York's claim was based on charters to the Duke of York in 1664 and 1674 giving him land as far east as the Connecticut River. New York had ceded land west of the Connecticut River to Connecticut and to Massachusetts allowing both of these colonies jurisdiction to land approximately 20 miles east of the Hudson River. (See map 3.10.) New York, however, still maintained the right to all land north of the Massachusetts border and west of the Connecticut River, the area that even-

settlers, who had bought their claims from New Hampshire, pay for them again. A major point of contention was that the settlers with New Hampshire grants felt they had grants issued by a representative of the king of England and they should be valid regardless of which colony claimed jurisdiction over the disputed area. If New York had honored the New Hampshire grants, history may have played out much differently. New York had simply done too many things wrong and alienated too many people.

New York was not looked upon as a good place to live by the lower class, and most of the settlers in the New Hampshire Grants fell into that category. New York had high taxes, and most of the good land in the Hudson Valley had been granted to speculators with very large landholdings who refused to sell. When they leased the lands, the terms were not favorable for the lessee. Much of the conflict between the Green Mountain Boys and New York was a conflict of Vermont farmers against New York landlords. Another factor working against New York's claim over Vermont was the fact that Congress wanted to limit the size of large states such as New York.

New York was unable to maintain any jurisdiction over Vermont, so in 1790 the legislature appointed a commission to establish boundaries. The boundaries they agreed to ran along town boundaries in the most southern part, then down the Poultney River, then through the deepest channel of East Bay and Lake Champlain to the Valentine-Collins Line near the 45th parallel. The major islands in Lake Champlain all went to Vermont. The slight westward extension of Vermont's southern boundary (seen only on large-scale maps) goes around the town of Pownal. When it had all been settled, this Vermont–New York boundary ran a little more than 20 miles east of the Hudson River, just about where Wentworth envisioned it. The boundaries were formally recognized by both New York and Vermont in 1790. New York consented to Vermont's admission to the Union in 1791.

When it was an independent republic, Vermont did not respect the borders of abutting entities and claimed land all the way to the Hudson River. Whether this was puffery or a real claim is not known; nonetheless, the deal that finally brokered the resulting border rested upon concessions by both New York and Vermont. Vermont agreed to give up its claim to land to the Hudson River, and New York agreed to Vermont's claim to land 20 miles east of the Hudson. The final result was a boundary that was much like that of Connecticut and Massachusetts that had been settled earlier.

With Canada. Not only did Vermonters not have any allegiance to New York or New Hampshire, they did not have much to the confederated United States government either. They negotiated with the British during the War for American Independence for admission to Canada. Vermonters, who already engaged in a lot of trade with Canada, were willing to side with whomever would give them the best deal. Cornwallis's defeat at Yorktown in 1783 and the treaty that year, which included Vermont in U.S. territory, dashed any realistic hopes of Vermont ever joining the British Empire, although some strident citizens kept hopes alive until the late 1780s.

Vermont's border with Canada was intended to be the 45th parallel as specified in the Treaty of 1783 and worked out between the United States and Great Britain. The actual border runs anywhere from one-quarter mile to a mile north of the parallel because of errors by surveyors Valentine and Collins. Their 1771–74 line was officially approved as the border between Canada and the United States by the Webster-Ashburton Treaty in 1842. The intention was for this international border to run east to the middle of Halls Stream which had been determined as the international boundary between Canada and the United States stemming from the Treaty of 1783. However, the northern border of Vermont did not stop at Halls Stream but continued on to the Connecticut River because Vermont's northern border was defined as the 45th parallel as surveyed by Valentine

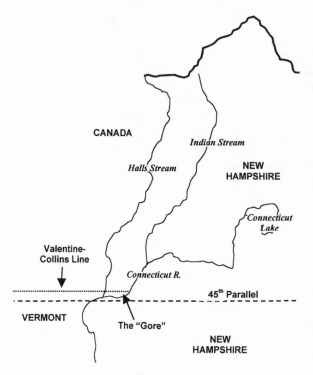

CANADA

Indian Stream

Halls Stream

NEW
HAMPSHIRE

Connecticut
Lake

Valentine-
Collins Line

Connecticut R.

45th Parallel

VERMONT

The "Gore"

NEW
HAMPSHIRE

Map 2.12. Head of Connecticut River

territorial disputes. Land speculators from both New Hampshire
and New York wanted the land, and
both colonies made grants, sometimes overlapping, in the area. New
Hampshire's governor Benning
Wentworth granted 138 towns, reserving huge portions in each for
himself. Most of the actual settlers
in Vermont came from New Hampshire, Massachusetts, and Connecticut, while very few came from
New York.

One proposal to resolve the
issue between New Hampshire and
New York was to divide the area
along the north-south running
Green Mountains (approximately
in the middle of Vermont), with
the western portion going to New
York and the eastern portion to
New Hampshire. Settlers east of
the mountains convinced settlers
on the west side to join with them
to resist control by either New York
or New Hampshire.

and Collins to the Connecticut River. The
different points where the 45th parallel and
the Valentine-Collins Line meet the Connecticut River can readily be seen on map
2.12. This creates an unusual area, often
called "The Gore," which will be discussed in
the following subsection.

With New Hampshire. New Hampshire claimed jurisdiction over land west of
the Connecticut River based on its assertion
that the Duke of York's grants were invalid.
Even if they were valid, New York had ceded
land to two other colonies to within 20 miles
of the Hudson, and so they felt the king would
agree with their claim to jurisdiction over
this land. New Hampshire lost its claim to
the land west of the Connecticut River in
1764 when the king established this colony's
western border at the Connecticut River.
This boundary was later confirmed by the
U.S. Supreme Court.

Economics played a major part in the
dispute over Vermont as it does in almost all

Vermont's border with New Hampshire
was set by the English Board of Trade and
accepted by George III in 1764. It is the low-
water mark on the western shore of the Connecticut River, right where New York thought
it should be all along, but New Yorkers ultimately did not benefit from this determination. New Hampshire worked out its differences with Vermont in 1782, and New York
did so in 1790.

The definition of the boundary between
Vermont and New Hampshire as the west
bank of the Connecticut and the inaccurate
survey of Valentine and Collins created an
unusual piece of Vermont called the "Gore,"
a land irregularity that belongs to Vermont.

As can be seen in Map 2.12 the Connecticut River goes north slightly past the
45th parallel but turns east and slightly south
before reaching the Valentine-Collins Line,
which is the north boundary of Vermont.
Then the river turns northward again where
it finally intersects with the Valentine-Collins

Line. Consequently, Vermont has a small slice of land, approximately 1¾ by 1 mile, jutting into New Hampshire called the "Gore." This area is bordered by the Valentine and Collins Line on the north, on the east and south by the Connecticut River, and on the west by Halls Stream. If Valentine and Collins had been accurate in finding the 45th parallel, this anomaly would not have occurred as that parallel meets the Connecticut River before the river gets to Halls Stream. Halls Stream and the Valentine-Collins Line are the boundary between the United States and Canada.

3

MID-ATLANTIC REGION

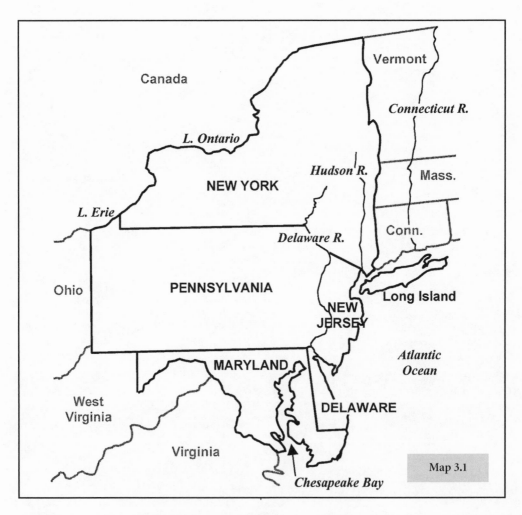

Canada

Vermont

Connecticut R.

L. Ontario

Hudson R.

Mass.

NEW YORK

L. Erie

Conn.

Delaware R.

Ohio

PENNSYLVANIA

Long Island

NEW JERSEY

Atlantic Ocean

MARYLAND

West Virginia

DELAWARE

Virginia

Chesapeake Bay

Map 3.1

Map is not to scale; boundaries are roughly drawn.

Delaware

Modern Delaware natives often joke that their small tidewater state consists of three counties at low tide and two at high tide. Notwithstanding its diminutive size, three men tried to encompass Delaware into their domains. They all failed, and Delaware defied the odds to become an independent colony, although it never had a charter from the king of England granting any land nor any right to establish a government.

The first person to attempt to gain control over Delaware (named for Baron De La Warr, Virginia's first governor) was Cecil Calvert, the second Lord Baltimore, who received a grant for land north of the Potomac River (the northern boundary of Virginia) and east to the Delaware River. (See map 3.1.) His 1632 grant encompassed the land that would become Delaware but excluded any land previously cultivated by Europeans, and this was to cause Calvert problems in claiming hegemony over the area. The second man to claim Delaware was the Duke of York, who based his claim on the somewhat nebulous idea that some Swedes cultivated the area as early as 1631, who were run out by the Dutch, and who were taken over by the duke's forces; ergo, the area was his. Since the area was cultivated by the Swedes, it was excluded from Calvert's charter. Scholars are not unanimous as to when the Swedes actually farmed the area. The duke's claim was enhanced somewhat because he was the brother of King Charles II. (The duke would become King James II in 1685.) The third claimant was William Penn, whose claim to Delaware was based on a grant from the Duke of York.

Calvert strongly contested the duke's claim by insisting that the Swedes did not have a permanent colony in Delaware until 1638, and since this postdated Calvert's 1632 grant, the area was his. The English Lords of Trade in 1685 ruled against Calvert and in favor of the duke. Calvert's claim was weakened by several factors: He had tolerated the Swedes in Delaware for forty years and had done nothing about them, the duke was the brother of the king, and Calvert was Catholic — Catholics were generally despised in the colonies and the mother country.

With Maryland. The dispute over Delaware centered on the Delmarva Peninsula, the land between the Delaware and Chesapeake bays. The Delmarva Peninsula derives its name from the first three letters from Delaware and Maryland, and the first and last letters from Virginia. In 1685 Charles II finally settled the matter on the peninsula by dividing the contested area equally between the Calverts and Penns. He decreed that a line should be drawn due west from Cape Henlopen (which appeared to be a cape when viewed from the sea), later called Fenwick Island, to Chesapeake Bay. At the exact center of this east-west line another line would be drawn slightly west of north to intersect with the westernmost tangent point of a 12-mile arc drawn around the town of New Castle. The boundary would then follow the arc briefly until a line could be drawn straight north to a latitude drawn from a point 15 miles south of Philadelphia. This due-north segment is only about 4 miles long. The survey of the north-south part of the line favored the Penn family, and hence, the state of Delaware, as it gave more land along the southern part of the line to Penn than he had ever claimed.

This boundary description doesn't seem like such a difficult matter to implement, but it was. The Calverts and Penns each located Cape Henlopen at different points on the map. The Penns used an old Dutch map that showed the cape about 25 miles south of the point where the Calverts claimed it was. (See map 3.2.) This place was later to be called False Cape and currently called Fenwick Island. The Penns won this battle as the line was eventually drawn at the more southern point. If the southern boundary of Delaware had been drawn at the more northerly point called "Cape Henlopen" on modern maps, the state would be much smaller than it is now but still larger than Rhode Island.

Local surveyors completed the survey of the east-west part of the line in 1750 and

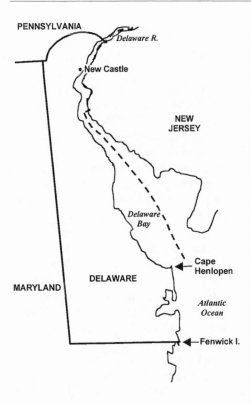

PENNSYLVANIA

Delaware R.

•New Castle

NEW
JERSEY

Delaware
Bay

Cape
Henlopen

DELAWARE

MARYLAND

Atlantic
Ocean

◄—Fenwick I.

Map 3.2. Delaware

worked on the north-south part of the line for three years beginning in 1760, but difficulties, largely caused by a considerable amount of swampy land, led the Penns and Calverts to employ two well-known English surveyors-astronomers-mathematicians, Charles Mason and Jeremiah Dixon, to complete the work. The line they surveyed, in addition to the east-west line surveyed in 1750, is the current Delaware-Maryland boundary.

Since the Mason-Dixon Line is so prominent in U.S. history, it should be noted that this north-south line and the east-west boundary between Maryland and Pennsylvania are the lines surveyed by Mason and Dixon. They did not survey the southern Delaware boundary, although it is often considered part of the Mason-Dixon Line in the sense that it divides the North from the South.

Pennsylvania and Maryland, represented by the Penns and Calverts, would continue to fight over their east-west bound-

ary for many years, but the boundary on the Delaware Peninsula was settled.

With Pennsylvania. King Charles II granted William Penn a charter for Pennsylvania in 1681. To separate Penn's land from the Duke of York's land on the Delaware River and Bay, the king decreed that a 12-mile arc be drawn from New Castle beginning at the Delaware River. A commission meeting in 1750 determined the courthouse spire as the center of the radius. This boundary, which still exists, is the only state boundary in the United States that consists of a circle segment. Two surveyors marked the arc in 1701 by placing three notches on both sides of trees. Due to the extreme difficulty of surveying an arc, this line is actually a series of compound curves with different radii.

The reason that Delaware came into Penn's domain was that he wanted an outlet to the sea. Penn's original grant, current Pennsylvania, while ample in size did not in Penn's eyes provide an adequate port allowing access to the sea. The later success of Philadelphia as a port belies this assumption. Nonetheless, Penn asked his good friend, the duke, for the land along the Delaware River and Bay which would give him control of the entrance to the Delaware River. The duke agreed, thus giving Penn not only Delaware but also the boundary dispute with the Calverts.

Penn divided Delaware and Pennsylvania each into three counties so that they would have equal representation in the legislative assembly. Delaware still consists of those same three counties. The Delawareans, however, never saw themselves as a part of William Penn's domain. They were different ethnically and culturally. Furthermore, they were not Quakers and resented the pacifistic positions of the Pennsylvanians because the Delawareans were very vulnerable to attacks from the sea by French and Spanish marauders, and the Pennsylvanians refused to help with defense. Although Penn made sincere attempts to keep the two areas equal in legislative representation, the Delawareans saw that Pennsylvania was quickly exceeding them in population, political power, and economic development, and they feared dominance by the Quaker community.

In the early 1700s, the schism became so great that Penn consented to let the Delawareans set up their own legislative assembly. Nonetheless, Delawareans continued to share a common governor with Pennsylvania until 1776. This situation of having one governor and two legislatures also occurred with New York and New Jersey, and with Massachusetts and New Hampshire. Penn hoped to unite the two areas under one governmental jurisdiction, an aspiration not shared by people in either Pennsylvania or Delaware. Therefore, the separation of Delaware from Pennsylvania was inevitable — even geography did not favor Delaware's union with Pennsylvania as the two areas had so little common border. However, Delaware would seem to fit in well with Maryland geographically, but after Penn won his battle with the Calverts, this was never a possibility. One can only speculate whether or not Delaware would be a separate state if the Calverts had won control of Delaware. The Delawareans, however, would have fought vigorously against being united with Maryland because they were bent on being independent early in their history.

One additional element of the Delaware-Pennsylvania boundary remained to be settled; that area is called the Delaware Wedge, the Thorn, or the Flat Iron. (See map 3.3.) Delaware's northern boundary was described as a 12-mile arc drawn around New Castle. This border designation was established when Charles II decreed the 12-mile arc to separate Penn's colony from land controlled by the Duke of York. Its western border extended from the westernmost extent of this arc (point *B* on map 3.3) to the center of the line drawn west from Cape Henlopen (line *B–C*). Maryland's eastern border was an extension of Delaware's western border north to Pennsylvania's southern border (line *A–B–C*). Pennsylvania's southern border was a latitude 15 miles from the southernmost part of Philadelphia and in the east

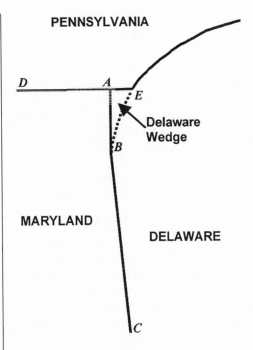

Map 3.3. Delaware Wedge

extended to the 12-mile arc drawn from New Castle (line *D–E*). From map 3.3 one can see that when the 12-mile arc is continued south from point E that it will not touch the north-south line (line *B–C*) until a point a few miles south of the Pennsylvania border. This left a small triangle of land, about 800 acres, over which no one had official jurisdiction. This triangle was bounded by the 12-mile arc on the east, Maryland's eastern boundary on the west, and Pennsylvania's southern border on the north.

Mason and Dixon had said this area belonged to Pennsylvania, which tried to exercise authority over it. However, the inhabitants of the Wedge paid taxes to and voted in Delaware, even though maps of that time showed the Wedge as a part of Pennsylvania. Delawareans adamantly refused to accept any jurisdiction over the area except their own. In 1849 U.S. engineers resurveyed this triangle of land and again assigned it to Pennsylvania. The citizens, however, still saw themselves as members of the First State. Tired of the strife and acrimony, Pennsylvania formally ceded the area to Delaware in 1921.

Delaware took little official notice of this transaction as they felt the Wedge had always been theirs.

With New Jersey. The boundary between Delaware and New Jersey is the low-water line on the New Jersey shore 12 miles north and south of New Castle. (See map 3.2.) Twelve miles south of New Castle the boundary goes to the middle of the Delaware River and the navigational channel of Delaware Bay. This Delaware–New Jersey boundary was a frequent subject of dispute until the U.S. Supreme Court decided in 1935 that Delaware included the Delaware River to the low-water mark on the New Jersey shore within 12 miles of New Castle. The reason for this shift in the boundary is based on the original charter to Penn, which included not only the 12-mile circle but also all islands in the river and the soil under the river within this radius. The Supreme Court determined this to include the river to the New Jersey side.

With Atlantic Ocean. The U.S. Geological Survey says that generally speaking the individual states recognize an offshore boundary of 3 nautical miles. The United States territorial sea limit contiguous zone has been set at 12 nautical miles but is expected to be extended to 24 nautical miles. The exclusive economic zone boundary is 200 nautical miles. (A nautical mile equals 1.15 land miles.)

Maryland

Without telling the Virginia authorities of his visit, George Calvert, the first Lord Baltimore, in 1629 sailed with his family into Jamestown. Calvert had twice tried to establish a colony in Newfoundland, but the bitterly cold climate and rocky soil had persuaded him that was not where he wanted to be. So he and his group sailed south to Virginia, intending to settle there. However, citizenship required that he take an oath to acknowledge the King of England as head of the church and state and renounce the pope. Since Calvert was Roman Catholic he could not do this, and the authorities asked him to depart. Leaving his family and servants in Virginia, Calvert sailed up Chesapeake Bay and found land that was not occupied by other Europeans. Some sources contend that Calvert never sailed far enough north to see Maryland, but he at least saw enough of the Chesapeake area that he determined that the future of his colony was in this area.

Calvert returned to England, where he received a grant from King Charles I in 1632 for land north of Virginia and the Potomac River. George Calvert died before he could return to the New World, but his oldest son Cecil Calvert received the grant. Cecil appointed his brother Leonard as governor of Maryland. Leonard and another brother, George, sailed in two ships with 300 men for their proprietary colony in 1634.

Virginians did not take kindly to the new colonists. Although they had not occupied the area granted to the Calverts, they claimed it historically and resented the interlopers. The Virginians were also anti-Catholic so resented the intrusion of "papists." This animosity would crop up in border disputes for years to come.

Maryland, named for the wife of Charles I and sometimes called Marie's Land in early histories, looks like it got caught in a squeeze play. (See map 3.4.) Its western

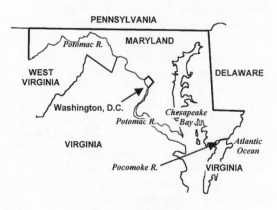

Map 3.4. Maryland

border looks like it just got hung out in the mountains for no apparent reason. Its eastern and southeastern borders are chopped up by Delaware and Virginia. Its northern and southern borders with Pennsylvania and Virginia are crammed to a distance of less than 2 miles apart near the city of Hancock on the Potomac River.

The original boundaries of Calvert's charter were the 40th parallel in the north, the headwaters of the Potomac River in the west, the Potomac River on the south, and the Delaware Bay in the east. Notwithstanding the seeming clarity of this boundary definition, Maryland lost just about every boundary dispute it encountered; it lost land to Virginia, Pennsylvania, and Delaware.

With West Virginia. Maryland's boundary with Virginia (now West Virginia) as defined by charter seemed clear enough — except when it came to determining precisely which stream was the headwater of the Potomac River. The Potomac River, at least, was a constant in Maryland's borders, although Virginia claimed that its charter gave it land north of the Potomac to the southern Pennsylvania border. Virginia did not get anywhere in pressing this claim and reluctantly recognized the existence of Maryland north of the Potomac River in 1638. The Maryland-Virginia border is the low-water line on the south shore of the river due to Maryland's 1632 charter description which drew its boundary from the north to the "further" bank of the Potomac, the "further" bank being the southern bank.

While Virginia lost out on its claim to land north of the Potomac, it did gain a little land from Maryland on the Delmarva Peninsula (the area between Chesapeake and Delaware bays). The line on the "Eastern Shore," as the peninsula is often called, was to be drawn east from the north point, called Watkins Point, of the bay into which the Pocomoke River emptied. In 1670 a commission consisting partly of Philip Calvert, representing Maryland, and Edmund Scarborough, the king's surveyor-general repre-

senting Virginia and a man with considerable land holdings on the Eastern Shore, met to mark the line. Instead of beginning the line at the north point of Pocomoke Bay, they traveled up the river to avoid marshy ground. This short trip began the eastward running of the line about 3 miles north of where it should have started. However, the line's incursion into Maryland was not yet finished. Instead of running a due-east line, the line runs north of east by 5 or 6 degrees. The surveyors apparently ran a compass line and did not compensate for the fact that magnetic north is west of true north for this area. The language of the agreement did not specify a "due-east" line, just that the line should begin at the north point of the bay and run east, but a true east-west line would be assumed.

However, if Calvert had been more attentive to detail, he likely could have gained about 15,000 acres more land for Maryland by insisting that the line begin at the north point of the bay and that it run due east. The current boundary between the two states travels up the Pocomoke River to the point settled upon by Calvert and Scarborough, then it heads east. There is some hint that Scarborough may have been deceptive in running the line. He was a staunch loyalist, a passionate Virginian, and had no love for Catholics.

The boundary across Chesapeake Bay is really an oddity. (See map 3.5.) The beginning point of the bay boundary on the west side was, by charter definition, the point where the Potomac River ended. The map shows two different points being selected to meet the definition with the most northern being the final choice. The boundary point on the east side of the bay was to be the north point of the bay into which the Pocomoke River emptied as mentioned above. The boundary between these two points is now very irregular, although that was not always the case as shown on map 3.5. The current boundary across Chesapeake Bay takes a course through Smith Island to the Pocomoke River. In its course it bisects some islands and changes course several times. The

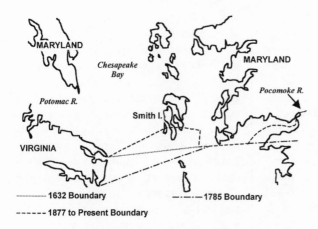

Map 3.5. Chesapeake Bay Boundaries

two states adopted different provisional boundaries over the years but were unable to come to a final determination of the boundary in the bay. They put the matter into the hands of a board of arbitration in 1874, and in 1877 this board determined the line as it is today. The reasons they chose what they did are not known, but apparently they settled on a boundary that was a compromise of previous existing provisional lines. A good deal of the dispute stemmed from the economic value, and hence taxes, from the rich fishery, including oysters, in the bay. It involves more than this, however, as considerable differences exist between Maryland and Virginia over conservation, with Maryland being the more conservation-minded of the two. The bay boundary, marked by orange and white buoys, was not finally settled upon until 1970.

The western boundary with Virginia, now West Virginia, was a different sort of problem. Calvert's charter stated the western boundary was to be the headwaters, or most distant tributary, of the Potomac River, then due north to the Pennsylvania border. Determining the headwaters of a river can be a very puzzling issue because as one travels up a river, determining which branch is still the main river becomes increasingly difficult. This was the case in determin-

ing which upper branch of the Potomac River constituted its headwaters. A dispute ensued between Thomas Fairfax, who held large tracts of land in this area, and the Calverts as to which branch was the headwaters. Fairfax entered into an agreement with Virginia to make the northern branch the headwaters and thus establish that as a boundary point.

The Calverts continued to argue for the southern branch and were basing their argument on the findings of Thomas Cresap, a man knowledgeable about local geography. Cresap determined that the southern branch was the true headwaters of the Potomac; it is in fact about 60 miles longer than the northern branch. It was a case of each party trying to obtain the most territory for their domain. (See map 3.6.) Virginia did not accept Cresap's determination, and the line remained uncertain until 1787 when the U.S. Supreme Court decided the northern branch was the true headwaters. This determination obviously favored Virginia. Cresap may have favored Maryland somewhat in his findings as he held a land grant from that colony near the border with Pennsylvania and was an officer in its militia. The South Branch is un-

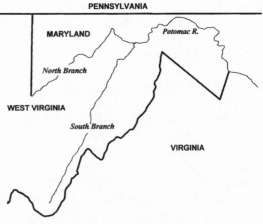

Map 3.6. Upper Potomac River Branches

questionably the longer of the two, and its headwaters are usually regarded as being further west, depending on which stream is deemed its headwaters.

Nonetheless, the North Branch was decreed as the headwaters, and this determination anchored the southern point of the western Maryland boundary. This western boundary, called the Deakins Line, does not run true north and is not a straight line. It has many offsets and is very irregular (as seen only on large-scale maps); according to Maryland officials it was not even intended to be an intercolonial line when run but rather was just a survey by Francis Deakins in 1788 to mark off land grants given to men who served in the Maryland military. The boundary line between the two states follows the margins of these land grants.

In 1910 Maryland brought suit against West Virginia in the U.S. Supreme Court to move the southern end of its western boundary to the Potomac Stone. This stone had been placed in 1897 and was considered as a more accurate marking for the headwaters of the North Branch of the Potomac River than the Fairfax Stone which had been placed in 1746. The Potomac Stone is 1¼ miles west of the Fairfax Stone. The Supreme Court denied Maryland's suit acknowledging that the Potomac Stone undoubtedly more accurately marked the headwaters, but nonetheless, the Deakins Line had long been regarded as the boundary by citizens living in the area and by official actions of the governments of Virginia, West Virginia, and Maryland. Much of the Deakins Line had been obliterated, so the court ordered it resurveyed and remarked. This was done, and the court accepted the results in 1912.

In 1859 Lt. N. Michler ran a true north-south line beginning in the south at the Fairfax Stone and found that his line met the Pennsylvania border three-quarters of a mile west of the Deakins Line. In the 1910 Supreme Court case mentioned above, West Virginia agreed to move the boundary to the line as surveyed by Michler if Maryland would agree to honor land titles previously granted in the area. Maryland refused to do so, and West Virginia withdrew its offer.

With Delaware. Maryland also lost land on the Delmarva Peninsula because the Duke of York, later to become King James II, claimed Delaware because he had conquered the Dutch who had previously conquered the Finns and Swedes who the duke claimed had settled the area in 1631. Although Delaware was land seemingly within Maryland's charter, the duke maintained that the Scandinavians had settled and farmed the area before Calvert obtained his charter, a charter which denied him any land previously under cultivation by a European nation.

The Scandinavian settlement had been wiped out when Calvert got his charter, but that did not matter according to the duke. Notwithstanding the arguments of when the area came under cultivation, the area had been settled by the Scandinavians for years, and because the Marylanders had done nothing about it, the duke felt they had no claim to the area.

William Penn later received Delaware from the duke. Delaware and Pennsylvania were unable to settle the boundaries on the peninsula, so King Charles II settled the peninsular matter in 1685 by decreeing that a line would be drawn across the peninsula from Cape Henlopen (now called Fenwick Island) due west to the Chesapeake side of the peninsula. At the exact center of this east-west line another straight line would be drawn north to the western extremity of the 12-mile arc around New Castle, then due north to the Pennsylvania border. This would determine Maryland's borders on the peninsula. Much litigation ensued determining where Cape Henlopen was located. The Calverts thought it was in one place, the Penns another. Old Dutch maps showed Cape Henlopen about 25 miles south of the place named Cape Henlopen on now-current maps. (See map 3.2.) After much arguing, Penn won this boundary battle, and the border was drawn from the more southerly point.

With Pennsylvania. Maryland's northern border with Pennsylvania is the one that caused the most irritation to the Calverts and that took the longest to resolve. The Calverts assumed the border was the 40th parallel because that is what their charter very clearly said. Marylanders established a fort on the Susquehanna River as near to the 40th parallel as they could determine and established that as the northern extent of their territory. Pennsylvanians contested the location of this fort as they felt it intruded into their territory. The dispute went to the Lord Chief Justice in England who determined that the southern boundary of Pennsylvania was to be the 12-mile arc drawn around New Castle, Delaware, and the beginning of the 40th degree. This was the wording used in Penn's original charter.

In the 1600s a degree of parallel was sometimes considered to be a strip of land 1 degree wide. Using this reasoning, the beginning of a degree would be the end of the previous degree, the first degree would begin at 0 parallel and end at the first parallel. Continuing this thinking, the beginning of the 40th degree would be the 39th parallel. The discussion of which parallel was the correct parallel was further complicated by the fact that the eastern end of the boundary was to meet the 12-mile arc drawn around New Castle, Delaware. (See map 3.2.) Neither the 39th nor 40th parallels met that arc.

The king urged the Penns and Calverts to settle their border dispute. Members of the two families met during the winter of 1682-83 but could not reach an agreement. Calvert held out for the 40th parallel, Penn wanted access to Chesapeake Bay and argued for the 39th parallel. The Penns probably never expected to achieve a boundary at the 39th parallel but used the unclear language as bargaining power to obtain a boundary as far south as possible.

Finally, in 1760 and after a lot of hostility and wrangling, the Penns and Calverts agreed to accept as their boundary a latitude line drawn from a point 15 miles south of the southernmost part of Philadelphia as the boundary between the two colonies. This did not give the Penn family all they wanted, as they did not get access to Chesapeake Bay, but at least it settled this boundary dispute except for some minor problems, and it did connect to the 12-mile arc around New Castle. The line was surveyed and marked in 1764 by noted English astronomers and mathematicians Charles Mason and Jeremiah Dixon.

Mason's and Dixon's first challenge was to determine the southern edge of Philadelphia as it was in 1760. They did this by examining old deeds and the testimony of residents. They determined that the southern edge of the city was the north wall of a house on the south side of what was then Cedar Street. They couldn't go south from here as that would put them in New Jersey. So they surveyed 31 miles west then 15 miles south to establish the point from which the Maryland-Pennsylvania boundary could be surveyed.

It is interesting to note that had Maryland's northern border been drawn at the 39th parallel, its border would have been just north of Washington, D.C., and Maryland would be only about one-half its present size. Had it been drawn at the 40th parallel, nearly 20 miles north of its present location, Philadelphia, the city so carefully laid out by William Penn, would have been predominantly in Maryland.

With Atlantic Ocean. The U.S. Geological Survey says that generally speaking the individual states recognize an offshore boundary of 3 nautical miles. The United States territorial sea limit contiguous zone has been set at 12 nautical miles but is expected to be extended to 24 nautical miles. The exclusive economic zone boundary is 200 nautical miles. (A nautical mile equals 1.15 land miles.)

Washington, D.C.

The seat of federal government met in several places during this country's early history. Congress, meeting in Philadelphia in 1783, received a number of generous offers for permanently locating the federal capital. Kingston, New York, offered 2 square miles; Annapolis, Maryland, offered 300 acres; New Jersey proposed the town of Nottingham, and Virginia offered the former Virginia colonial capitol and ancillary buildings in Williamsburg.

Requirements for siting the national capital were that it be centrally located and be on a navigable river with access to the Atlantic Ocean. Considering this criteria, the best offer was a combination from Maryland and Virginia, as they jointly offered to cede up to 100 square miles straddling the Potomac River for the capital.

Virginia, and Maryland to some extent, had considerable interest in seeing that the capital was located in the South where southerners could better influence lawmakers concerning their agrarian and low-tariff agenda rather than letting the capital reside in a city like Philadelphia that was oriented to mercantile interests and high tariffs. The Virginia-Maryland property seemed to be a good location as it was centrally located, in an area between the North and the South, and had access to the sea.

President George Washington, accepting the generous gift from Maryland and Virginia, issued a proclamation in 1791 stating that the capital boundaries would begin at a place on the west bank of the Potomac River called Jones's Point. Lines were then drawn east and west at 45 degree angles from true north for 10 miles; both lines then turned 90 degrees to the north, where they ran another 10 miles and met to form the northern corner.

Congress re-ceded to Virginia that portion of the district in their state in 1846. (See map 3.7.) The southern boundary of the district then became the high-water mark of the Potomac on the Virginia side. The reasons for the retrocession of the district south of the Potomac was that the people living there felt their needs were not being attended to by Congress. Their perception was accurate, as

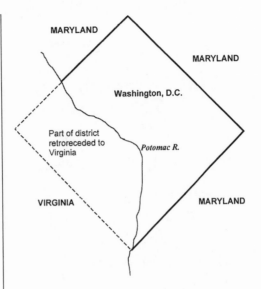

Map 3.7. Washington, D.C.

the trans–Potomac area had never received much attention from federal officials on the north side of the river. They checked with Virginia to see if that state would take them back. After receiving affirmation they successfully petitioned Congress for the retrocession.

The issue of the location of the capital arose again in 1869 when Missourians made a pitch for moving the capital to St. Louis. Strong support also arose during this time for locating it in Cincinnati, Chicago, and Kansas City. Part of the argument for relocating the capital was that by the mid-nineteenth century the original site was no longer centrally located.

New Jersey

New Jersey has natural water features forming all but the north border. (See map 3.8.) Therefore, it might seem that New Jersey would have had little in the way of boundary disputes, but that was not the case. While its boundary problems were not as extensive as some states, they did exist.

New Jersey was originally part of the grant given by Charles II in 1664 to the Duke of York. The extent of the duke's grant, one

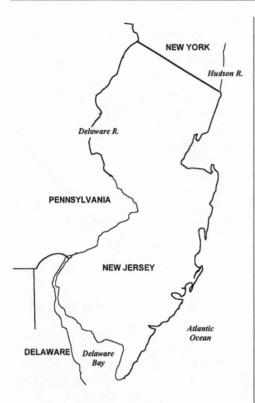

NEW YORK

Hudson R.

Delaware R.

PENNSYLVANIA

NEW JERSEY

Atlantic
Ocean

DELAWARE   Delaware
Bay

Map 3.8. New Jersey

of the shortest and most hastily prepared, consisted of all territory lying between the Connecticut and Delaware rivers. (See map 3.1.) The Connecticut River makes a reasonable eastern boundary line, as it runs as far north as the 45th parallel. The Delaware River, however, peters out around the 42nd parallel and leaves a lot of room for potential boundary problems. After getting his grant, the duke quickly sent a fleet of four ships to the New World to take possession of his grant from the Dutch, who occupied not only New Jersey but also Manhattan Island, the western end of Long Island, the Hudson River Valley as far north as Albany, and the area where the Delaware River emptied into Delaware Bay. (See map 3.10.) The Dutch, realizing they were much too weak to resist, quickly gave in to the duke's forces.

The duke granted New Jersey to John Berkeley and George Carteret in 1664, two friends who had helped the royal family during difficult times in England. Berkeley soon

went bankrupt and sold his share to two Quakers, one of whom also went bankrupt and further divided the colony. One of the men receiving part of the divided colony was William Penn, who would later receive the grant for Pennsylvania. During this time New Jersey was divided into East and West, satisfying the interest of shareholders, including Carteret. This division, however, had nothing to do with the ultimate boundaries of the colony. Carteret and Berkeley were also proprietors in the Carolina grants of 1663 and 1665. Berkeley would also be a governor of Virginia in 1676.

With New York. In his grant to Berkeley and Carteret the Duke of York drew a line on a Dutch map from a branch of the Delaware River near 41 degrees 40 minutes north latitude to the Hudson River near the 41st parallel. One source said the duke thought he was drawing a boundary along a river, and therefore thought the area he was granting was an island, so he called it New Jersey to honor Carteret's native island of Jersey. Maps of the New World in the 17th century were very inaccurate, and the duke never saw his New World possessions.

The grant to Carteret and Berkeley specified that the northern border was defined in the east by the point of the 41st parallel on the Hudson River and on the west by the northernmost branch of the Delaware River at 41 degrees 40 minutes. These points were located in 1686 by surveyors, but no line was marked so its location remained in doubt. In 1719 commissioners were appointed by New York and East New Jersey who located a point at 41 degrees 40 minutes on the Fishkill Branch of the Delaware River. They did not locate 41 degrees on the Hudson because a New York commissioner complained that the astronomical instrument being used was not accurate enough. He was most likely responding to pressure from residents in the general area who feared their land might fall into New Jersey's jurisdiction.

No further action was taken until 1769 when conflicts along the border area motivated the king to appoint commissioners to resolve the boundary issue. New Jersey claimed a strict interpretation of 41 degrees 40 minutes on the Delaware River and 41 degrees on the Hudson River, whereas New York put forth several different boundary possibilities. In October 1769 the commissioners adopted the western point of the line as the Mahackamack Fork of the Delaware River at latitude 41 degrees 21 minutes 37 seconds and the eastern point as a rock on the Hudson River at 41 degrees.

The commissioners placed the western point where they did because a map by Nicholas Vischer, considered the most accurate when the duke made the grant to Berkeley and Carteret, showed the Mahackamack Fork at latitude 41 degrees 40 minutes and concluded that the duke intended this point to be the western terminus of the line. Two members of the commission refused to concur, arguing that if Vischer's map was going to be used for the western point that it should also be used for the eastern point which placed the 41st parallel at the north end of Manhattan Island, approximately 8 miles south of the present east end of the line. This argument did not prevail, and although both colonies were dissatisfied with the decision, New York adopted the commission's determination in 1771 and New Jersey the following year. The king in council approved it in 1773.

The location of the western end selected by the commissioners is at the point where the Delaware River sharply changes direction from running northeast to going northwest. To put the western point at 41 degrees 40 minutes would have put the west point further upriver, creating an awkward slice of New Jersey to the northeast of Pennsylvania.

Staten Island, near New Jersey's northeast corner, presents an interesting boundary interpretation. When considering the island's close proximity to New Jersey, it seems like it would naturally be a part of New Jersey rather than New York, and since New Jersey's eastern boundary was supposed to be the Hudson River, one would think the is-

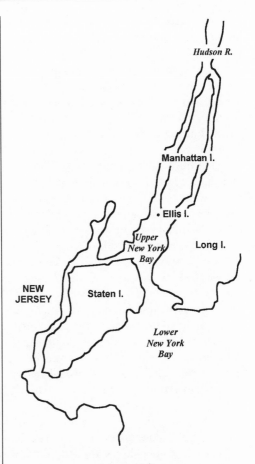

Map 3.9. Staten Island

land would belong to New Jersey. (See maps 3.9 and 3.10.)

The story concerning how it became a part of New York has three different scenarios. One is that when the duke granted New Jersey to Berkeley and Carteret, an upset New York governor, Richard Nicolls, told the duke he had given away the best and most productive part of his colony. The basis for Nicolls' statements was that at the time the duke's land effectively consisted of Manhattan Island, western Long Island, and New Jersey. The interior of New York was Indian country and seemed likely to remain so for quite some time and thus of little value. Nicolls was so furious with the duke's grant that he resigned as governor. The story claims the duke, reacting to Nicolls' resignation, then withdrew Staten Island from the grant.

The second story is that many years after the grant New York businessmen, fearing commercial competition from New Jersey, claimed an arm of the Hudson flowed on the west side of the island, and it therefore belonged to New York. It takes a considerable stretch of the imagination to argue this point, but logic was apparently not paramount in determining the issue.

The third story is that New York's original charter included all small islands in adjacent waters and thus it claimed Staten Island. New Jerseyans argued that at 60 square miles, the island was not small and therefore was not covered in New York's charter. Whichever story is true, the fact is that Staten Island is a part of New York and not New Jersey.

An overriding fact was that New Yorkers were very acquisitive and fearful that New Jersey might control some of the commerce, and they did everything they could to negate any New Jersey claims. Until the mid-nineteenth century New York claimed all waters right up to the New Jersey shore, denying them the opportunity to build piers or wharves. New York in 1834 finally gave in on this point and allowed New Jersey territorial rights to the mid-point of the Hudson and the waterways north and west of Staten Island; the island, however, remained a part of New York.

This was not the end of problems between New Jersey and New York concerning an island. In 1834 the two states entered into a curious agreement that gave New York jurisdiction over the 3 acres of Ellis Island, entry point for millions of immigrants, that was above the high-water line. New Jersey, however, received the submerged land around the island. As years went by the size of the island was increased as soil, rock, and debris were brought in to enlarge it by approximately 25½ acres.

In the 1990s New Jersey sued for their right to claim the landfilled part of the island as theirs, basing their claim on the 1834 agreement. The U.S. Supreme Court agreed in 1998 by awarding New Jersey jurisdiction over the landfilled part of the island settling the long-standing dispute. Political jurisdiction over any part of the island doesn't mean much, however, because the federal government owns all of the island. New Jersey will derive some revenue from tax on gift items sold on the island. Probably more important is the fact that New Jersey has prevailed over New York in the area of bragging rights.

With Atlantic Ocean. The U.S. Geological Survey says that generally speaking the individual states recognize an offshore boundary of 3 nautical miles. The United States territorial sea limit contiguous zone has been set at 12 nautical miles but is expected to be extended to 24 nautical miles. The exclusive economic zone boundary is 200 nautical miles. (A nautical mile equals 1.15 land miles.)

With Delaware. The boundary separating Delaware from New Jersey was a frequent subject of dispute until the U.S. Supreme Court decided in 1935 that Delaware included the Delaware River to the low-water mark on the New Jersey shore within 12 miles of New Castle. (See map 3.2.) The Supreme Court's decision was based on the wording of the original charter specifying that Delaware had jurisdiction over all land within the 12-mile circle around New Castle and that this included the land under the river to the New Jersey shore within the 12-mile radius. South of the arc the boundary follows that main ship channel of the river and bay. North of the arc the boundary with Pennsylvania is in the river, although it is not clear whether it is in the middle of the main channel or the physical center of the river.

With Pennsylvania. The Delaware River was the western boundary of New Jersey because it was a part of the Duke of York's grant, and the western boundary of his grant was specified as the Delaware River. Penn's charter further specified the river as Pennsylvania's eastern boundary. No disputes have occurred over this boundary. Sources are quiet as to where in the river the boundary is located, but maps indicate the boundary is in the middle of the river and moves to the side of islands to place them entirely in one state or the other.

New York

King Charles II of England was very generous to his brother James when he granted him land in the New World. The grant included all territory between the Delaware and Connecticut rivers, part of Maine, all of Long Island, and the islands of Martha's Vineyard and Nantucket. (See maps 2.1, 2.8, 3.1, and 3.10.) The size of the grant was unrealistic, unwieldy, and soon reduced. Maine, Martha's Vineyard, and Nantucket were not useful possessions as they added to administrative costs and produced little revenue. The duke effectively gave up his claim to these lands when he became King James II in 1685 and attempted to establish an all-encompassing royal colony in New England that officially became part of Massachusetts in 1691.

The king didn't think it was important that part of his grant was already claimed by the Dutch since England did not acknowledge Dutch claims to the area the latter called New Netherland, an area that in Dutch minds generally encompassed Rhode Island, Connecticut, New York, Vermont, New Jersey, Delaware, Pennsylvania, and western Massachusetts. The Dutch did, however, occupy some of the area, so James, who was the Duke of York and Lord High Admiral of England, sent a fleet of four warships to the New World in 1664 to subdue the Dutch and lay claim to his colony. The duke didn't like the Dutch anyway because they had slighted him when he briefly resided in Holland, and they were competitors for African trade.

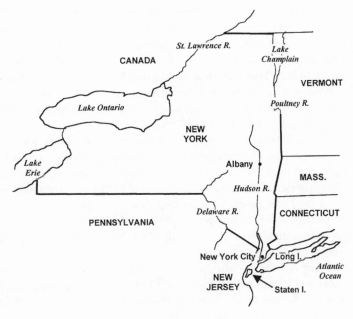

Map 3.10. New York

New Netherland governor Peter Stuyvesant, realizing the weakness of his defenses, capitulated at the appearance of the English ships and gave up Dutch claim to land settled along the Delaware and Hudson rivers and on the western end of Long Island. After Dutch capitulation, the area along the lower end of the Hudson River was renamed New York.

The Dutch, not willing to have the English in control of what they considered their domain, reentered New York in force in July 1673, causing it to surrender. The English retook the city in October 1674. All of this caused little change in the culture or economic activity of the city. Anglicization was a slow process that took a long time.

The duke, who never visited the colony and exercised little personal direction over it, appointed Richard Nicolls, the commander of the English fleet, governor of the colony. The duke showed little interest in his new possession and made some unwise decisions concerning his colony.

With New Jersey. In 1664, the same year he received the grant, the duke sold New

Jersey to John Berkeley and George Carteret. The duke was not being altruistic; the two men had been faithful to the royal family and were owed a favor. Giving away this area so incensed New York governor Nicolls that he resigned stating that the duke had given away the best part of his colony.

The grant to Carteret and Berkeley specified that the northern border was defined in the east by the 41st parallel on the Hudson River and in the west by the northernmost branch of the Delaware River at 41 degrees 40 minutes. These points were located in 1686 by surveyors, but no line was marked, so its precise location remained in doubt. In 1719 commissioners were appointed by New York and East New Jersey who located a point at 41 degrees 40 minutes on the Fishkill Branch of the Delaware River. They did not locate 41 degrees on the Hudson because a New York commissioner complained that the astronomical instrument being used was not accurate enough. He was probably responding to pressure from residents in the area who feared their land might fall into New Jersey's jurisdiction.

No further action was taken until 1769 when the king appointed commissioners to resolve the boundary issue because of shootings and beatings and the unwillingness of property owners in the contested area to pay taxes to either colony. New Jersey claimed a strict interpretation of 41 degrees 40 minutes on the Delaware River and 41 degrees on the Hudson River, whereas New York put forth several different boundary possibilities. In October 1769 the commissioners adopted as the western point of the line as the Mahackamack Fork of the Delaware River at latitude 41 degrees 21 minutes 37 seconds and the eastern point as a rock on the Hudson River at 41 degrees north latitude.

The commissioners placed the western point where they did because a map by Nicholas Vischer, considered the most accurate when the duke made the grant to Berkeley and Carteret, showed the Mahackamack Fork at latitude 41 degrees 40 minutes. Two members of the commission refused to concur,

arguing that if Vischer's map were going to be used for the western point that it should also be used for the eastern point, which placed the 41st parallel at the north end of Manhattan Island, approximately 8 miles south of the present east end of the line. While both colonies were dissatisfied with the decision, New York adopted the commission's determination in 1771 and New Jersey the following year. The king in council approved it in 1773.

The location of the western end selected by the commissioners is at the point where the course of the Delaware River changes from running northeast to going northwest. To put the western point at 41° 40' would have put the west point further upriver, creating an awkward slice of New Jersey to the northeast of Pennsylvania.

The two states have had recent jurisdictional problems over an island in New York harbor. In 1834 the two states entered into a curious agreement that gave New York jurisdiction over the 3 acres of Ellis Island that was above water. (See map 3.9.) New Jersey, however, received jurisdiction over the submerged land around the island. As years went by the island was increased as material was brought in enlarging it by approximately 25½ acres.

New Jersey sued for their right to claim the landfilled part of the island as theirs, basing their claim on the 1834 agreement. New York's claim to all the island was based on the idea that millions of immigrants had entered the U.S. through the island. All of them had been told that they were entering through New York. In addition, people living on the island always voted in New York, and children born on the island had always been registered in New York. Nonetheless, in 1998 the U.S. Supreme Court agreed with New Jersey's claim — the 1834 agreement was upheld. Political jurisdiction over any of the island has little meaning because the federal government owns all of the island. New Jersey will derive some revenue from tax on gift items sold on the island. Probably more important is the fact that New Jersey has prevailed over New York in the area of bragging rights.

Staten Island, which is much closer to New Jersey than New York, has always been a part of New York. (See maps 3.9 and 3.10.) Early in its history, New York sought to control all commerce on the Hudson River and surrounding waters. They, therefore, sought to deny to New Jersey all opportunities to participate in trade. New York did this by claiming the charter to the Duke of York gave the state all small islands in the harbor and all water rights up to the high-tide line on the New Jersey shore. New Jersey officials countered that at 60 square miles Staten Island was not small. Finally, in 1834, the two states worked out a deal whereby New Jersey received territorial rights to the center of the Hudson and the waterways north and west of Staten Island, while New York retained the right to the island.

With Pennsylvania. The east-west border between New York and Pennsylvania was somewhat of a problem due to different interpretations of William Penn's charter. His charter said his grant was 3 degrees of latitude high from the *beginning* of the 40th degree to the *beginning* of the 3 and 40th degree.

The Penn family interpreted this as running from the 39th parallel to the 42nd parallel, interpreting a degree of parallel as 1 degree wide, and the beginning of the 40th degree was the 39th parallel because parallels began at 0 — the beginning of the first degree was 0 parallel, the beginning of the 2nd degree was the first parallel, and so on. This was an occasional understanding of a degree in the 17th century. Consequently, Penn labored to establish his southern boundary with Maryland, as detailed elsewhere, at the 39th parallel. He was unsuccessful, as that boundary was finally placed near 39 degrees 44 minutes.

Some uncertainty and confusion exists about why the New York–Pennsylvania boundary was placed at the 42nd parallel. One source says New York's governor and surveyor general interpreted the New York–

Pennsylvania boundary as being the 43rd parallel ignoring the *beginning* part. Another source, however, says that after the French and Indian War the Penns ceased to press for that boundary and in 1774 asked the crown to approve a boundary drawn along the 42nd parallel. This would make sense if Pennsylvania's southern boundary began at the beginning of the 40th degree (the 39th parallel), as the 42nd parallel would then constitute a height of 3 degrees, the stipulation in Penn's charter. It doesn't make sense, however, if the Penns were somehow expecting a northern boundary of the 43rd parallel because people just don't give up land, especially if their neighbor is willing to concede it.

For Pennsylvania to accept a northern boundary at the 42nd parallel doesn't make much sense from another standpoint. In 1760 the Penns and Calverts settled on the southern Pennsylvania boundary as being north of the 39th parallel (approximately 39° 44'). Some sources indicate that the Penns pressed for a more northern boundary than the 42nd parallel because they wanted to gain enough frontage on Lake Erie for a port. Further supporting the idea for a more northern Pennsylvania–New York boundary is that Penn's charter stipulated that his colony was to be 3 degrees high. Once the southern boundary was placed at a point higher than the 39th parallel, it is reasonable that the Penns would expect their colony to remain 3 degrees of latitude high. However it came about, the two colonies did settle upon the 42nd parallel as their boundary. A 1783 map shows this boundary running from the Delaware River to Lake Erie, although surveyors representing the two states didn't run and mark the line until 1786–87. Legislatures of both states approved this line.

Another border issue with Pennsylvania involved what later became known as the Erie Triangle. (See map 3.14.) In the interest of fostering harmony among the forming states, of promoting the confederation of those states, and of gaining support in Congress for its claim to the area north of Massachusetts to the Connecticut River, New York in 1780 agreed to cede its claim to western lands, the boundaries of which were very vague, to the United States to be used for the benefit of states that joined the confederation. Since the Duke of York's charter granted land only to the Delaware River in the west the astute reader may wonder on what grounds New York claimed any territory west of that river; New York's claim was based on its conquest and dominance of the Iroquois.

The location of New York's western boundary was not defined in 1780 other than the stipulation that it not be east of a meridian line drawn 20 miles west of the most westerly part of the Niagara River. In 1781 the state agreed to limit its jurisdiction to a meridian line drawn from the western end of Lake Ontario, which is where New York's western boundary is today, and cede all land beyond this to the federal government. This was at a time when the 45th parallel was discussed as the border between the United States and Great Britain, and New York expected its north border would be the 45th parallel. In 1782, however, negotiations between the two countries established a boundary between them as being along the 45th parallel to the St. Lawrence River, then up that river, across Lake Ontario, up the Niagara River, and across Lake Erie, thereby depriving New York of a lot of land it expected to receive north of the two lakes and the St. Lawrence River. New York probably didn't mean for the line from the western edge of Lake Ontario to be drawn south of Lake Erie to the 42nd parallel but instead through the center of the lake to where it would meet the northwestern border of Pennsylvania. Nonetheless, the official interpretation was to draw the border to the 42nd parallel. Surveyors completed this line in 1791, and New York lost the "triangle." Pennsylvania bought the more than 200,000 acres in the Erie Triangle from the federal government in 1792.

Massachusetts also laid a weak claim to the Erie Triangle. Its claim was based on an interpretation of their 1629 and 1691 charters that gave them land to the western sea that was not under the jurisdiction of another state or nation. Massachusetts released its claim to the triangle in 1786.

With Canada. The northern border was generally established by negotiations conducted in 1782 by the United States and Great Britain and formally embraced by the Treaty of 1783. Since the 1783 treaty was frequently vague in defining boundaries, adjustments had to be made by the 1814 Treaty of Ghent and the 1842 Webster-Ashburton Treaty.

Before 1782 the United States and Britain had discussed a boundary between the two countries as the 45th parallel all the way to the Pacific Ocean. Such a boundary would have preserved for Britain the valuable trapping around Lake Superior, the Columbia River, and the fur trade of the Pacific Northwest. The United States and New York would have gained prized land in what is now southern Quebec. This plan fell through largely because U.S. negotiators realized more was to be lost by such a deal than gained. Nonetheless, New Yorkers were a bit crestfallen when, in 1782, a preliminary agreement was struck between the United States and Great Britain to draw the boundary along the 45th parallel only to the St. Lawrence River, then along that river, through Lake Ontario, along the Niagara River, and through Lake Erie. This agreement was formally ratified by the Treaty of 1783 and modified by later treaties.

As indicated, part of the northern boundary of New York was intended to exactly follow the 45th parallel. Unknown to the treaty negotiators, however, was that the 45th parallel had been incorrectly surveyed by Valentine and Collins in 1771–74. For the most part the line runs a quarter of a mile to a mile north of the 45th parallel but with a slight dip below the parallel for about 30 miles immediately east of the St. Lawrence River. This line was disputed by the United States and Great Britain until it was finally settled by the Webster-Ashburton Treaty in

1842, which established the incorrectly surveyed line as the true boundary between the two nations.

An interesting sidelight of the Valentine-Collins Line is that the survey crew submitted a sundries bill for large purchases of wine, rum, and brandy. Therefore, one can speculate whether the inaccuracy of the line they marked was due to inadequate instruments, inadequate techniques, or inadequate restraint.

The resolution of this boundary was partly a common-sense matter. Settlers along the 45th parallel had long seen themselves as either American or British based on the Valentine-Collins Line. The line was really important to the United States because it had built Rouse's Fort on Lake Champlain thinking it was south of the 45th parallel. The fort was an important part of the U.S. strategic defenses of the north boundary and built at a cost of over a million dollars. When the line was accurately surveyed, the fort was north of the parallel and in jeopardy of being dismantled. The land between the line and the 45th parallel constitutes a total of 61 square miles between the St. Lawrence River and Hall's Stream on the New Hampshire border. New York's part of this border ends in the east at the deep-water channel of Lake Champlain.

At the point where the 45th parallel, as surveyed, meets the center of the St. Lawrence River the international boundary follows the center of that river, the center of Lake Ontario, the center of the Niagara River, and the center of Lake Erie. The treaties mentioned previously determined to which country various islands belonged.

With Vermont. The Duke of York's original charter set his eastern boundary at the Connecticut River. Even though he claimed all land west of the Connecticut River, he ceded jurisdiction west of that river to Connecticut and to Massachusetts, in both cases to approximately 20 miles east of the Hudson River. The duke never, however, ceded land west of the Connecticut River and

north of Massachusetts. This area, later to become Vermont, was to be a land of strife and contention for many years.

Between 1750 and 1764 New Hampshire governor Benning Wentworth granted 138 towns in southwest Vermont. He was claiming jurisdiction of this area for New Hampshire based on the fact that New York had given both Connecticut and Massachusetts jurisdiction to within 20 miles of the Hudson River and figured this would apply to New Hampshire as well. Besides, New Hampshire considered the duke's charter invalid respecting its provision to the Connecticut River. The New Hampshire governor was not being altruistic in the grant for towns, as he was reserving large parcels within each for himself.

New York speculators also granted land in Vermont, and sometimes the New York grants overlapped the New Hampshire grants. Most of the New York grants were given to speculators, and thus New York placed few settlers in the area, whereas most of the New Hampshire grants were settled by farmers. The settlers with New Hampshire grants felt that since their grants were made by an official appointed by the king that their grants should be valid regardless of the jurisdictional conflicts by the two colonies. New York officials, however, did not honor the New Hampshire grants and insisted that the settlers buy the land from the New York speculators. Since they had paid for the land once, this naturally infuriated the settlers and considerable conflict ensued. It began with lawsuits brought by both sides. For its part, New York felt it had solid grounds to claim the area based on treaty language.

The animosity escalated with surveyors and settlers being driven out. One New Hampshire grantee was taken from his home by a New York sheriff. New York deputies killed at least two men in another encounter. The settlers formed an armed band called the "Green Mountain Boys" led by Ethan Allen. This group stirred so much trouble that New York officials offered a reward for Allen's capture. Although they were greatly feared, the

Green Mountain Boys used threats and intimidation more than any other tactic to accomplish their goals. The Vermonters eventually established an independent republic owing no allegiance to either New York nor New Hampshire.

New York formed a commission in 1790 to resolve the Vermont issue and establish a boundary. The boundary they established began at the Massachusetts border and then ran along town boundaries that had been granted by New Hampshire. This caused the boundary to go west ever so slightly from the northwest corner of Massachusetts then head north along the western margin of nine New Hampshire towns to the Poultney River, down the middle of its channel to East Bay, then through the deepest channel of East Bay and Lake Champlain to the international boundary with Canada (roughly the 45th parallel). This line puts the border slightly over 20 miles east of the Hudson River, just about where the New Hampshire governor thought it should be all along.

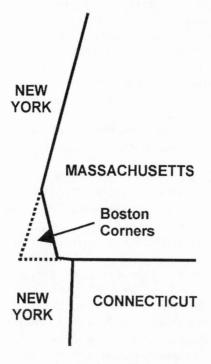

Map 3.11. Boston Corners

With Massachusetts. The border with Massachusetts was established before the border with Vermont. This border was also the scene of considerable conflict as settlers and speculators from both colonies vied for the area. Mobs formed on both sides bent on inflicting violence on each other. They engaged in burning homes, barns, fields, and forests. Some homes were robbed and ransacked. Sheriffs of both colonies jailed settlers from the other colony. At least one man was murdered. This conflict had mostly abated by the mid–1700s when New York and Massachusetts agreed to their common border in 1750. Official settlement notwithstanding, border conflict continued for a few additional years.

The New York border with Massachusetts is mostly a straight line nearly parallel to and approximately 20 miles east of the Hudson River. Since the area west of the Connecticut River was settled mostly by people from Massachusetts, New York finally realized the futility of trying to establish control and jurisdiction over that area.

The extreme southern part of the New York–Massachusetts boundary makes a sharp turn to the southeast and was much more easily resolved than the rest of the border. This change in direction was made to cut off an area called "Boston Corners" from Massachusetts and place it in New York. (See map 3.11.) In 1848 the inhabitants of this community petitioned Massachusetts for release to New York. The request was granted in 1853 and agreed to by the U.S. Congress in 1855. The reason for the request was that geography of the area isolated Boston Corners citizens from Massachusetts. In order for them to conduct any official business with Massachusetts they had to travel through New York and Connecticut. This was a boundary issue where common sense prevailed rather than state hubris.

With Connecticut. The New York boundary with Connecticut is another situation where the duke's charter gave him jurisdiction to the Connecticut River, but he was never able to enforce it. The border negotiated between the two colonies was mostly to be 20 miles east of the Hudson River and approximately parallel to it. The two colonies agreed that the line should start at the mouth of Byram Brook (or River), and follow it upstream to a "wading place," then northwest about 8 miles, then run nearly parallel to Long Island Sound for 12 miles, then turn northwest again until it came to a point approximately 20 miles west of the Hudson River, then turn north to the Massachusetts line. This put part of the Connecticut line to within about 8 miles of the Hudson River. To compensate for this loss, the colonies agreed that an equivalent strip called "The Oblong," about 1¾ miles wide and consisting of 61,440 acres, would be added to New York's eastern boundary beginning at the line paralleling Long Island Sound and running all the way to the Massachusetts border. (See map 3.12.)

The protrusion of Connecticut so close to the Hudson River was due to the New Haven Colony, founded in 1638. New Haven preferred independence from all other political jurisdictions, but it knew they did not have the resources to remain that way. Its absorption into Connecticut in 1664 was due to a preference to unite with Puritan Connecticut rather than possibly be absorbed into Anglican New York.

Although the duke's charter clearly gave him Long Island, New York and Connecticut contended for control of the eastern part of Long Island because Connecticut had established some towns there. Connecticut's claim was based on a grant to William Alexander Stirling. When the Duke of York died, his agent mortgaged the land to men from New Haven and Saybrook. Connecticut eventually absorbed Saybrook and New Haven. No one, however, ever bothered to pay off the mortgage, and the Duke of York bought the patent from Stirling's heirs, thus reclaiming possession of the entire island. This, coupled with the Duke of York's charter giving him Long Island, was enough for a commission in 1644 to confirm the duke's hegemony over the island.

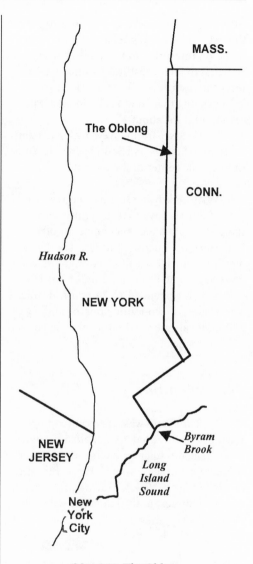

Map 3.12. The Oblong

New York also gained control over Fishers Island in Long Island Sound. (See map 2.2.) This island lies about 2½ miles from the southeastern Connecticut shore and would seemingly belong to that state. Connecticut apparently had control of the island until near the end of the War for American Independence, but at that time New York began to assume control of the island based on the interpretation of the Duke of York's 1664 charter giving him jurisdiction over all small islands. A joint New York–Connecticut committee met in 1878–79 to resolve the ownership of the island. After maintaining that they should have ownership of the island based on interpretation of their charter and nearness to their coastline, Connecticut representatives ceded all claim in 1880 acknowledging that New York had actual possession of it for about a century.

The line separating New York and Connecticut in Long Island Sound generally runs through the center of the channel.

With Atlantic Ocean. The U.S. Geological Survey says that generally speaking the individual states recognize an offshore boundary of 3 nautical miles. The United States territorial sea limit contiguous zone has been set at 12 nautical miles but is expected to be extended to 24 nautical miles. The exclusive economic zone boundary is 200 nautical miles. (A nautical mile equals 1.15 land miles.)

Pennsylvania

William Penn was a persecuted English Quaker who wanted to establish a colony where religious toleration was the norm, very unlike most other colonies. He had tried to do this in West New Jersey, where he had a financial interest in the late 1670s with some

other Quakers, but this venture was not successful. With his goal of a colony based on religious toleration still in mind, in 1681 he received a charter for Pennsylvania from King Charles II of England. Penn received the proprietary grant of lands in payment for a debt the crown owed his father. This grant came after all of the coastal land from New Hampshire to South Carolina had been granted, so Penn received interior lands. The grant's boundaries were fairly precise: The province was to be 3 degrees of latitude high and 5 degrees of longitude wide. The eastern boundary was the Delaware River, the northern was the *beginning* of the 43rd parallel, the southern was the *beginning* of the 40th parallel and the 12-mile arc around New Castle, Delaware, and the western boundary 5 degrees west of the Delaware River.

Border disputes involved the entire Penn family (William's second wife, Hannah, and their sons John, Thomas, and Richard; Penn's son by his first wife was disinherited) on all borders except the Delaware River. The disputes involved Maryland, Delaware, Virginia, Connecticut, and New York.

With Delaware. Penn was happy with his grant but concerned that he did not have a port on the Atlantic Ocean. He acquired Delaware from the Duke of York to give him control of the Delaware Bay and Delaware River and thus ready access to the sea. A 12-mile arc had previously been drawn from the courthouse spire at New Castle, Delaware, to separate the duke's lands from Penn's lands. This arc is still part of Pennsylvania's southern border and is the only state border in the United States that is a circle segment. (See maps 3.2 and 3.13.) The Delawareans, however, were never happy being a part of Pennsylvania. Penn granted them the

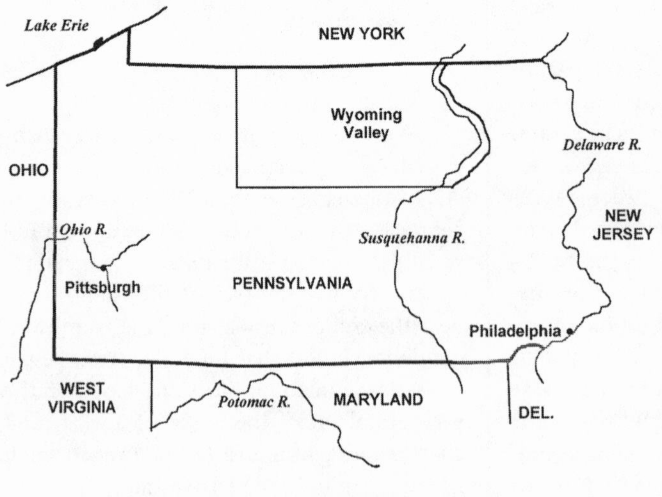

Map 3.13. Pennsylvania

right to a separate legislature in the early 1700s, although the two areas continued to share a common governor until 1778.

With Maryland. The border with Maryland was contested by the Penns and Calverts for many years. Penn's charter said his southern boundary was the *beginning* of the 40th degree of latitude, which is in effect the 39th parallel, and extended to the *beginning* of the 43rd parallel, which is the 42nd parallel. When a degree of latitude is considered as 1 degree in width, which was occasionally the case in the 17th century, the beginning of 1 degree is the end of the previous degree because the first degree begins at 0 and ends with the first parallel, the second begins where the first ends, and so on. This conflicted with Calvert's charter, which predated Penn's. Calvert's charter stated that his northern border was the 40th parallel without saying that it was the *beginning* of that parallel. Resolving this problem took three-quarters of a century.

The resolution of the border would come about not by a strict reading of the charters, which of course was impossible, but rather by where everyone involved sort of figured it would be. All of the players involved figured that the 40th parallel was somewhere near the head of Chesapeake Bay, near the latitude of New Castle, and they knew that it was to connect with the 12-mile circle drawn around New Castle. Near the head of Chesapeake Bay was where John Smith's map of 1624 placed the 40th parallel. That was where all of the following thought it would be: Charles I who granted Maryland to the Calverts, the Calverts who received that grant, Charles II who granted Pennsylvania to Penn, Penn who received that grant, and James II and Queen Anne who later confirmed Penn's grant.

The players, therefore, kind of knew where the border was to be, but no one knew exactly where to place it. In 1760, the Penns and Calverts agreed to an east-west boundary 15 miles south of the southernmost edge of Philadelphia, latitude 39 degrees 44 min-

utes. This border did intersect with the arc around New Castle, a point that was mentioned in Penn's charter. It also kept Philadelphia in Pennsylvania, and the solution kept Maryland from being squeezed so small that it would hardly be a viable state at all. If the 40th parallel had been used as the boundary, a large part of Philadelphia would have been in Maryland. If the 39th parallel had been used, Maryland's northern border would have been just north of Washington, D.C. The state would have lost Baltimore and all of its western land. A factor in the resolution of the dispute was that Pennsylvania Quakers had more political muscle than Maryland Catholics.

With West Virginia. Pennsylvania's border with West Virginia was settled when that state was still a part of Virginia. Pennsylvanians encountered some border conflicts with the Virginians. Virginia's land claims dated back to 1609 and the original charter granted to the London Company. This charter included a 400-mile north-south coastline centered on Old Point Comfort (approximately the 37th parallel, just south of Hampton, Virginia), and extended all the way to the western sea (Pacific Ocean). When Virginia became a royal province in 1624, all unoccupied land reverted to the crown. Nonetheless, Virginia continued to claim all territory not assigned to another colony — and even some land included in the charters of other colonies.

Virginians settled the southwestern part of Pennsylvania before any Pennsylvanians settled there. Then, as now, possession counts for a lot. In addition, the Virginians had played a large part in defending the Pennsylvania frontier during the early years of the French and Indian War, whereas the pacifistic Pennsylvania Quakers did not help defend their western frontier. Also, Virginians had built roads and forts in the area. In addition, George II in 1749 chartered a half million acres in southwestern Pennsylvania to the Ohio Land Company, some of whose members were Virginians. Therefore, the

Virginians felt entitled to the area regardless of what Penn's charter claimed. The two colonies finally settled their differences at the behest of the Continental Congress. The result was that commissioners from both Virginia and Pennsylvania met in 1779 and agreed to extend the Mason-Dixon Line 5 degrees from the Delaware River (the point originally intended by Penn's charter) and north from that point. In the agreement Pennsylvania agreed to recognize land titles of the settlers from Virginia.

The western part of the West Virginia–Pennsylvania border is a straight line drawn from the west end of the east-west border due north to the 42nd parallel which ends in Lake Erie. In early discussions of the border with Virginia, the Virginians wanted this line to conform to the contours of the Delaware River, probably thinking this definition best met the language of Penn's charter. Fortunately for surveyors this was not the result of negotiations between the two colonies, and a straight north-south line was chosen.

This north-south border does create an interesting anomaly, however. The fact that the border is drawn 5 degrees of longitude west from the Delaware River, and no further, creates a thin strip of land about 64 miles long and approximately 16 miles wide at its southern, and widest, point. It would seem, from a common-sense point of view, that it would have made much more sense for the southern border of Pennsylvania to have extended another 16 miles to the Ohio

River, thereby including this thin finger of land in Pennsylvania's jurisdiction. Boundaries, of course, were not drawn with common-sense political geographical divisions in mind but, in this case, were developed in adherence to a charter as best as it could be interpreted.

With Ohio. The boundary with Ohio was created by Pennsylvania's western boundary as 5 degrees longitude west of the Delaware River and the decision to draw a straight line north from the end of Pennsylvania's southern boundary. This boundary was in place before Congress created the Northwest Territory in 1787.

With Canada. The international boundary in Lake Erie is the center of the lake, the result of a treaty between the United States and Great Britain worked out in 1782 and signed in 1783. This boundary was confirmed by treaties in 1814 and 1842.

With New York. Penn's charter specified his northern border as the *beginning* of the 43rd parallel, i.e., the 42nd degree. The New York governor at one time apparently was ready to accept the 43rd parallel, but this idea was short-lived, and the 42nd parallel became the acknowledged boundary. A 1783 map shows the 42nd parallel as the boundary, and surveyors representing Pennsylvania and New York in 1786–87 ran and marked the line on that parallel.

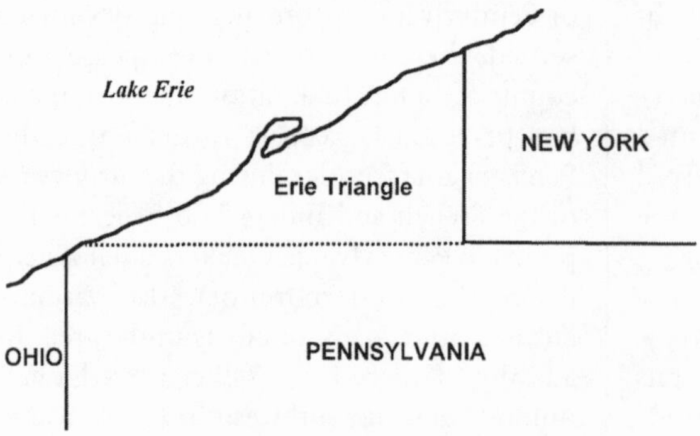

Once the 42nd parallel had been agreed upon, one more adjustment needed to be made to bring Pennsylvania's boundaries to their modern form. This involved a tract of land called the "Erie Triangle." This area is formed by drawing a line south from the west end of Lake Ontario to the 42nd parallel. The area of this triangle is over 200,000 acres. (See map 3.14.) Pennsylvania wanted a port on Lake Erie and with the northern boundary drawn at the 42nd parallel, Pennsylvania had only

Map 3.14. Erie Triangle

4 or 5 miles of land fronting Lake Erie, and none of that provided a suitable port.

Two colonies had some claim to the area. New York claimed the area because it lay north of the 42nd parallel, the line agreed to as the boundary between Pennsylvania and New York. The story about why New York finally ceded the area to the United States is complex. In 1780 New York agreed to cede western lands to the federal government to promote the developing Federal Confederation but did not define the boundary other than to say it was not east of a meridian line drawn 20 miles west of the Niagara River. In 1781 the line was defined when New York agreed to a western boundary drawn due south from the west end of Lake Ontario.

This was at a time when the 45th parallel was considered a possibility as the boundary between the United States and Great Britain and New York was declaring that it was willing to limit its borders to the meridian drawn at the west end of Lake Ontario from the 45th parallel to Lake Erie. Unfortunately, the north and south points were not clearly identified. An agreement was formulated in 1782 and ratified by the Treaty of 1783 that made the border between England and the United States as ascending the St. Lawrence River from the 45th parallel, across Lake Ontario, up the Niagara River, and across Lake Erie. The boundary was the middle of the watercourses in all cases. Confusion existed as to the location of New York's western border south of Lake Erie. Was it along the watercourses as New York maintained, or did it run from the meridian at the west end of Lake Ontario to the 42nd parallel? The latter interpretation was adopted, and the line was drawn in 1791 establishing New York's western boundary. Thus the area ceded by New York included the 200,000 acres called the Erie Triangle. Pennsylvania eagerly bought this area from the federal government in 1792 for $151,640.25.

Massachusetts also claimed the triangle based on its sea-to-sea charter; Massachusetts released its weak claim in 1786.

With New Jersey. Colonial charters defined the Delaware River as the western boundary of New Jersey and the eastern boundary of Pennsylvania, so this river was a long-standing established boundary. Sources are silent as to where in the river the boundary is placed — the center of the main channel or the center of the river. Maps suggest that the center of the river as the boundary, skirting islands to place them in one state or the other.

And Connecticut. Pennsylvania and Connecticut are not adjacent states but they did have a major border conflict. How could this be? Connecticut was 200 miles to the east and separated from Pennsylvania by New York. Connecticut's 1662 charter was one of those which granted land from sea to sea, excepting any territory held by another colony. Europeans of this era thought the North American continent was very narrow, perhaps only a few hundred miles wide. General opinion was that the distance from the Atlantic to the Alleghenies was about 300 miles, so it was assumed the distance from these mountains to the Pacific was about the same. Other sources, however, claim the English kings were aware the distance from ocean to ocean was more like 3,000 miles, and these ocean-to-ocean grants were made to claim as much land as possible to strengthen the British claim in her territorial contests with France and Spain. Connecticut's sea-to-sea provision excluded New York but not Pennsylvania, which had not been chartered in 1662.

Connecticut could lay a claim to all of Pennsylvania between the 41st and 42nd parallels but did not press the issue and had, in fact, listed its western boundary as New York in official documents. In 1750 a land speculating business called the Susquehanna Company began looking around for some new land. They knew of Connecticut's tenuous claim to the northern part of Pennsylvania and bought land between the 41st and 42nd parallels and 120 miles wide beginning at a point 10 miles east of the Susquehanna

River from the Indians in northern Pennsylvania. (See map 3.13.) They then sold parcels
to settlers who were tired of coaxing a living
from the thin and rocky New England soil.

The company pressured Connecticut
officials to establish towns in the area, called
the "Wyoming Valley." Connecticut did so,
causing sharp conflicts between 1769 and
1784, called the "Pennamite Wars," resulting
in much posturing, violence, and some
bloodshed. Both Pennsylvania and Connecticut made land grants in the area. The
Susquehanna Company settlers who came
into the valley were from other colonies and
were openly hostile to the Pennsylvania
Quakers.

A special commission set up in 1782 by
the new federal government decided that the
contested area belonged to Pennsylvania.
Part of the resolution was that the grants of
land made by the Susquehanna Company
were upheld, and the Pennsylvanians who
held titles to the same land received cash settlements. Disputes continued into the early
1800s, but no reversal of the 1782 court action occurred.

4

UPPER SOUTH REGION

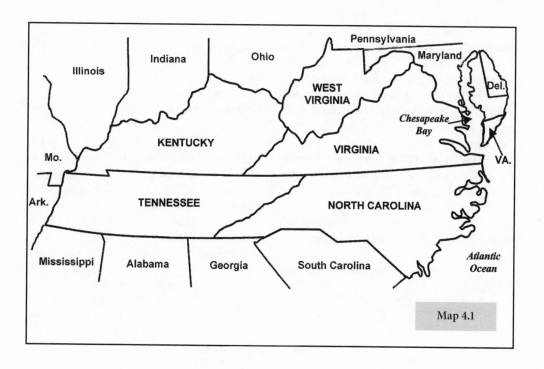

Map is not to scale; boundaries are roughly drawn.

Kentucky

When Virginia extended to the Ohio and Mississippi rivers, it seemed inevitable that the eastern and western parts of Virginia would separate; the differences in the two areas were great. The eastern part consisted of a settled planter class that held slaves and was urbane and educated. In contrast, in the early years the area west of the Appalachian Mountains consisted of people on the move who felt crowded when they could see the smoke rising from the chimney of their neighbors. Their economy was largely hardscrabble subsistence farming rather than producing commodities for market. Agitation for separation began as early as 1784.

Other problems existed as well: The easterners didn't pay much attention to the needs of the westerners, mostly the need for defense against Indians, and the westerners resented it. Communication was also very slow between the two areas. The capital, Richmond, was far away from the westerners, and its interests were oriented to the eastern establishment. Nonetheless, it was Virginia that was involved in determining many of Kentucky's boundaries before the latter became a state in 1792. (See map 4.2.)

With Ohio, Indiana, and Illinois. When Virginia established the Kentucky District in 1776 in its western region, it set the district's northern boundary at the northern shore of the Ohio River. Eight years later, when Virginia ceded to the federal government all land it claimed north of the Ohio River, it defined the ceded land's southern boundary as the river's north shore. Later interpretation placed the boundary specifically at the low-water mark on the north shore of the river. The Virginia cession established that river as Kentucky's boundary with the future states of Ohio, Indiana, and Illinois.

Years later Ohio brought suit claiming the center of the river as the boundary. The U.S. Supreme Court affirmed in 1820 that the low-water mark on the northern shore, as it existed in 1784, was the boundary between the two states. This ruling was later extended to Indiana and Illinois. Determining, many years later, where the low-water line was in 1784 was an impossible task. The exact placement of this boundary was very slow in coming to fruition. The Supreme Court ruled in 1985 that the boundary between Kentucky and Indiana is "a series of straight lines between sequentially numbered geodetic points."* The boundary between Kentucky and Ohio and Illinois had not been as clearly defined by 1992 as that between Kentucky and Indiana. All islands in the river belong to Kentucky.

Rivers often alter their channel, and the Ohio River has done this in one notable place opposite the entrance of the Green River, near Evansville, Indiana. In 1792 the Ohio River flowed north of an island called Green River Island, an area of 2,000 acres opposite the mouth of Kentucky's Green River. Over time the channel shifted to the south, and the island became attached to Indiana. This naturally created

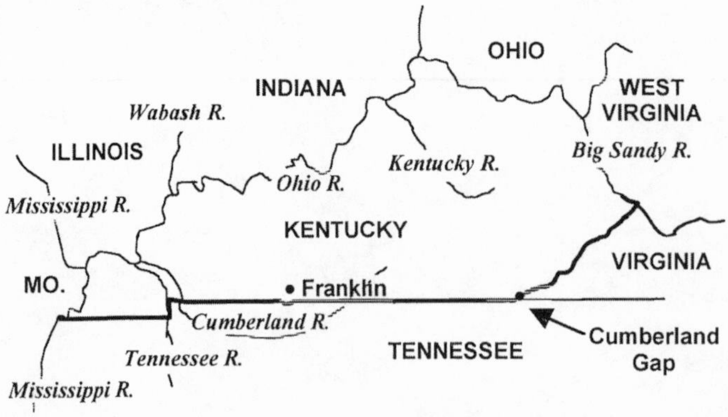

Map 4.2. Kentucky

*Kleber, John E., ed., *The Kentucky Encyclopedia* (Lexington: The University Press of Kentucky, 1992), p. 103.

contention between the states as to who had jurisdiction over the area and resulted in an 1890 U.S. Supreme Court ruling upholding Kentucky's claim to the island because the area was a part of Kentucky in 1792. (See map 4.3.)

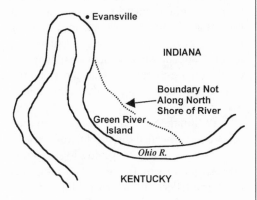

Map 4.3. Green River Island

With Missouri. Kentucky's border with Missouri along the Mississippi River was fairly easy to determine. The Treaty of 1763 established the western boundary of Great Britain as the Mississippi River. Twenty years later the Treaty of 1783 set the western boundary of the newly formed United States as the center of the river. The river boundary is not the actual center of the river but has been defined as center of the deepest channel.

The boundary does not follow the center of the channel in all places now. The Mississippi River meanders and thus changes its course. The U.S. Supreme Court has ruled that boundaries do not change when a meandering river changes course due to catastrophic events, but boundaries do move when the changes occur due to natural meandering.

The westernmost part of Kentucky, called the "New Madrid Bend" or "Kentucky Bend," juts noticeably into Missouri where the Mississippi River takes a northbound course creating a circular area of about 10 square miles before the river heads south again. (See maps 4.4 and 4.5.) Ownership of this piece of land was never a problem be-

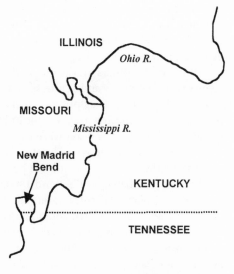

Map 4.4. New Madrid Bend

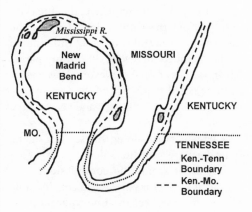

Map 4.5. New Madrid Bend Detail

tween Kentucky and Missouri, but Tennessee attempted to claim the area since it was attached to their state. This anomaly will be taken up in the discussion of the boundary with Tennessee.

With Tennessee. The border between Virginia and North Carolina was established as the parallel of 36 degrees 30 minutes from the Atlantic Ocean to the Pacific Ocean when a group of men received a charter for Carolina in 1665. The western extent of this domain ended at the Mississippi River by the Treaty of 1763 and also excluded land given to the Chickasaw Indians between the Tennessee and Mississippi rivers. When Virginia and North Carolina ceded their western lands, this parallel became the boundary between Kentucky and Tennessee.

Although the official location of the border between Kentucky and Tennessee was very clear, the skill and techniques of the many surveyors attempting to survey the line and the instruments they used were often flawed. Surveyors conducted at least nine surveys along the Kentucky-Tennessee portion of the border between 1799 and 1860. Surveyors used blazes on trees, mounds of rock or earth, and other impermanent markers to denote the line they surveyed. When later surveyors tried to determine where the previous crew had ceased their work they often could not find the markers. They were then forced to begin where the line was reputed to be. As a consequence, the line is irregular from the Cumberland Gap to the Tennessee River and is up to 12 miles north of the intended 36 degree 30 minute parallel. In fairness to the surveyors, however, it must be noted that much of the terrain they marked was thickly forested and very mountainous.

Irregularities along this section of the boundary are not due solely to surveying problems. It seems the commissioners in charge of surveying parties had considerable discretion to deflect the line to accommodate influential inhabitants along the border who wanted to remain in one jurisdiction or the other. One such significant deflection, called the "Simpson Triangle," occurs in Simpson County, Kentucky, south of the city of Franklin. Map 4.6 shows the broad V deflection with the bottom of the V near the town of Black Jack, Tennessee, and the

boundary extending northwest and northeast from there. One story explaining this anomaly is that a property owner was dismayed to learn that surveyors were to pass his property to the north and make him a Tennesseean. He therefore informed the weary crew that a sumptuous meal and a barrel of fine Kentucky whiskey awaited them if he remained a Kentuckian. This story may be apocryphal as the official surveying log does not contain any mention of why this deflection occurs, and the reason may simply be due to the discretion of the commissioners rather than bribery.

Within the Simpson Triangle occurs another anomaly called the "Middleton Offset." (See map 4.6.) The surveying log contains no mention of why the boundary takes this northern deflection inside the Simpson Triangle. Speculation is that the owner of a 100-acre farm wished to remain in Tennessee, and the surveyors honored his wish.

A jog to the north just east of the Cumberland River has no easy explanation. (See map 4.7.) A letter from the Stewart County (Tennessee) Historical Society said no one knows why the boundary jogs north at this point. The only possibility given was that an influential landowner or landowners persuaded surveyors to alter the line so as to keep them in Tennessee. Considering other discretionary changes in the boundary be-

Map 4.7. Chickasaw Lands

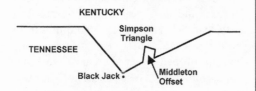

Map 4.6. Simpson Triangle and
Middleton Offset

tween these two states this seems a plausible explanation.

The Kentucky-Tennessee border extending from the Tennessee River to the Mississippi River was not part of the original surveys because this area belonged to the Chickasaw Indians. (See map 4.7.) Thomas Walker stopped his survey at the Tennessee River, traveled down that river, then down the Ohio and Mississippi rivers to a place where the parallel of 36 degrees 30 minutes would be if extended to the Mississippi River. In 1818 Andrew Jackson helped negotiate the purchase of this land from the Indians. When this boundary was surveyed it was done so on the parallel of 36° 30'. The actual boundary is not precisely on the parallel and is not perfectly straight due to errors in surveying.

In 1819 Kentucky sought to correct its boundary with Tennessee between Cumberland Gap and the Tennessee River by moving it south to the intended 36° 30' parallel. Tennessee understandably refused to make any adjustments. Their argument was based on the rights of property owners in the disputed area between the parallel and the Walker Line. The two states named a joint commission that resolved the issue by declaring the Walker Line from Cumberland Gap to the Tennessee River as the proper boundary, but that the 36° 30' parallel was to be the line from there to the Mississippi River.

The joint commission that settled the boundary also gave to Kentucky the right to the soil of all unappropriated land between the parallel of 36° 30' and the Walker Line. This gave Kentucky the right to sell this land for revenue while denying it jurisdiction. This also required another survey to determine just where the parallel was located.

The drawing of the border between the Tennessee and Mississippi rivers, however, creates the interesting anomaly mentioned earlier — the New Madrid (or Kentucky) Bend. (See maps 4.4 and 4.5.) An earthquake in 1811 changed the course of the Mississippi River creating this 10-square-mile circular patch of land. The boundary was drawn to the westernmost part of the river as that had

been determined as the boundary line's terminus in 1799–1800 by the Walker survey crew. Natural calamities do not usually result in boundary changes, but this is an exception to the general rule. This area is accessible by land only from Tennessee.

With Virginia and West Virginia. The boundaries with Virginia and West Virginia were set in 1776 when the Virginia House of Delegates created the Kentucky District and defined the boundary in this area as beginning in the Cumberland Gap at a point called "seven pines and two black oaks," then running northeastwardly along the crest of the Cumberland Mountains to the Russell Fork. From there the line heads on a straight 45-degree line to the crossing of the Tug Fork, then heads down the Tug Fork to the Sandy River, along the west bank of each of these two streams to the north bank of the Ohio River. The last half of the above-described boundary is the current boundary with West Virginia and was determined when that area was still a part of Virginia. Kentucky and Virginia appointed commissioners in 1798 to more clearly define the Kentucky-Virginia boundary. They made no substantive changes.

North Carolina

Carolina was originally a part of the large 1606 grant to the Virginia Company and later a 1629 grant to Robert Heath. Heath did not develop his grant, so King Charles II revoked the grant and in 1663 granted Carolina to eight Englishmen to whom he was in debt due to help they provided him to gain the throne after the Protectorate of the Cromwells. Two of these men were George Carteret and William Berkeley who also received grants from the Duke of York for New Jersey in 1664. The 1663 grant was generally from Albermarle Sound (the 36th parallel) in the north to what is now the Georgia-Florida state line and bounded on the west by the South Sea

(Pacific Ocean). When the grantees realized that the grant did not include an area called the Southern Plantation on the northern shore of Albermarle Sound, they approached the king to extend their grant northward. He did so in 1665, including that area and generally establishing the parallel of 36 degrees 30 minutes as the boundary between Carolina and Virginia. (See map 4.8.) Virginia unsuccessfully contested this change. The new grant also extended the southern boundary to the 29th parallel, about 100 miles further south than originally.

With Virginia. The wording of the 1665 charter specified that the boundary between Virginia and Carolina begin in the east at the north end of Currituck Inlet (or river), and run due west to Weyanoke (also called Wyonoak) Creek. The assumption was that both of these places were close to the parallel of 36° 30'.

The Carolina proprietors were eager to run the line, but Virginia officials were not, as they still disputed the line having been moved north one-half degree from the 36th parallel. The crown pressured both colonies to settle their boundary disagreement and run the line. Virginia finally agreed to run the line at the more northerly parallel in 1680. In the years between 1665 and 1680 the location of Weyanoke Creek was lost: No one in the area associated that name with any of the creeks. Virginia argued that a creek called Wicocon was the proper creek.* The Car-

olina proprietors argued for the Nottoway River. The Wicocon was the more southerly of the two; both colonies were pressing their case in an attempt to gain the most land. The difference was considerable as it involved an east-west a strip about 15 miles wide.

Finally, in 1715, the governor of Carolina, in a spirit of compromise, proposed to the governor of Virginia a three-part means of settling the dispute. Virginia's governor agreed. The proposal was that (1) if the due-west line from Currituck Inlet should meet the Chowan River between the mouths of Nottoway River and Wicocon Creek, the line should continue west, (2) if the line from Currituck Inlet should meet the Chowan River south of its confluence with Wicocon Creek, then it should run from that point up the Chowan to the confluence with the creek and then at that point continue due west, (3) if it met the Blackwater River north of the Nottoway River, then it should run down the Blackwater to the Nottoway and then due west. (See map 4.9.)

This seemingly convoluted and difficult agreement at least was clear enough that the two colonies could press on with surveying and marking the boundary, and both accepted the proposal. The line was finally run in 1728 with the determination of the point of 36 degrees 30 minutes on Currituck Inlet (the point chosen is actually a few miles north of the parallel). There the commis-

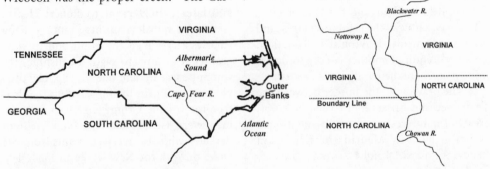

Left: Map 4.8. North Carolina; *right:* Map 4.9. Jog in North Carolina–Virginia Boundary

*The author was unable to locate a creek by this name on current maps.

sioners set a cedar post and the surveying began due west across the Dismal Swamp. The commissioners, having done their work in establishing the point of departure, then circled the swamp and met the surveyors on the western side.

The survey crew encountered the Blackwater River, and as per the third alternative of the agreement, they went down that river to its confluence with the Nottoway River at which point they continued their due-west course. On current maps this slight jog in the boundary can readily be seen. The remainder of the boundary is a nearly due-west line all the way to the northwest corner of North Carolina.

With Atlantic Ocean. The eastern boundary of North Carolina includes all islands and offshore lands of which the Outer Banks are notable. The U.S. Geological Survey says that generally speaking the individual states recognize an offshore boundary of 3 nautical miles. The United States territorial sea limit contiguous zone has been set at 12 nautical miles but is expected to be extended to 24 nautical miles. The exclusive economic zone boundary is 200 nautical miles. (A nautical mile equals 1.15 land miles.)

With South Carolina. The king bought Carolina from the proprietors in 1729 when they divested themselves of the colony except that one proprietor kept his one-eighth interest. Division into north and south immediately followed. The boundary between the two Carolinas contains a lot of direction changes even though it was intended to be quite straightforward. According to an agreement worked out by the Board of Trade and the two colonial governors in 1730, the line was to begin at a point about 30 miles southwest of Cape Fear River, then run northwesterly and generally parallel with the river to the 35th parallel, and then run due west. This was a compromise between the South Carolinians who wanted the Cape Fear River as the boundary and the North Carolinians who wanted the more southerly Pee Dee River as the boundary. Part of the argument of the North Carolina governor in arguing for the Pee Dee River is that a river would make a natural boundary and obviate the expense in running a line over land. The same argument can be made for the Cape Fear River as well, but of course the North Carolina governor was not in favor of this. North Carolina's governor, fearing excessive survey costs, convinced the South Carolina governor to agree to a straight line from the coast to the 35th parallel rather than one paralleling precisely the contours of the Cape Fear River.

Commissioners from the two colonies met in 1735 and agreed to a line beginning just as described above. By 1737 they had successfully run it to what they thought was the 35th parallel, but they were not accurate in determining the location of the parallel and stopped about 11 miles short of it. The agreement also contained a provision that if the west line along the 35th parallel should intersect the Catawba Indian lands, the line should go north around them and return to the 35th parallel. This did indeed happen as shown in map 5.13.

The two colonies haggled over the boundary for 25 years, but by 1763 both had accepted the 1735–1737 line as at least a temporary boundary and were ready to continue the boundary. Authorities in England suspected the 1735–1737 line had stopped short of the 35th parallel and sent instructions in 1763 for the new commissioners to ensure they began at the 35th parallel. In 1764 commissioners from the two provinces met to run a due-west line. Ignoring instructions to first ensure they were at the 35th parallel, they simply began where the 1735–1737 crew stopped and did not check the latitude. They ran the line west about 62 miles to the north-south-running Salisbury-Charlotte Road. At this point the commissioners were tired and asked for time to rest. One of the commissioners was ordered to continue the line until it struck the Catawba lands, but he did not do so.

The Catawba lands are essentially a square standing on a point. (See map 5.13.)

If the 1764 line had extended to the Catawba boundary, the ensuing northern boundary would have been northeast instead of slightly east of north.

In 1771 the English Board of Trade and the Privy Council recommended that the boundary continue along the Salisbury-Charlotte Road to the Catawba lands, around those lands (the Catawbas had indicated they wanted to remain in South Carolina) to where the Indian lands intersect the Catawba River, then up the middle of that river to the confluence of its southern and northern branches. From there the boundary was to run due west to the Saluda Mountains, sometimes called the Cherokee Mountains. This line was completed in 1772. The east-west portion of this line was about 15 miles north of the 35th parallel.

The amount of land each colony lost and gained by the 1764 and 1772 surveys nearly balanced. South Carolina was a slight winner though because the west line from the Catawba River runs north of west rather than due west. Some sources say the line around the Catawba lands was intended to return to the 35th parallel, but when they realized it didn't and also realized it balanced the loss to South Carolina of the 1764 survey, they made a decision not to change it.

Both colonies became distracted by the War for American Independence and did not undertake the boundary issue again with any vigor until the early 1800s when they were states and entered into an agreement to settle the remainder of their boundary. As commissioners began to run the line, they realized the agreement needed some modifications in order to run a practical and natural boundary and to avoid creating inconveniences for citizens along the western part of the boundary. After a couple of conferences to modify the original agreement, the resulting line extended from the end of the 1772 line to a ridge separating the drainage of forks of the Pacolet and Saluda rivers, then the line encircled three springs of the Saluda keeping this area in South Carolina. The line then followed mountain ridges to where it intersected a 1797 Cherokee boundary line. From that point it ran straight to a rock on the east bank of the Chattooga River which marked the 35th parallel and the point of contact of the North Carolina, South Carolina, and Georgia boundaries. The line from the end of the 1772 line was run and marked in 1815.

With Georgia. North Carolina's border with Georgia was the subject of much dispute. Georgia's 1732 charter specified its northern border as the northernmost part of the Savannah River, then due west to the Mississippi River. Georgia interpreted the northernmost part of the Savannah as the head of the Keowee River. The head of the Keowee is above the 35th parallel although the exact location of the parallel was not known at that time. (See map 5.8.) This, of course, conflicted with North Carolina's southern border, which its charter placed at the 35th parallel along its western portion.

In 1803 Georgia created Walton County in its northeastern corner, a county that extended above the 35th parallel. Fierce disputes arose among people living in the area as to which state had jurisdiction. Militia from the two states fought a few skirmishes, called the "Walton War," over the area in the early 1800s. North Carolina wanted to settle the boundary, but Georgia refused to participate because North Carolina insisted that all existing land grants in the area be honored. Georgia made no claims to land north of the 35th parallel, and North Carolina made no claims south of that parallel; however, they disagreed on the location of that parallel. Each state had surveyors determine the parallel, with North Carolina's being more accurate than those from Georgia. Georgia surveyors had taken observations to determine the parallel but had done so inaccurately and had put the parallel north of its true position. Georgia was sure it had accurate readings for the parallel and in 1806 asked the U.S. Congress to settle the matter. Congress oddly enough refused to intervene and told the states to settle their own boundary problem.

In 1807 both states appointed commissioners and scientists to determine the parallel. They discovered that Georgia's Walton County was indeed north of the 35th parallel. The Georgia commissioners recommended to their legislature that the act creating the county be rescinded. The legislature, however, was unwilling to lose an entire county, and in 1809 it ordered a new survey with new commissioners, new scientists, and new instruments. North Carolina refused to participate in a new survey as they considered the location of the parallel settled by the 1807 survey. Georgia then proposed that Andrew Ellicott, a person not associated with either state, locate the parallel. North Carolina agreed, and Ellicott did so in 1811 and concurred in the location of the parallel as determined by the 1807 scientists. He marked the parallel with a large stone on the east bank of the Chattooga River that marks the common point for North Carolina, South Carolina, and Georgia.

Georgia finally accepted the mass of evidence that they were wrong. Surveying and marking the line took place in 1819. Surveyors began at Ellicott's rock and went west. They traveled only about 30 miles when they neared the line surveyed by Montgomery (his first name could not be determined) in 1818 when he surveyed east from Nickajack. The 1819 surveyors were 661 yards north of Montgomery's Line. Not knowing what to do, they simply went due south to connect with Montgomery's Line, creating the boundary jog that can be seen only on large-scale maps called "Montgomery's Corner." After the War Between the States, Georgia checked the location of the line and found that it was too far south. The state tried to have the line moved, but too much time had elapsed for it to have a case.

With Tennessee. North Carolina's 1789 act ceding its western lands established the border with Tennessee. That document specified the line as beginning at Stone Mountain on the Virginia border, then following the crest of the mountains south-westerly to the Georgia border. In 1799 a joint commission marked this line to where the Hiwassee Turnpike crossed the Smoky Mountains, about 4 miles north of the Hiwassee River. They stopped there because of uncertainty regarding the boundary of Cherokee lands. Another joint commission resumed the line in 1821 and ran a straight line rather than following the mountain crest. The mountains are not easily identifiable along the southern end of the border, and the surveyors apparently decided on an easier course by marking a straight line to the Georgia border. This part of the line was intended to run due south but is actually 6 degrees west of south probably due to the line being run with a compass and without proper compensation for the deviation of the needle from true north.

Tennessee

The Volunteer State was initially included as a part of the Virginia charters of 1606 and 1609. Then in 1663 it became part of Carolina when Charles II gave a grant to some of his friends to whom he owed a favor. The king divided Carolina into north and south in 1729; the boundaries for North Carolina were the parallels of 36 degrees 30 minutes in the north and 35 degrees in the south all the way to the Pacific Ocean, except for the extreme eastern portion which ran from the 35th parallel southeast to the Atlantic Ocean. (See maps 4.1 and 4.8.) When the Treaty of 1783 limited the United States to the Mississippi River, the area that would become Tennessee was the western part of North Carolina.

The pioneers who ventured west across the Appalachian Mountains into Tennessee soon became disgusted with the easterners and wanted to establish their own government. In the eastern part of modern Tennessee frontiersmen established the State of Franklin in 1784, but it lasted only five years. In the minds of the men who established Franklin, the easterners were "ignorant of the back country's needs and indifferent to its dangers."* Such a concern was similar to that of the people who traveled west from Virginia and settled Kentucky. Sensing they were not going to be able to govern the western part of their colony, the easterners agreed to cede the western counties to the federal government in 1789 shortly after North Carolina entered the Union.

Congress organized this land cession into the Territory of the United States South of the Ohio River in 1790; it is usually known simply as the "Southwest Territory." With the exception of the reference to slavery, the provisions of the Northwest Territory governed the Southwest Territory. The territory was short-lived as Congress admitted Tennessee as the sixteenth state in 1796. (See the section on Illinois in chapter 6 for information about the Northwest Territory.)

Tennessee has had a lot of neighbors to contend with. With eight bordering states, Tennessee shares with Missouri the distinction of having the most neighboring states in the Union. Its many neighbors notwithstanding, its border disputes have been modest compared to those of some of the New England states. Tennessee's basic borders were established while it was still part of North Carolina: the parallels of 36 degrees 30 minutes in the north, the 35th degree in the south, the Mississippi River in the west, and the Great Smoky Mountains in the east. When ceding its western counties, North Carolina set the Unaka Mountains (today this is a series of mountains generally called the "Great Smoky Mountains") as the border between it and Tennessee. However, even with Tennessee's basic boundaries established the precise location of them on the ground caused problems.

With Kentucky. Tennessee's boundary with Kentucky has more changes in direction than the wind, and nearly all of them are north of the parallel of the intended line

of 36 degrees 30 minutes, a situation that favors Tennessee. However, the extreme western part of the boundary, between the Tennessee and Mississippi rivers is very close to the 36° 30' parallel. The reasons for the boundary changes are several: surveying errors, the extreme difficulty of surveying in heavily forested and steeply mountainous country, and the apparent discretion of the original surveyors, Thomas Walker and Richard Henderson, to vary the line to accommodate influential settlers along the line who wished to remain in one jurisdiction or the other during their 1779-80 survey. The boundary is 5¾ miles north of 36° 30' at the eastern end and 12½ miles north of it at the Tennessee River. The surveyors miscalculated proper allowance for variance of true north from magnetic north, and so the line gets further from the intended parallel as it goes west. (See map 1.2.) It began too far north because the surveyors had the same problem when they surveyed the Virginia–North Carolina line.

It is interesting to note that the language of the Tennessee constitution still places the boundary on the parallel of 36° 30', but it contains the following saving clause: "Provided that the limits and jurisdiction of this State shall extend to any other land and territory now acquired by compact or agreement with other States, or otherwise, although such land and territory are not included within the boundaries hereinbefore designated."

Kentucky, when it realized the border was north of 36° 30', took action in 1819 to get this boundary put at the intended parallel. Tennessee, of course, refused to cooperate since most of the line, called the "Walker Line," was as much as 12 miles north of the parallel. A joint commission in 1819 eventually agreed to keep the boundary at the old Walker Line between Cumberland Gap and the Tennessee River, put the boundary at 36° 30' in the newly acquired Chickasaw lands

*Dykeman, Wilma, Tennessee: A Bicentennial History (New York: W. W. Norton & Company, Inc., 1975), p. 66.

between the Tennessee and Mississippi rivers, and give Kentucky the right of soil on all unoccupied land between the Walker Line and the 36° 30' parallel. The right of soil meant Kentucky could sell and gain revenue from unowned land but had no political jurisdiction over it. This naturally necessitated another survey to determine the correct location of the parallel between the Tennessee River and Cumberland Gap to see just how much land Kentucky could sell.

The jog to the north near the Cumberland River has no easy explanation. (See map 4.10.) A letter from the Stewart County (Tennessee) Historical Society said no one knows why the boundary jogs north as this point. The only possibility given was that an influential landowner or landowners persuaded surveyors to alter the line so as to keep them in Tennessee. Considering other changes in the Tennessee-Kentucky line, this is a reasonable explanation.

With Virginia. Tennessee's border with Virginia is much more difficult to explain than its border with Kentucky. North Carolina's charter stipulated that its border with Virginia was to be the 36 degrees 30 minutes north latitude, so the border between Tennessee and Virginia should theoretically be on that parallel as well. It is a few miles north of that parallel and has several deflections from a straight line that are difficult to understand.

Instructions to Walker and Henderson told them to begin surveying where Joshua Fry and Peter Jefferson had ended their work near Steep Rock Creek (now Laurel Fork of the Holston River). The first task for Walker and Henderson was to determine if the Fry-Jefferson Line was on the 36° 30' parallel; if not, they were to correctly locate the parallel then continue due west to the Tennessee River. Walker and Henderson could not locate the point where the Fry and Jefferson line ended. They took observations, however, and determined they were on the 36° 30' parallel. They surveyed west, and after about 45 miles they had a disagreement. Henderson decided they were 2 miles too far south; Walker felt they were on the correct parallel. The two teams agreed to survey two parallel lines. The Henderson crew ended their survey at the Cumberland Mountains, whereas the Walker crew continued to the Tennessee River.

North Carolina in 1790 agreed to the more southerly Walker Line saying the small amount of mountainous country wasn't worth sending out new commissioners and surveyors. Tennessee, when it separated from North Carolina, claimed the territory between Walker's and Henderson's line saying North Carolina's actions in boundary matters were not binding for Tennessee once it was a separate jurisdiction.

In 1802 commissioners from both Virginia and Tennessee met and agreed to run a line halfway between the Walker and Henderson line from the top of White Top Mountain, the presumed northeast corner of Tennessee, to the top of the Cumberland Mountains, the southwest corner of Virginia. Surveyors marked the line, and both states accepted it. In 1856 the boundary was again an issue, and both states appointed commissioners to re-run and re-mark the line of 1802. Their orders were that they were to start at the top of White Top Mountain and run all the way west to the Cumberland Mountains on the parallel of 36° 30'. These

Map 4.10. Tennessee

instructions posed several problems. One was that the line as it ran through the town of Bristol, which was thought to be accurate, was 6 minutes north of 36° 30'. Another problem was that the eastern part of this line did not end on the top of White Top Mountain but about 3 miles southwest of it and 8 miles north of 36° 30'. Since the commissioners could not comply with their instructions, they simply chose to re-run and re-mark the 1802 line with all its irregularities. The western end of the line did end at the summit of the Cumberland Mountains. This work was completed in 1859.

Virginia sued in the U.S. Supreme Court in 1890 to have the line moved to the correct parallel, but the court would not allow it and declared the 1802 line as the true boundary. The court has frequently denied boundary changes when they have been in place for a long time and are generally acknowledged.

The preceding several paragraphs explain the history of the boundary of Tennessee and Virginia but do not adequately explain its deflections from a due west line. The largest offset is called the "Denton Valley Offset," and sometimes the "Iron Mountain Notch," in the extreme northeast corner of Tennessee. (See map 4.11.) This area has a couple of legends associated with it, both of which come from historical societies in Virginia. The first says that a lady who lived in the area made an agreement with the surveyors to allow them to spend the night in her house if they would keep her in Tennessee. The second is that the surveyors developed quite a thirst for alcohol and left to find a moonshine still in the mountains. They took off northward with all their gear and finally found one. They drank themselves into a torpor and spent the night where they found the still. The next morning they forgot they had left their original line and simply proceeded to continue the survey west from that point. They eventually sobered up enough to realize their error and dropped back to the original line. Whether or not either story is true is speculative.

Three other offsets, ranging from about

½ mile to 1 mile, occur between the Denton Valley Offset and the Cumberland Mountains, these can be seen only on large-scale maps. While no official explanation is available, these offsets are likely due to accommodations to residents or perhaps north-south corrections after astronomical observations so as to return to what surveyors assumed to be the correct parallel.

With North Carolina. The Tennessee boundary with North Carolina is mostly a series of mountain ranges as per the North Carolina cession agreement. From north to south these mountains are the Stone, Unaka, Bald, Smoky, and Unicoi, collectively often called the "Great Smoky Mountains." The intent was for this border to follow the crest of mountains all the way to the Georgia line. Surveyors ran the northern part of the line in 1799 but stopped at the Hiwassee Turnpike, about 4 miles north of the Hiwassee River. When surveyors returned in 1821 to finish the line to the Georgia border, they ignored their instructions to follow the crest of the mountains and simply ran a line south to the Georgia border. Their intent was to run a due-south line, but the line they ran is actually about 6 degrees west of south due most likely to running a compass meridian and not accurately figuring the deviation of the needle from magnetic north. (See map 1.2.) In defense of the surveyors not following their instructions, it must be acknowledged that the mountains are mere hills here, and following them would have been very difficult. Tennessee benefited from this straight line because they got a valuable mining area that would likely have been included in North Carolina if the line had been run according to the cession agreement.

With Georgia. The southern boundary by charter was to run along the 35th parallel as per the 1730 agreement between North and South Carolina, and it does in most places. James Camack ran the border with Georgia in 1818. It is south of the 35th parallel by as much as a mile in places because of faulty determination of the parallel. As late as 1940 Georgia attempted to have the line run correctly along the 35th parallel but was rebuffed in its attempt as the boundary had been generally accepted for over a hundred years. The U.S. Supreme Court has consistently refused to alter boundaries, even when incorrectly placed, once they are generally recognized.

With Alabama. Moving west to the Tennessee boundary with Alabama, the line continues slightly south of the 35th parallel, its intended position. The line as surveyed varies north and south of the true parallel. When the line reaches Pickwick Lake in northwest Alabama it is about 1½ miles north of the 35th parallel. Neither state has concerned itself with getting the boundary on the exact parallel, and both have been content to accept the boundary as surveyed by the several different surveyors who marked it.

With Mississippi. The boundary with Mississippi was first run in 1818–1819. Mississippi decided that the 35th parallel had not been located correctly and that, if it were, Memphis (Tennessee) might be in Mississippi. Mississippi's hope was without fruition, however, as a surveyor they hired decided the parallel was actually south of the previous line. Tennessee ordered a new line run in the mid–1830s which would have gained Tennessee about 300 square miles of land. This line, called the Thompson Line, was never agreed to by Mississippi. In 1837 the two states appointed commissioners to settle the boundary question. They ultimately chose a line defined by numbers of chains and links north of Thompson's line. Both states adopted this line as official, although it is slightly south of the true location of the 35th parallel.

With Missouri and Arkansas. The western boundary of Tennessee with Missouri and Arkansas generally follows the channel of the Mississippi River as per the Treaty of 1783. The line does not always follow the river's channel because it is a meandering river and changes its course. So some Tennessee land is actually across the river in Missouri and Arkansas, and those states claim some land on the Tennessee side of the river. The U.S. Supreme Court has consistently ruled that rapid changes in a watercourse do not alter a boundary; however, boundaries can be altered by gradual changes in a watercourse.

Virginia

A 1606 grant from King James I to a group of merchants called the Virginia Company included all land between the 34th and 45th parallels, approximately from Cape Fear, North Carolina, to Bangor, Maine, but only 100 miles inland. The Virginia Company established Jamestown in 1607. In 1609 a new charter for a larger grant of land redefined the boundaries as beginning on the Atlantic coast at Old Point Comfort (a point of land southeast of Hampton, Virginia) and then extending 200 miles north and south of that point. The southern boundary would thus extend from near Wilmington, North Carolina, due west to the South Sea (Pacific Ocean). The northern boundary would begin on the Atlantic coastline east of Philadelphia, Pennsylvania, and run northwest, not west, to the South Sea — a really generous chunk of real estate. Many people believed that the new continent they were populating was very narrow, perhaps only 600 or so miles wide, so the granters apparently had no idea the grants were so extensive.

Virginia's grant was subsequently reduced many times to provide for new charters from the crown. One of the major reductions was the Northwest Territory which eventually became the states of Ohio, Indiana, Illinois, Michigan, Wisconsin, and part of Minnesota. New York, Massachusetts, and Connecticut also claimed part of the Northwest Territory based on sea-to-sea charters, but their claims were all extinguished between 1781 and 1786.

With North Carolina. Another reduction of Virginia was the 1663 charter from King Charles II of England to eight men to whom he was indebted for political support. He granted them land south of Virginia beginning at the 36th parallel that they named Carolina. The grantees soon realized that this would not give them some valuable land called the Southern Plantation on the north side of Albermarle Sound. They petitioned the king to move the line to the north. An amended charter in 1665 moved the boundary to the north end of Currituck Inlet, and from there it went straight west to Weyanoke (also called Wyonoak) Creek, both of which were assumed to be about 36 degrees 30 minutes north latitude, then all the way to the South Sea. Virginia, of course, contested this change in boundary, but without positive result.

Virginia finally agreed in 1680 to meet with Carolina to settle the boundary issue, but by this time the location of Weyanoke Creek was lost. Residents in the area knew of no creek by that name. The colonies each specified streams they thought was the creek — Virginians thought it was Wicocon Creek.* The Carolinians thought it was the Nottoway River, the most northerly of the two. Resolution of the boundary was stalled again.

When a new governor came to Carolina in 1715 he proposed three possible resolutions to the boundary dispute, or "the dividing line" as it was called, that were accepted by the Virginia governor. All the scenarios had the same starting point on the north shore of Currituck Inlet and running west. Then the options were: (1) If the line met the Chowan River between Wicocon Creek and the Nottoway River, it was to continue west. (2) If it met the Chowan River south of Wicocon Creek it was to go up the river to the creek mouth then continue due west. (3) If it reached the Blackwater River, a stream north of the Nottoway, it was to descend down the Blackwater to the confluence with the Nottoway River then go due west. (See map 4.9.)

Commissioners from both colonies met in 1728, argued about the location of the starting place on Currituck Inlet, and settled on a point then let the surveyors mark the line west. The surveyors came to the Blackwater River, so option number three went into effect causing a ½-mile southern jog approximately 60 miles from the Atlantic Ocean. The line continues more-or-less due west, a few miles north of 36° 30', until it meets the northeast corner of Tennessee. The entire Virginia–North Carolina border has several deflections from a straight line. Some of these appear to be adjustments made when surveyors realized their line had moved north or south of the intended boundary. At other times, however, the line will move from a straight course for only a few miles then return to the course it was on. This is likely due to discretion the commissioners had in altering the line to accommodate the wishes of residents who wanted to remain in one jurisdiction or the other. Another reason for change may be due to slight changes from the end of one survey and the beginning of another. Most of these changes can be seen best on large-scale maps.

With Tennessee. Continuing west along Virginia's southern boundary the boundary with Tennessee begins with a sharp jog to the north for about 2 miles, then continues due west for about 15 miles, then jogs back to the south continuing on a west course at about the same parallel as it was before making the northward jog. The irregularities and offsets in the boundary between Virginia and Tennessee are difficult to explain, but the offset in the extreme northeast corner of Tennessee, called the "Denton Valley Offset" or "Iron Mountain Notch," has two interesting legends associated with it; both come from historical societies in Virginia. The first is that a woman who lived in the area offered a night's lodging to the sur-

---

*The author has been unable to locate a creek by this name on modern maps.

veyors if they would alter the line so she could remain in Tennessee. The other is that the surveyors went looking in the mountains for a moonshine still. They took all their gear, and when they found the still they set up camp and began to drink heavily. The next morning they forgot they had left their original line and began surveying from where they spent the night. After they sobered up they realized their error and returned to the original line. (See map 4.11.)

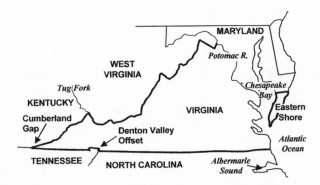

Map 4.11. Virginia

Three other offsets occur in the line between the northeast corner of Tennessee and the southwest corner of Virginia. Two of these cannot be seen except on large-scale maps. They vary from ½ to about 1 mile and may be due to surveyors accommodating the wishes of residents along the line or perhaps to corrections after making astronomical observations and returning to what they considered the correct parallel.

With Kentucky. Commissioners determined in 1799–1800 that the Kentucky border would begin on the Tennessee border at the top of the Cumberland Mountains, near Cumberland Gap, at a place called "seven pines and two oaks" and head northeast along the crest of the highest part of the Cumberland Mountains to the Russell Fork, then run 45 degrees northeast until it intersected the principal branch of the Sandy River called the "Tug Fork." This is where Virginia's boundary with Kentucky currently ends. However, before the separation of West Virginia in 1863, the boundary continued down that branch to the Sandy River and on to the north shore of the Ohio River. The boundary is along the west shore of both the Tug and Sandy.

With West Virginia. In 1863 the boundary of Virginia was again altered. Sectionalism had existed between eastern and western Virginians since the early 1800s, and talk among western Virginians of separating from the easterners was frequent. The issue came to a head in 1861 when Virginia considered seceding from the Union. When the secession issue came to a vote, the westerners soundly voted against the proposition, while the easterners wholeheartedly supported it. The reasons are not hard to find — eastern plantations were dependent on slave labor and bound to the slave culture, whereas the predominantly small-scale farmers of western Virginia were not. Virginia's vote to secede from the Union forced the hand of the westerners, who then advocated separating from Virginia.

The westerners took a vote of selected counties, and the results were overwhelmingly in favor of dismemberment from Virginia. The task was then to determine just what counties would separate. A core group of counties of strong Union sentiment were identified. (See map 4.12.) The West Virginia State Constitutional Convention added more counties along the southeast to "round out" their proposed state. Counties along the Potomac River in the northeast were added to protect the right-of-way of the Baltimore and Ohio Railroad, so important to Union interests. Voters in many of these added counties had little or no say as to whether they wished to be included in the new state.

The upshot of all this is that the boundary with West Virginia takes an irregular course following old county lines from the Tug Fork all the way to the Potomac River, where the Virginia boundary with West Virginia ends.

Jefferson and Berkeley counties in the extreme northeast part of West Virginia opposed dismemberment from Virginia because their culture and economics were more in line with Virginia than West Virginia. Hoping to regain control of these two counties Virginia tried to get them returned shortly after the War Between the States, but Virginia's suit in the U.S. Supreme Court failed.

With Maryland. Virginia was incensed when George Calvert, the first Lord Baltimore, received his grant for land north of the Potomac River in 1632. Although they had not made use of that land, Virginians still claimed it as part of their territory. Furthermore, they resented such a close intrusion of Roman Catholics. Nonetheless, Virginia reluctantly acknowledged the existence of Maryland in 1638.

Both colonies disputed the location of their boundary along the Potomac River. Calvert's 1632 grant specified the boundary as going to the "further" bank of the Potomac; hence, the boundary was the southern bank. Just where along that bank was a point of contention until 1930, when a commission consisting of members from both states met and agreed to a boundary at the low-water mark on the south shore of the Potomac River.

This boundary extends to Smith Point, the southern point on the south shore of the river on Chesapeake Bay. From there the line takes an irregular course across the bay to the Pocomoke River on the Delmarva Peninsula. Reasons for such a course are not very clear but appear to be due to a long series of negotiations between the two states to gain control over the important fishery resources in the bay and the setting of provisional boundaries at various places. Since the two states could not settle the boundary problem they appointed a three-man board of arbitration in 1874. The board's determination is the current boundary and seems to be a compromise of the various provisional boundaries, some as early as 1632, that the two states had recognized over the years. The

current line is marked by orange and white buoys in the bay and patrolled by both states. (See map 3.5.)

The line across the peninsula, however, was clearly defined in Calvert's charter as running east from Watkins Point, which was identified as beginning at the north point of the bay into which the Pocomoke River emptied. A commission consisting of Edmund Scarborough, representing Virginia, and Philip Calvert, representing Maryland, met in 1670 to run the line across the peninsula. Instead of beginning at the north point of the bay, they traveled up the river to avoid marshy ground. This change began the eastward running of the line about 3 miles north of where it should have started, resulting in a loss of land for Maryland. However, Maryland's loss of land was not yet over. When they finally began running the eastward line they did not run it due east but rather north of east. Whether this was due to deceitfulness on the part of Scarborough or to careless surveying is not known. Scarborough was intensely loyal to the king, not fond of Catholics, and a devoted Virginian. The line was run using a compass, and the surveyors may have not known the deviation of the compass from magnetic north for this area. (See map 1.2.) The result, however, is that these two aspects of running the line on the peninsula cost Maryland territory to which it was entitled. (The Delmarva Peninsula is named for its constituent states, Delaware, Maryland, and Virginia, and contains letters from each of their names.)

With Atlantic Ocean. The U.S. Geological Survey says that generally speaking the individual states recognize an offshore boundary of 3 nautical miles. The United States territorial sea limit contiguous zone has been set at 12 nautical miles but is expected to be extended to 24 nautical miles. The exclusive economic zone boundary is 200 nautical miles. (A nautical mile equals 1.15 land miles.) Virginia's eastern boundary along the Atlantic Ocean includes all offshore islands. In 1970 Virginia and North Carolina agreed to extend their boundary due east into the ocean.

West Virginia

All of West Virginia's boundary battles, except one, were fought by Virginia. The exception is their common boundary. The reason Virginia fought those battles is because, until 1863 during the War Between the States, Virginia encompassed both states. The war brought to focus differences between east and west Virginians that had been bubbling for many years. Talk of sectionalism within Virginia began during the early 1800s and was based principally upon three issues. One was that slaves were taxed less than other property including animals. Westerners didn't own but very few slaves while eastern Virginia was dependent on them. This meant a greater tax burden for the westerners. The second reason was representation in the General Assembly. Slave population was considered in determining the number of representatives in the General Assembly, thereby adding political clout to the easterners. The third reason was that the eastern part of the state was greatly favored in the funds distributed for public works, and all public buildings were in the east.

Also of consideration was the socioeconomic status of the two areas. Eastern Virginians were plantation oriented, educated, and urbane, while the westerners were mostly subsistence farmers on small plots of land with little formal education. The big issue, however, was slavery — easterners were oriented to the slave culture and dependent on it, while westerners did not own slaves for the most part and had no interest in maintaining the institution of slavery.

With Virginia. When southern states were seceding from the Union in 1860 and 1861 they put great pressure on Virginia to join them. When Virginians voted on secession it was greatly supported in the eastern part of the state, while in the west it was voted down by a margin of 4-to-1. This forced the hand of the western Virginians advocating separation from Virginia. They held a vote in counties with known strong pro–Union sentiment. The resulting vote was strongly in favor of separation from Virginia by more than a 20-to-1 margin.

The next step for the separatists was to determine just what counties were to be included in the dismemberment. The modus operandi was to include counties with strong Union sentiment and avoid counties with slaves and strong confederate leanings. The Constitutional Convention called by the separatists identified a block of core counties early in the process. (See map 4.12.) The convention added more counties to the south and east of the original block. The southern counties were added to "round out" the bottom of the new state, while those east of the original block were added to give West Virginia control over the right-of-way of the Baltimore and Ohio Railroad. The inclusion of the northeast counties put all of the railroad right-of-way in states loyal to the Union. The map shows the approximate distribution of counties in the three areas.

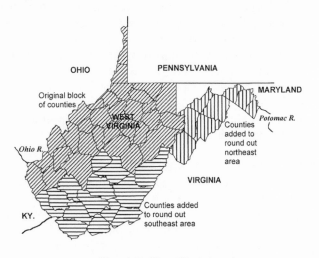

Map 4.12. West Virginia

The voters in many of the added counties had no voice in the decision to include them in West Virginia. Virginia sued in the U.S. Supreme Court shortly after the war to get Berkeley and Jefferson counties (the two most eastern counties as seen on map 4.12) returned to it, but the suit was unsuccessful. A result of the northeast extension is that part of West Virginia is connected to the rest of the state by a narrow neck of land only 15 miles wide at its narrowest. The resulting irregular border between West Virginia and Virginia is thus caused by the margins of the counties that existed in 1863 when the dismemberment became final and West Virginia became a state.

The remainder of West Virginia's borders were determined by Virginia before the war.

With Kentucky. When Virginia defined the boundaries of the Kentucky District in 1776, it named the Big Sandy River and its main branch as part of the boundary. The Levisa and Tug forks come together at Louisa, Kentucky, to form the Sandy River; however, which fork constituted the main branch of the Sandy had never been determined. In 1779 a joint commission met to determine which of the two forks was the larger. The weather was rainy and miserable, so the commissioners spent a lot of time indoors keeping warm with an ample supply of whiskey. Heavy rain in the drainage of the Tug Fork, normally the smaller of the two streams, caused it to be unusually large, and the commissioners decreed it as the main branch of the Sandy. This determination lost about 1,000 square miles to Virginia and thus to West Virginia. The boundary on both the Sandy and Tug is the west bank.

With Ohio. The West Virginia–Kentucky boundary continues all the way to the north bank of the Ohio River, where the boundary with Ohio begins. When Virginia transferred the territory north of the Ohio River to the federal government in 1784 the north bank of that river became the north-

ern boundary. In 1820 the U.S. Supreme Court determined that the boundary with Ohio was the low-water line on the north bank of the river and not the center of the river as Ohio claimed.

With Pennsylvania. Virginia claimed land in what is now southwestern Pennsylvania in the early 1700s. Virginia's claim was based on the fact that they had settlers in the area and they had fought and defeated the Indians there while the pacifistic Pennsylvania Quakers had done nothing. Virginia's claim received no support, however, as William Penn's charter from the king clearly gave him hegemony over the area. Penn's charter was stated as 5 degrees longitude beginning at the Delaware River and extending west and 3 degrees latitude high starting at the beginning of the 40th parallel. It took a lot of haggling, mostly with Maryland, to determine the southern border of Pennsylvania. This line was finally determined in 1760 as 15 miles south of Philadelphia and was run by English mathematicians Charles Mason and Jeremiah Dixon. Virginia eventually agreed to an extension of the Mason-Dixon Line as its border with Pennsylvania if Pennsylvania would agree to honor land claims granted by Virginia. Pennsylvania did, and the matter was settled. The line was thus run 5 degrees west of the Delaware River and stopped at a point 16 miles east of the Ohio River. The line was then run north pursuant to charter provisions to where it encountered Lake Erie. The rigid adherence to Pennsylvania's charter created the odd-shaped 64-mile northern thrust of West Virginia between the western border of Pennsylvania and the Ohio River.

With Maryland. King Charles I in 1632 granted Lord Baltimore land north of the Potomac River and extending to the "First Fountain" of the Potomac River and then north. A dispute naturally arose over which branch of the Potomac constituted the headwaters of that stream. (See map 3.6.) The North Branch and the South Branch are the two major tributaries of the Potomac River. Maryland favored the more southerly of the two, while Virginia favored the more northerly.

The U.S. Supreme Court determined in 1787 that the northern branch was the proper boundary. This ruling was in spite of the fact that the southern branch is about 60 miles longer than the northern branch. This ruling awarded a considerable amount of land to Virginia and, ultimately to West Virginia.

Maryland and West Virginia also disputed the placement of the border along the Potomac. As part of a 1910 suit in the U.S. Supreme Court, West Virginia and Maryland tried to get the boundary along the Potomac moved to benefit their respective states. Maryland argued to move it to the high-water mark on the south shore. West Virginia asked that the line with Maryland be moved to the high-water line on the north shore. The low-water line on the south shore had been the line for years, and the court ruled that the line should remain there.

The line running north from the headwaters of the Potomac River to the Pennsylvania boundary was marked in 1787 by Francis Deakins. He was not surveying a state boundary but rather merely surveying and placing property lines. Consequently, the Deakins Line is not straight.

A joint commission employed Lt. N. Michler in 1859 to run an astronomically correct north-south line beginning at the southwest corner of Maryland. This line showed the Deakins Line meeting the Pennsylvania border three-quarters of a mile east of a true north-south line. West Virginia agreed to moving the line if Maryland would honor existing land claims in the area. Maryland refused to do this, and West Virginia backed out of the deal. Maryland could have gained a small triangular piece of land three-quarters of a mile wide at the top and about 37 miles long if it had accepted the Virginia offer.

Maryland sued in the U.S. Supreme Court in 1910 to move the southern end of the line to a place called the Potomac Stone, then regarded as the true headwaters of the North Branch of the Potomac River. The Potomac Stone was about 1¼ miles west of the Fairfax Stone, the latter long regarded as the southern point of the Deakins Line. From the Potomac Stone Maryland wanted an astronomically correct north-south line run to the Pennsylvania border. The court ruled in 1910 to leave the boundary where Deakins placed it and since much of the Deakins Line was obliterated, to have it resurveyed and remarked. The court's reason for not moving the line was that it had long been regarded as the true boundary by citizens living along it and by the states of West Virginia and Maryland and that to move it would create hardships and inconvenience to citizens in the area and create the possibility of extensive litigation.

5

LOWER SOUTH REGION

Map 5.1

Map is not to scale; boundaries are roughly drawn.

Alabama

Spaniards were likely the first Europeans to visit the Alabama coast in 1505, and Spaniard Hernando De Soto explored interior Alabama in 1540. The state has been under the control of four different nations: Spain, France, Great Britain, and the United States. The first European settlement was on Mobile Bay by the Spanish in 1559, but it was abandoned by 1561. The French were the next to take an interest in the area when René-Robert Cavelier, Sieur de La Salle, explored the Mississippi River and claimed the entire drainage for France in 1682. He called the area Louisiane to honor his king Louis XIV. The French established a settlement in Biloxi (Mississippi) in 1699, and by 1702 they moved the seat of government east to Mobile (Alabama) and later moved the capital to New Orleans (Louisiana). By 1717 the French colony of Louisiana extended along the Gulf Coast to include New Orleans, Biloxi, and Mobile. French hegemony never extended east of the Perdido River, the current west boundary of Florida, because Spain was dominant in Pensacola (Florida).

Alabama was not only a part of four different countries but also two territories and was included in the Carolana grant to Robert Heath in 1629, the Carolina grants of 1663 and 1665, and the Georgia grant to James Oglethorpe in 1732.

France maintained dominance over this area until the Treaty of 1763, when all of Louisiana east of the Mississippi River was ceded by France to Great Britain. Great Britain divided Florida into two colonies, East and West Florida, with the Chattahoochee and Apalachicola rivers as the boundary between them. (See map 5.3.) The northern boundary was given as the 31st parallel until the West Florida governor realized that his northern boundary did not include some substantial settlements along the Mississippi River. He asked the English Board of Trade to move that boundary north. They subsequently moved it to a line due east from the mouth of the Yazoo River, latitude 32 de-grees 28 minutes. (See map 5.3.) In this same 1763 treaty France ceded Louisiana west of the Mississippi River to Spain, and Great Britain ceded the Isle of Orleans to Spain in exchange for Florida. (The Isle of Orleans consisted of the area bounded on the west by the Mississippi River, on the south and east by the Gulf of Mexico, and on the north generally by lakes Maurepas, Pontchartrain, and Borgne. [See map 8.9.])With Great Britain and the United States involved in war, Spain captured Mobile in 1780 and Pensacola in 1781, so by that year Spain controlled all of West Florida.

West Florida, which included southern Alabama, became an asylum for loyalists to the crown during the War for American Independence. West Florida was a rough and tumble frontier colony without the refinements, culture, or education found in the Atlantic seaboard colonies.

The Treaty of 1783 ended the War for American Independence and set the western boundary of the United States at the Mississippi River. The United States maintained that its southern boundary with Spain was at the 31st parallel, while Spain claimed it was 32° 28' since British West Florida had extended that far north. (See map 5.2.) Pres-

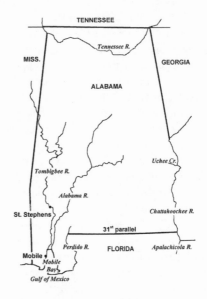

Map 5.2. Alabama

ident George Washington sent Thomas Pinckney to Spain to negotiate a treaty concerning this boundary. Among other aspects, the 1795 treaty Pinckney negotiated established the boundary between the two nations at the 31st parallel, although no one knew exactly where that parallel was located.

In 1798 the U.S. Congress created Mississippi Territory with boundaries of the Mississippi River in the west, the Chattahoochee River in the east, the 31st parallel in the south, and the parallel of 32° 28' in the north. (See map 5.10.) Based on its 1732 charter, Georgia claimed all land north of the 31st parallel as far as the Mississippi River, but the federal government said that since the land between the parallels of 31° and 32° 28' had recently been part of Great Britain's colony of West Florida, it was federal land and not part of Georgia. Mississippi Territory gained area in 1802 when the U.S. purchased from Georgia land from the parallel of 32° 28' to the Tennessee border and added it to the territory.

As settlers went into Mississippi Territory, differences began to develop between the settlements along the Mississippi River and those along the Tombigbee River in the central part of the territory (now western Alabama). It was a familiar story that was seen with Virginia-Kentucky and North Carolina–Tennessee: The newest group of settlers, in this case those along the Tombigbee, felt the territorial government in the Mississippi Valley was not responsive to their needs and was just too far away. Alabamans petitioned Congress as early as 1803 to divide the territory because they had different interests and customs from the settlers along the Mississippi River. One proposal was to divide the territory with an east-west line into northern and southern sections, but this didn't get far as the schism was definitely east versus west, so a north-south dividing line was ultimately adopted.

The tensions between the western and eastern parts of the territory were exacerbated after Indian land cessions in 1814 when settlers began to flow into the eastern part of Mississippi Territory. The settlers on the Tombigbee, who had heretofore favored division of the territory, now saw a projected population shift favoring their area and possible removal of the territorial capital to St. Stephens on the Tombigbee.

Conversely, the settlers along the Mississippi River, who had previously favored admission as a single state, became so alarmed at the prospect of being dominated by the eastern part of the territory that they now pushed for division of the territory. Despite differences held by officials in the territory, Congress favored division, as they considered the territory too large to enter the Union as a single state. The plan Congress adopted was for immediate statehood for the western part of the territory (Mississippi), and territorial status for the eastern part (Alabama). The only remaining issue was the boundary, which is discussed in the next subsection. Congress admitted Mississippi as the twentieth state in 1817. Alabama became the twenty-second state in 1819.

With Mississippi. When Georgia sold its western lands to the federal government in 1802 it stipulated that the area was to be formed into one political unit. Dissention formed in Mississippi Territory, and pressure mounted in the east part of the territory to divide it. The westerners did not want to do this initially, and the territorial delegate submitted several bills to Congress to admit the territory as a single state. These bills passed the House but never the Senate. Senators rejected the bills because they felt the area was too large to enter the Union as a single state.

Territorial officials finally realized that the territory was not going to be admitted as one state and that advantages existed in having two states because the area would then have four senators instead of just two. Georgia was asked to consent to a division of the territory, and it agreed. Now the question was where to divide it.

Some settlers in the eastern part of the territory wanted the boundary placed along the Pearl River. (See map 5.10.) Those in the western part of the territory wanted the Tombigbee River as the boundary. A Pearl River boundary would have made Mississippi very small and given it no frontage on the Gulf of Mexico. A boundary along the Tombigbee River would have given Mississippi jurisdiction over the city of Mobile and put the Tombigbee drainage basin within two political jurisdictions. The thought of losing Mobile was anathema to the easterners.

An idea had been advanced in Congress years earlier to divide the territory somewhere to the west of the Tombigbee. This idea finally prevailed, and in the 1817 act, creating the state of Mississippi, Congress specified the boundary with Alabama as up the Tennessee River from the southern boundary of Tennessee to the mouth of Bear Creek, then in a straight line to the northwest corner of Washington County, Alabama, then due south of the gulf.

Congress inserted a provision that if that part of the line south of the northwest corner of Washington County infringed on the Mississippi counties of Wayne, Greene, and Jackson, the line was to be moved so it struck the gulf 10 miles east of the Pascagoula River. A trial line struck the gulf a little more than 6 miles east of the Pascagoula and did infringe on those counties, so the line was moved east to strike the gulf 10 miles east of the river. John Coffee and Thomas Freeman ran this line in 1820. They located the northwest corner of Washington County, then Coffee ran the line north to Bear Creek and Freeman ran the line south to the gulf. Meeting the criteria for the boundary created a slight bend in the line at the northwestern corner of Washington County. The bend no longer occurs there because Washington County was reduced in size in 1847 when Alabama created Choctaw County.

With Tennessee. The 1817 act of Congress creating Alabama Territory specified its northern boundary simply as the southern boundary of Tennessee. The southern boundary of Tennessee is supposed to be the 35th parallel, but the line as surveyed and

marked is anywhere from 1 to ½ mile away from the parallel due to inaccurate surveying. The boundary is about 1 mile south of the parallel in northeast Alabama, then crosses north of the parallel just west of the Alabama county line dividing Limestone and Lauderdale counties. The line is ½ mile north of the parallel in northwest Alabama. Thomas Freeman surveyed and marked this boundary beginning in 1807 and ending in 1839. In 1818 James Camack and James Gaines, acting for Georgia and Tennessee respectively, established the northwest corner of Georgia on the 35th parallel. The exact location they determined is about a mile south of the parallel. It is also south of the Tennessee town of Nickajack, and near the top of Nickajack Mountain.

With Georgia. Nor did Alabama have much to do with establishing its eastern boundary. This boundary was set when Georgia sold its western lands to the federal government in 1802. The Chattahoochee River part of the boundary was given as the western bank of that river as far north as the Great Bend above Uchee Creek. (See map 5.2.) From that point, the line ran to the Indian town of Nickajack near the Tennessee border. Georgia commissioners determined that Miller's Bend was the "Great Bend" referred to and in 1826 unilaterally ran a straight line from there to the point determined in 1818 by James Camack and James Gaines as the northwest corner of Georgia on the 35th parallel. This point is near the top of Nickajack Mountain. Alabama commissioners disputed the 1826 line, claiming it did not meet the definition called for in the 1802 Georgia cession agreement. Alabama maintained the proper bend in the Chattahoochee was 30 to 40 miles north of Miller's Bend. This argument did not prevail, and in 1840 Alabama formally accepted the line as run by Georgia in 1826. Later the two states disputed whether the 1802 cession agreement referred to the Chattahoochee's high-water mark, Georgia's claim, or low-water mark, which was Alabama's claim. The issue ended in the U.S. Supreme Court, which rendered a decision in 1859 setting the boundary at the mean-water line on the western shore.

With Florida. The Treaty of San Lorenzo (often called Pinckney's Treaty) negotiated by Thomas Pinckney in 1795 established the boundary between the United States and Spain at the 31st parallel. The two nations appointed Andrew Ellicott and Esteban Minor to survey and mark the boundary. They began in 1797 at the Mississippi River and worked east. They completed the 31st parallel as far as the Chattahoochee River by 1799. The line deviates by as much as a mile from the true location of the parallel.

During the War of 1812 the United States, fearful that Great Britain would occupy Spanish West Florida, added to Mississippi Territory the area between the Perdido and Pearl rivers (the area between the west boundary of present-day Florida and the southern boundary between Louisiana and Mississippi) and south of the 31st parallel. (See map 5.3.) U.S. troops invaded and held the area in 1813, although Spain did not officially relinquish it until 1819. This established the boundary between Florida and Alabama south of the 31st parallel at the Perdido River.

Sentiment existed as early as 1821 in Alabama to annex the western panhandle of Florida, i.e. between the Perdido and Apalachicola rivers, and many eastern Floridians seemed eager to rid themselves of the area. By 1868 serious negotiations took place when Florida commissioners offered the area for $1 million. Both sides then cooled to the idea. Alabamans disliked the deal because they thought it was too much money for an area consisting of sand banks and gophers, and they would have access to Pensacola harbor without having political jurisdiction over it. Floridians didn't like the deal because the thought of losing such an excellent harbor as Pensacola became repugnant.

With Gulf of Mexico. Alabama has jurisdiction over all islands within 6 leagues (about 18 miles) of the shore. Its gulf boundary, however, is limited to 3 nautical miles, about 3.45 land miles. Alabama thought that provisions of the 1953 Submerged Lands Act would allow it to claim a 3-league (about 9 miles) gulf boundary. The U.S. Supreme Court ruled in 1960 that was not the case because nothing in Alabama's enabling act justified its claims to 3 leagues. Florida and Texas do have gulf boundaries extending for 3 leagues. See those states for why this is the case. The point from which gulf boundaries are measured is the mean low-tide line.

Florida

Spaniards were the first known Europeans to visit Florida when Ponce de León landed there in 1513. Spaniards settled St. Augustine in 1565, the oldest continuously occupied European settlement in North America. Florida was very important in Spain's colonial empire as it served as an important protective link in Spain's trade route to the riches of Mexico. Spain had such a vast empire that it could not be settled nor adequately administered or protected. In 1763 Spain ceded its lands east of the Mississippi River and south of the 31st parallel to Great Britain, except for the Isle of Orleans. (The Isle of Orleans consisted of the area bounded on the west by the Mississippi River, on the south and east by the Gulf of Mexico, and on the north generally by lakes Maurepas, Pontchartrain, and Borgne. [See map 8.9.])

Britain created two colonies out of the area it received from Spain: East Florida and West Florida. East Florida, which comprised most of what is currently the state of Florida, was bounded mostly just as the state is today, except that in the west the boundary was the Chattahoochee and Apalachicola rivers rather than the Perdido River. (See map 5.3.)

West Florida was bounded on the west by the Mississippi River, on the south by the Gulf of Mexico, on the east by the Chattahoochee and Apalachicola rivers, and on the north by the 31st parallel. The governor of

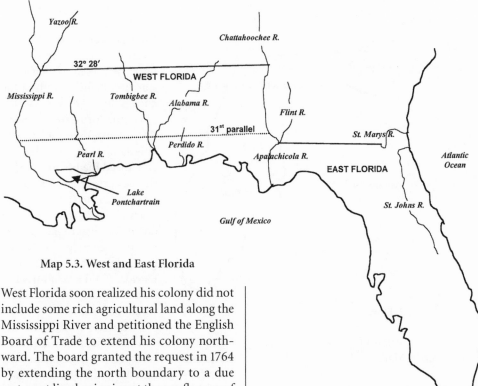

Map 5.3. West and East Florida

West Florida soon realized his colony did not include some rich agricultural land along the Mississippi River and petitioned the English Board of Trade to extend his colony northward. The board granted the request in 1764 by extending the north boundary to a due east-west line beginning at the confluence of the Yazoo and Mississippi rivers, latitude 32 degrees 28 minutes, and extending east to the Chattahoochee River. Most of West Florida is outside the boundaries of the state of Florida and within the boundaries of Alabama and Mississippi, where it is discussed further.

In the Treaty of 1783 ending the War for American Independence, Great Britain acknowledged the thirteen American colonies (Georgia being the most southern) as free and independent and retroceded the two Florida colonies to Spain. The treaty also specified the boundary as the 31st parallel from the Mississippi River to the Chattahoochee or Apalachicola rivers. (Confusion existed as to what to call the river; it is now the Chattahoochee above the confluence with the Flint River and the Apalachicola below it.) The boundary then continues down this river to the confluence with the Flint, then a straight line to the head of St. Marys River and down the middle of this river to the Atlantic Ocean. A lot of details were yet to be ironed out, but this 1783 treaty established most of Florida's boundaries when the United States later acquired Florida from Spain. Spain ceded the area to the United States in 1819, but the United States did not take formal possession until 1821.

The United States created the Territory of Florida in March 1822 out of all the land east of the Mississippi River ceded by Spain — East and West Florida. After about 15 years of being a territory, ideas of statehood surfaced, and the question arose as to whether it should be one or two states. The eastern part of the territory favored two states along the line of the old Spanish division of the area. Middle Florida, the area between the Apalachicola and Suwannee rivers, wanted one state. (See map 5.4.) In the western part of the panhandle some were in favor of annexing to Alabama. In the years leading to statehood, eastern Floridians came together to form one state with the current bound-

Map 5.4. Florida

aries. Florida was admitted as the twenty-seventh state in March 1845.

With Alabama. Florida's boundary with Alabama was quite easy to determine. The Treaty of 1783 established the 31st parallel as the boundary between the United States and Spanish Florida. The 31st parallel was thus already an accepted boundary before Congress began dividing the area into states. Congress passed an act in 1831 establishing the 31st parallel as the boundary between Florida and Alabama. The Perdido River became a boundary when, in 1812, Congress added the area below the 31st parallel and between the Pearl and Perdido rivers to Mississippi Territory. This added area eventually became parts of the states of Mississippi and Alabama and thus put this part of the Florida-Alabama boundary at this river. The boundary in the Perdido is in the middle of the river.

With Georgia. The boundary with Georgia was more difficult to settle than that with Alabama. The initial English Board of Trade draft for the new colony of East Florida after 1763 had the northern bound-

ary running from the confluence of the Flint and Chattahoochee rivers to the mouth of the St. Johns River near the present site of Jacksonville, slightly south of the current line. The East Florida governor protested, saying this removed too much valuable land from Florida, and convinced the board to move the eastern terminus of the straight line to the head of St. Marys River, then running down that river to the Atlantic Ocean. (See map 5.5.) While this didn't add a lot of land to Florida, it did give it jurisdiction over all the area that would become Jacksonville.

Andrew Ellicott and Esteban Minor, commissioners for the United States and Spain respectively, established the boundary with the United States and Spain from the Mississippi River to the Atlantic in 1797–1799. Beginning at the Mississippi, they completed and marked the line as far east as the confluence of the Flint and Chattahoochee rivers when problems with Indians necessitated that they cease their work. They then traveled to the St. Marys River to find its source. The St. Marys has no easily identifiable source; some possibilities are indicated in map 5.5. All emanate from Lake Okefenokee and could be considered as sources of the river. After careful consideration the two men agreed that the northern prong best fit the definition as the source of the river. They built a mound, called "Ellicott's Mound," 10 feet in diameter at the base and 5 feet high, as close to the source as they could get and from which the source of the river, about 2 miles away, could be pinpointed. Having done this, they quit their work without surveying and marking the line back to the confluence of the Flint and Chattahoochee rivers.

In 1817 a member of the Georgia legislature claimed an error had occurred in establishing the northern prong as the source of the St. Marys. Georgia was eager to have the southern prong (*B* on map 5.5) denoted the source as the state would gain 1.5 million acres by such a designation. Other officials claimed the middle prong (*A* on map 5.5) was the correct head of the river. Georgia ordered several new surveys in the 1820s, all of which confirmed the northern prong as the source of the river. Finally convinced, Georgia agreed to surveying and marking the line from the confluence of the Chattahoochee and Flint rivers to Ellicott's Mound in 1859. It was 1866 when Georgia officially accepted the boundary. The boundary in the St. Marys is in the middle of the river.

The north-south part of the boundary between Florida and Georgia is the middle of the Chattahoochee River. This was the long-standing boundary first established by the Treaty of 1783. However, the boundary in the Chattahoochee River between Georgia and Alabama is the mean-water line on the western bank rather than in the middle. This is where Georgia's 1802 cession agreement put that part of the boundary.

With Atlantic Ocean and Gulf of Mexico. Florida's statutes specify its ocean boundary as 3 nautical miles (about 3.45 land miles) or the edge of the Gulf Stream, whichever is greater. The gulf boundary is specified as 3 leagues, about 9 miles. The reason for the 3-league gulf boundary is that when Congress admitted Florida as a state it approved Florida's 1868 constitution which specified a boundary of 3 leagues in the gulf.

Florida's Atlantic Ocean boundary is limited by the 1953 Submerged Lands Act. Florida also encompasses all of the Florida Keys to the westernmost Dry Tortugas Islands. The point from which gulf and ocean boundaries are measured is the mean low tide line.

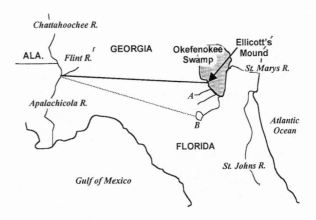

Map 5.5. Source of St. Marys River

Georgia

Georgia was originally part of a 1629 English grant to Sir Robert Heath for a land he called "Carolana." Since Heath did not develop his grant, Charles II regranted the land in 1663 to eight men to whom he owed favors. They renamed the land "Carolina." This grant was amended in 1665 to include land as far south as the 29th parallel, about 30 miles north of what is now Orlando, Florida. In 1729 the crown bought Carolina from the eight proprietors. It was immediately divided, and Georgia became part of South Carolina. Then in 1732 George II granted Georgia to James Oglethorpe and 20 associates who planned to populate the land with people who had fallen on economic hard times but who were of good character.

The boundaries of the 1732 grant were along the northernmost part of the Savannah River in the north, the southernmost part of the Altamaha River in the south, and lines drawn parallel from the heads of these river systems all the way to the South Sea (Pacific Ocean). This created a province about 50 miles wide at the coast, broadening to about 100 miles in the interior, and then a long band of land about 60 miles wide from the heads of the rivers to the Pacific. This area can be inferred from map 5.6 by following the Savannah and southern branch of the Altamaha rivers to their heads and drawing lines to the west. Although this area was

Map 5.6. Georgia Territory

With Florida. The Treaty of 1783 between the United States and Great Britain established the boundary between those two nations, as it relates to Georgia, as a line beginning in the middle of the Chattahoochee River on the 31st parallel, south along the middle of that river to the confluence of the Flint River, then straight to the head of St. Marys River, then down the middle of that river to the Atlantic Ocean. The United States and Spain both acknowledged this boundary line in 1795 after Great Britain's 1783 retrocession of Florida to Spain.

taken from South Carolina, that state was happy to relinquish its status as a buffer between the United States and Spanish Florida.

In 1752 Oglethorpe and his associates surrendered their charter, which had stipulated that the colony would revert to the crown after 21 years, and the king established a royal colony. In 1763 the boundaries of Georgia were altered by proclamation of George III. The southern boundary was extended to the St. Marys River and the 31st parallel, with the western boundary limited to the Mississippi River. The northern boundary remained the same as specified in the 1732 grant. Although it no longer extended to the Pacific Ocean, Georgia was still a very large area. (See map 5.6.)

After the War for American Independence, states holding large expanses of western lands ceded them to the federal government to help finance the new confederated government. Georgia was not willing to give away the lands but was willing to sell them for $171,428, an offer that was refused. Georgia continued to maintain jurisdiction over its western lands until 1802, when it struck a deal to sell the lands to the federal government for $1,250,000, a whole lot more than Georgia's original offer.

Georgia's western lands eventually formed most of the states of Alabama and Mississippi. In spite of the reduction in Georgia's area, it remains the largest state east of the Mississippi River.

It is interesting to note that Georgia's boundary with Florida is along the middle of the Chattahoochee, but Georgia's boundary with Alabama along the same river (to be discussed later) is the mean-water line on the western bank of that river.

Determining the head of St. Marys River posed a problem as that river drains from many small branches of the Okefenokee Swamp before it forms anything resembling a river. Andrew Ellicott, representing the United States and Captain Esteban Minor, representing Spain, were appointed commissioners in 1796 to run and mark the boundary between the two nations. By 1799 they had completed their work from the Mississippi River as far as the Flint and Chattahoochee rivers when Indian threats caused them to cease surveying. They then sailed up the St. Marys River to determine the main channel and head of that river. They decided the northern prong was the source, and they built a mound on dry land and located the head of the river in relation to that mound, about 2 miles away. (See map 5.5.) They did not complete the survey back to the confluence of the Chattahoochee and Flint rivers.

A Georgia legislator disputed the determination for the head of the St. Marys in 1817. He felt the southern prong of the river (*B* on map 5.5), south of Ellicott's Mound, was the proper head of the St. Marys River. Some Georgia officials argued for the middle prong (*A* on map 5.5) as the river's source. Georgia ordered additional surveys in the 1820s, all of which supported the northern prong as the proper source of the river, and both states finally agreed on the northern prong. The line was run and marked in 1859–60. The boundary in the St. Marys runs along the middle of the river.

With Alabama. When Georgia ceded its western lands to the U.S. in 1802 it described the cession as south of Tennessee and west of the Chattahoochee River from where it crosses the boundary between the United States and Spain (the 31st parallel), then running up the western bank of this river to the great bend above Uchee Creek, then in a straight line to Nickajack, ending at the southern boundary of Tennessee. (See map 5.7.) In 1826 Georgia commissioners determined that a bend in the river called "Miller's Bend" was the one referred to in the cession agreement. Alabama commissioners refused to agree, and Georgia commissioners refused to change their minds. Georgia in 1826 ran the line unilaterally from Miller's Bend to Nickajack without the participation of Alabama. The Alabama legislature finally accepted the line as run by Georgia in 1840. Surveyors established the 35th parallel and the northwest corner of Georgia in 1818. This point is a little more than a mile from the south bank of the Tennessee River and due south of the Tennessee town of Nickajack and near the top of Nickajack Mountain.

With Tennessee. Georgia's 1732 charter specified its northern border as the source of the Savannah River, but this point was not then known. Then in 1787 the Beaufort Convention put Georgia's northern boundary on the same parallel as the presumed southern border of South Carolina, i.e., the 35th parallel. This conformed well with the southern borders of Tennessee and North Carolina, which were also along the 35th parallel according to their charters.

Map 5.7. Georgia

Mathematician James Camack, working for Georgia, and James Gaines, working for Tennessee, established the point on the 35th parallel marking the northwest corner of Georgia in 1818. The point they established was 1 mile and 28 poles south of the south bank of the Tennessee River and due south of the center of the old Indian town of Nickajack. The location of the parallel was not accurate, as it is south of the true position of the parallel at this point. Later in 1818 this line was run east by a surveyor named Montgomery to within 30 or so miles of the northeast Georgia corner.

With North Carolina. Some settlers moved into the French Broad River area in 1803 and, not realizing they were within the boundaries of North Carolina, they petitioned the General Assembly of Georgia to be incorporated into that state. Georgia sought the cooperation of North Carolina to survey the area, as both states recognized the 35th parallel as their boundary. Commissioners and surveyors from both states met in 1807, but crude instruments and a lack of skill produced conflicting results for the location of the parallel. In 1818 Andrew Ellicott fixed the 35th parallel on the Chattooga River at a point known as Ellicott's Rock, a common point for North Carolina, South Carolina, and Georgia. Ellicott's determination was actually several hundred feet north of the 35th parallel.

In 1819 Georgia and North Carolina appointed commissioners and surveyors (Camack was one) to run their boundary. Both parties met at Ellicott's Rock on the Chattooga River in September. They ran the line just 30 miles west when they came to near where Montgomery's earlier line, run westward from Nickajack in 1818, stopped. They had a problem. Although the two lines were supposed to be on the 35th parallel, they were 661 yards apart. The commissioners had no formal instructions concerning this situation, so they simply ran a straight line south of their line to join with Montgomery's line, creating Montgomery's Corner in Towns County, Georgia, and Clay County, North Carolina. The Montgomery's Corner jog can be seen only on large-scale maps.

Georgia asked Camack to double check the location of the 35th parallel in 1826. Now equipped with better instruments, Camack determined that the correct parallel was 2,500 feet north of his 1819 line; neither state

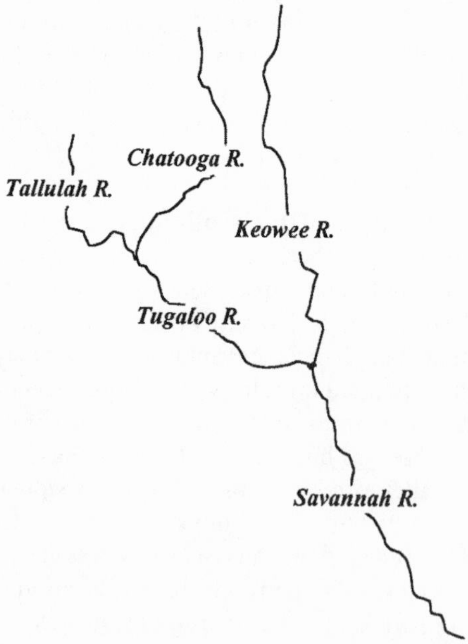

Map 5.8. Savannah River Head

accepted this 1826 line. Georgia made unsuccessful attempts to have the line relocated in 1887 and 1971, but nothing was done. Now that over 180 years have elapsed since the boundary was established, it is unlikely that it will ever be moved.

With South Carolina. When the king split Georgia from South Carolina in 1732 he specified the boundary as the most northern stream of the Savannah River all the way to its source. The two colonies soon got into a dispute over what constituted the most northern stream of the Savannah. South Carolina advanced the argument that the Savannah ended where the Keowee and Tugaloo met because above that confluence there was no river called Savannah. It was an idea worth advancing, but it didn't have much logical support, so the argument became whether the Keowee or Tugaloo-Chattooga river systems were the most northern stream of the Savannah. (See map 5.8.)

This issue was not resolved until the 1787 Beaufort Convention, where the delegates determined that the Tugaloo-Chattooga system best met the definition. It is not clear why they arrived at this determination because the Keowee is now known to be the most northern source of the Savannah. It could be that the precise locations for the sources simply were not known in 1787.

South Carolina claimed land as far south as the 29th parallel when Georgia was created. Since Georgia's southern boundary was the Altamaha River, South Carolina still claimed land south of the Altamaha to the 29th parallel. British officials never intended that South Carolina should have any claim to land south of Georgia, but it was not until the Beaufort Convention that South Carolina formally gave up its claims to that area.

The Beaufort Convention was vague enough that the U.S. Supreme Court had to interpret it in 1922. The court determined that the boundary in the Savannah, Tugaloo, and Chattooga rivers was in the middle of the river at ordinary stage except when islands were encountered. The boundary then shifted to midway between the island and the South Carolina shore at ordinary stage, thereby awarding all islands to Georgia.

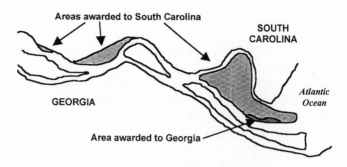

Map 5.9. Lower Savannah River

The Savannah River has altered its course over time due to natural causes and the work of humans. The increasing importance of industry and commerce, especially in the lower parts of the Savannah, created the need for a precise location of the boundary as the river neared the sea. Georgia brought suit in the U.S. Supreme Court in 1977 as it claimed the right to about 3,000 acres of land that had become attached to the South Carolina shore because of changes in the river's channel. The court appointed a special master who listened to a host of experts from both states offering as evidence charts, maps, charters, and other documents in an effort to support their cases. After careful consideration the special master made several recommendations to the court, most of which were adopted. (See map 5.9.)

The result was that the court awarded Georgia only 195 of the contested 3,000 acres. The determination was that the 1787 convention had meant to form a permanent boundary, not one that constantly shifted. Therefore as new islands formed after 1787 in South Carolina's half of the river, those islands belonged to South Carolina. If a new island formed in the middle of the river, both states had claim to a part of it. Barnwell Island, near the mouth of the Savannah, had become attached to South Carolina and was awarded to that state based on the fact that South Carolina had exercised jurisdiction over it and Georgia had not protested this until the late 1970s. Georgia was awarded land near the mouth of the river.

Determining the exact boundary was important not only for commerce and industry but also because of the Submerged Lands Act of 1953 and federal legislation in 1976 which gave coastal states a portion of offshore leasing revenues. Also important were laws that pertained to commercial and sport fishing in the river and bay.

With Atlantic Ocean. The U.S. Geological Survey says that generally speaking the individual states recognize an offshore boundary of 3 nautical miles. The United States territorial sea limit contiguous zone has been set at 12 nautical miles but is expected to be extended to 24 nautical miles. The exclusive economic zone boundary is 200 nautical miles. (A nautical mile equals 1.15 land miles.) The point from which ocean boundaries are measured is the mean low tide line.

Mississippi

The early history of Mississippi is a lot like that of Alabama in that it is linked with the British colony of West Florida and the land Georgia sold to the federal government. It is also linked with the international politics and policies of Spain, France, and Great Britain.

Spanish explorers were likely the first Europeans to visit Mississippi in the early 1500s when Hernando De Soto trampled through the interior in 1540. In 1682 René-Robert Cavelier, Sieur de La Salle, claimed the region drained by the Mississippi River for France and named it Louisiane for King Louis XIV. The first European settlement in Mississippi was Fort Maurepas, now Ocean Springs (just east of Biloxi), established by the French in 1699. By 1717 French influence extended along the gulf coast from the Isle of Orleans (the area bounded on the west by the Mississippi River, on the south and east by the Gulf of Mexico, and on the north generally by lakes Maurepas, Pontchartrain, and Borgne [see map 8.9]) on the Mississippi River to the city of Mobile in Alabama but not very far inland.

The Treaty of 1763 ended the French and Indian War and also ended France's influence on the North American continent as it ceded land west of the Mississippi River to Spain and ceded land east of the river and north of the 31st parallel to Great Britain. Great Britain also received the land south of the 31st parallel from Spain and promptly divided it into two colonies: East Florida and West Florida with their boundaries set at the Chattahoochee and Apalachicola rivers. (See map 5.3.) The governor of West Florida was not pleased that his territory did not include some heavily populated prime agricultural land along the Mississippi River and petitioned the English Board of Trade to expand his colony northward. The board did this in 1764 when they moved the border north to the confluence of the Mississippi and Yazoo rivers, latitude 32 degrees 28 minutes, then due east to the Chattahoochee River. (See map 5.10.)

In the Treaty of 1783 Great Britain ceded the Floridas back to Spain, while the United States was casting covetous eyes toward this area. The United States and Spain disputed this border, with the United States claiming the 31st parallel and Spain claiming the boundary in the west should be 32° 28' because that was where the British had placed it in 1764. Thomas Pinckney negotiated the Treaty of San Lorenzo with Spain in 1795 that formally settled the boundary dispute by placing it at the 31st parallel.

Congress created Mississippi Territory in 1798 with both east-west boundaries extending from the Mississippi to Chattahoochee rivers, with the southernmost extending along the 31st parallel and the northernmost along the parallel of 32 degrees 28 minutes, a fairly small area. (See map 5.10.) The federal government bought Georgia's western lands in 1802, and two years later it added to Mississippi Territory all the land between the Mississippi River and the western border of Georgia and north of the original territory to the southern boundary of Tennessee. The territory was further augmented in 1812 when the U.S. government annexed the land between the Perdido and Pearl rivers south of the 31st parallel. (See map 5.10.)

As is often the case, differences arose among widely scattered settlers as Mississippi Territory's population increased. Polarization became apparent between the settlements along the Mississippi River and those along the Tombigbee River in present western Alabama. Division came in 1817 when Congress admitted Mississippi as the twentieth state.

With Alabama. When Georgia sold its western lands

Map 5.10. Mississippi Territory

to the federal government the agreement contained a clause that the ceded area was to be formed into one state. As Mississippi Territory gained settlers, however, a division arose between those living along the Mississippi River and those living along the Tombigbee River. The western community, in this case the older, had the most developed economy and the most political clout. The settlers along the Tombigbee felt the settlers along the Mississippi didn't attend to their needs and wanted a separate government. The western settlers did not want to divide the territory.

Bills to admit the territory as one state passed the U.S. House of Representatives but always failed in the Senate. Senators were against admitting the area as one state because they felt it was too large. The mood of western territorial citizens was for one state. The Senate made it clear that admittance as one state was not going to happen, so the consent of Georgia to a division of the territory was asked for and received.

The next question, then, was to determine where the boundary should be. Officials advanced several ideas. One proposal, for example, was to run a line directly north from the head of Mobile Bay, a plan that would have placed the city of Mobile in Mississippi. (See map 5.10.) This plan was attacked not only because it would put Mobile in Mississippi but also because such a plan would put the Tombigbee-Alabama river drainage basin under two different political jurisdictions, thus confusing administration of the area. Another plan would have used the Pascagoula River as part of the boundary, but this was too far west for the westerners. (See map 5.11.)

Early in the deliberations a member of the Select Committee of the House had suggested a boundary placed west of the Tombigbee River. This proposal was originally rejected because such a division of the territory would give Alabama more than half. Mississippians were finally convinced that, although this was true, the western land was considerably more fertile than the eastern

land, making this a fair division. This division west of the Tombigbee finally prevailed, and Congress set the eastern boundary of Mississippi as beginning at the southern Tennessee boundary, then up the Tennessee River to the mouth of Bear Creek, then in a straight line to the northwest corner of Washington County, Alabama, then due south to the Gulf of Mexico.

The agreement contained a provision that if the due-south portion of the boundary encroached upon the Mississippi counties of Wayne, Greene, and Jackson, the line was to shift east to hit the gulf 10 miles east of the mouth of the Pascagoula River. When surveyors ran a preliminary line in 1820 they discovered that a due-south line did infringe upon the Mississippi counties, so the terminus of the line was moved east in accordance with the agreement.

With Gulf of Mexico. Mississippi's gulf boundary is 3 nautical miles into the gulf, about 3.45 land miles. It does, however, have jurisdiction over all islands within 6 leagues, about 18 miles, of the shore. Missis-

Map 5.11. Mississippi

sippi thought that provisions of the 1953 Submerged Lands Act would allow it to claim a 3-league gulf boundary, about 9 miles. The U.S. Supreme Court ruled in 1960 that this was not the case because nothing in Mississippi's enabling act justified its claims to 3 leagues. Florida and Texas do have gulf boundaries extending for 3 leagues into the gulf. (See the information on those states for why this is the case.) The point from which gulf boundaries are measured is the mean low tide line.

With Louisiana. The 31st parallel was a well-established boundary long before Louisiana and Mississippi took shape as states because Great Britain, in 1763, had originally established this as the border between its new colony of West Florida and the other colonies. It was also a contested boundary between the United States and Spain beginning in 1783, and then it was finally established as a boundary in 1795.

The United States bought the Louisiana Purchase from France in 1803. Excluded from the purchase, in the eyes of Spain, was all land east of the Mississippi River and south of the 31st parallel. (See map 5.3.) The United States, however, claimed as part of the Louisiana Purchase land as far east as the Perdido River (the current west boundary of Florida), but it did nothing to force the issue of ownership. Many American settlers moved into the former British colony of West Florida. (See map 5.3.) They eventually revolted and claimed independence from Spain. U.S. president James Madison claimed Florida from the Perdido to the Mississippi in 1810 and instructed District of Orleans Governor William C. C. Claiborne to occupy the area as part of his district.

In 1811 the settlers between the Pearl and Perdido rivers and south of the 31st parallel petitioned Congress to be attached to the Territory of Mississippi. They didn't like the idea of being aligned with the District of Orleans. That territory was much too French for them, and they cited differences in manners, customs, language, and politics. Al-

though Claiborne felt his district had a good claim to West Florida as far as the Perdido River, in the interest of compromise he said that he would agree to limit his district at the Pearl River. Congress agreed, and in 1812 formally added the land below the 31st parallel and between the Mississippi and Pearl rivers to Louisiana. Congress that same year added the area between the Pearl and Perdido rivers to Mississippi Territory. These two acts established this part of the boundary between the two states.

The border between Mississippi and Louisiana along the Mississippi River is complex. The boundary between the two states does not always follow the middle of the river's main channel. The Mississippi frequently floods and consequently does not always stay in its channel. The general rule, adopted by the U.S. Supreme Court, is that when a river boundary changes its channel by natural and gradual processes the boundary follows the changing course of the river. If, however, the river changes its channel suddenly, then no change of boundary occurs. One such sudden change in the channel is the Albermarle Bend, about 15 miles north of Vicksburg, but others exist as well. This fact puts some of Mississippi west of the current channel of the river and some parts of Louisiana east of it.

The general rule of the Supreme Court, however, does not prevent states from working out agreements to cede lands to each other where a watercourse has inconveniently separated them from the original state. In 1909 Congress gave Mississippi and Louisiana authority to cede to each other tracts of land that were separated from the main body of each state. It appears this has not happened, at least not in all cases, because many tracts are on the "wrong" side of the river. Parcels of land that have been separated from their original political jurisdiction by changes in a river and now lying seemingly within the territory of another jurisdiction are sometimes called "exclaves." The river boundary is mostly in the middle of the channel as per the Treaty of 1783, where the western boundary of the United States was given as the middle of the Mississippi River.

The boundary between Mississippi and Louisiana in the gulf was determined by the Supreme Court in a 1905 case. Congress admitted Mississippi giving it jurisdiction over islands within 6 leagues (18 miles) of the coastline. Mississippi later claimed jurisdiction over some islands and fishery areas that Louisiana also claimed. The court ruled in favor of Louisiana, stating that Louisiana's jurisdiction included all islands within 3 leagues (9 miles) of its coastline, and since Louisiana became a state 5 years before Mississippi, Congress could not give Mississippi any area that was already Louisiana's. See the discussion under Louisiana in chapter 8 for a more detailed explanation.

With Arkansas. The Arkansas-Mississippi boundary shares the same problems as that of Mississippi and Louisiana. The river has changed course over time, and now each state has some land on the other state's side of the river. Congress gave the same authority to Arkansas and Mississippi to cede land to the other as in the case of Louisiana and Mississippi. The boundary is in the middle of the channel as per the Treaty of 1783, where the western boundary of the United States was given as the middle of the main channel of the Mississippi River. The same Congressional action also authorized Mississippi and Arkansas to cede tracts of land separated from the main body of their states. Just as in the case of the Mississippi-Louisiana border, this has apparently not happened with Arkansas in all cases, judging from the many tracts on the "wrong" side of the river.

With Tennessee. The boundary between Tennessee and Mississippi was established when the king put the southern boundary of Carolina, which then included Tennessee, at the 35th parallel. Two different surveyors ran the original line between Mississippi and Tennessee in 1818 and 1819. Mississippians thought that if the line were run

correctly Memphis just might be in Mississippi. Tennessee, of course, refused to participate in any new survey they thought might move their southern boundary northward. Mississippi's governor, nonetheless, ordered a new survey to determine the accurate location of the 35th parallel. This new survey determined that the true parallel was a few miles south, not north, of the 1818–1819 line. Therefore, Tennessee's interest in the boundary location was renewed with the possibility that it might gain land. They had a new line run in the mid-1830s using the new location of the 35th parallel as the proper line. This line, known as the Thompson Line, was never sanctioned by Mississippi. The two states named commissioners in 1837 to run and mark the permanent boundary between the two states. They ran a line that was north of the Thompson Line, but to the disappointment of the Mississippians, it was south of Memphis. The boundary is slightly south of the 35th parallel, which favors Tennessee.

South Carolina

First what is now South Carolina was a part of the Virginia grant, then part of a grant called "Carolana," and then a part of a grant called "Carolina." Finally it became a separate colony in 1729 when Carolina was split by King George II into north and south.

In 1629 Charles I granted to Robert Heath all territory between the 31st and 36th degrees north latitude and from sea to sea. Heath named the land Carolana, but since he did not develop the grant, Charles II revoked it in 1663 and re-granted the area to eight men who had helped him regain the crown and to whom he owed favors. They called the land Carolina; it had the same boundaries as Carolana. The eight proprietors of Carolina were not happy with the size of their grant, so in 1665 the king enlarged the already generous boundaries to 36 degrees 30 minutes latitude in the north, and to 29 degrees in the south, about a half de-

Map 5.12. South Carolina

gree north of Orlando, Florida. This southern boundary extended well into Spanish territory, but since no one tried to settle south of the Savannah River, no conflicts arose.

The Carolina grant was so large that it was impossible to administer from one location, so an informal north-south division occurred. This division was formally acknowledged by the king in 1729 when he divided Carolina into North and South at about where the North Carolina–South Carolina border is today. (See map 5.12.) In that year the crown bought out seven of the eight proprietors. The eighth proprietor, George Carteret, eventually received title to land in North Carolina. At the time of the division Carolina extended south into the northern part of Florida, so on paper at least, South Carolina controlled a large chunk of land. South Carolina was a buffer area between British America and Spanish America.

King George II reduced South Carolina's size in 1732 when he granted to James Oglethorpe and twenty associates land extending from the Savannah to the Altamaha rivers and extending west from the heads of these two rivers to the South Sea. (See map 5.6.) Although greatly reduced in size, South Carolina was happy to lose its status as a buffer between the United States and Spain. Since the Georgia grant was only to the Altamaha, South Carolina still claimed land south of that river to the 29th parallel and made some land grants there, actions the crown never intended.

With North Carolina. South Carolina is fortunate in that it had only two political jurisdictions to contend with in resolving its boundaries. First, of course, was with North Carolina when Carolina was divided by the king. Instructions from Great Britain stipulated the two provinces be divided by a line beginning at the sea 30 miles southwest of Cape Fear River and parallel to it to its source and then west to the Pacific Ocean. (See map 4.8.) It stipulated that if the Waccamaw River was within 30 miles of Cape Fear River, then that river should be the boundary. The Waccamaw is 50 or so miles from Cape Fear River at its mouth but less than 30 miles from it in the upper reaches. So, what to do? North Carolina naturally wanted to use the Waccamaw as the boundary as that would give it more land. South Carolina wanted a border based on the Cape Fear River to enhance its domain. South Carolina had lost considerable land in the grant to Oglethorpe and was tenacious in trying to preserve as much area as possible.

After several rounds of negotiations, the two sides agreed to begin on the coast 30 miles southwest of Cape Fear River and run a straight line northwest, generally about 30 miles from the river, to the 35th parallel. This line was surveyed and marked in 1735–1737, but the survey crew was very inaccurate in locating the 35th parallel, as they stopped about 15 miles south of it. Survey work ceased until 1764, when the boundary was extended from the end of the 1735–1737 line west to the Catawba Indian lands.

Two major problems stem from the 1735–37 line. First was that British officials in England suspected that the northwest line had not reached the 35th parallel and instructed the 1764 crew to check and ensure they were at the correct parallel before they began their survey work to the west. Either they did not check the end point of the earlier survey, or if they did, then they made the same error as the previous crew. In any event, they began where the 1735–1737 crew ended their work. The other problem was that they did not survey all the way to the

Catawba lands. They stopped at the Salisbury-Charlotte Road, slightly east of the Catawba lands, complaining of fatigue and asked to halt their work. (See map 5.13.) Their request was granted, but they were instructed to have one of the surveyors finish the line to the Catawba lands. This did not happen.

In later years everyone involved in the boundary placement realized the 1764 boundary was south of the 35th parallel. In an effort to compensate South Carolina for land it lost in that survey, the Board of Trade recommended in 1771 that the boundary continue north from the end of the 1764 line around the Catawba lands until reaching the point where the Catawba lands boundary intersected the middle of the Catawba River. The line was then to continue up the middle of that river to the confluence of its northern and southern branches and then go due west until reaching the Saluda Mountains, also called the "Cherokee Mountains." This point is the intersection of South Carolina's Spartanburg and Greenville counties. This east-west line, surveyed and marked in 1772, compensated South Carolina nearly equally for the land lost in the 1764 survey, except that since the line actually runs north of west, South Carolina gained more than it lost.

Survey work halted until 1815, when the line was continued. A series of negotiations ensued to complete the boundary along natural features and without causing undue hardship for citizens along the boundary who originally would have been in North Carolina and would have had to cross the Saluda Mountains to do business in that state. The two states ultimately agreed to continue the boundary from the end of the 1772 line north of three springs forming the Saluda River and then essentially along the Saluda Mountains to a point where the ridge intersected a 1797 Cherokee boundary. From that point the boundary ran straight to Ellicott's Rock on the east bank of the Chattooga River which had been determined by Andrew Ellicott to be on the 35th parallel. The rock

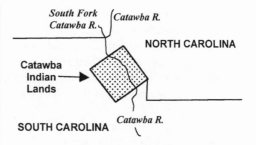

Map 5.13. Catawba Lands

is actually a few hundred feet south of the parallel.

A straight line was substituted for the north-south Salisbury-Charlotte Road line in 1815. An 8-mile line was surveyed and marked slightly east of the old line along the road.

With Georgia. The grant for Georgia to James Oglethorpe and twenty associates in 1732 specified boundaries as along the most northern stream of the Savannah River to the most southern stream of the Altamaha and from the heads of these rivers all the way west to the South Sea. (See map 5.6.) Determining what series of streams was meant by "most northern stream of the Savannah" provided a point on which the two colonies could not agree for several years.

South Carolina argued that the Savannah River ended where the Keowee and Tugaloo rivers met to form the Savannah. (See map 5.8.) They did not get anywhere with this argument, and it boiled down to which of the two river systems best met the charter description of "most northern stream." Commissioners met in Beaufort, South Carolina, in 1787 and negotiated an understanding that made the Tugaloo and Chattooga rivers the boundary above the Savannah. This settlement preserved a sizable piece of land, current Oconee County, for South Carolina. The Beaufort Convention agreement was still vague, however, and did not become comprehensible until the U.S. Supreme Court interpreted it in 1922.

The court's interpretation made the middle of the Savannah River the boundary except where islands occur. The boundary shifts to the middle of the river on the north side of all islands not only in the Savannah but also the Tugaloo and Chattooga rivers, thereby preserving all islands to Georgia. This river boundary ends at the 35th parallel.

Boundary problems between Georgia and South Carolina arose again in 1970 brought on by the increasing importance of industry, commence, and transportation, especially in the extreme lower portion of the Savannah River. The river changed its course over time due to various causes, so the question arose over whether the boundary was along the course of the river as it was in 1787, in 1922, or at some other time. Georgia sued in the U.S. Supreme Court in 1977 to settle the issue. Both states brought in experts in the form of geographers, historians, and others to support their case. Witnesses introduced new and old maps, court decisions, charters, and other documents to a special master appointed by the court to handle this issue. The special master rendered a decision, most of which was adopted by the court, that determined the boundary in the lower river mostly in favor of South Carolina, although some land on the South Carolina side were awarded to Georgia. A total of 3,000 acres was disputed in the lower part of the river; of that amount the court awarded South Carolina all but 195 acres. (See map 5.9.)

Precise determination of the boundary at the mouth of the Savannah was also important because in the 1953 Submerged Lands Act coastal states received title to the water up to 3 miles offshore. Also the 1976 Coastal Zone Management Act necessitated states to create economic zones.

With Atlantic Ocean. The U.S. Geological Survey says that generally speaking the individual states recognize an offshore boundary of 3 nautical miles, about 3.45 land miles. The United States territorial sea limit contiguous zone has been set at 12 nautical miles but is expected to be extended to 24 nautical miles. The exclusive economic zone boundary is 200 nautical miles. (A nautical mile equals 1.15 land miles.) The point from which ocean boundaries are measured is the mean low tide line.

6

GREAT LAKES REGION

Map is not to scale; boundaries are roughly drawn.

Illinois

The problem of how to deal with new territory the United States would acquire appeared as early as 1780. The sense was that new states should be small, about the size of the original states. However, after James Monroe traveled west, he wrote Thomas Jefferson that the area was miserably poor and contained extensive plains that could not sustain even a bush. He felt the area could not support many people and that states there would need to be larger for them to support a sufficient number of people to entitle them admittance into the Union.

Ordinance of 1787. The Ordinance of 1787 established the framework by which Congress created all territories of the United States. Congress amended it several times to refine its workings, but the ordinance ranks high on the list of seminal documents that have helped organize the United States. Its precepts were used as recently as 1959 with the admission into the Union of Alaska and Hawaii.

For our immediate interest the ordinance established the Northwest Territory, which was the area west of Pennsylvania, and north and west of the Ohio River, east of the Mississippi River and that extended north to the international boundary with British America. Several of the original thirteen states laid claim to some part of this area, with Virginia's claim being the largest, but all of the interested states ceded their land to the federal government. New York ceded its claim in 1781, Virginia in 1784, Massachusetts in 1785, and Connecticut in 1786. The reasons for these cessions were to provide land to help the federal government with his huge war debt, to pay for the operation of governments in the new areas, and to appease the states without western land holdings.

The Ordinance of 1787 was the document created to establish the framework by which new areas would become states on an equal footing with the original thirteen, and provided for territorial government until they met the conditions for statehood. This ordinance made provision for as few as three states and a maximum of five in the Northwest Territory, officially called in the ordinance the "Territory of the United States Northwest of the River Ohio." It outlined the borders for each that will be discussed under the five states in this region. (See map 6.2.)

Virginia had originally proposed that ten states be created from the Northwest Territory, but it was asked to alter this request to three to five. Both George Washington and Thomas Jefferson suggested boundaries for states in the Northwest Territory, and Jefferson even proposed a list of names. Congress adopted neither the names nor the boundaries suggested by the two men.

In 1800 Congress created Indiana Territory as that part of the Northwest Territory west of a line from the confluence of the Kentucky and Ohio rivers to Fort Recovery, near Greenville, Ohio, and then north to the international boundary, essentially the current western Ohio boundary. (See

Map 6.2. Northwest Territory

map 6.5 later in this chapter.) Then in 1809 Congress created Illinois Territory from Indiana Territory. Illinois Territory consisted of all the former Northwest Territory west of the current Illinois-Indiana boundary all the way to the international boundary. (See map 6.3.)

The borders outlined in the Ordinance of 1787 for the "western state," eventually to become Illinois, were roughly drawn at the Mississippi River in the west, Ohio River in the south, the Wabash River and north from Vincennes in the east, and the international boundary in the north. (See map 6.3.) However, the ordinance provided for the creation of five states if Congress so desired, and it did, so Illinois Territory was reduced in size when Illinois became a state.

With Wisconsin. The Northwest Ordinance provided that if five states were created, the northern boundary of the southern tier of states was to be an east-west line drawn from the extreme southern point of Lake Michigan. (See map 6.8 later in this chapter.) None of the southern tier of states— Illinois, Indiana, and Ohio— have northern borders drawn by this definition, so strict adherence to this element of the ordinance was obviously not a goal of Congress.

The original statehood memorial submitted to Congress in 1817 by Illinois territorial delegate Nathaniel Pope specified the southern extremity of Lake Michigan as the northern border for the proposed state of Illinois. However, shortly after introduction of the memorial, Pope changed the northern boundary to the parallel of 42 degrees 30 minutes, which is the present location and 61 miles north of the southern extremity of Lake Michigan. (See map 6.4.) Pope apparently did this without consulting any officials in Illinois, but no one there complained. Neither did Pope consult any of the people living in the affected area.

The east-west line as specified in the ordinance would have deprived Illinois of any port on Lake Michigan, and the state would have suffered greatly from this. Pope appar-

Map 6.3. Illinois Territory

Map 6.4. Illinois

ently recognized this fact and decided to take care of the oversight. Wisconsin was not even a territory at that time, so organized opposition presented no challenge to this change — although people living in the area largely favored Wisconsin jurisdiction when that territory raised the issue in later years.

A good deal of the thrust of Pope's argument in convincing Congress of this change from the 1787 ordinance was that without port facilities on Lake Michigan, Illinois would look south for its economic links because of the dominance of the Mississippi and Ohio rivers. If this were the case, then Illinois would likely side with the southern states in any sectional dispute that might occur. The problems of slavery, states rights, and possible secession were important issues even in the early 1800s, and so those arguments carried considerable weight. Because of Pope's forceful and energetic efforts, an area roughly equal in size to Massachusetts was added to Illinois. The boundary is not a straight line precisely on the parallel. Instead, it zigzags slightly north and south of the parallel due to being run by a surveyor using a compass.

With Lake Michigan. The boundary in the lake is from the Illinois-Indiana line to the center of the lake, then north along the center of the lake to the parallel of 42° 30', then west. (See map 6.16 later in this chapter.)

With Indiana. The ordinance specified the basic Illinois boundary with Indiana as the Wabash River to Fort Vincent's, latter changed to Vincennes, then due north to the international boundary. When it became apparent to officials that such a definition would place some land east of the river in Illinois, creating awkward jurisdictional problems, they changed the definition to read due north from a point on the Wabash where a due north line from Vincennes would last touch the northwest shore of the river. This change kept all land east of the river in Indiana. The river boundary is defined as the middle of the river as it existed in 1816. The Wabash does not keep a constant channel, and Illinois has a few parcels of land on the east side of the river. Since the U.S. Supreme Court has ruled that a boundary follows normal meanderings, the assumption is that these parcels were created by cataclysmic events such as flooding.

With Kentucky. When Virginia ceded the territory northwest of the Ohio River to the federal government in 1784, it specified that the north shore of that river was the boundary between it and the states to be formed across the river. When Virginia granted independence to Kentucky, the same boundary was in force. Ohio brought suit in the U.S. Supreme Court challenging this north shore definition with the intent to establish the center of the Ohio River as the boundary. The court ruled in 1820 that the boundary was the low-water mark on the north shore as it existed in 1792 when Virginia passed the act allowing Kentucky to become a separate state. This ruling was later extended to Illinois and Indiana. In 1991 the Supreme Court ruled that the boundary was at the low-water mark on the north shore of the river, without specifying where that low-water mark was. All islands in the river belong to Kentucky.

With Missouri. The Treaty of 1783 establishing the western boundary of the United States defined the center of the Mississippi River channel as the boundary, and this established the Illinois boundary with Missouri. A 27-square-mile tract of Illinois land is on the west side of the Mississippi River near Chester, Illinois, due to an abrupt change in the river's course in 1881. The Supreme Court has ruled that sudden changes in the course of a river do not change boundaries, whereas gradual changes do change boundaries. Each of these two states have land on the opposite side of the river.

With Iowa. The Treaty of 1783 defined the western boundary of the United States as the middle of the Mississippi River channel. Current maps do not show that either of these states have land on the opposite side of the river.

Indiana

The state that eventually became Indiana began as a part of the Northwest Territory. (See map 6.2.) In 1800 Congress created Indiana Territory defined as all of the Northwest Territory west of a line from the mouth of the Kentucky River to Fort Recovery (just west of Greenville, Ohio) and then north to the international border, essentially the current line between Indiana and Ohio extended north to the Canadian border. (See map 6.5.) The area east of the line, what would become Ohio plus the area north of it, retained the name Northwest Territory. (See the Illinois section for more detail on the Northwest Territory.)

The Ordinance of 1787 set up the Northwest Territory and provided that at least three and as many as five states would be created from it. So it was no surprise to Indiana officials when in 1805 Congress created Michigan Territory from Indiana Territory. Michigan Territory consisted of the peninsula that is now Michigan and that portion of the Upper Peninsula that lay east of the Straits of Mackinac. (See map 6.6.) Congress further reduced Indiana Territory in 1809 when it created Illinois Territory. Indiana Territory now consisted of its current area plus part of the Upper Peninsula between the northern extension of its western and eastern boundaries. (See map 6.6.)

Upon achieving statehood in 1816, Indiana's area was pared down to the current boundaries which were specified in the Ordinance of 1787 for the middle state and are very close to what they are currently, the major exception being the boundary with Michigan. (See map 6.7.)

With Michigan. The Northwest Ordinance specified that if more than three states

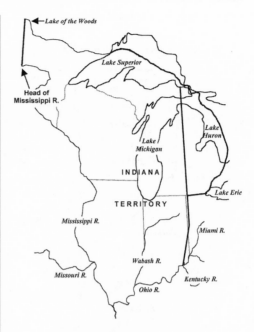

Map 6.5. Indiana Territory

Map 6.6. Territorial Changes as of 1809

were created from the Northwest Territory, the northern boundary of the southern tier of states was to be an east-west line drawn from the southern extremity of Lake Michigan. (See map 6.8.) The original bill to admit Indiana as a state contained language to this effect. The U.S. House of Representatives

Map 6.7. Indiana

framers of the amended bill erred in their geography as the mouth of the St. Joseph River was north of the 42nd parallel. The current boundary still provides Indiana with important commercial contact with Lake Michigan, something it would have been denied had the Ordinance Line been strictly adhered to.

In 1816, when the Indiana statehood bills were being considered, Michigan had no territorial delegate in Congress and, thus, did not protest the boundary change to north of the southern extremity of Lake Michigan. Besides, the area in question was undeveloped, and its future potential could not be seen. Arguing that the southern extremity line was an immovable boundary, Michigan did protest the boundary in 1818, 1831, and 1834, but without effect. Certainly one can argue that fairness could not be attained by denying Indiana access to the lake when Michigan had so much access not only to Lake Michigan but also to Lake Huron and Lake Superior and some access to Lake Erie.

With Ohio. When Congress created Indiana Territory it specified its eastern boundary as from the mouth of the Kentucky River to Fort Recovery then north to the international boundary. When Ohio became a state in 1803, Congress defined its boundary with Indiana as due north from the confluence of the Miami and Ohio rivers. (See map 6.7.) This line was surveyed between 1798 and 1817 by compass. The U.S. Coast and Geodetic Survey examined the line in 1891 to see if it was seriously in error. They found the

amended the bill several times and by the time it passed this chamber the northern boundary was put at the 42nd parallel. However, by the time the bill had gone through the Senate, the boundary had been moved approximately 15 miles south to a point 10 miles north of the southern extremity of Lake Michigan, which is where it is today. Michigan officials did not make any serious objections to the change in Indiana's northern border.

The reason for the 42nd parallel in the House bill was to provide Indiana with a port at the mouth of the St. Joseph River, but the

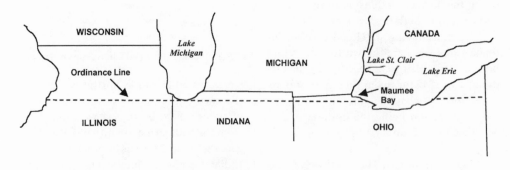

Map 6.8. Ordinance Line

line was slightly irregular as one might expect from a line run by compass. They reported that a true meridian drawn from the mouth of the Miami would cut about 100 square miles from Indiana. The location of the line was already well established and was not moved.

With Kentucky. In the early 1780s Virginia ceded to the federal government all its land north and west of the Ohio River. Virginia stipulated that the boundary was the north shore of the river. When Kentucky became a state in 1792 its north boundary became the low-water mark on the north shore of the river as it existed in that year.

A problem with the boundary occurred when Ohio brought suit in the U.S. Supreme Court to establish the center of the Ohio River as the boundary between it and Virginia and Kentucky. The court ruled in 1820 that the boundary was the low-water mark on the north shore as it existed in 1784 for Virginia and as it existed in 1792 for Kentucky. This ruling was later extended to Illinois and Indiana. Determining the location of the 1792 low-water mark was an impossible task. The Supreme Court ruled in 1985 that the boundary was a series of straight lines connecting geodetic points based on 1927 North American Datum. (The North American Datum is a geographic position based on Meade's Ranch in central Kansas that has specific values of latitude and longitude. This point is used in a system of triangulation for determining specific points on the earth's surface.) All islands in the river belong to Kentucky.

A disagreement arose concerning ownership of Green River Island, an area consisting of about 2,000 acres lying just southeast of Evansville, Indiana. (See map 4.3.) Over time Green River Island was no longer really an island but was separated from Indiana by nothing more than a slough. Indiana wanted it, but Kentucky maintained that the river ran north of the island in 1792, and it therefore belonged to Kentucky. Both states appointed commissioners to settle jurisdiction of the island, but they could not reach an agreement. The issue ended in the U.S. Supreme Court, which ruled in favor of Kentucky in 1890. In its ruling the court noted that Indiana had not prosecuted a claim against Kentucky in the many years since becoming a state, and Kentucky by legislative act had repeatedly asserted its claim over the island.

With Illinois. Indiana's boundary with Illinois originally ran up the Wabash River to Fort Vincent's (later named Vincennes), then due north. This definition would have included some land west of the river in Indiana, creating awkward jurisdiction over an area that could be more easily governed by Illinois. Therefore, officials wisely modified the boundary definition in the 1816 statehood bill as along the middle of the Wabash River, as it was in 1816, from the Ohio River to a point where a due-north line drawn from Vincennes would *last* touch the northwestern shore of that river, then due north to Lake Michigan. The Wabash has not kept its channel; consequently, Indiana has a few parcels of land on the west side of the river. Since the U.S. Supreme Court has ruled that a boundary follows normal meanderings, the assumption is that these parcels were created by cataclysmic events such as flooding.

With Lake Michigan. The boundary in the lake runs from the Indiana-Illinois line toward the center of the lake to the point where it intersects the east-west line drawn 10 miles north of the southern extremity of the lake. (See map 6.16 later in this chapter.)

Michigan

As the first political jurisdiction created north of the southern tip of Lake Michigan, Michigan began life as a territory encompassing the Lower Peninsula on which it now sits and that portion of the Upper Peninsula north and east of the Straits of Mackinac. (See map 6.6.) In 1818 when Illinois became

Map 6.9. Michigan Territory

1800s placed the southern tip of Lake Michigan, from which the northern boundary of Ohio was to be drawn according to the Ordinance of 1787, above the 42nd parallel, and an east-west line drawn from that point would place the boundary well above the bay. However, when Ohio was forming its state constitution and defining its boundaries prior to becoming a state in 1803, officials heard from a backwoodsman familiar with the area that the southern tip of Lake Michigan was well below the 42nd parallel and perhaps far enough below that an east-west line would strike Lake Erie east of Maumee Bay, putting the bay in Michigan and not Ohio.

Armed with this information, those at the constitutional convention inserted a clause that if the southern tip of the lake were found to be at a latitude where an east-west line would strike Lake Erie east of Maumee Bay, the boundary would be on a line drawn from the southern tip of Lake Michigan to the north cape of the bay. This would ensure Ohio jurisdiction over the bay whatever the latitude of the southern tip of Lake Michigan. When Congress admitted Ohio to the Union, it did not formally accept nor reject this provision — simply because not enough was known of the area's geography to take action. Therefore, Ohio became a state with an indefinite northern boundary. All this happened before Congress created Michigan Territory.

The area under contention, 6 to 8 miles wide and known as the "Toledo Strip," was the source of bitter, but bloodless, conflict between Michigan and Ohio for years. (See map 6.12.) It heated up in the 1830s, causing a lot of strident newspaper articles, impassioned oratory, and comical antics by many persons on both sides of the controversy.

At first the dispute over the strip was of little importance, as the inland area was not developed and had few people in it. Its future

a state, Michigan Territory was given all the remainder of the Northwest Territory not encompassed by the states of Ohio, Indiana, and Illinois. Then in 1834 its jurisdiction was increased to include Iowa and the area west to the Missouri and White Earth rivers. (See map 6.9.) (The discussion under Illinois provides more information on the Northwest Territory and the Ordinance of 1787.)

Michigan Territory was reduced by the creation of Wisconsin Territory in 1836. Congress often created very large territories knowing that these territories would be reduced in size and sometimes reshaped to some degree. Throughout its history, Michigan never pretended to want jurisdiction over any land other than the Lower Peninsula and that part of the Upper Peninsula north and east of the Straits of Mackinac. It did, however, insist that its southern boundary on the Lower Peninsula be an east-west line drawn from the southern tip of Lake Michigan. When Congress created Michigan Territory, its southern boundary was defined as this east-west line, called the Ordinance Line; Michigan was content. (See map 6.8.) However, herein lies the seeds of a major controversy with Ohio.

With Ohio. From its infancy as the eastern part of the Northwest Territory, Ohio wanted jurisdiction over Maumee Bay. (See map 6.12.) This didn't seem to be a problem because highly regarded maps of the early

potential was not yet readily apparent. Because of the trading affiliations Detroit had with the small settlement at the bay, Michigan exercised what little governmental jurisdiction the area had. Maumee Bay thus had some early importance as a trading center, but its real value was in the future and greatly increased with the building of the Erie Canal.

Michigan maintained that the east-west line of the Ordinance of 1787 was inviolable and immovable, and it insisted that the boundaries of the ordinance be followed. Ohio argued that it had made its desire for the bay known from the beginning and in fact assumed that Congress had assented to the provision when it accepted Ohio into the Union in 1803. Ohio also argued, after Illinois and Indiana were admitted to the Union, that the boundaries in the ordinance were guidelines and that Congress was not strictly bound by them, and this certainly had proven to be the case as the northern boundaries of neither Indiana nor Illinois conformed to the stipulation of an east-west line drawn from the southern tip of Lake Michigan.

Michigan was at a great disadvantage in this dispute with Ohio because Michigan was merely a territory with one delegate in Congress, while Ohio was a state and thus had two senators and a few representatives. Illinois and especially Indiana had supported Michigan early in the dispute, but Michigan kept hammering at the idea that the Ordinance Line must be adhered to, the result of which would alter the northern boundaries of both Illinois and Indiana. Both states subsequently turned on Michigan and joined with Ohio, thus aligning the Congressional delegations of three states against Michigan. Because of this situation, Michigan wanted admittance to the Union without the boundary being settled, feeling it would get a fairer hearing in the Supreme Court, which adjudicated boundary disputes between states, rather than in the Congress, which settled matters between a state and a territory.

Many governmental officials felt that Michigan's case was strong. Former president John Q. Adams, known to openly declare his feelings about important matters, declared his support for Michigan: "Never, in the course of my life have I known a controversy of which all the right was so clearly on one side, and all the power so overwhelmingly on the other; never a case where the temptation was so intense to take the strongest side, and the duty of taking the weakest so thankless."*

Notwithstanding this golden oratory, a presidential election was looming, and President Andrew Jackson was unwilling to incur the wrath of the three states upon the Democratic Party by siding with Michigan. Congress eventually proposed that as a condition for statehood Michigan must accept 9,000 square miles of additional land in the Upper Peninsula, give up its claim to the 468-square-mile Toledo Strip, and agree to the existing northern Indiana boundary. (See map 6.10.) Michigan was incensed at such an

Map 6.10. Michigan

---

*John T. Faris, The Romance of the Boundaries (New York: Harper and Brothers Publishers, 1926), p. 283.

idea, as it considered the Upper Peninsula land an American Siberia, a worthless barren wasteland inaccessible for most of the year, and wanted nothing to do with it. However, Michigan still wanted the Upper Peninsula east of the Straits of Mackinac.

The government had a surplus of money in 1836 that it was going to distribute to the states; territories would not share in the distribution. Michigan, if it were admitted as a state, would gain $400,000 as its share of the surplus; if it did not enter the Union, it would forever lose this opportunity. This added incentive finally tipped the scales, and Michigan voters agreed to the boundary that Ohio wanted. Michigan entered the Union in 1837 $400,000 richer and with additional land in the Upper Peninsula that held extremely valuable mineral resources but were unknown at the time.

If the Ordinance Line had been strictly enforced, the northeast portion of Ohio would have been a part of Michigan, creating the awkward situation of having some Michigan land completely separated from the main body of the state. (See map 6.8.)

With Indiana. The northern boundary of Indiana also violated the Ordinance Line as specified in the Ordinance of 1787, but Michigan never made more than a minor protest over this incursion into its territory. The area was undeveloped and had no obvious port facilities, so it didn't seem as valuable as Maumee Bay.

Indiana at one time proposed a boundary far enough north to encompass the mouth of the St. Joseph River with the expectation of developing a port there. The bill passed by the House authorizing Indiana to frame a constitution specified a boundary at the 42nd parallel, which would not have included the river's mouth. However, by the time the bill was reported out of Congress, the Senate had lowered the boundary 15 miles and placed it 10 miles north of the southern tip of Lake Michigan where it is today.

It is doubtful that Michigan was even aware of Indiana's incursion into its territory in 1816 when Indiana entered the Union. Later, when Michigan was fervently contesting the boundary with Ohio, it was also demanding the 10-mile strip of land that Indiana owned north of the Ordinance Line. This, of course, incurred the animosity of the Indiana congressional delegation.

Why Congress moved the line where it did is only conjecture, but it seems likely that it was to give Indiana at least some commercial contact with Lake Michigan. Some very important Indiana cities are located along this margin of the lake.

With Wisconsin. When Congress created Wisconsin Territory in 1836 it set the Menominee and Montreal rivers as the boundary with Michigan Territory with the expectation that Michigan would eventually accept the deal giving it the Upper Peninsula. When Congress first created Wisconsin Territory the assumption, based on early maps, was that these two rivers formed a more-or-less continuous waterway, with both having headwaters in Lake of the Desert. Surveyors soon discovered that the waterway was not continuous and recommended some changes in the boundary definition; some were adopted, and some were not. The resulting boundary definition heads up the middle of the main channel of Menominee River to the Brule River and up this river to Lake Brule and along its south shore, then in a straight line to mid-channel between Middle and South islands in the Lake of the Desert, then in a direct line to the headwaters of the Montreal River as marked on a survey by Captain Thomas Cram, and down this river to Lake Superior. (See map 6.15 later in this chapter.) This is the boundary that exists today.

The boundary with Michigan in Lake Michigan is from the Menominee River up Green Bay into the lake then generally along the center of the lake. (See map 6.16.)

With Minnesota. The Michigan-Minnesota line runs from the Montreal River to the northeast extremity of Minnesota. (See map 6.16.)

With Canada. The international boundary with Canada was worked out in several treaties between the United States and Great Britain beginning with the Treaty of 1783, then again in 1812 with the Treaty of Ghent, and the details were finalized by the Webster-Ashburton Treaty in 1842. In general, the boundary is along the centers of lakes Superior, Huron, and Erie and the watercourses connecting them. Islands are assigned to either country as worked out by the treaty negotiators, who generally awarded an island to the country that would have the greater part of an intersected island.

Ohio

The first area carved out of the Northwest Territory was Ohio. (See map 6.2.) The Northwest Territory was first partitioned in 1800 when Congress created Indiana Territory with a boundary roughly where the Ohio-Indiana boundary is today. The area east of the line, later to become Ohio, retained the name Northwest Territory, and its jurisdiction extended north to the international boundary with British America. (See map 6.11.) Three years later Ohio entered the Union with the boundaries it has today, but the placement of its approximately 65-mile northern boundary with Michigan took many years to resolve. (See the Illinois section for more information about the Northwest Territory and the Ordinance of 1787.)

With Michigan. The state constitution of Ohio was purposefully indefinite concerning the land portion of its northern boundary. That boundary, according to the Ordinance of 1787, was on an east-west line drawn from the southern tip of Lake Michigan, called the Ordinance Line. In the early 1800s authoritative maps placed the southern tip of the lake as far north as the 42nd parallel. Ohio was willing to accept that line as a boundary, assuming it was that far north.

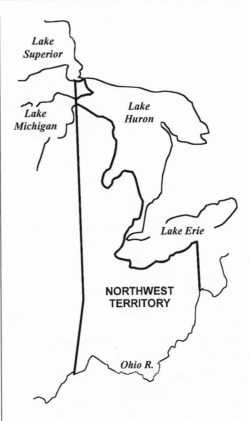

Map 6.11. Ohio 1800–1803
(Northwest Territory)

However, Ohio officials received information from a backwoodsman suggesting that the southern tip of the lake was much further south than originally thought.

If that were the case, officials were concerned that the Ordinance Line would strike Lake Erie east of Maumee Bay, thus putting the bay in Michigan and not Ohio. (See map 6.8.) Ohioans were adamant about retaining the bay because of its excellent harbor. The bay became increasingly important in later years with the building of the Erie Canal. They, therefore, inserted a proviso in their state constitution that if a true east-west running of the Ordinance Line didn't include the bay in Ohio then their northern boundary should be a line drawn from the southern tip of Lake Michigan to the northern cape of Maumee Bay, thereby ensuring that the bay would be in Ohio regardless of the location of the tip of Lake Michigan.

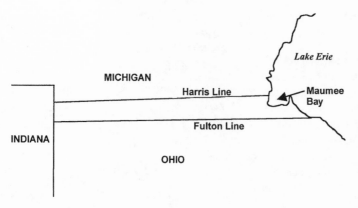

Map 6.12. Toledo Strip

Congress accepted the Ohio constitution but took no formal action on the boundary proviso. Ohioans naturally assumed that the proviso had been accepted and that Maumee Bay was in Ohio. Congress created Michigan Territory in 1805 and specified its southern boundary as the Ordinance Line. (See map 6.8.) The stage was set for a dispute over an area of 468 square miles called the Toledo Strip. (See map 6.12.) The settlers at Maumee Bay were separated by many miles of wilderness from the settled portion of Ohio and were closely tied commercially with the settlement at Detroit about 45 miles away to the north-northeast. As a consequence, Michigan provided the area with what little government it possessed.

Congress authorized a survey of the Ordinance Line in 1812, but the United States and Britain were at war, so the survey was not commenced until 1817 when William Harris undertook the task. It was the intent of Congress that the line be surveyed in accordance with Ohio's enabling act (not its constitution), which defined Ohio's northern boundary as an east-west line drawn from the southern tip of Lake Michigan. Instead, Harris surveyed a line from the southern tip of Lake Michigan to the northern cape of Maumee Bay as per the proviso in the state constitution, thus ignoring the explicit instructions from Congress. (See map 6.12.) Whether he did this due to malice or favoritism depends on whether one reads

Michigan or Ohio histories of the dispute. The Ohio legislature quickly accepted the Harris Line as official. Michigan, just as quickly, memorialized Congress complaining that the line had not been run properly and asked for another survey.

The secretary of the federal treasury ordered another survey in the summer of 1818. Surveyor John Fulton undertook this project and ran an east-west line from the southern tip of Lake Michigan to Lake Erie. (See map 6.12.) The two lines were approximately 5 miles apart at the Indiana border and 8 miles apart where they reached Lake Erie. Both Ohio and Michigan sent militia to the area, and a lot of posturing, chest beating, and fiery oratory ensued, but no blood was shed and probably none intended.

Michigan became militant in insisting on the Ordinance Line as the northern boundary for all the southern tier states—Illinois, Indiana, as well as Ohio—and thus incurred the animosity of all those states in the boundary dispute with Ohio. The northern boundaries of Indiana and Illinois had already been settled, and both of them were north of the Ordinance Line. As a result, Michigan was at a great disadvantage in pressing the issue in Congress, as it had only one territorial delegate while the three states had twenty-nine representatives and six senators.

Another complication was the upcoming 1837 presidential election. President Andrew Jackson was promoting his protégé Martin Van Buren to succeed him and did not want to anger the thirty-five electoral votes in the three states. Another piece of the puzzle was that Michigan wanted to become a state. Jackson dispatched commissioners to attempt settlement of the dispute; they failed. Congress finally proposed a plan that

Michigan would be admitted to the Union if it would accept the Harris Line as its border with Ohio and accept 9,000 square miles of additional land in the Upper Peninsula in exchange for the loss of the Toledo Strip. (See map 6.10.)

Michigan at first rejected this idea as it had no desire for any more land in the Upper Peninsula. (Michigan traditionally claimed the Upper Peninsula north and east of the Straits of Mackinac.) However, it did strongly covet the land to the Ordinance Line. At this time, 1836, the federal government had a huge budget surplus it was going to distribute to the states—territories were not included in the distribution. Michigan's portion, if it became a state, amounted to about $400,000. This added incentive was enough to tip the scales of Michigan voters in favor of accepting the Harris Line and gaining land in the Upper Peninsula that, unknown at the time, was rich in valuable minerals.

In fairness to Ohio, the intent of Congress was most likely to give Maumee Bay to Ohio. The best maps of the early 1800s placed the southern tip of Lake Michigan north of the bay, and as Congress discussed the boundary, this was what they were looking at and intending. Also, the northern boundaries of both Illinois and Indiana had been settled prior to the Ohio-Michigan dispute without regard to a strict interpretation of the Ordinance Line. For perspective, realize that in the Ohio-Michigan conflict Congress was interpreting the Northwest Ordinance, and part of this interpretation was the meaning of specific phrases. For example, did the mention that two states could be formed north of the Ordinance Line mean this line should be the boundary or merely that the states should be north of it?

With Canada. The boundary with Canada is the center of Lake Erie in accordance with treaties of 1783, 1812, and 1842.

With Pennsylvania. Pennsylvania's western boundary was established as 5 de-

Map 6.13. Ohio

grees of longitude from the Delaware River as per its 1681 charter to William Penn from England's King Charles II. This boundary was fixed before Ohio became a state and thus part of its defined boundary. Virginia, when it still claimed the Northwest Territory, had argued for the western boundary of Pennsylvania to follow the contours of the Delaware River, but this would have created a surveyor's nightmare, and common sense prevailed when a straight north-south line was adopted.

With West Virginia and Kentucky. These two state's boundaries with Ohio were established when they were part of Virginia at the time that state ceded its land northwest of the Ohio River to the federal government in 1784. When Virginia ceded this area to the federal government the assumption was that the low-water mark of the north bank of the river was the boundary. Ohio later sued in the U.S. Supreme Court asking that the middle of the river be declared the boundary. The court ruled in 1820 that the boundary was the low-water line on the north shore of the river as it was in 1784. Since the river's course in 1784 was impossible to determine, the court ruled in 1985 that the boundary was the low-water mark on the north shore without specifying where that mark was.

With Indiana. When Indiana Territory was split off in 1800, the boundary was defined as from the confluence of the Kentucky and Ohio rivers, then to Fort Recovery, near present-day Greenville, Ohio, then due north to the international boundary. Ohio changed this in its constitution to be a due-north line from the mouth of the Miami River where it enters the Ohio River. This boundary is the first principal meridian of the General Land Office.

Wisconsin

In the creation of territories, it was common for large tracts of land to be organized as a territory, then for the area to be repeatedly broken down and reshaped into smaller territories, and eventually into states. This was certainly the case for the Northwest Territory and Wisconsin. This area was initially a part of the Northwest Territory, then Indiana Territory, and then Illinois Territory. When Illinois entered the Union in 1818, Wisconsin became attached to Michigan Territory, which at that time extended west to the Mississippi River, but in 1834 Congress extended its western boundary to the Missouri and White Earth rivers and south to include Iowa.

In anticipation of Michigan's 1837 entry into the Union, Congress created Wisconsin Territory in 1836 with its western boundary still the Missouri and White Earth rivers and south to include Iowa. (See map 6.14.) In 1838 the territory's western boundary was reduced to the Mississippi River and north to Lake of the Woods, the original western boundary of the Northwest Territory. Congress created Iowa Territory at the same time. (See map 7.2.) (For additional detail and discussion concerning the Ordinance of 1787 and the Northwest Territory, see the discussion in the Illinois section.)

Since Wisconsin was the fifth entity created from the Northwest Territory, it had every expectation of getting all the Northwest Territory's remaining land. This was not to be the case. Wisconsinites felt they lost land they reasonably expected to receive to Minnesota in the west, to Michigan in the northeast, and to Illinois in the south. Their pique at losing land to these latter two states is difficult to understand because Illinois was a state long before Wisconsin became a territory, and Michigan was well on the road to statehood when Congress created Wisconsin Territory. These facts did not prevent Wisconsin from contesting the boundaries with both these areas.

With Illinois. When Illinois submitted its constitution to Congress for admittance to the Union in 1817 it specified the southern tip of Lake Michigan as its northern boundary as per the Ordinance of 1787. The Illinois delegate, Nathaniel Pope, soon amended the document, apparently without consulting officials in Illinois, to move the northern boundary to the parallel of 42 degrees 30

Map 6.14. Wisconsin Territory

minutes, 61 miles to the north of the southern extremity of Lake Michigan. His reasons for doing this are based on his belief that Illinois needed a commercial connection to the Great Lakes and thus the northern states. His argument was that an Illinois without a harbor on the lake was commercially aligned with southern states because of the Ohio and Mississippi rivers and that in the event of a sectional conflict, being talked about even in the early 1800s, Illinois would naturally align itself with the southern states.

This argument prevailed in Congress, which admitted Illinois with the amended northern boundary. It also seemed a reasonable idea. After all, why should a jurisdiction to the north have untold miles of lake frontage while a budding state had none? The disputed area, slightly smaller than Massachusetts, consists of 8,500 square miles of rich agricultural, mining, and industrial land.

Wisconsin territorial officials soon developed reasons why it wasn't a plausible idea to give this land to Illinois as it pointed to the language of the ordinance that clearly stated the northern boundary of the southern tier of states was to be an east-west line drawn from the southern tip of Lake Michigan, and people living in the disputed area preferred to be in Wisconsin. It was obvious to Wisconsin officials that the framers of the ordinance did not intend Illinois to have lake frontage. The protestations of Badger State officials obviously did not prevail, although they continued until 1847 when action toward recovering this area finally died.

With Iowa. The Wisconsin boundary with Iowa, like all Mississippi River boundaries, was established in the Treaty of 1783 when the western boundary of the United

Map 6.15. Wisconsin

States was set at the middle of the main channel of the river. Iowa was a part of both Michigan and Wisconsin territories before Congress created the Iowa Territory in 1838. Both Wisconsin and Michigan territories knew that Iowa was attached to them strictly for temporary governance, and so Wisconsin raised no objections when it was detached.

With Minnesota. The Wisconsin boundary with Minnesota was difficult to establish. Since Wisconsin was the fifth political entity created from the Northwest Territory, it expected that it would get the remainder of the territory, i.e., a western boundary of the Mississippi River and north to Lake of the Woods, since the Ordinance of 1787 specified a maximum of five states. Congress did not constrain itself by a strict interpretation of the ordinance regarding the northern boundary of three of the states, and it was not to be bound strictly in the number of states either. Although Wisconsin Territory originally extended all the way to the Missouri and White Earth rivers, Wisconsin knew this was a temporary situation and never claimed any land beyond the Mississippi River.

Two major settlement areas developed in what is now Wisconsin — the southeastern area near Lake Michigan, and along the Mississippi and St. Croix river valleys. (See map 6.15.) The two areas had no commercial nor social connections, and the people in the St. Croix Valley wanted nothing to do with the people to the southeast but rather to cast their fortunes with a new territory to be created. Another reason they didn't want to be a part of Wisconsin was political: Some of the St. Croix leaders figured that they would likely become important figures in a new territory but would hold no sway in Wisconsin.

Notwithstanding the feelings of the citizens of the St. Croix Valley, Wisconsin's del-egate to Congress, Morgan L. Martin, in 1846 introduced a bill in Congress to enable his constituents to form a state government and constitution. The bill claimed boundaries to the Mississippi River and north to the international boundary, thus including the St. Croix area.

The bill went to the House Committee on Territories, which amended the bill and altered its boundaries by greatly reducing Wisconsin's area in the northwest. The enabling act for Wisconsin statehood passed by Congress specified a northwest boundary through the center of Lake Superior, up the main channel of the St. Louis River to the first rapids above an Indian village according to Nicollet's Map, then due south to the St. Croix River and down the main channel of that river to the Mississippi River. (See map 6.15.)

Through the maneuvering of St. Croixan William Holcombe, the Wisconsin constitutional convention made a proposal that further reduced the boundaries in the northwest by taking the due-south line from the St. Louis River and extending it all the way to the Mississippi River. Holcombe was working diligently trying to separate the St. Croix area from Wisconsin. The voters rejected the constitution with these boundaries.

A second constitutional convention adopted a preference, in lieu of the boundaries in the enabling act, for a northwest boundary running from the rapids in the St. Louis River to the confluence of the Rum and Mississippi rivers. The Rum enters the Mississippi 20 to 25 miles above Minneapolis–St. Paul. This proposal would have put the entire St. Croix Valley in Wisconsin and also the city of St. Paul. This, of course, stirred the animosities of the St. Croixans.

Congress ultimately rejected both the Rum River preference and the St. Croix proposal to run the due-south line to the Mississippi

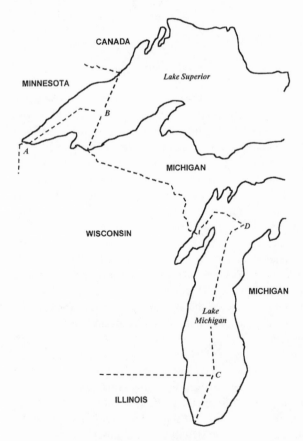

Map 6.16. Lake Boundaries

rather than the St. Croix River. Congress admitted Wisconsin into the Union with the boundaries as listed in the enabling act, and these are the current boundaries.

The story concerning this northwest boundary is not yet complete, however. The government employed George R. Stuntz in 1852 to run and mark the line from the St. Louis to the St. Croix rivers. When he conducted his survey the water in Lake Superior was higher than normal, so the first rapids of the river, actually a place where the river meets the lake in a narrow bay, were not visible. Stuntz was assured by a native Chippewa chief that this was where the first rapids were. Since he could see no rapids, Stuntz traveled upstream about a half mile to a place he identified as rapids, and here he began his survey south. Wisconsin thereby gained an area about ½ mile wide and 42 miles long that was not intended in the enabling act.

The boundary with Minnesota in Lake Superior is along the middle of the lake from points *A* to *B* as seen on map 6.16.

With Michigan. Wisconsin was very disappointed in not having the Upper Peninsula west of the Straits of Mackinac. (See map 6.10.) This 9,000-square-mile area was given to Michigan to compensate for its loss of the Toledo Strip in its dispute with Ohio. The deal was made even more bizarre by the fact that Michigan did not want the area and considered it a wasteland. On the other hand, Wisconsin did want the area, after all it was attached to Wisconsin and separated from peninsular Michigan by the Straits of Mackinac. Nonetheless, national politics dictated that Michigan end up with the Upper Peninsula area. When Congress worked out the plan to give the area to Michigan, current maps of the time indicated a nearly continuous waterway separating the area from Wisconsin, and Congress specified a boundary consisting of the middle of the Montreal and Menominee rivers and Lake of the Desert that was presumed to be the headwater of both of them. Michigan entered the Union in 1837 with this northwest boundary. (See map 6.15.)

Captain Thomas Jefferson Cram accepted the surveying job of marking this boundary in 1840. He soon discovered that no continuous waterway existed and that it would be impossible to precisely follow the official boundary description. He offered several suggestions for accurately describing the boundary. Some of his suggestions were accepted. The resulting boundary, as it exists today, is through Lake Michigan and Green Bay, ascending the main channel of the Menominee River to the Brule River, along the southern shore of Lake Brule, then on a direct line to the center of the channel between Middle and South Islands in the Lake of the Desert; then a straight line to the headwaters of the Montreal River and down the main channel of this river to the middle of Lake Superior.

The boundary with Michigan in Lake Michigan is along the center of the lake. It begins as a continuation of the Wisconsin-Illinois boundary to the center of the lake, point *C* on map 6.16. Then additional points were plotted running to point *D*. It then turns west and continues up the approximate center of Green Bay to the northern boundary of Wisconsin.

7

North Central Region

Map 7.1

Map is not to scale; boundaries are roughly drawn.

Iowa

The Hawkeye State came under control of the United States with the Louisiana Purchase. When political organization came to the area that eventually became Iowa, it was included in the territories of Louisiana, Missouri, Michigan, and Wisconsin before acquiring its own status as a territory in 1838. Iowa Territory included the area from Missouri north to the international border and from the Mississippi River to the Missouri River in the heartland of the Dakotas. (See map 7.2.)

Talk concerning statehood began as early as 1839. Proposed state boundaries at that time would have placed the northern boundary as far north as the Minnesota River in what became southern Minnesota, with the western boundary the Missouri River, the eastern boundary the Mississippi River, and the southern boundary the still-disputed boundary with the state of Missouri. (See map 7.3.) The Iowa territorial legislative assembly, however, was occupied with trying to organize a territory and was unwilling to seriously consider statehood and the proposed boundaries their state might have. More compelling was the fact that most Iowans at the time did not want the financial burden of statehood. By 1844, however, as Congress proposed distributing a budget surplus to the states the financial factor was overcome. Territories would not participate in the upcoming revenue sharing, so territories considering statehood had a considerable incentive to enter the Union. With this new incentive in hand, the Iowa legislative assembly accepted the 1839 boundary proposal.

Congress considered this boundary proposal too large. An Ohio congressman suggested different boundaries that were later accepted by Congress. His proposal would have placed the western boundary along the meridian of 94 degrees 30 minutes (about 25 miles west of Des Moines), north to the 45th parallel (about where Minneapolis–St. Paul is located), and then east to

Map 7.2. Iowa Territory

the Mississippi River. (See map 7.3.) The southern boundary was the state of Missouri. The people of Iowa, however, refused to accept these boundaries and voted them down. Illinois Congressman Stephen Douglas offered a set of compromise boundaries (discussed in the next subsection) that Iowans finally accepted. Congress admitted Iowa to the Union in 1846 as the twenty-ninth state with the boundaries it has today.

With Minnesota. The 1839 proposed boundaries would have started the northern

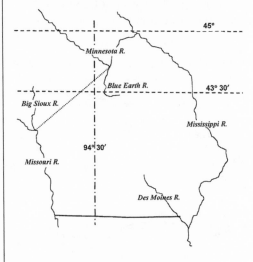

Map 7.3. Iowa Boundary Proposals

boundary of Iowa at the confluence of the Missouri and Big Sioux rivers and run from there to the Minnesota River near Mankato, Minnesota, then down that river to the Mississippi, then down that river all the way to the northern Missouri border. (See map 7.3.) This proposal would have placed a sizeable chunk of Minnesota in Iowa. Iowans claimed that this created "natural" boundaries for their state.

Congress rejected the 1839 proposed boundaries, and Iowans rejected the proposal by the Ohio congressman mentioned previously. Then Stephen Douglas, who was active in state and territorial formation, proposed that Iowa be bounded in the west by the Missouri River and in the north by the parallel of 43 degrees 30 minutes. The Iowa convention soon adopted these boundaries. A good part of the argument favoring the boundaries proposed by Douglas was that Iowans saw that the area between 94° 30' and the Missouri River was growing much more rapidly than the area in the north, and so gaining the western land was more important than keeping land to the north. Congress passed an act in 1846 adopting the boundaries proposed by Douglas.

With Wisconsin and Illinois. The Iowa boundary with Wisconsin and Illinois was defined in the Treaty of 1783 that established the western boundary of the United States and by the fact that these states entered the Union before Iowa with their western boundaries defined as the main channel of the Mississippi River.

With Missouri. Missouri became a state in 1821 with a defined, but unclear, northern boundary. The state's enabling act specified the northern boundary as an east-west line passing through the rapids of the Des Moines River, also called the "Indian Boundary Line." A dispute arose between Missouri and Iowa Territory because they differed over the definition of "the rapids of the river Des Moines." Missouri maintained the reference was to rapids in that river, which seems obvious from the quoted phrase. Iowa, on the other hand, claimed the reference was to the Des Moines Rapids in the Mississippi River. This part of the argument somewhat favored Iowa because rivermen in the area had long referred to rapids in the Mississippi as the Des Moines Rapids.

Since Missouri did not agree with Iowa's interpretation of "rapids of the river Des Moines," they ordered a line run in 1836 by Joseph C. Brown. (See line *4* on Map 7.4.) Brown found what he considered rapids in the Des Moines River and ran his line from there. Another aspect of the argument between Iowa and Missouri was the reference to the Indian Boundary Line. This, too, favored Iowa. The federal government had ordered a line run in 1816 by John C. Sullivan to delineate an Osage land cession (line *1*, map 7.4). The difference in these two surveys is a sizeable chunk of land about 10 miles wide by 200 miles long.

This long-standing boundary dispute ended in the U.S. Supreme Court in 1846. The court ruled three years later that the 1816 Sullivan Line was the true boundary and ordered it resurveyed and remarked. This work was done and accepted in 1851. The Sullivan Line is not a true east-west line as it runs 2 degrees north of east due to er-

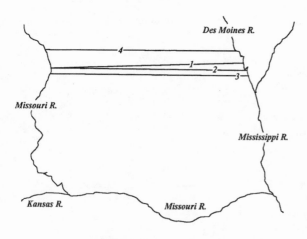

Map 7.4. Iowa-Missouri Boundary

rors in surveying. Line *2* on map 7.4 shows where a correct east-west line should have been placed; line *3* is a line advocated by Iowa but never allowed. The settlement of the border at the Sullivan Line was especially important to Iowans who lived in the disputed area as they did not want to become part of Missouri, a slave state.

Notwithstanding earlier border problems, the two states amicably agreed to a slight alteration of their Des Moines River boundary in 1939 to where the channel of the river was in that year.

With Nebraska. The western Iowa boundary was in essence a compromise. The territorial boundary was in the middle of the Dakotas while one of the early proposals for a state boundary was the longitude of 94 degrees 30 minutes west of Greenwich. Iowans liked the earlier boundary but rejected the 94° 30' proposal. Stephen Douglas struck a happy compromise when he suggested the Missouri and Big Sioux rivers as the western boundary. (See map 7.5.) By adopting this proposal Iowans established their boundary with Nebraska as the Missouri River. Hawkeye State officials liked this proposal because they realized the land west of 94° 30' was gaining population faster than area they originally wanted north of their final northern boundary of 43° 30'.

Both Franklin K. Van Zandt and Daniel H. Ehrlich say that in 1943 Iowa and Nebraska agreed to alter their common boundary to coincide with the main channel of the Missouri River as it was at that time and that Congress approved this change that same year. The river has apparently changed its course since then because DeLorme maps from both states (dated 1996 and 1998) show that several pieces of Iowa are on the west side of the river and several pieces of Nebraska are on the east side. Ehrlich's 1976 article has a map that shows several exclaves

Map 7.5. Iowa

and a table stating that Iowa has an estimated 3,760 acres on the west side of the river and Nebraska has nearly 20,000 acres on the east side of the river.

With South Dakota. A proposal for the western boundary of Iowa in 1839 would have had it running from the confluence of the Big Sioux and Missouri rivers directly to near where Mankato, Minnesota, is today. (See the dotted line on map 7.3.) A later proposal would have put Iowa's western boundary at the longitude of 94 degrees 30 minutes, about 25 miles west of Des Moines. Neither of these proposals was accepted by Iowans. Stephen Douglas, proposed a compromise solution for Iowa's western boundary as the Missouri and Big Sioux rivers to the parallel of 43 degrees 30 minutes and then west to the Mississippi River. Iowans, seeing that population was growing more rapidly in the west than in the north, accepted this boundary, and Iowa was eventually admitted to the Union with this boundary, thus creating the peculiar jog in South Dakota's eastern boundary where it abuts the northwest corner of Iowa.

Minnesota

Most of Minnesota came very close to not being a part of the United States. During the latter part of the War for American Independence, negotiators from Great Britain and the United States discussed several proposals to separate the two countries. One suggestion was to draw the boundary along the 45th parallel from the Connecticut River to the Mississippi River. The proposal would have placed southern Ontario in the United States and large chunks of Michigan and Wisconsin and most of Minnesota under British rule. This idea failed mostly because it would have created an unnatural boundary with areas difficult to govern because of water barriers and geography. U.S. negotiators had proposed a water route all the way from the St. Lawrence River to Lake of the Woods, and this was the boundary principle adopted, although the details were not easily arrived at. The details as they relate to Minnesota are discussed under the Canada subhead.

Minnesota was formed partly from the Northwest Territory (the Northwest Territory extended westward to the Mississippi River and north to Lake of the Woods), partly from the Louisiana Purchase, and partly from an agreement with Great Britain in 1818 that set the international boundary at the 49th parallel. While the boundaries of the Louisiana Purchase were vague, they generally included the drainage basin of the Mississippi

River west of that river. The drainage basin of the Red River of the North, in northwestern Minnesota and northeastern Dakota, drains to Hudson Bay in Canada so was not part of the Louisiana Purchase. (See map 1.1.)

The state is a bit of an anomaly because a maximum of five states were to be created from the Northwest Territory according to the Ordinance of 1787. Congress, however, played loose with the interpretation of the ordinance as it related to several states, which gave an element of common sense, equity, and justice to boundary drawing. For example, if Wisconsin, the fifth state created from the Northwest Territory, had gotten all the remainder of the territory, it would have been exceptionally large, as it would have included that part of Minnesota east of the Mississippi River, and Indiana and Illinois would have been denied frontage on Lake Michigan if the ordinance had been followed exactly. (A more detailed discussion of the Northwest Territory and Ordinance of 1787 is in the Illinois section of chapter 6.)

Before gaining territorial status from the leftovers of Iowa Territory in 1849, Minnesota had been part of the territories of Louisiana, Indiana, Illinois, Michigan, and Wisconsin. The extent of Minnesota Territory was from Iowa to the international border and from Wisconsin to the Missouri and White Earth rivers. (See map 7.6.)

In 1856, as Minnesotans were talking about statehood, much discussion in the territory centered on whether to divide it on an east-west or north-south line. The east-west line would have been placed near the 45th or 46th parallel and run from Wisconsin to the Missouri River in what is now central South Dakota (approximately the southern one-third of present-day Minnesota). (See map 7.6.) Politics played an important part in the resolution of this question and is taken up in the following discussion of both Dakotas.

Officials favoring the north-

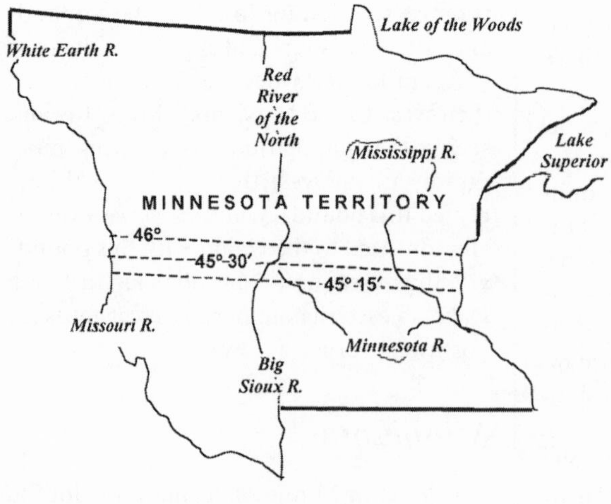

Map 7.6. Minnesota Territory

south boundary won the day as the Minnesota state enabling act passed by Congress in 1857 defined the state boundaries as Iowa in the south, Wisconsin in the east, Canada in the north, and in the west by a line from the international boundary south through the main channel of the Red River of the North and Bois de Sioux rivers, then through Lakes Traverse and Big Stone, and from the foot of Big Stone Lake by a line due south to the Iowa border. (See map 7.8.)

With Canada. The international border with our northern neighbor has an interesting history and contains one of the most unusual aspects of the entire northern border — a northern projection into Lake of the Woods called the Northwest Angle, an area of about 124 square miles consisting mostly of water and several small islands. This is the most northern part of the 48 conterminous states. A 1783 treaty between Great Britain and the United States defined the Minnesota-British boundary as from Lake Superior through the middle of Long Lake and then along the waterway between it to the most *northwestern* part of Lake of the Woods. Geographic knowledge of the area was very scant at the time; Lake of the Woods was thought to be oval with a narrow northwest end rather than its actual irregular shape. The treaty also said the boundary was to go from this point on the lake due west to

the Mississippi River, an impossibility since the river does not extend that far north. The two countries realized in 1794 that the river probably didn't go that far north and agreed to settle the matter amicably by drawing the boundary from the most northwest point of Lake of the Woods south to the head of the Mississippi River.

Recognizing these problems, and others notwithstanding, the border had been defined, and it became the burden for future diplomats and surveyors to make the best use of the information they had. The Treaty of Ghent in 1814 provided for surveying the international boundary. The commissioners completed survey work as far as Lake Superior, but the commission was disbanded in 1827 before completing the line to Lake of the Woods.

This commission, however, did discuss the boundary. As specified in the 1783 treaty, the boundary was to leave Lake Superior and enter a lake called Long Lake. The first problem was to determine which body of water was that lake. The British offered the St. Louis River, entering at the extreme western end of Lake Superior (Duluth) then ascending the Vermillion River to the Grand Portage as meeting the definition. The United States countered that the Kaministikwia River, well east of the modern boundary, met the definition. After years of wrangling the two sides settled on the Pigeon

Map 7.7. Minnesota-Canada Boundary

River as meeting the criteria for the Long Lake. (See map 7.7.) Then surveyors had to establish the line from there to Lake of the Woods. The British wanted a line that traversed an old trade route, slightly to the south of the water route and one with many portages, while the U.S. team insisted on a boundary that was a true water route and thus better met the treaty criteria. The United States won this argument.

Once the line reached Lake of the Woods, the task centered on determining the most northwest part of the lake. A British surveyor located four places as possibly being the most northwest point. British officials were not satisfied with the surveyor's findings and hired a German astronomer to locate the northwest point. His determination was that an inlet in the northwest part of the lake, one of the points previously identified by the British surveyor, was the most northwest point. This was finally accepted by both sides and established the point from which a line could later be drawn to the 49th parallel.

The remainder of the northern boundary hinged originally on an understanding of the northern boundary of the Louisiana Purchase. The northern extent of the Louisiana Purchase was very vague; the French insisted they had not precisely defined the boundary. President Thomas Jefferson found this difficult to believe and found in the 1713 Treaty of Utrecht language he believed indicated the 49th parallel as the northern boundary between French Louisiana and British North America. Great Britain did not contest this understanding, and the two countries tacitly agreed in 1818 to this parallel as the boundary as far west as the crest of the Rocky Mountains.

The two countries dissolved previous boundary commissions, and their findings were put in limbo until the 1842 Webster-Ashburton Treaty. This treaty finally settled the boundary from the Atlantic Ocean to the Rocky Mountains. Lord Ashburton (Alexander Baring), who was more interested in effecting a settlement of the border than any-thing else, took very little interest in preserving for Britain land north of Minnesota as he felt it was a wasteland of rock and water. Thus, he generously agreed to U.S. interpretations of the 1783 treaty and most of the determinations of the commission established by the 1814 treaty. Daniel Webster and other American negotiators were quite determined to get the line as far north as possible and considered the area valuable as a mineral region. Their perseverance paid off as the future Mesabi Iron Range became U.S. property.

With Lake Superior. The boundary in the lake runs north of Isle Royale as per the 1783 treaty and affirmed by the Webster-Ashburton Treaty. The lake boundaries with Wisconsin and Michigan are along the center of the lake. (See map 6.16.)

With Wisconsin. Wisconsin was disappointed in not getting all of the remaining Northwest Territory land that extended to the Mississippi River. Congress felt doing so would create an unmanageably large state. However, one other proposal would have reduced Wisconsin's area even more as it would have taken the remainder of the Northwest Territory after Congress created the first four states and divided it to create two nearly equally sized states. This idea failed because it would have denied one of the states access to Lake Superior.

Working against Wisconsin's desire to have the Mississippi River as its western boundary was that settlers along the St. Croix River wanted to be separate from Wisconsin. (See map 7.8.) They were lumberjacks, fur traders, and squatters who saw themselves as affiliated with people along the upper Mississippi River and different from people in far away southeast Wisconsin. They lobbied diligently by proposing a boundary that ran from the St. Louis River southeasterly to the easternmost part of Lake St. Croix then due south to the Mississippi River. This would have placed all of the St. Croix Valley within a new territory they hoped would be created by Congress. Politics was also a factor as the leading citizens in the St. Croix Valley expected to receive government positions if a new territory were created.

Another boundary proposal was to include all of the St. Croix Valley in Wisconsin by running the border from where the St. Louis River enters Lake Superior (Duluth) southwesterly to about 15 miles above Minneapolis–St. Paul and then down the Mississippi River.

Neither of these proposals prevailed. When Congress passed an enabling act for Wisconsin to become a state, it specified its boundaries as from the first rapids in the St. Louis River due south to the St. Croix River and then down this river and the Mississippi River. After much discussion and counter proposals, this was the boundary adopted to separate Wisconsin from Minnesota Territory in 1848 when Wisconsin entered the Union. The wishes of the settlers in the St. Croix Valley were thus thwarted as the area was divided.

With the boundary definition determined, the task remained for it to be surveyed. An unusually high water level in Lake Superior in 1852, when the survey was made, caused Minnesota to lose a small slice of land. The boundary was to run due south from the first rapids of the St. Louis River, but the high water conditions obliterated the first rapids, so the surveyor proceeded upriver about a half mile to what he determined as rapids and began his line there. Minnesota thus lost a thin slice of land to Wisconsin.

With Iowa. An 1839 boundary proposal would have created a roof-like northern boundary for Iowa. The proposal was for this boundary to begin at the confluence of the Missouri and Big Sioux rivers and run from there to the Minnesota River near Mankato, Minnesota, then down that river

Map 7.8. Minnesota

to the Mississippi, then down that river all the way to the northern Missouri border. This proposal would have placed a sizeable chunk of Minnesota in Iowa. Iowans claimed that this created "natural" boundaries for Iowa. (See map 7.3.) This didn't happen. The northern boundary finally adopted by the Iowa legislature, suggested by Stephen A. Douglas, placed this line at the parallel of 43 degrees 30 minutes.

With North Dakota and South Dakota. An early proposal, favored by citizens living in southern Minnesota Territory, which then encompassed the Dakotas, was to split the territory along an east-west line somewhere near the 45th or 46th parallel. (See map 7.6.) Minnesota's representative in Washington, Henry M. Rice, did not like this idea, and he worked hard, and effectively, for a north-south boundary line. His 1856 proposal was mostly a water boundary along the Red River (later called Red River of the North to distinguish it from the Red River separating Oklahoma and Texas) and the Bois de Sioux River to Lake Traverse, then along the Big Sioux River to the Missouri River. (See map 7.8.)

In early 1857 the chairman of the Committee on Territories, to which Rice's bill had been referred, substituted a boundary line extending from Lake Traverse to Big Stone Lake and then due south from the southern tip of that lake to the northern Iowa boundary. This change moved South Dakota's boundary slightly to the east, thus cutting off a slice of real estate from Minnesota. The boundary in all rivers is the main channel, and in lakes it is the center.

Rice had political motives in pushing for the north-south boundary as he figured such a state would be Democratic. Since he was a Democrat, he had aspirations to become one of the U.S. senators from Minnesota.

A change in the channel of the Red River of the North near Fargo, North Dakota, caused about 20 acres of Minnesota land to be placed on the North Dakota side of the river. Minnesota and North Dakota agreed to transfer of this land to North Dakota; Congress consented in 1961.

Nebraska

The area of the United States increased greatly with the acquisition of the Louisiana Purchase in 1803; Nebraska was included in this area. (See map 1.1.) Some early explorers, however, considered the land less than a prize. Explorers Zebulon M. Pike and Stephen H. Long considered the area west of the Missouri River a desert and vast wasteland unfit for farming.

Nonetheless, the U.S. government went systematically about organizing the enormous area. Nebraska was part of the territories of Louisiana and Missouri and was an unorganized area called Indian Territory before Congress created the Territory of Nebraska in 1854. The territory extended from the Missouri and White Earth rivers in the east to the crest of the Rocky Mountains in the west and from the 40th parallel to the 49th parallel. (See map 7.9.) Congress reduced the size of the territory in 1861 when it created Colorado Territory mainly for miners, and then two days later, largely in anticipation of ultimate statehood for Nebraska, it created Dakota Territory. The organization of Idaho Territory in 1863 further reduced the size of Nebraska Territory. (Compare maps 7.9 and 10.6.)

Agitation for statehood began as early as 1858 because Nebraskans were eager to join the Union. It became the thirty-seventh state in 1867. However, before that, some Cornhuskers flirted with the idea of joining with Kansas.

With Kansas. Congress granted statehood to Kansas in 1861 with its north border at the 40th parallel, which was the boundary between Kansas and Nebraska territories. Nebraskans living between the 40th parallel and the Platte River sent representatives to the Kansas constitutional convention with the possibility of getting that area included in Kansas. (See map 7.10.) The Platte River was wide enough that crossing was difficult and thus created a natural barrier to populations on either side. Because of this it also created a natural boundary between whites and Native Americans. Many Nebraskans south of the Platte

Map 7.9. Nebraska Territory

were willing to join with Kansas and abandon the area north of the river to Native Americans. Nebraskans were also concerned about how long it might take for them to be admitted as a state. Antislave Kansans initially liked the idea of Nebraskans joining with them because they thought they might need the southern Nebraskans to gain control of the state. When that proved not to be the case the Kansans quickly cooled

Map 7.10. Nebraska

to the idea. This effort to join with Kansas was also unsuccessful because Kansans were mostly Republicans while Nebraskans were mostly Democrats, and Kansas officials feared losing political control if they included their neighbors to the north. The end result was that the northern boundary of Kansas was left at the 40th parallel where Congress had put it when creating the Nebraska and Kansas territories in 1854.

The reasons Congress chose the 40th parallel as the boundary between Kansas and Nebraska are not known. One source indicated it was chosen to avoid dividing some Indian land, but this has not been confirmed. Iowa officials may have applied some pressure to put the boundary at that parallel because they felt that such a division would likely place a seat of government close to their western border and thus open a market for Iowa products. Missouri officials also favored a division at the 40th parallel. Some speculation exists that placing the boundary at the 40th parallel, and no further north, would enhance the possibility of Kansas becoming a slave state.

With Colorado. Kansas entered the Union in 1861, and Congress created Colorado Territory a month later. Kansans were willing, even eager, to get rid of the western part of their territory with a few different boundary possibilities being considered. The one finally chosen was selected to ensure that miners were not part of farmer-dominated

Kansas, discussed in detail in the Kansas section of Chapter 8.

Since Colorado creates a notch in Nebraska, one must wonder why. The first boundary proposals for Colorado Territory had lines of latitude and longitude for all boundaries except its western boundary, which was the Colorado and Green rivers. This boundary was later changed to a line of longitude as well. Congress seemed intent on making all the boundaries straight and keeping Colorado Territory, and state, rectangular. This created part of Nebraska's notch in its western and southern borders. Congress could just as easily have put the notch in Colorado's northeastern corner, which was a part of Nebraska Territory, but the sense in Congress was that Colorado needed a lot of area because so much of it seemed barren. A rule of thumb at the time was that any land west of the 100th meridian was mostly useless for farming and would not be able to support much population. About one-half of Nebraska is east of that line so Congress could easily have thought that Colorado was in greater need of land than Nebraska.

With Wyoming. Dakota Territory extended to the Rocky Mountains in the early 1860s. (See map 7.14.) When Congress created Idaho Territory in 1863, it placed the boundary between it and Dakota Territory at the 27th meridian west of Washington. The reason for this choice is not given. When Congress created Montana Territory in 1864, it reshaped Idaho Territory and gave the area south of Montana, essentially Wyoming, back to Dakota Territory. (See map 9.12.) In 1867 the legislature of Dakota Territory formed the county of Laramie, putting its east boundary at the 27th meridian west of Washington. The boundary between Nebraska and Wyoming was thus prefigured by both the placement of the boundary between Idaho and Dakota territories and the creation of Laramie County.

With South Dakota. When Nebraska entered the Union in 1867 its boundary with South Dakota was defined as ascending the Missouri River from the mouth of the Big Sioux River to the Niobrara River, up that river to the Keya Paha River, then to the 43rd parallel, and then west on that parallel to the 27th meridian west of Washington. (See map 7.10.)

Because of the problems associated with a boundary along small, meandering streams such as the Niobrara and Keya Paha, Congress in 1882 redefined this boundary as ascending the Missouri River to the 43rd parallel and along that parallel as before, thus eliminating the two small rivers as a boundary. Dakota Territory had little say in this change as Congress had control over the boundary changes involving territories. Since Nebraska was already a state, it had to agree to the alteration of its boundary; the change added land, and Nebraska agreed. Nebraska was one of three states to gain major pieces of land after entering the

Union. Others were Ohio, which gained the Toledo Strip, and Missouri, which gained the Platte Purchase in its northwest corner.

Nebraska had earlier, in 1870, gained a small piece of land from Dakota Territory. A 5-square-mile piece of land near Sioux City had been cut off from Dakota by a sudden change in the Missouri River, and Congress wisely added it to Nebraska. (See map 7.11.)

In the early 1900s Congress approved another change in the Nebraska–South Dakota boundary (this time with consent of South Dakota since it was then a state) to the middle of the main channel of the Missouri River as it existed in 1905. Both states requested this change.

With Iowa. When it entered the Union in 1846 Iowa's western boundary was already set as the Missouri River. The Missouri River is a meandering watercourse and changes its channel from time to time. Iowa and Nebraska entered into an agreement in 1943 to change their common boundary to the main channel of the river as it existed in that year except for an area called "Carter Lake," near downtown Omaha, that was created by an avulsion in 1877. (See map 7.12.)

Since 1943 the river has apparently been active in shifting its course. DeLorme maps from both states (dated 1996 and 1998) show

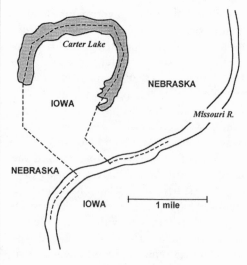

Map 7.11. Dakota Area Added to Nebraska

Map 7.12. Carter Lake

that several pieces of Iowa are on the west side of the river and several pieces of Nebraska are on the east side. Daniel H. Ehrlich's 1976 article has a map that shows several exclaves and a table stating that Iowa has an estimated 3,760 acres on the west side of the river and Nebraska has nearly 20,000 acres on the east side of the river in Iowa.

With Missouri. The act admitting Missouri as a state in 1821 defined its western boundary as a north-south line drawn from the confluence of the Missouri and Kansas rivers. (See map 8.10*A*.) However, in the 1830s Missourians wanted the rich bottomlands between their northwestern boundary and the Missouri River, land that was then set aside for Native Americans. Missouri senators were able to convince Congress to change Missouri's northwest boundary to the Missouri River. The line is in the middle of the main channel. Since this boundary was established before Nebraska became a territory or state, it was a preexisting boundary for Nebraska.

The river didn't stay put, however, and its changes caused land from each state to be on the opposite side of the river. The two states entered into negotiations in the early 1970s and more than twenty years later finally arrived at the Nebraska-Missouri Boundary Compact. This agreement put the boundary between them in the channel of the river as it existed in the late 1990s. In the compact the two states simply ceded to the other any land that was on their side of the river. The agreement also notes that work by the U.S. Army Corps of Engineers has stabilized the channel, but if changes in the course of the river should occur, the two states will enter into negotiations to resolve boundary problems. Nebraska first passed the compact in 1972 but no action was taken by Missouri. Missouri passed a compact bill in 1990; Nebraska passed a similar bill in 1998, and the U.S. Congress passed a joint resolution in 1999 giving its seal of approval to the compact. DeLorme maps for both Nebraska and Missouri dated 1996 and 1998 still show exclaves at Evan's Island and Rulo Bend, so it

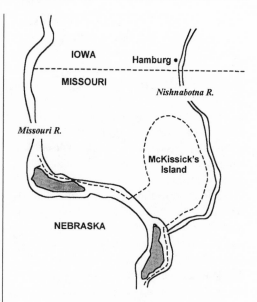

Map 7.13. McKissick's Island

is not certain that boundary changes have occurred for these areas.

An important exception to the boundary compact is an area known as McKissick's Island. (See map 7.13.) This "island" is not really an island at all: It is land that is now firmly attached to Missouri. It was attached to Nebraska until July 5, 1867, when the river cut a new channel over a twenty-four-hour period of flooding and high water. Surveyors from both states surveyed and marked the old river channel in 1895, but Missouri decided to contest the ownership of this area and brought suit against Nebraska in the U.S. Supreme Court. The court decreed in 1904 and 1905 that McKissisk's Island was indeed a part of Nebraska. In these suits the court reaffirmed the basic principle that gradual changes in a river channel change boundaries, but that sudden changes do not change boundaries.

The residents of McKissick's Island, who are totally cut off from Nebraska, have frequently voiced concerns about taxation, fire and police services, and flood control. Sentiment exists in the area for annexation to Missouri, although this will probably never happen. The residents of this area do most of their unofficial business in Hamburg, Iowa, as they are cut off from the greater part of Missouri by the Nishnabotna River.

North Dakota

The Dakota area was part of the Louisiana Purchase and a part of the territories of Louisiana, Missouri, Michigan, Wisconsin, Iowa, Minnesota, and Nebraska before Congress created the Dakota Territory in 1861. It also spent some time as unorganized territory that the whites called "Indian Territory." It lost land to Idaho Territory in 1863, and gained land (essentially, Wyoming) back from Idaho Territory in 1864. (See map 9.12.) The Dakota Legislative Assembly of 1867-68 decided that they no longer wanted their territory to be so large. They memorialized Congress asking for a new territory to be formed out of the southwest portion of their territory. Reasons they cited were the remoteness from eastern Dakota, the new Union Pacific Railroad that would give that area easy communication with Nebraska, the lack of direct lines of travel between the eastern and western part of Dakota, and the size of Dakota Territory as then constituted was too large to be effectively governed. Congress agreed and created Wyoming Territory in July 1868. Congress transferred small territorial areas to Nebraska in 1870 (map 7.11) and the area between the Keya Paha River and 43rd parallel in 1882 (map 7.10), and to Montana in 1873 (map 9.6).

By 1868 the boundaries of Dakota Territory were essentially the extent of the two states as we know them today. (See map 7.14.) This was a large area, and several early proposals developed to divide it. In 1877 Senator Alvin Saunders of Nebraska introduced a bill in the U.S. Senate to divide the territory vertically along the 100th meridian, a line that would have divided the territory into two nearly equal halves. His argument for such a line was that the eastern part of the territory was mostly agricultural whereas the western part was mostly mining. Dakotans were against this idea, and it did not go anywhere. Another proposal, and by far the most popular, was to divide the territory horizontally along the 46th parallel, a line that would also create two nearly equal areas.

Notwithstanding all the talk about dividing the territory, the first statehood bill, introduced in 1879 by Territorial Delegate Jefferson P. Kidder, proposed admitting the territory as a single state. This bill was never reported out of committee. A minority in the territory continued to lobby for nondivision, but the majority feeling was strongly in favor of division, with that division being along the 46th parallel.

The reasons offered for division were that those in the northern and southern parts of the territory had no social or mercantile relationships, travel was difficult between the two areas, and the territorial capital in the extreme southeastern part of the territory was a long way from any part of the territory above the 46th parallel. Their economic interests were also oriented differently. The northerners had markets to the east in Minneapolis and St. Paul in Minnesota and a shipping port at Duluth, Minnesota, while the southerners had markets in Chicago, Illinois, and St. Louis, Missouri.

Another proposal would have admitted the southern part of the area as a state and left the northern part as a territory. The

Map 7.14. Dakota Territory

southern part of the territory had enough population for statehood by 1880. This plan died in favor of admitting both as states largely because when Democrats controlled Congress they didn't want to admit any part of the Dakotas fearing the area would send Republicans to Congress, upsetting the delicate balance of power. North Dakota finally entered the Union in 1889, the same time as South Dakota. President Benjamin Harrison signed the bills consecutively but refused to declare which one he signed first. As a convention, North Dakota is listed as the thirty-ninth state to enter the Union, while South Dakota is listed as the fortieth state.

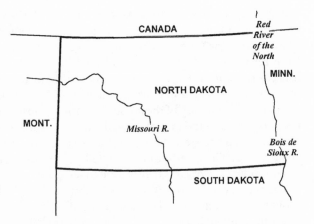

Map 7.15. North Dakota

The proposal for admitting the southern part as a state called it "Dakota," and the northern part with the name "Pembina Territory." However, a convention meeting in Fargo in 1882 felt that neither part of the territory had the exclusive right to the name Dakota and, therefore, suggested that the names be North Dakota and South Dakota.

A proposal advanced by Dakota Territory governor Nehemiah G. Ordway put a whole different wrinkle in the division scheme. Addressing the territorial legislature in 1881, he suggested extending the western boundary into Montana and Wyoming and then dividing the territory into three states. This idea received no support.

With South Dakota. Early in territorial history the leaders in the south planned for a division along the 46th parallel. (See map 7.15.) Dakota Territory had a natural east-west split as settlers in the northern and southern parts of the area had little to do with each other. Population in the south concentrated around the confluence of the Big Sioux and Missouri rivers, whereas the northern population concentrated along the Red River of the North. The railroads ran east and west, further cementing ties of each area to the east. Further, officials in the south feared the influence of the Northern Pacific Railroad, which tended to dominate politics in the north.

All of the most popular division proposals placed the boundary along the 46th parallel. Objections eventually surfaced pointing out the potential problems such a boundary would create because the 7th standard parallel, a little less than 7 miles south of the 46th parallel, had already been surveyed, and county lines had already been placed on this line. To place the boundary on the 46th parallel would disrupt property and political boundaries and likely cause litigation. North Dakota gained a sizeable piece of land when the boundary was placed on the 7th standard parallel. Even so, South Dakota is the larger of the two states.

With Montana. When Congress created Idaho Territory out of Dakota Territory in 1863, it put the border at the 27th meridian west of Washington. Just why Congress chose that meridian is not disclosed, but one can speculate that Congress was looking to the future when Dakota Territory would be divided into two states, and the resulting total area of each of those states would be about equal to other central plains states.

An interesting anomaly that relates to the western Montana border is an area called the "Lost Dakota Territory." Boundary definitions sometimes created strange anomalies, and this happened in the southwestern part of Montana. Often when the boundaries of a new jurisdiction were described they would be in reference to the boundaries of established jurisdictions. The northern boundary of a new area might simply be described as the southern boundary of the jurisdiction to the north of it. In the case of a small parcel of land in southwestern Montana, this was not the case. The creation of a isolated 4-square-mile piece of land that is sometimes called the "Lost Dakota Territory" came about because of the boundary definitions of three different territories.

First of all, the creation of Montana Territory in May 1864 defined its southern boundary along the 45th parallel from the 27th to the 34th longitude west of Washington, then south along the 34th longitude to the parallel of 43 degrees, 30 minutes, then west along this parallel to the crest of the Rocky Mountains, and then north along these mountains. (See map 9.6.) At this same time the remainder of Idaho Territory east of the Rockies and east of the 33rd meridian was attached to Dakota Territory.

Four years later Idaho Territory was further reduced when Congress created Wyoming Territory and defined the new territory's western boundary as the 34th meridian west of Washington rather than the 33rd meridian. The boundary definitions of Idaho, Montana, and Wyoming territories thus left a small triangular chunk of land about 4 miles long on the north and 2 miles long on the east side that was not included in any one of them and technically still belonged to Dakota Territory but over 300 miles east of the territory.

Once Congress realized this anomaly, the Dakota representative in Congress introduced a bill to attach the area to Montana. This made sense because the boundary line between Idaho and Montana was along the crest of the Rocky Mountains in this area. Congress passed the bill in 1873.

With Canada. The international boundary at the 49th parallel stems from the Treaty of Utrecht separating Hudson's Bay Company territory from French Louisiana. This parallel as a boundary between the U.S. and Great Britain was proposed by negotiators in 1814 and 1818 but was not then formally adopted. Finally, in 1842, the Webster-Ashburton Treaty formally recognized the 49th parallel as the boundary between the two nations from Lake of the Woods to the Rocky Mountains.

With Minnesota. An important discussion was going on in the 1850s about whether to split Minnesota Territory on a north-south or east-west axis. Minnesota territorial delegate Henry M. Rice in 1856 wanted an east-west split of Minnesota Territory, which then included the Dakotas. Rice had political motives in wanting the north-south boundary line. He figured such a division would create a Democratic Minnesota, and he aspired to be a U.S. senator from that state. The boundary he proposed was the main channel of the northward running Red River of the North, then south along the main channel of the Bois de Sioux River to Lake Traverse, then to the headwaters of the Big Sioux River and down that river to the Missouri River. (See map 7.8.) Map 7.6 shows some of the proposals to split the territory on an east-west axis.

The southern part of this boundary was subsequently altered, a change that affected South Dakota but not North Dakota. North Dakota's eastern boundary remained as originally proposed — the Red River of the North and Bois de Sioux River.

By mutual agreement, and with the consent of Congress, about 20 acres of land were transferred by Minnesota to North Dakota in 1961. A portion of the Red River of the North near Fargo, North Dakota, was moved for flood control, and access from Minnesota was very difficult.

South Dakota

South Dakota, along with its northern sibling, traveled the long territorial road of being part of the Louisiana Purchase then the territories of Louisiana, Missouri, Michigan, Wisconsin, Iowa, Minnesota, and Nebraska. At times the Dakotas were in two different territories with the Missouri River as a dividing line. The Dakota area was not under organized government at all from 1858 to 1861 and was simply called the "Land of the Dakotahs."

Congress organized Dakota Territory in 1861. At the time of organization the territory included the two Dakotas along with sizeable parts of Montana and Wyoming. (See map 7.14.) It was reduced in size in 1864 by the loss of Montana and the northern part of Wyoming, then increased in 1864 when most of modern Wyoming was added once again, then reduced again in 1868 to encompass only the two states that would become North and South Dakota. (See maps 7.14 and 9.12.) Refer to the North Dakota section in this chapter for general information and for further details concerning Dakota Territory.

With Minnesota. South Dakota's eastern boundary with Minnesota was formed when Minnesota became a state in 1858. At that time Minnesota Territory encompassed the Dakotas and discussion was whether to divide the huge territory along an east-east or north-south line. Due to the efforts of the Minnesota territorial delegate to Congress, that body agreed to a north-south boundary. The delegate, Henry M. Rice, proposed a line along the Red River of the North, Bois de Sioux River, Lake Traverse, from there to the headwaters of the Big Sioux River and down that river to the Missouri River. (See map 7.8.)

The Committee on Territories altered this line to run from Lake Traverse to Big Stone Lake to its southern outlet, then a straight line due south to the Iowa border. Congress adopted this line, thereby adding a slender strip of land to what would become the state of South Dakota. The boundary travels along the center of the lakes and rivers.

With Iowa. Congress approved boundaries for Iowa at the 45th parallel in the north and longitude 94 degrees 30 minutes in the west. The citizens of Iowa, however, voted down the constitution with these boundaries. Congressman Stephen Douglas then proposed boundaries at the parallel of 43 degrees 30 minutes in the north and the Missouri and Big Sioux rivers in the west. The Iowa constitution convention adopted these boundaries, and the people approved the constitution containing them. Congress quickly approved the constitution, and Iowa entered the Union in 1846 with these boundaries thus forming part of South Dakota's eastern boundary.

With Nebraska. When Congress reduced Nebraska Territory in 1861 by forming the territories of Colorado and Dakota, the boundary with the latter territory was defined as ascending the Missouri River to the Niobrara River, ascending that river to the Keya Paha River, and ascending that river to the 43rd parallel and west along that parallel. (See map 7.16.) In 1882 Nebraska officials decided that using the Keya Paha and Niobrara, small meandering rivers, was unsatisfactory. So they convinced Congress to change the boundary as up the Missouri River to the 43rd parallel and then east on

Map 7.16. South Dakota

that parallel thus removing the boundary from these small rivers. (See map 7.16.) South Dakota lost land in this change, but since Nebraska was a state and Dakota only a territory it didn't have much say in the decision.

With Wyoming and Montana. South Dakota's boundary with Wyoming and Montana is the 27th degree of longitude west of Washington. It was specified as such for Dakota Territory and for the two Dakota states. Stephen Visher, who researched House and Senate documents, says he was unable to discover why this meridian was chosen. It seems reasonable, however, to think that Congress had a nebulous overall plan as to how the regions might be divided into states when it chose this meridian. Congress tended to choose meridians and parallels a lot in the West because it knew so little about the area, and these arbitrary lines made for easy boundary placement. This meridian is also the western boundary of Nebraska.

A jog of slightly less than a mile in South Dakota's western boundary occurs at the junction of the Wyoming and Montana borders. This is due to two different survey parties determining the 27th meridian from different locations.

With North Dakota. Some sentiment existed in Dakota Territory for creating one state. Most officials and key players, however, saw a division of the territory. The major settlements, along the Red River Valley in the northeast part of the territory, and along the Missouri and Big Sioux rivers in the southeast, were separated by 400 miles and different economic philosophies. The southern area was settled by homesteaders with conservative ideas, whereas the northern area was controlled by large bonanza farms and industry in the form of the Northern Pacific Railroad. Railroad connections in both areas were to the east, further cementing ties in that direction.

An informal division along the 46th parallel had been tacitly assumed since the 1860s. Formal petitions for division of the territory began in the 1870s. Some Dakotans, however, still preferred a single state. Factors other than economic and cultural division were active in splitting the territory: Congress likely would not have permitted a single state to be admitted to the Union because it would have been too large. Also, local politicians favored a split because two states created twice as many political positions.

A constitutional convention meeting in Sioux Falls in 1885 judiciously proposed a boundary along the 7th standard parallel. County lines had already been surveyed using this parallel, and a boundary along the 46th parallel would have meant additional surveys of all affected counties. The 7th standard parallel is a little less than 7 miles south of the 46th parallel, so adopting this as the boundary created quite a loss of land to South Dakota. Nonetheless, South Dakota is the larger of the two states.

Congress admitted both Dakotas to the Union in 1889. President Benjamin Harrison signed the bills consecutively but would not say which one he signed first to determine the order of their entry into the Union. As a convention South Dakota is listed as the fortieth state, while its northern sister is listed as the thirty-ninth.

8

SOUTH CENTRAL REGION

Map is not to scale; boundaries are roughly drawn.

Arkansas

Hernando De Soto was likely the first European to visit Arkansas in the early 1540s. Since then this southern state has seen a lot of changes in governance. It was part of the area claimed for France by René-Robert Cavelier, Sieur de La Salle, in 1682 when he descended the Mississippi River and named it "Louisiane." It was Spanish for a while, then back in French possession when the United States bought the Louisiana Purchase in 1803. (See map 8.8.)

Arkansas became a part of the District of Louisiana in 1804 when the Louisiana Purchase was broken into two districts. The two districts were the District of Louisiana, consisting of all the Louisiana Purchase north of the 33rd parallel, and the District of Orleans, consisting of all land south of that parallel. In 1812 Arkansas became part of the Missouri Territory, and in 1819 Congress created the Arkansas Territory, consisting of the present state and Oklahoma as far as the 100th meridian. (See map 8.2.) Arkansas became the 25th state in June 1836.

With Mississippi and Tennessee. The Arkansas boundary with Mississippi and Tennessee was established in 1783 when the western boundary of the United States was put at the middle of the main channel of the Mississippi River. The Arkansas state enabling act simply restated that the boundary was to be the middle of the river. The river, however, was not willing to remain in the same channel throughout time and has changed its course. The U.S. Supreme Court has ruled that sudden changes in the course of a river do not alter state boundaries but that gradual changes do alter the boundaries. Maps show that Arkansas has land on the east side of the river, and Tennessee and Mississippi have land on the west side of the river.

Congress authorized Mississippi and Arkansas in 1909 to fix river boundary lines between them and exchange land that had been separated from either state by changes in the channel of the river. Since many tracts of land are on the "wrong" side of the river, it is very doubtful that any exchanging has taken place.

With Louisiana. In 1804 the United States divided the huge Louisiana Purchase into the District of Orleans and the District of Louisiana. While considerable confusion existed as to the location of the west boundaries of the districts, and some confusion over the east boundary of the District of Orleans, the dividing line of the two districts was clearly placed at the 33rd parallel. When Louisiana became a state in 1812, this parallel became its northern border and, thus, the southern boundary of Missouri Territory and later Arkansas Territory. When Arkansas became a state, this parallel remained its southern border. (See map 8.3.)

With Texas. A boundary was established between the future states of Arkansas and Texas before either was a political entity. In the 1819 Adams-Onís Treaty, the United States and Spain negotiated an international boundary; the result of these negotiations, as they had an impact on the future states of Arkansas and Texas, was a boundary that ascended the Sabine River to the 32nd parallel, then due north to the south side of the Red River, then west along that river to its source. (See map 8.14.) The United States and Mexico reaffirmed this boundary in 1828 after

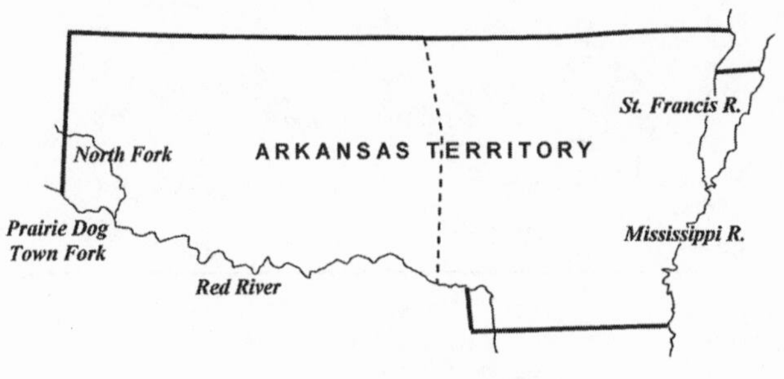

Map 8.2. Arkansas Territory

Map 8.3. Arkansas

Mexico achieved its independence from Spain in 1821. The 1836 enabling act admitting Arkansas as a state specified the boundary with the emerging Republic of Texas as the south side of the Red River where it met the Mexican boundary line (the one specified in the Adams-Onís Treaty), then to the northwest corner of Louisiana. At the time Congress admitted Arkansas as a state Texas had declared its independence from Mexico and set up a provisional government. The United States recognized the new Republic of Texas in late 1836.

With Oklahoma. The boundary between Arkansas and Oklahoma is the result of treaties the United States made with the Choctaw and Cherokee Indians. The treaty with the Choctaws was negotiated in 1825 and specified the boundary as a north-south line established at 100 paces, about 100 yards, east of old Fort Smith and running from the Arkansas River just north of Fort Smith south to the Red River. This boundary was first surveyed in 1825. When it was resurveyed in 1857 the surveyors discovered it ran west of south rather than due south as intended. The error may be due to not knowing the deviation of the compass from true north. (See map 1.2.) Rather than correcting the line, officials ordered the 1825 line remarked. To compensate the Choctaws for land mistakenly taken from them, Congress

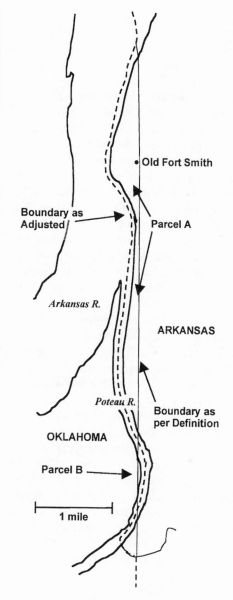

Map 8.4. Fort Smith

in 1875 ordered the computation of the land between the line as run and the line as intended. This calculation was 137,500 acres, for which the Choctaws were paid the paltry sum of 50 cents an acre. At that time the federal government was selling land for more than $2.50 an acre. The boundary as it now exists meets the Red River 4.6 miles further west than originally intended.

This part of the boundary created an

anomaly in the Fort Smith area. About 130 acres of Oklahoma land was between the Arkansas River and the eastern Arkansas boundary (parcel *A* on map 8.4). It also put a really small sliver of land on the west side of the Poteau River in Arkansas (parcel *B*). Congress passed legislation in 1905 to add land between the Arkansas. River and the boundary to Arkansas and to remove the parcel west of the Poteau from its jurisdiction and add it to Oklahoma. Congress could make this change without the consent of Oklahoma because it was not yet a state. The new boundary is the dashed line on map 8.4.

The part of the west boundary north of Fort Smith involved an agreement with the Cherokees who had previously been moved from their native lands in the east to the northwest corner of Arkansas. Although authorities tried to keep whites out of the Cherokee area, it was an impossible task. The problem became so acute that the Cherokees asked to be moved further west. In 1828 the Cherokees and the United States negotiated a treaty whereby the Indians would cede their land in Arkansas and gain title to land in what would become the state of Oklahoma. This treaty stipulated an eastern boundary of Cherokee lands as a straight line from the most northern point of the Choctaw line at the Arkansas River to the southwest corner of Missouri. The southwest corner of Missouri had been established in 1821 when Congress admitted it to the Union. This line was surveyed in 1871 and resurveyed in 1877.

With Missouri. When Congress admitted Missouri as a state in 1821 much discussion centered around its boundaries. An early proposal was for its southern boundary to be entirely at the parallel of 36 degrees 30 minutes, an extension of the Kentucky-Tennessee boundary. An energetic, politically active, and influential plantation owner who lived south of 36° 30' along the Mississippi River wanted to be a part of the new state and not part of Arkansas Territory. His considerable influence prevailed, and Congress altered the southern boundary to begin at the middle of the main channel of the Mississippi River at the 36th parallel, then run due west to the middle of the St. Francis River, then up the middle of this river to the parallel of 36° 30', thus creating an area called the "Bootheel." Then the line ran due west to a line running due south from the middle of the confluence of the Kansas and Missouri rivers. This political maneuvering by Missouri established the northern boundary of Arkansas without it having much voice in the matter because it was a territory, and Congress could change territorial boundaries however it chose.

Kansas

Francisco Vásquez de Coronado was probably the first European to visit Kansas when he and his expedition traveled through interior states looking for gold in 1541. The area became part of the United States with the Louisiana Purchase in 1803. (See map 8.8.) Then it was part of the Missouri Territory until Congress created Kansas Territory. The latter territory extended from Missouri to the Rocky Mountains and from the 37th to 40th parallels, except that New Mexico Territory intruded to the 38th parallel in the southwest corner. (See map 8.5.)

Congress created Kansas Territory in the Kansas-Nebraska Act of 1854, which created both the Kansas and Nebraska territories with the

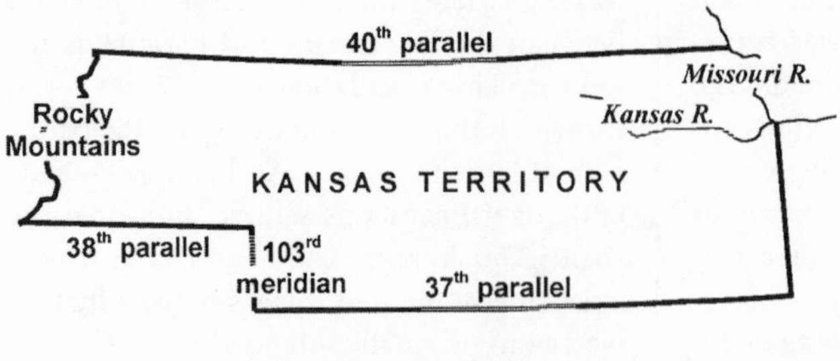

Map 8.5. Kansas Territory

boundary between the two set at the 40th parallel. The choice of the 40th parallel was apparently chosen to avoid division of Cherokee Country. The choice could also have been done with the idea of dividing the area into future states. The act altered one of the provisions of the Missouri Compromise of 1820. This act stated that slavery was prohibited north of the parallel 36 degrees 30 minutes. The Kansas-Nebraska Act gave both these territories the option to vote whether or not they wanted to legalize slaveholding. The vote in Kansas brought on a border war of such strife and blood-letting between people from southern states who wanted to extend slavery into Kansas and those from northern states who were determined to stop the spread of slavery that the term "Bleeding Kansas" entered the lexicon of U.S. history. Slavery was never an issue in Nebraska.

With Nebraska. As mentioned previously, the congressional act establishing Kansas and Nebraska territories set the boundary at the 40th parallel. Why this parallel, and not some other, was chosen is not clear other than easily to avoid division of Cherokee land. When statehood talk began in Kansas some settlers living between the 40th parallel and the Platte River wanted to be included in Kansas. (See map 7.10.) Therefore, they sent delegates to the state constitutional convention that met at Wyandotte (near present Kansas City, Kansas) in 1859. Some Kansans also wanted to include that area, but the convention did not seat these delegates since they were not part of the call for delegates. They did, however, allow them to join in the proceedings and present their case.

The advocates for including in Kansas the area between the Platte River and the 40th parallel argued that the Platte made a perfect northern border between whites and Indians. Another reason was that the convention was considering placing the western boundary somewhere around the 102nd meridian (about where the present western boundary of Kansas is located), and they wanted to augment the state with the additional land in the north. For the Nebraskans a reason for joining Kansas was that they wanted to be part of a state and not a territory. Nebraska achieved statehood in 1867.

Kansans finally rejected the proposal of adding the area north of the 40th parallel out of fear of losing political control: the Nebraskans were mostly Democrats, while the Kansans were mostly Republicans. Kansans were also concerned that the capital might be located north of the 40th parallel if they included the northerners. Ultimately, the Wyandotte delegates decided to retain their northern boundary at the 40th parallel as specified in the 1854 act. Some of the delegates even expressed the altruistic notion that they didn't want to take rich land from Nebraska and impair that territory's chances for statehood.

With Missouri. In the east, Kansas is bounded by Missouri. The line currently runs from the 40th parallel down the center of the Missouri River to its confluence with the Kansas River then due south to the northeast corner of Oklahoma. The Kansas-Missouri boundary was established by Missouri before Kansas became a territory.

When Missouri became a state in 1821 its western boundary was a north-south line from the middle of the confluence of the Missouri and Kansas rivers from Iowa to Arkansas. Missourians lobbied Congress to alter this boundary by extending the northwest portion to the Missouri River between its confluence with the Kansas River and the Iowa boundary. (See maps 8.10 and 8.12.) The boundary along the Missouri River is the center of the main channel. This change ultimately cost Kansas some rich farmland, but this was many years before Kansas was organized as a territory or state.

The Missouri River does form a natural boundary, although it does not always remain within its banks as flooding often causes the channel to relocate. The U.S. Supreme Court has repeatedly ruled that a boundary does not change in a river when the channel changes due to a catastrophic even such as flooding. It must have been such an event that placed a large section of Missouri west of the river in the area immediately west of the Missouri city of St. Joseph. (See map 8.6.)

Other shifts in the river also created land on the "wrong" side of the river. Recognizing the concomitant jurisdictional problems, legislatures of the two states agreed in 1949 to swap land that was on the "wrong" side of the river. Congress approved these exchanges in 1950. An exception to the agreement, however, was the above-mentioned section west of St. Joseph. Other than this one place, the boundary between the two states is in the river.

With Oklahoma. When Congress created Kansas Territory it considered establishing the southern boundary as an extension of the southern boundary of Missouri, thus putting the boundary at the parallel of 36 degrees 30 minutes. Instead, Congress moved the boundary north to the 37th parallel, thereby adding ½ a degree to what was then Indian Territory and fixing the Kansas-Oklahoma boundary. Congress moved the boundary because of the influence of Stephen A. Douglas, who may have been influenced by an 1854 map from the Commissioner of Indian Affairs Office that showed the 37th parallel as the dividing line between the Osage and Cherokee reservations.

With Colorado. Kansas Territory extended to the Rocky Mountains, but considering the vast expanse of land and poor communications, this was much too large an area for one jurisdiction to administer. Another consideration in limiting the western extent of Kansas, even more important than communication or administration, was the fact that many of the delegates to the 1859 Kansas constitutional convention in Wyandotte had no interest in forming a state that large.

Many of the delegates were convinced that the western land was worthwhile only as habitat for prairie dogs, owls, buffalo, rattlesnakes, and Indians, and totally unsuited for agriculture. The area was also populated by scruffy, unkempt miners and free-living cattlemen, reprobates the delegates felt were inherently incompatible with the farmers in the eastern part of the territory. Some talk circulated at the convention of limiting the western boundary at about where Hays, Kansas, is today, about 145 miles east of the present western border. (See map 8.7.) This would have created a nearly square state with

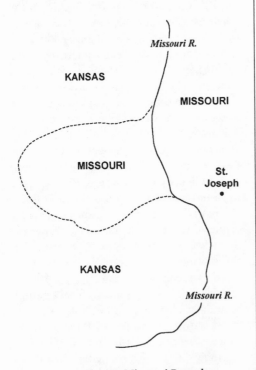

Map 8.6. Kansas-Missouri Boundary

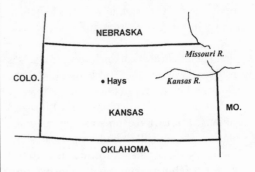

Map 8.7. Kansas

homogeneous climate and soil. After all the earlier warfare over slavery, the delegates were attentive to keeping considerable sameness in the people to be included in the new state.

Other delegates, however, were willing to extend the western boundary to include ranch land they felt would round out the state's food-producing industry. They prevailed, and the delegates finally settled upon the 25th meridian west of Washington for the western boundary. This is the first instance where a Washington meridian was used for a state boundary. This meridian is 2.81 miles west of the 102nd meridian west of Greenwich. This meridian had also been mentioned as the eastern boundary of the proposed State of Jefferson, one of the early ideas for forming a territory in the Colorado area.

Slavery politics also figured heavily in the decisions regarding the western border of Kansas. Southern Democrats generally favored including in Kansas the area extending to the Rocky Mountains so as to enlarge an area they felt would be a slave state. The antislavery Republicans naturally favored excluding that area with the idea of limiting any area that might become a slave state.

Louisiana

Spaniards were mostly likely the first Europeans to visit Louisiana as Hernando De Soto explored the area in 1541. However, it was the French who established a lasting presence when René-Robert Cavelier, Sieur de La Salle, descended the Mississippi River in 1682, claimed the entire river drainage basin for France, and named it "Louisiane" for King Louis XIV of France.

France held the area until 1763, when it ceded the land west of the Mississippi River to Spain. The following year France, defeated in the French and Indian War, ceded its land east of the Mississippi, except for the Isle of Orleans which remained Spanish, to Great Britain. This ended France's empire in North America. The Isle of Orleans included the area bounded on the west by the Mississippi River, on the south and east by the Gulf of Mexico, and on the north generally by lakes Maurepas, Pontchartrain, and Borgne. (See map 8.9.)

In the years following 1763 Spain captured the Gulf of Mexico towns of Biloxi, Mississippi; Mobile, Alabama; and Pensacola, Florida. When Great Britain was defeated in its war with the American colonies and granted them independence in 1783, it also ceded its colonies of East and West Florida to Spain. (See map 5.3.) Spain maintained the northern boundary of West Florida was the parallel where the Yazoo River entered the Mississippi River, then east to the Chattahoochee River because that it where it had been when Great Britain possessed the area. The United States, however, maintained the boundary was at the 31st parallel because in its treaty with Great Britain in 1783 it negotiated the boundary at that parallel.

Spain and the United States simply chose to disagree over this boundary until 1795 when Thomas Pinckney negotiated a treaty with Spain that officially placed the western part of the boundary between the two countries at the 31st parallel. This established this part of Louisiana's boundary with Mississippi.

Louisiana in 1800 had a strange identity: It was a French-speaking colony under Spanish control when, in that year, Spain ceded it back to France. Neither France nor Spain had been successful in settling the area with very many people. Their interest in the New World was mostly extractive — removing furs and gold — rather than settling it with farmers. Both countries had lost money in Louisiana.

Thomas Jefferson sent James Monroe to Paris to assist the American minister to France Robert R. Livingston in negotiations with the French. The goal of the Americans was to effect one of four plans: (1) purchase East and West Florida and the Isle of Orleans, (2) purchase the Isle of Orleans only, (3) purchase land on the eastern bank of the Mississippi River for a fort, or (4) gain the right of navigation on the Mississippi River and deposit of goods at New Orleans. The American negotiators were surprised when France offered to sell the entire Louisiana area to the United States. (See map 8.8.) Unknown to the Americans, Napoleon was eager to get rid of a money-losing endeavor and at the same time gain funds to finance his European expansion. The huge area known as the Louisiana Purchase became U.S. territory in 1803. Spain thus gained a new aggressive neighbor west of the Mississippi River along hundreds of miles of indefinite border—the drainage basin of the Mississippi River west of the river.

The year following the purchase of Louisiana the United States divided the area into the District of Louisiana, consisting of all the area north of the 33rd parallel, and the District of Orleans, consisting of all land south of that parallel. Then in 1805 the United States organized the District of Louisiana into the Territory of Louisiana. Congress admitted Louisiana as the eighteenth state in 1812.

With Texas. The act of admitting Louisiana as a state specified the western boundary as the middle of the Sabine River, including all islands, to the 32nd parallel, then due north to the 33rd parallel. (See map 8.9.) Texas at this time was Spanish territory, and Spain and the United States disputed the location of the boundary. The generally accepted western boundary of the Louisiana Purchase was the drainage basin of the Mississippi River. The Sabine River was not part of the Mississippi's drainage basin, so a strict interpretation would have placed the boundary east of it. The United States, however, insisted on a boundary with Spain at the Sabine.

The entire boundary between the two countries was a matter that demanded resolution. In 1819 John Q. Adams of the United States and Don Luis de Onís of Spain negotiated a treaty defining the boundary between the two countries. (See map 8.14.) The treaty as it pertains to Louisiana was for the boundary to be along the western bank of the Sabine to the 32nd parallel, then

Map 8.8. Louisiana Purchase

Map 8.9. Louisiana

due north. This shifted the western boundary of Louisiana from the middle of the river to the western bank. In 1848 Congress consented to moving the boundary back to the middle of Sabine River, Sabine Lake, and Sabine Pass (the channel that connects the lake to the gulf). The 1819 treaty also specified that the boundary run due north from where the Sabine River intersected the 32nd parallel to the Red River, thus establishing all of Louisiana's western boundary. This boundary was reaffirmed with Mexico in 1828 after that country achieved its independence from Spain.

With Arkansas. The boundary with Arkansas was the obvious outgrowth of the division of the Louisiana Purchase into the District of Orleans and the District of Louisiana, which placed the dividing line at the 33rd parallel. That parallel remained a boundary in the act admitting Louisiana as a state, which specified its northern boundary as the 33rd parallel.

With Mississippi. The 1783 treaty between the United States and Great Britain specified the western boundary of the United States as the center of the main channel of the Mississippi River to the 31st parallel, then east along that parallel. This established most of Louisiana's boundary with Mississippi. Maps clearly show that some Louisiana land is east of the river, and some Mississippi land is west of the river. The Supreme Court has ruled that slow changes in the channel of a river also change any boundary formed by the river. Changes formed by sudden, catastrophic action do not change boundaries. The parts of each state that are on the "wrong" side of the river, therefore, must have been caused by catastrophic action such as floods. Congress gave Louisiana and Mississippi authority in 1909 to cede land to the other where changes in the river have separated land from the main body of each state. Since so many tracts of land are on the "wrong" side of the river, often called "exclaves," it is doubtful that any exchanging has taken place.

Understanding how Louisiana got the area below the 31st parallel and between the Mississippi and Pearl rivers is complicated. Americans had been moving into West Florida (map 5.3) for some time and continued to do so. In 1810 these settlers revolted against Spanish rule, formed an independent government, and asked to become part of the United States. President James Madison ordered District of Orleans governor William C. C. Claiborne to take possession of West Florida for the United States.

In 1811 settlers of West Florida below the 31st parallel (map 5.3) petitioned Congress for permission to join Mississippi Territory. They were Americans, and the District of Orleans was predominantly French, a situation they claimed was destined to cause constant strife and disagreement for both sides if they were to be joined to that district. Mississippi territorial delegate George Poindexter recommended adding the area to Mississippi Territory, which at this time did not have any area bordering the gulf. His reasons were not only that it would respect the wishes of the residents but also that adding West Florida to the District of Orleans would create an area wielding too much control over Gulf of Mexico commerce.

Many Louisianians were not sure how much of West Florida they wanted because it included too many Anglo-Americans, so the first congressional act submitted to admit Louisiana as a state did not include any land east of the Isle of Orleans. Just a few days later an additional act was submitted that would add the Florida parishes, an area east of the Isle of Orleans, south of the 31st parallel, and west of the Pearl River to Louisiana. ("Parish" is the term given by Louisiana to a governmental unit that most states call a county.) The reason they were not added initially was to give the Louisiana legislature the opportunity to vote on whether or not to include them in the new state. While some Louisianians wanted to exclude the parishes, many, like Governor Claiborne, wanted to include land all the way to the Perdido River. (See map 5.3.) Claiborne felt that removing all of West Florida from Louisiana was extreme, but he was willing to compromise by setting the boundary at the Pearl River. This proposal carried the day in the Louisiana legislature. The United States House agreed and approved this proposal in 1812, annexing the area between the Mississippi and Pearl rivers, about 5,000 square miles, to Louisiana. That same year Congress attached the land between the Pearl and Perdido rivers to Mississippi Territory.

The border between Louisiana and Mississippi in Mississippi Sound and Chandeleur Sound was problematic. Mississippi's boundaries included all islands within 6 leagues (18 miles) of the shore. Louisiana's boundaries included all islands within 3 leagues (9 miles) of the coast. These definitions caused a problem off Mississippi's southwestern coast because some islands fell within the scope of the boundary definitions of both states.

Louisiana brought suit against Mississippi in the U.S. Supreme Court to settle the boundary in this area. Mississippi argued that Congress obviously intended it to have jurisdiction over islands within 6 leagues to compensate it for the small area of coastline. Louisiana naturally disagreed.

The court settled the matter in favor of Louisiana. It decreed in 1905 (202 U.S. 1) that the deep-water channel in the two sounds was the boundary of Louisiana when it was admitted to the Union in 1812 and Congress could not take land away from Louisiana when it admitted Mississippi in 1817 with the 6-league boundary definition. This boundary is officially described as the deep-water channel from the Pearl River, then into Lake Borgne and exiting this lake at its northeast corner, passing north of Grand Island into the Mississippi Sound, and then passing between Cat Island and Isle a Pitre to the gulf.

With Gulf of Mexico. Louisiana's Gulf of Mexico boundary had not been much of an issue until oil fields were discovered in the gulf, but the boundary was usually con-sidered as 3 nautical miles (about 3.45 land miles), which is fairly common. However, after the discovery of the oil fields, Louisiana argued for a boundary of 3 leagues (9 miles). Louisiana's enabling act to enter the Union said its offshore boundary includes all islands within 3 leagues of the coast. Louisiana argued in 1960 before the U.S. Supreme Court that its gulf boundary was 3 leagues. Federal attorneys argued that the enabling act pertained only to islands and not to the water within that distance. A Supreme Court decision (80 S.Ct. 961) agreed and ruled against Louisiana so its gulf boundary is only 3 nautical miles. However, Louisiana does have jurisdiction over islands 3 leagues from its shore. (Texas does have a gulf boundary of 3 leagues, see that state for an explanation.)

Missouri

With eight contiguous states, Missouri shares with Tennessee the distinction of having the greatest number of bordering states. However, since it was only the second state formed west of the Mississippi River (Louisiana was the first), it had relatively few boundary problems. It had no other abutting states except east of the Mississippi River, and the boundary there was well established.

Although Missouri didn't have many state or territory boundary problems, except with Iowa, it did encounter a lot of different proposals on its journey to becoming a state. The story begins when Congress created the Missouri Territory in 1812 that included all of the former Territory of Louisiana, which was the remainder of the Louisiana Purchase after Louisiana became a state in 1812. A movement soon began to form a state.

Interested parties advanced many boundary proposals. The first well-defined proposal placed the southern boundary at 36 degrees 30 minutes, the northern boundary at the 40th parallel, and the western boundary about 24 miles east of where the north-south western boundary is today. (See *A* on map

8.10.) This proposal would have created a much smaller state than exists because it would not only have reduced the land in the west but also the north boundary would have been about 40 miles south of the current boundary.

Citizen agitation for a larger area convinced the territorial legislature to expand the proposed state boundaries in the south, west, and north. (See *B* on map 8.10.) This proposal met rejection in the U.S. Congress because the proposed state was too large and its boundaries poorly defined. The territorial legislature reduced the boundaries as shown in *C* on Map 8.10, and Congress admitted Missouri with those boundaries as the twenty-fourth state in 1821. (See *D* on map 8.10 and map 8.12)

With Illinois, Kentucky and Tennessee. The Treaty of 1783 established the Mississippi River as the western boundary of the United States. Consequently, the boundary of Missouri with Illinois, Kentucky, and Tennessee was already set at the middle of the river's main channel for all these states when Congress admitted them to the Union. If the river had kept its channel, all would have been well, but that was not the case. The U.S. Supreme Court has ruled that slow changes in a river's channel changes boundaries, but that rapid or catastrophic changes — whether natural or man-made — do not. Maps show that all these states have some land on the "wrong" side of the river.

Even these fairly lucid court rulings don't cover all situations. Missouri and Kentucky disputed ownership of some 15,000 acres in the Mississippi River called Wolf Island. (See map 8.11.) The parcel was originally an island in the river but had subsequently become attached to Missouri. Since the location of the main channel determined to whom the island belonged, the question arose as to whether the channel originally ran on the east or west side of the island. Both states produced maps to support their claim. In 1870 the U.S. Supreme Court ruled in favor of Kentucky.

A dispute also arose between Missouri and Illinois over a sandbar in the Mississippi River called "Arsenal Island" located between St. Louis and Cahokia, Illinois. It was considered a no-man's land where both states contended for jurisdiction and where men fought duels with impunity. The island was awarded to Illinois, but the fickle river ultimately settled the problem when it simply washed the sandbar downstream during a flood.

With Arkansas. The original proposal for Missouri's southern boundary was to

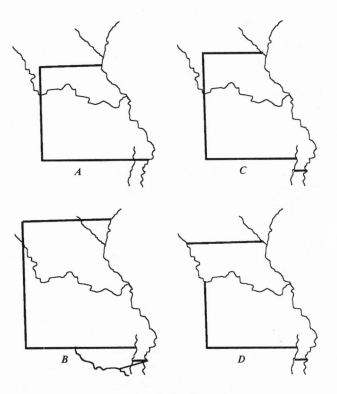

Map 8.10. Early Missouri

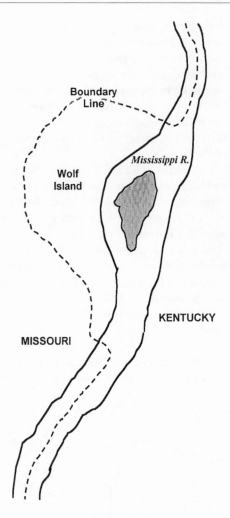

Map 8.11. Wolf Island

Map 8.12. Missouri

well-organized state and not part of Arkansas Territory. His influence, along with that of family and friends, tipped the scales, and the Missouri territorial legislature included his plantation in the new state by defining the southern boundary as starting at the middle of the Mississippi River at the 36th parallel and running due west to the center of the St. Francis River, then up the middle of the river to parallel of 36° 30', then due west to a north-south line drawn from the center of the confluence of the Missouri and Kansas rivers.

With Oklahoma, Kansas and Nebraska. The act admitting Missouri as a state defined its western boundary as a north-south line drawn through the confluence of the Missouri and Kansas rivers from the parallel of 36° 30' to a latitude drawn west from the rapids in the Des Moines River. This created the western boundary shown. (See C on map 8.10.) In the 1830s Missourians began to covetously eye the rich bottomlands between their northwestern boundary and the Missouri River, and many settlers intruded onto this Indian land. This triangular piece of land can be seen in D of map 8.10 and in map 8.12.

Missourians resented that this land was reserved for use by Indians and memorialized Congress to stop sending Indians there, which it did in 1833. Influential Missouri

place it along the parallel of 36 degrees 30 minutes. Several influential people south of this line wanted to be included in Missouri. The first scattered group that wanted inclusion lived along the White and Black rivers. This is the area to the west of the Bootheel. (See B on Map 8.10.) This group was unsuccessful. The Bootheel is the protrusion in southeastern Missouri.

The other group that wanted inclusion lived between the Mississippi and St. Francis rivers. The story is that John Hardeman Walker, a wealthy, energetic, politically-oriented plantation owner living between those two rivers was intent on being included in the new state. He wanted to be a part of a

senators convinced the Committee on Indian Affairs to favor annexing the area to Missouri. Congress agreed, and in 1837 added the 3,000-square-mile Platte Purchase to Missouri. The Sauk, Fox, and Potawomie Indians living in the area agreed to exchange the area for land elsewhere, and their titles to the Platte Purchase were extinguished. The western boundary was thus altered to run from the confluence of the Missouri and Kansas rivers up the middle of the Missouri to the latitude line forming the northern boundary of Missouri.

Missouri and Kansas agreed in 1950 to change their common boundary in the Missouri River to midchannel of the river as it existed that year. Congress agreed. An exception to this is an area immediately west of the Missouri city of St. Joseph where a part of Missouri is on the west side of the river. (See map 8.6.)

Missouri and Nebraska signed a boundary compact in 1990 and 1998 respectively ceding to the other all land that was on their side of the Missouri River and establishing the boundary as the channel in the river. De-Lorme maps for both Missouri and Nebraska, dated 1998 and 1996 respectively, show exclaves at Evan's Island and Rulo Bend, so the author is not sure whether boundary changes have occurred for those areas.

An exception to the Missouri-Nebraska compact was an area called McKissick's Island that was previously awarded to Nebraska in U.S. Supreme Court cases decided in 1904 and 1905. (See map 7.13.) McKissick's Island is discussed further in the Nebraska section in chapter 7.

With Iowa. Missouri's northern boundary was more difficult to locate than the others. The state enabling act specified a northern boundary passing through the rapids of the Des Moines River and also called this line the "Indian Boundary Line." John C. Sullivan surveyed this line in 1816 and fixed the limit of the Osage cession of 1808 (line *1* on map 7.4). This line is not a true east-west line but was recognized by Missouri as its boundary at statehood in 1821.

In 1836 Missouri authorized the survey of a new line. Joseph C. Brown established a line about nine or ten miles north of the Sullivan Line which the Missouri General Assembly readily accepted as its northern boundary (line *4* on map 7.4). How Brown determined this line is not known because the Des Moines River had no easily identifiable rapids, but that is presumably the reference point from which he established his line.

When Congress created the Territory of Iowa in 1838 it defined its southern boundary simply as the northern boundary of Missouri. However, it did authorize a commission consisting of representatives of Missouri and Iowa Territory to participate in a survey to determine the boundary line. Missouri declined to participate; nonetheless Albert Lea, apparently at the behest of the federal government, directed a new survey.

Lea determined that more than one line could be seen as the boundary. (See map 7.4.) The one farthest north was the Brown Line (line *4* on map 7.4) and was favored by Missouri. The Sullivan Line lay south of this by 9 or 10 miles (line *1*). The federal government recognized this line, and Iowa Territory initially accepted this line as well. A third line, still farther south, was an east-west line drawn from what was considered the Des Moines Rapids in the Mississippi River (line *3*). Iowa's advocacy for the more southerly line did not win approval in Congress.

Disputes between Missouri and Iowa became intense. People living in the disputed area were unsure concerning the validity of their property rights and to whom they should pay taxes. Naturally, they didn't want to pay taxes to either jurisdiction, but they knew they would eventually have to do so. Missouri sent its militia to the area, determined to enforce its claim to the Brown Line.

Congress admitted Iowa as a state in 1846 without the boundary being settled. Then the dispute became a matter for the

U.S. Supreme Court to decide when the states brought suit in 1847 to decide the boundary. The court determined that no rapids existed in the Des Moines River and that this boundary stipulation was not a factor to consider. The court's 1849 ruling established the boundary as the old Sullivan Line (line *1* on map 7.4). This was the boundary accepted in the original enabling legislation and was the boundary that had generally been recognized. The Sullivan Line was also somewhat of a compromise as it is nearly in the middle of the extreme boundaries advocated by the two states.

Iowa state enabling legislation established the northeastern part of the boundary as along the middle of the Des Moines River to the Missouri River. The two states agreed in 1939 to change the boundary along the Des Moines River to the middle of the river as it existed in that year; Congress agreed.

Oklahoma

Formation of the states of Texas, Arkansas, Missouri, Colorado, and Kansas and the Territory of New Mexico formed the boundaries of Oklahoma. For years Oklahoma was Indian Territory and was thus basically an unorganized space as other areas around it became organized. This fact notwithstanding, the precise location of the boundaries required some working out.

When President Thomas Jefferson made the Louisiana Purchase in 1803, one of his plans for the area was that it be a place for displaced American Indians. The area set aside for Indians was narrowed down through the years, and Congress contracted it to what is now called Oklahoma when it created Indian Territory in 1834, a place supposedly off-limits to white settlers. During the settlement of the West, the whites constantly pressured the federal government to release Indian lands for white settlement. They felt that Indians had no right to the land as they didn't use it "properly" and had no concept of private ownership. Consequently Congress relented in 1890 and formed Oklahoma Territory. Congress admitted Oklahoma as the forty-sixth state in 1907.

With Missouri. The short segment of Oklahoma's east border with Missouri results from the statehood enabling act defining part of Missouri's western border as a north-south line drawn from the center of the confluence of the Kansas and Missouri rivers. This line extends to the parallel of 36 degrees 30 minutes.

With Arkansas. All of Oklahoma's eastern boundary with Arkansas is the result of treaties between Native Americans and the federal government. The southern portion, between the Arkansas and Red rivers, is the result of an 1825 treaty with the Choctaws. (See map 8.13.) The treaty described the line as a north-south line 100 paces east of old Fort Smith running from the Arkansas River to the Red River. This line was surveyed in 1825 and resurveyed in 1857. The latter survey revealed that the line did not run due south as intended from the Arkansas River but veered to the west. Rather than correcting the line, officials ordered the 1825 line remarked. In 1875 Congress ordered the computation of the land between the line as run and a due-south line. This calculation added

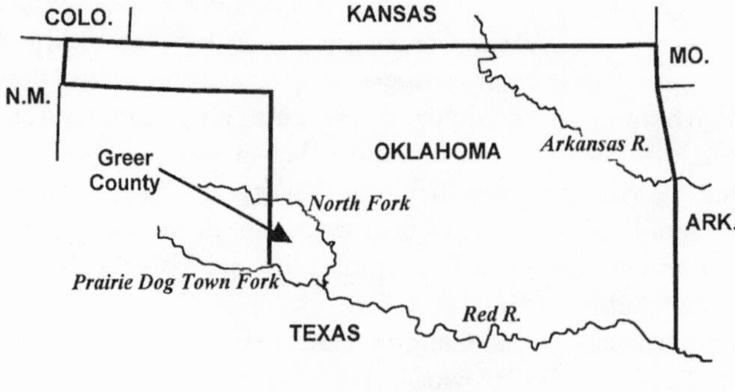

Map 8.13. Oklahoma

137,500 acres, for which the Choctaws received 50 cents an acre. The line as run hits the Red River 4.6 miles further west than intended.

The northern part of the line, from the Arkansas River to the southwest corner of Missouri, is the result of an 1828 treaty with the Cherokees. Whites had been encroaching on Cherokee lands in northwest Arkansas and causing problems. Fed up with this situation, the Cherokees asked to exchange this land for land farther west. The federal government agreed, and the 1828 treaty granted them land in Oklahoma. The treaty specified the eastern boundary of the Cherokee land as from the most northern point of the Choctaw boundary on the Arkansas River to the southwest corner of Missouri.

Congress made an adjustment in Oklahoma's east boundary between the years of 1905 and 1909 by transferring about 130 acres of Choctaw land lying between the Arkansas and Poteau rivers to Arkansas. The Choctaws received a little over $23,000 for this land. (See map 8.4.)

With Texas. The boundary with Texas was the most difficult to settle due to different interpretations requiring adjudication in the U.S. Supreme Court. A good deal of the Oklahoma-Texas boundary was established by the Adams-Onís Treaty in 1819 that specified part of the boundary between the U.S. and Spain as the Red River to the 100th meridian and then due north along that meridian. (See map 8.14.) The treaty did not mention which part of the Red River the negotiators had in mind, but John Q. Adams's personal notes indicate clearly that the south bank was the intended boundary.

The first crux in the interpretation of this boundary came about in interpreting which of two branches of the Red River, about 44 miles east of the 100th meridian, was considered an extension of the river.

Map 8.14. Adams-Onís Line

Texas argued in favor of the more northerly branch, while the federal government argued for the more southerly branch. The U.S. Supreme Court, after years of litigation, ruled in 1896 that the southern branch, Prairie Dog Town Fork, fit the definition in the treaty and other documents and, thus, made Greer County, with an area of about 2,380 square miles, a part of Oklahoma. (See map 8.13.)

The precise location of the Red River boundary was not a problem between Texas and the United States during Oklahoma's territorial days. However, when oil was discovered near the river and in the bed of the river in 1918, the exact location of the boundary became important, mostly for tax purposes.

Texas argued that the center of the river's channel was the boundary. It based this contention on the fact that several treaties the United States had made with Indians gave the center of the river as the boundary. The federal government countered that the Adams-Onís Treaty and related documents had firmly established the south bank as the boundary notwithstanding any treaties the government had made with Indians.

Determining what "south bank" meant was not easy to settle either. The Red River is a meandering river for much of its course. It is a puny stream during dry times and can flood at other times. The U.S. Supreme Court, when settling the case in 1921, ruled that the south "cut bank" of the Red River was the boundary between Oklahoma and Texas. A "cut bank" was defined as a bank a few feet high, usually very steep, within which the river flows except during exceptional times. During low-water levels the actual edge of the water may be many feet from the cut bank.

Identifying the boundary continued to be a problem. In 1996 Texas and Oklahoma formed a boundary commission to settle the border between the two states. The commission determined that the permanent boundary was to be the vegetation line along the south bank of the Red River except for the Texoma area (a lake southeast of Ardmore, Oklahoma). In the Texoma area the boundary is along the south bank of the Red River as it existed before the construction of Lake Texoma. Texas adopted the commission's ruling in 1999, but inquiry by the author to Oklahoma was not answered, so it is not clear if it adopted the ruling or not.

Boundary issues aside, who owned the bed of the river was an early question that had to be resolved. States own the bed of navigable rivers within their borders, but the federal government owns the bed of nonnavigable rivers. This ruling was very important in determining tax revenues from the production of oil in the river. Oklahoma made a strong case that the river was navigable by pointing out that the Red River was navigated by river boats for over a hundred years and that Congress had appropriated money to keep it navigable. Nonetheless, the U.S. Supreme Court concluded that the river was not navigable and that north shore land owners had ownership only to the medial line between the cut banks. This same 1923 decision confirmed that the federal government owned the southern half of the river bed.

Nothing came easily in settling the Oklahoma-Texas boundary. The 1819 treaty specified the 100th meridian west of Greenwich as a boundary. But where on the ground was that meridian? Surveys made in 1852, 1857–59, 1860, 1892, and 1902 attempted to locate the meridian. None of these lines agreed with one another, and none was truly at 100 degrees. Both states claimed different surveys as the boundary, each favoring a line enhancing its claim to territory. It wasn't until 1919, when the two states were arguing about the Red River boundary, that the issue of the 100th meridian became a renewed point of contention. The question ended in the U.S. Supreme Court, and in 1926 the court determined that none of the previous surveys accurately located the meridian but that the boundary was indeed the true position of the 100th meridian. The court in 1927 directed geodetic and astronomic engineer Samuel S. Gannett to locate and mark the meridian. Gannett did so and filed his report in 1929; the court accepted it in 1930. None of the boundary lines surveyed before Gannett had become an accepted boundary. If that had been the case, it would have been the boundary even though not accurately placed on the 100th meridian.

In 1819, after the Adams-Onís Treaty, the Oklahoma Panhandle was a part of Texas as the boundary between the United States and Spain extended along the 100th meridian from the Red River to the Arkansas River in the north. (See map 8.15.) This was also the boundary of the Republic of Texas and the United States from 1836 to 1845.

Texas, however, ultimately didn't want this area. The Missouri Compromise of 1820 established the line of 36 degrees 30 minutes as the parallel above which slavery could not exist in western states. Texas considered itself a slave state and didn't want any land above the 36° 30' parallel, so it ceded this land and other land to the federal government in 1850. (See map 8.15.) The Oklahoma Panhandle, about 5,740 square miles called the "Public Land Strip," was a no-man's land attached to no state or territory until the federal government made it a part of Oklahoma Territory in 1890. (See map 8.13.) This cession by Texas of land between the meridians of 100 degrees and 103 degrees and north of 36° 30' thus set the boundary of Oklahoma in this area. John H. Clark surveyed this boundary in 1859–60. Both Texas and Congress confirmed it in 1891.

With New Mexico. Surveyors marked Oklahoma's boundary with New Mexico, known as the "Cimarron Meridian," in 1881. It begins at the parallel of 36° 30' and runs to the 37th parallel. It is more accurately located than the western boundary of Texas, also supposedly located on the 103rd meridian. The two meridian lines are 2.2 miles apart at the northwest corner of Texas. The reason for the difference is because they were surveyed by different crews. Cimarron County, the westernmost county in the Oklahoma Panhandle, is the only county in the United States that touches four states— Kansas, Colorado, New Mexico, and Texas.

With Colorado. Enabling legislation for both the territory and state of Colorado placed its southern boundary at the 37th parallel. The entire southern Colorado boundary was surveyed three times: 1868, 1874, and 1902–03. Everyone considered the 1868 line official, but since later surveys located the line at different places, residents were in a quandary about in which jurisdiction they resided. Congress passed a resolution declaring the 1902–03 line as official. President Theodore Roosevelt, however, sent the resolution back, claiming that Congress could not alter a state boundary once it had become well established. New Mexico sued Colorado in 1919 to determine the official boundary. In 1925 the U.S. Supreme Court upheld the entire 1868 line as official, thus establishing Colorado's boundary with Oklahoma a well as with New Mexico. The line between Oklahoma and Colorado is not perfectly on the 37th parallel and has a jog in it that may be due to surveying errors or a surveying correction.

With Kansas. The president signed legislation in 1854 establishing Kansas Territory. The logical southern boundary of that territory would have been an extension of the southern Missouri border at the parallel of 36 degrees 30 minutes, but Cherokee lands

extended north of 36° 30' in Oklahoma, so the boundary was placed at the 37th parallel. This put Oklahoma's northern boundary at the 37th parallel as far west as the 25th meridian west of Washington, the western border of Kansas.

Texas

Before entering the Union, the Lone Star State was a republic that nearly became an independent nation. Texas was a part of the Spanish empire from the time Spaniards first arrived in 1517 and became a part of Mexico when that country overthrew Spanish control in 1821. Texans were content for many years to be part of Mexico since Mexico did not closely govern its northern area. This changed in 1830 when Mexico banned immigration from the United States. Texas was populated mostly with Anglos, and Mexico feared it would lose this area if Anglos continued to enter it.

Texans held conventions in the early 1830s with the intent to separate from Mexico and form their own government. Many Texans just wanted to scare Mexico and return to the liberal Mexican constitution existing before the ban on immigration. The die was cast, however, and the momentum for separation became too great to stop. After the Alamo defeat in 1836 Texans rallied to defeat the Mexican army and force the Mexican surrender. Texas was free of Mexico and became the Republic of Texas in 1836, bounded as shown on map 8.15.

The question then became whether Texas would unite with the United States or absorb the remaining northern states of Mexico and establish a nation of its own. A referendum in 1836 indicated that most Texans were in favor of annexation to the United States, from which most of them had emigrated, but many influential politicians were against it. Also working against annexation was the fact that northern U.S. states didn't want Texas in the Union fearing it would become a slave state, a reasonable assumption

Map 8.15. Republic of Texas

since most Texans came from the South. However, sentiment in the United States about Texas statehood changed in the early 1840s, largely due to the fear that Texas and Great Britain were becoming much too friendly and to the growing sentiment in the United States of Manifest Destiny — the idea that the United States should expand to the Pacific Ocean.

A joint resolution was introduced into Congress stipulating that Texas could become a state if it would meet three conditions: (1) leave its boundary adjustments to the United States, (2) cede its public property to the United States, and (3) allow prohibition of slavery in any part of it north of the parallel of 36 degrees 30 minutes — the Missouri Compromise line. Texas agreed to these stipulations. In this agreement Texas was given authority to divide into as many as five states. As can be seen on map 8.15, some of its territory was well above 36° 30' (the current northern boundary of Texas).

Great Britain, France, and Mexico all used their influence to keep Texas an independent republic. Mexico, previously antagonistic toward Texas, much preferred an independent republic on its northern border than an expanded United States. While all this was occurring in the higher political levels, a movement was growing among Texans to unite with the United States. Notwithstanding fear in Congress that annexation of Texas would cause a war with Mexico, Congress admitted Texas as the twenty-eighth state in 1845. The precise locations of many Texas boundaries were unsettled at the time of statehood, but generally they were those the Republic of Texas claimed. War with Mexico to settle part of the border began soon after and lasted from 1846 to 1848.

With Louisiana. When the United States purchased Louisiana from France in 1803, it created a vast, indefinite boundary with Spain. The first boundary problem was in Louisiana near the Gulf of Mexico. The traditional boundary between France and Spain, when they controlled the area, was the Arroyo Hondo, a Red River tributary between the Sabine and Natchitoches rivers. General James Wilkinson and Simón de Herrera, the U.S. and Spanish military commanders, negotiated an agreement creating a buffer area called "Neutral Ground" between the Arroyo Hondo and the Sabine River. The arrangement lasted until 1819 when a more permanent agreement became effective.

In 1819 American John Q. Adams and Spaniard Don Luis de Onís negotiated the treaty bearing their names. This treaty delineated the boundary as beginning at the Gulf of Mexico, running up the west bank of the Sabine River to the 32nd parallel, then due north to the Red River, then along this river to the 100th meridian, then due north to the Arkansas River, along this river to its source, then due north to the 42nd parallel, then due west to the Pacific Ocean. (See map 8.14.)

Part of this treaty described the boundary of modern Texas, and some of it described the boundaries of the Republic of Texas.

This treaty effectively established the boundary between Texas and Louisiana except that Congress moved part of the boundary to the middle of the Sabine River, Sabine Lake, and Sabine Pass (the outlet of the lake into the gulf) in 1848.

With Gulf of Mexico. The Texas gulf boundary is 3 leagues, about 9 miles, including islands. Texas is one of two gulf states, the other is Florida, that have a 3-league boundary in the gulf. The reason for this is that when Congress admitted Texas to the Union it did so affirming the gulf boundary Texas claimed and that was thee leagues. Louisiana, Mississippi, and Alabama have gulf boundaries of 3 nautical miles, about 3.45 land miles. (See those states as to why this is so.) The point from which gulf boundaries are measured is the mean low-tide line.

With Mexico. Some influential early Texans advocated a boundary with Mexico about 700 miles south of the Rio Grande. The reason for such a southerly line was that they considered the Rio Grande an indefensible boundary. Most Texans after 1836, however, saw their boundary with Mexico as the Rio Grande. Mexico recognized the Nueces River, north of the Rio Grande, as the boundary. (See map 8.15.) In 1845 both Texas and Mexico claimed the area between the Rio Grande and Nueces River. The Mexican War settled this issue, and the treaty ending the war established the boundary as the deepest channel of the Rio Grande.

The Rio Grande is a meandering river that frequently floods and consequently changes its course, often putting land claimed by each country on the "wrong" side of the river. Both countries appointed commissioners to deal with this problem, and after five years of work the commission reported their results in 1912. They recommended that cut-offs caused by the meandering river be transferred to the country on whose side of the river they lay, except that cut-offs of more than 650 acres and having a population over 200 would not be transferred. Congress confirmed the recommendations of the commission. The Texas-Mexico boundary follows the Rio Grande all the way from the Gulf of Mexico to the parallel of 31° 47'. Both countries have built canals in strategic places to help control the meandering nature of the river.

With New Mexico. The Republic of Texas claimed its southern and western border was the Rio Grande all the way to its source, then due north to the 42nd parallel. (See map 8.15.) New Mexico had a claim to independence from Texas based partly on the fact that it was a separate Mexican state before Texas was settled. U.S. troops occupied land between the Rio Grande and 103rd meridian (the current north-south portion of the west Texas boundary) after the Mexican War. (See map 8.16.) Texas tried to assert its claim to the river by attempting to establish counties there after the war. The military government in New Mexico, however, rebuffed the Texans and, with the encouragement of local politicians and business leaders, oversaw the organization of the area as a territory of the United States. Citizens in New Mexico were eager to form their own government and did not want to be part

Map 8.16. Texas

of Texas. Texans naturally objected as they had claimed this area for years.

By 1850 it seemed that Texas and the federal government were headed for open hostility concerning boundaries when aging statesman Senator Henry Clay introduced a bill to settle the Texas–New Mexico boundary problem. The proposal was that Texas give up some of its claim to lands for which the federal government would pay Texas $10 million. To some Texans the idea of selling any sacred Lone Star State land was repugnant. Texas, however, was deeply in debt stemming from its days as a republic. Eventually, U.S. senator Sam Houston and influential Texans who controlled the state legislature realized the wisdom of accepting the offer. Texans endorsed the plan in an 1850 referendum. During the debate Houston claimed that it was a good deal because Texas already had more desert than it needed.

The agreement provided a northern boundary along the 36° 30' parallel from the 100th meridian to the 103rd meridian, then south along that meridian to the 32nd parallel, then west to the Rio Grande, then along that river to the Gulf of Mexico. (See map 8.15.) John H. Clark was directed to survey the 103rd meridian and the 32nd parallel in 1859. His survey was not very accurate. At the parallel of 36° 30' his line is longitude 103° 2' and at the 32nd parallel it is 103° 4', both points farther west than intended. Many disputes occurred along this line, and to settle the matter Congress, in a joint resolution in 1911, made the 103rd meridian and the 32nd parallel as surveyed by Clark the official boundary. The reason for such a determination was that both Texas and the United States had accepted the Clark line as the official boundary.

The Texas–New Mexico Rio Grande boundary is from ½ to 2½ miles west of the current channel of the river. The boundary is sinuous and follows an old riverbed as the river was in 1850. New Mexico sought this change in a 1920 U.S. Supreme Court case asking that the boundary be where the river was in 1850 before an 1864 avulsion; Texas agreed.

With Oklahoma. The boundary with Oklahoma has a varied history. Texas agreed to cede land north of 36 degrees 30 minutes in 1850 partly because it needed the $10 million and partly because the Missouri Compromise of 1820 had established the parallel of 36° 30' as a line above which slavery would not be allowed in western lands. Texans had little interest in land where slaves would not be allowed. The Oklahoma Panhandle thus became part of Oklahoma because Texas didn't want the area and the United States bought it.

The Adams-Onís Treaty established the 100th meridian as the boundary between Spain and the United States. (See map 8.14.) Finding just where this boundary was on the ground was a big problem. Surveys made in 1852, 1857–59, 1860, and 1902 all located it at different places, none of which was accurate. Both Texas and Oklahoma claimed different surveys as the official boundary, each favoring the one that enhanced its claim to territory. The location of the 100th meridian became a hot item in 1919 when the two states were disputing other boundary matters. The issue found its way to the U.S. Supreme Court in 1926. The court determined that none of the previous surveys accurately located the meridian, and that the boundary was indeed the true position of the 100th meridian. The court in 1927 directed geodetic and astronomic engineer Samuel S. Gannett to locate and mark the meridian. Gannett conducted his survey largely at night to avoid aberrations caused by heat waves. Gannett filed his report in 1929; it was accepted by the court in 1930. The court will not change a boundary that has been established and accepted, but in this case that had not happened, so the court determined that the boundary should be where it was intended to be.

The Greer County dispute also required court intervention to settle. (See map 8.13.) The 1819 treaty said the boundary ascended the Red River to the 100th meridian. The river divides into two major forks about 44 miles east of the 100th meridian. Texas argued that the North Fork was the extension of the river. The federal government argued that the south fork, called "Prairie Dog Town Fork," was the true extension of the river. The U.S. Supreme Court, after years of litigation, ruled in 1896 that the southern branch was the one referred to in the treaty and other documents and thus put Greer County in Oklahoma.

The Red River boundary was not a problem between Texas and the United States during Oklahoma's territorial days, but when oil was discovered near the river and in the bed of the river in 1919 the exact location of the boundary and ownership became important for obvious tax revenue considerations. Texas argued that the center of the river's channel was the boundary. They based their interpretation on the fact that several treaties the United States had made with Native Americans specified the center of the river as the boundary. The federal government countered that the Adams-Onís Treaty and related documents had firmly established the south bank as the boundary notwithstanding any treaties the government had made with Indians.

In reality the Adams-Onís Treaty had not delineated exactly where in the river the boundary was located, but Adams's notes clearly showed that the south bank was the intended location. Determining what "south bank" meant, however, was not easy to settle. The Red River is a meandering river for much of its course, it is a meager stream during dry times and can overflow its banks at other times. The U.S. Supreme Court, when settling the case in 1921, ruled that the south "cut bank" of the Red River was the boundary between Oklahoma and Texas. The court defined "cut bank" as a bank a few feet high, usually very steep, within which the river flows except during exceptional times. At low-water levels the actual edge of the water may be a considerable distance from the cut bank.

Notwithstanding the court ruling in 1921, identifying the boundary continued to be a problem. In 1996 Texas and Oklahoma formed a boundary commission to settle the border between the two states. The commission determined that the permanent boundary was to be the vegetation line along the south bank of the Red River except for the Lake Texoma area (a lake southeast of Ardmore, Oklahoma). In the Texoma area the boundary is along the south bank of the Red River as it existed before the construction of Lake Texoma. The agreement actually puts the boundary in the current channel in a portion of the Texoma area. Texas adopted the commission's ruling in 1999, but inquiry by the author to Oklahoma was not answered, so it is not clear if it adopted the ruling or not.

While this ruling settled the matter of the boundary between the two states, it didn't settle who owned the bed of the river. States own the bed of navigable rivers within their borders, but the federal government owns the bed of nonnavigable rivers. This ruling was very important in determining tax revenues from the production of oil in the river bed. Oklahoma made a strong case that the river was navigable by pointing out that river boats had navigated the Red River for over a hundred years and that Congress had appropriated money to keep it navigable. Nonetheless, in a seeming non sequitur, the U.S. Supreme Court concluded that the river was not navigable and that Oklahoma land owners had ownership only to the medial line between the cut banks. This same 1923 decision confirmed that the federal government owned the southern half of the river bed.

With Arkansas. The 1819 Adams-Onís Treaty established the north-south and east-west borders with Arkansas. (See map 8.14.) The U.S. Supreme Court ruling concerning Oklahoma also affected the east-west part of the border of Texas with Arkansas as it placed it at the south cut bank of the river. The north-south boundary is an extension of the Texas boundary with Louisiana, which the 1819 treaty specified as a due-north line from where the Sabine River intersected the 32nd parallel to the Red River.

9

ROCKY MOUNTAIN REGION

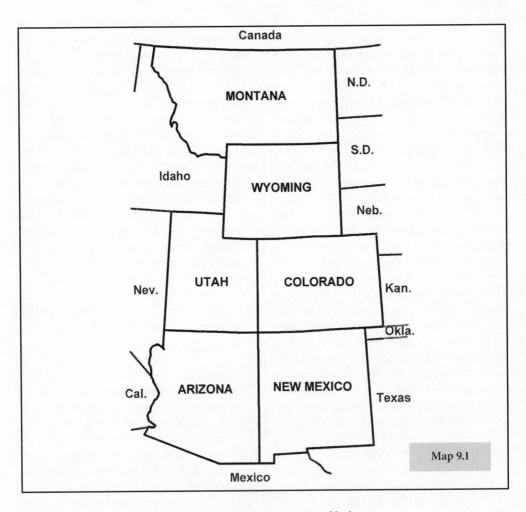

Map is not to scale; boundaries are roughly drawn.

Arizona

In the Treaty of Guadalupe Hidalgo, Mexico ceded to the United States land comprising California, Nevada, and Utah; large parts of Arizona and New Mexico; and a part of Colorado. (See map 1.1.) Arizona was first included in New Mexico Territory when Congress organized that territory in 1850. Efforts to gain separate territorial status for the western part of New Mexico Territory came as early as 1855 when people there realized they had no organized protection against outlaws, no judiciary system, and little representation or influence in the territorial legislature at Santa Fe.

Many different schemes developed to divide New Mexico Territory. Some of them would have created an east-west dividing line; others would have created a north-south line. The proposals for an east-west line would have created two horizontal, elongated territories, with New Mexico Territory being the northernmost and Arizona Territory the southernmost. People from slave states favored such a division; those from nonslave states did not.

The first territorial proposal with a shape near that of present Arizona came in 1862 when James M. Ashley, chairman of the House Committee on Territories, introduced a bill that eventually organized Arizona Territory. The bill specified the dividing line of New Mexico Territory as an extension of the western Colorado border. (See map 9.1.) This, coupled with the straight-line northern boundary of Arizona and New Mexico, created the phenomenon called "Four Corners," the only place in the United States where four states meet at one point. By 1863, when Congress created Arizona Territory, the slave states had seceded from the Union, and congressmen from the states remaining in the Union had the votes necessary to divide New Mexico Territory any way they wanted.

Arizona had four territorial governments, although the federal government did not recognize the first three. The first was established in Tucson in 1860. The second, established in 1862, was recognized by the Confederate States of America. The commander of volunteers from California who defeated Confederate forces in 1862 proclaimed the third. Congress organized the 1863 government.

With Mexico. The Arizona boundary with Mexico, as per the Treaty of Guadalupe Hidalgo in 1848, was along the Gila River in the area that would eventually become the territory and state of Arizona. U.S. officials, basing their understanding on an inaccurate map, thought the line would be drawn well south of the Gila, but when the surveyors met to actually mark the line, their interpretation of the treaty was different from what the negotiators thought they were specifying. (See maps 9.2 and 9.7.) Since the U.S. thought the boundary should be further south, the two countries naturally got into a boundary dispute. In an attempt to settle the matter, the United States sent James Gadsden, diplomat and railroad entrepreneur, to Mexico. His main purpose was to negotiate for more land from Mexico to allow for a railroad route. Another intent was to gain a port on the Gulf of California, but this latter effort failed. The United States paid $10 million for the Gadsden Purchase, an area which

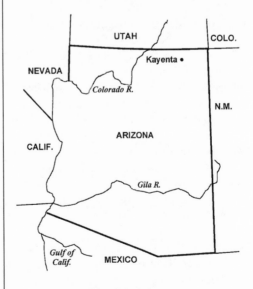

Map 9.2. Arizona

was largely barren, deserted, and desolate. Mexico agreed to the transaction only because it needed the money.

The purchase, consisting of 29,640 square miles, moved the line south in Arizona to the parallel of 31 degrees 20 minutes, west to the 111th meridian, then a straight line to a point on the Colorado River 20 miles below the confluence of the Gila and Colorado rivers, then up the Gila to the confluence of the two rivers. (See map 9.7.)

With California. Congress defined the western boundary of the Territory of New Mexico in 1850 as the state of California as far north as the 37th parallel. California's eastern boundary had been defined earlier in 1850 as the 120th meridian from the 42nd to 39th parallels, then a straight line to where the Colorado River crossed the 35th parallel, then down that river to the international boundary with Mexico. So the western boundary of Arizona Territory was this oblique line nearly paralleling the Sierra Nevada Mountains to the Colorado River and then down that river to the international boundary. (See map 9.7.) This has remained as Arizona's western boundary except for the area awarded to Nevada in 1866 mentioned in the following subsection.

The Colorado River frequently floods and thus has changed its course from time to time causing boundary disputes between Arizona and California that needed resolution. In 1963 the two states agreed to fix their common boundary in the river so that further channel shifting would not affect it. The two states appointed commissioners who attempted to place the boundary so as to effect equitable distribution of land that was in question. The location of the boundary is generally in the river's midchannel as shown in 1962 aerial photographs. Map 10.3 shows a variance of this general rule.

With Nevada. Arizona's boundary with Nevada Territory in 1863 was the 37th parallel, which was also the boundary when Arizona was part of New Mexico Territory.

In 1866 Congress attached the area north and west of the Colorado River and longitude 37 degrees west of Washington to Nevada. (See map 10.8.) Agitation for this change began in 1865 when Nevada senators introduced a bill to move Nevada's eastern border one more degree east. At this point the bill did not include any area south of the 37th parallel. This bill passed the Senate, but the session ended before the House could consider it. The bill was revived in 1866, but this time it included an additional provision to add land to southern Nevada by continuing Nevada's eastern border south of the 37th parallel to the Colorado River and down that river to the California border. This bill became law in spite of protests by Arizona and Utah delegates in Congress. The area taken from Utah and Arizona territories can be seen in map 10.8 labeled as "Additions of 1866." Considering that this region is where the city of Las Vegas sprouted, the loss to Arizona was indeed great.

The reason Congress added part of Arizona Territory is not known, but it was probably recognizing the fact that Nevada is a very arid region and that it would need a lot of land to support a state-sized population. Even with the loss, Arizona is slightly larger than Nevada.

With Utah. The 37th parallel became the boundary between Arizona and Utah largely as a political compromise that revolved around the slavery issue. When it came time for Congress to divide the Mexican Cession, the boundaries of California were well established, so Congress decided to divide the rest of the area into two territories—New Mexico and Utah. (See maps 9.7 and 9.10.) Illinois senator Stephen Douglas, chairman of the Committee on Territories, suggested the 38th parallel as a dividing line, but he was agreeable to 37 degrees 30 minutes or the 37th parallel to include most of the Mormon settlements in Utah. Southern congressmen in 1850, who were eager to extend slavery into the western territories, were in favor of 36 degrees or 36 degrees 30 minutes. An amendment to make the line at this latter parallel failed by only one vote. The 37th parallel was decided upon as a compromise between southerners and northerners.

The boundary has a 2,000-foot jog, seen only on large-scale maps, northwest of the Arizona city of Kayenta that is probably due to a correction after the survey line wandered from its intended course. (See map 9.2.)

In 1865 the Utah territorial legislature asked Congress to move its southwestern boundary to the Colorado River. (See areas *A* and *B* on map 9.3.) The argument used by Utah officials was that having land abutting this part of the river would give them access to navigable waters of the river. The logic was good because in 1865 the western boundary of Utah was one degree further west than it is today and moving its southern border to the Colorado River would have given Utah control over the river as far south as Laughlin, Nevada. The river was navigable for about 50 miles upriver to Boulder City, Nevada. Nonetheless, the request never got out of committee.

Between 1897 and 1910 Utah, after becoming a state, made several additional attempts to acquire that part of Arizona Territory north of the Colorado River known as the "Arizona Strip," or sometimes "The Strip." (See area *B* on map 9.3.) Utah first tried to persuade the Arizona legislature to cede it the area. That failed, so Utah asked Congress to award it the area. Utah was trying to use its power as a state to the disadvantage of a territory — Arizona. None of these tactics worked; the Arizona territorial legislature adamantly refused, and all requests to Congress fell on deaf ears. Utah's reasoning for the area was not without merit, however. It claimed the sparsely settled area was cut off from Arizona and that what few settlements existed there were mostly Mormon with strong ties to Utah. Both asser-

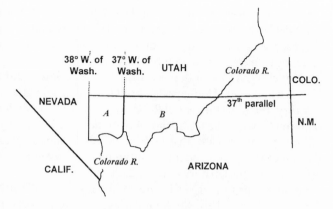

Map 9.3. Arizona Strip

tions were true but were not enough to overcome a generally negative feeling in Congress toward the polygamous Mormons. Utah made one more attempt to get The Strip in 1919 after Arizona became a state but was rebuffed again.

With New Mexico. The Arizona boundary with New Mexico was set when Congress created Arizona Territory from New Mexico Territory in 1863. It put the boundary as a straight line extending south from the western boundary of Colorado. This boundary is at the 32nd longitude west of Washington. It is part of the "Four Corners" phenomenon and is the only place in the United States where four states meet at a common point. (See map 9.1.)

Colorado

When citizens in the Rocky Mountain area of Kansas Territory met in 1859 to organize a government separate from Kansas Territory, they were sharply divided about whether to form a territory or a state. The faction advocating territorial status won out because of the tax burden statehood would place on the citizens. They named their government the "Territory of Jefferson" and proposed generous boundaries of the 102nd and 110th meridians and the 37th and 43rd parallels. These boundaries were greater than Colorado's current boundaries by 2 degrees in the north and 1 degree in the west. The first tentatively proposed western boundary was the Colorado and Green rivers. (See map 9.11.) However, this was changed to the 110th meridian.

When the U.S. House passed a bill for a territory straddling the central Rocky Mountains in 1861 they called it "Idaho." When the bill reached the Senate, that body changed the name to Colorado Territory. The boundaries given for the territory were the 25th and 32nd meridians west of Washington and the 37th and 41st parallels; the boundaries remained the same when Colorado achieved statehood in 1876. (See map 9.4.)

Colorado consists of land from the Louisiana Purchase, the 1848 Mexican Cession, and the 1850 cession from Texas. (See map 1.1.) The formation of Colorado Territory took land from the territories of Utah, New Mexico, Kansas, and Nebraska.

The creation of Colorado Territory, like many other territories in the West, was delayed because of the squabbling between the North and the South over the extension of slavery into western territories. When southern states seceded from the Union in 1860 and 1861 the way was cleared for the organization of new territories, Colorado being one of them. Others were Dakota Territory and Nevada Territory (1861), Arizona Territory and Idaho Territory (1863), Montana Territory (1864), and Wyoming Territory (1868).

The act creating Colorado Territory had some interesting features. It had a provision

that all Indian land was excepted from the boundaries of the territory until any tribe consented to be a part of the territory; it gave the territory the right to divide itself if it so chose, and it had a provision whereby it could attach a portion of another territory. Colorado is one of three states with boundaries consisting entirely of lines of latitude and longitude — the other two are Utah and Wyoming.

With New Mexico. Congress placed the southern boundary of Kansas Territory at the 37th parallel until it reached the 103rd meridian where it went north to the 38th parallel then continued west to the crest of the Rocky Mountains. (See map 8.5.) Organizers of territorial status in Colorado placed their proposed southern boundary entirely at the 37th parallel, thus slightly reducing the size of New Mexico. New Mexico, of course, objected to this loss and argued mightily to keep it. (See map 9.7.) Illinois senator Stephen Douglas, chairman of the Committee on Territories, argued against this loss of New Mexico's land. The arguments advanced by the New Mexico territorial delegate and Douglas were that the people in the disputed area were of Mexican birth, culture, and language and had always been under the governance of New Mexico. Douglas also argued that New Mexico was legally slave territory, whereas Colorado was not, and to attach the disputed area to Colorado would deny the people there from owning slaves. Further investigation revealed that only twenty-four people lived in the disputed area, and none of them owned slaves. The other arguments for keeping the area in New Mexico were valid.

When Congress organized Colorado Territory in 1861 it put the southern boundary at the 37th parallel, since the argument to keep the area above the parallel in New Mexico was weak. Another factor in deciding on this parallel was that Congress seemed to be governed by a desire to form a rectangular territory. See the paragraphs concerning Utah in the Arizona section of this chap-

Map 9.4. Colorado

ter for further discussion on why the 37th parallel was settled upon as the boundary.

The boundary as surveyed in 1868 by E. N. Darling is not straight and runs both north and south of the true parallel. Complications in land surveys and obliteration of some markers caused Colorado in 1899 to order a resurvey of the line. Neither New Mexico nor the federal government participated in this survey. Congress ordered the entire Colorado southern boundary resurveyed by H. B. Carpenter in 1902. This survey showed the deficiencies in the 1868 line. New Mexico sued in the U.S. Supreme Court in 1919 to have the boundary moved to this new line, but the court upheld the original line in a 1925 decree because it was well established and acknowledged by all participants. An offset noticeable on most maps is evident in Colorado's Archuleta County and can be attributed to surveying errors or a correction in alignment.

With Utah. The original bill introduced in Congress in 1861 to create Colorado Territory placed the western boundary at the Green and Colorado rivers, which is west of the present boundary. (See map 9.10.) A later amendment placed the western boundary at the 33rd meridian west of Washington, 1 degree west of the present boundary. Congress finally settled on the 32nd meridian west of Washington as the boundary.

Since the eastern boundary of Utah Territory had been the crest of the Rocky Mountains, one wonders why the western boundary of Colorado was placed so far west of the mountains. One reason for the shift was likely due to the fact that the 32nd meridian was nearly equidistant from the two emerging population centers of Salt Lake City and Denver and was in a desolate area with little population, none of which was white. Another reason could be that since Colorado Territory was organized to accommodate miners, Congress felt the territory should ensure that potential mining areas be included in it. Also, the Mormons were generally despised in Congress, and so Congress

probably felt no remorse in reducing their territory. One might also suspect that Congress didn't want important metals such as gold and silver falling under Mormon jurisdiction since Utah also lost the important mining area of Pahranagat to Nevada.

The Utah-Colorado boundary has a slight offset in the Colorado county of Montrose. It is not a sharp right-angle turn but rather a gradual shift to the west as the line heads north. This jog is probably due to a correction in the line after surveyors noticed they were off the intended meridian.

With Wyoming. The Colorado-Wyoming boundary is at the 41st parallel and was put there by Congress. The 1859 proposed boundaries for the Territory of Jefferson placed the northern boundary at the 43rd parallel. This would have included the area traversed by the future Union Pacific Railroad. Congress apparently thought these boundaries were too generous and pared them back to the 41st parallel.

Congress did not specifically state why they chose the 41st parallel, but in dividing up the West Congress was always looking at how the area would be parceled into individual states. It felt the area was extremely desolate and that a lot of land was needed to sustain a population large enough to form a state. Colorado's claim to the 43rd parallel would have created a state larger than Congress apparently deemed necessary to sustain such a population. Furthermore, they probably felt that those 2 degrees would be needed by a state to the north of Colorado. This is speculation on the part of the author, but it makes sense from what is known about the workings of Congress in the creation of western states.

With Nebraska. Colorado's border with Nebraska essentially was established in the agreement with Kansas and Colorado when Congress set their common border. Congress seemed intent on making Colorado rectangular. It also saw Colorado as an unproductive area in that it was not considered arable, so Congress wanted to give Colorado enough land in the hope that it could support itself. These two factors ultimately created the notch in Nebraska's southwest corner. Obviously, the notch could have been placed just as easily in the northeast corner of Colorado, but because of the reasons already mentioned, this did not happen.

With Kansas. The Territory of Kansas extended to the Rocky Mountains, but Kansans had no interest in the western area. It was a land of loose-living cattlemen and unkempt miners. The settled farmers in the eastern part of the territory did not want the western ruffians included when Kansas became a state. Delegates to the Kansas constitutional convention considered a western boundary near Hays, Kansas (map 8.7), but later pushed it further west to the 25th meridian west of Washington to incorporate rich ranch land they thought would round out their food-producing industry. This was the first instance of a meridian west of Washington being used for a state boundary.

With Oklahoma. When Congress created Kansas Territory in 1854, it considered putting its southern boundary at 36 degrees 30 minutes but later changed it to the 37th parallel. When Colorado Territory split from Kansas, this boundary was already at that parallel. So this parallel remained the boundary line between Colorado Territory and what was then Indian Territory.

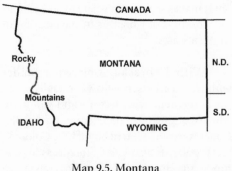

Map 9.5. Montana

Montana

Mining interests were the impetus behind the formation of several territories and states in the Rocky Mountains, and Montana was one of them. West of the Continental Divide, this northern Rocky Mountain area was originally part of the Oregon Country and part of the territories of Oregon, Washington, and Idaho. (See map 1.1.) East of the divide it was originally a part of the Louisiana Purchase, and later the territories of Louisiana, Missouri, Nebraska, Dakota, and Idaho. For a while it was not part of an organized territory and was simply known as "Indian Country."

When Montana was a part of Idaho Territory, miners on the east side of the Rocky Mountains demanded their own territory in 1863. The territorial capital at that time was in Lewiston, a considerable distance west over rugged and sometimes impassable mountains. (See map 10.7.) Idaho territorial officials agreed, and they petitioned Congress to create a new territory east of the mountains and 113th meridian to be called "Jefferson." The original proposal for the boundary between Idaho and the proposed new territory was to be the above-named meridian and the crest of the Rocky Mountains, but this didn't happen. The details are in the Idaho subsection following.

With Canada. The boundary with Canada along the 49th parallel was proposed at that parallel as early as 1814 but was not finally adopted until the 1842 Webster-Ashburton Treaty established this parallel as the boundary from Lake of the Woods in Minnesota to the crest of the Rocky Mountains. This secured Montana's boundary east of the Rocky Mountains; west of the mountains took some additional negotiations. (See map 9.5.) Britain and the United States could not agree on the boundary west of the mountains and finally agreed in 1818 to jointly occupy the Oregon Country, which was the area north of the 42nd parallel west of the Rocky Mountains and to the parallel 54 degrees 40 minutes in the north. In 1846 the two countries agreed to extend the 49th parallel as the boundary from the Rocky Mountains to the Strait of Georgia between the state of Washington and British Vancouver Island. (For additional information see the discussion in the Washington section in chapter 10.)

With North Dakota and South Dakota. When Congress created Idaho Territory in 1863 it put the border between it and Dakota Territory at the 27th meridian west of Washington. Just why Congress chose that meridian is not disclosed, but one can speculate that Congress was looking to the future when Dakota Territory would be divided into two states with the resulting total area of each of those states being about equal to other central plains states and its propensity to place western boundaries along parallels and meridians. This boundary was already established when Congress created Montana Territory in 1864.

Boundary definitions sometimes created strange anomalies, and this happened in the southwestern part of Montana. Often when the boundaries of a new jurisdiction were described they would be in reference to the boundaries of established jurisdictions. The northern boundary of a new area might simply be described as the southern boundary of an existing jurisdiction to the north of it. In the case of a small parcel of land in southwestern Montana, this was not the case. An isolated 4-square-mile piece of land that is called the "Lost Dakota Territory" came about because of the boundary definitions of three different territories.

First of all, the creation of Montana Territory in May 1864 defined its southern boundary along the 45th parallel from the 27th to the 34th meridian west of Washington, then south along the 34th meridian to the parallel of 43 degrees 30 minutes, then west along this parallel to the crest of the Rocky Mountains and then north along these mountains. (See map 9.6. Note that the Lost Dakota Territory is not shown in proper

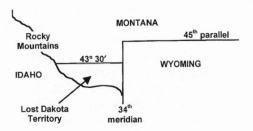

Map 9.6. Lost Dakota Territory

scale in this map, but it does adequately show the area where the territory was located.) At this same time the remainder of Idaho Territory east of the Rockies and east of the 33rd meridian was attached to Dakota Territory.

The second territory to exclude the Lost Dakota Territory was Idaho Territory because a part of its eastern boundary was described as along the crest of the Rocky Mountains. The third was Wyoming Territory because Congress defined its western boundary in 1868 as the 34th meridian west of Washington. So all three territorial definitions excluded a small triangular chunk of land about 4 miles long on the north and 2 miles long on the east that still technically belonged to Dakota Territory, the closest part of which was more than 300 miles to the east. Once Congress realized this anomaly, the Dakota representative in Congress introduced a bill to attach the area to Montana. This made sense because the boundary line between Idaho and Montana was along the crest of the Rocky Mountains in this area. Congress passed the bill in 1873.

With Wyoming. Montana's border with Wyoming at the 45th parallel is an arbitrary line that was placed there mostly likely because it was easy to draw on a map. Nonetheless, this boundary does have some rationale. People in Idaho Territory in 1864 were aware of the phenomenon of what would become Yellowstone National Park. Those in the area north of Yellowstone had the glitter of gold in their eyes and were not necessarily interested in a land that looked more like hell than anything. Seeing this area as a potential tourist mecca was not important in the 1860s. Therefore, the decision was made in Congress to draw the line arbitrarily along the 45th parallel thinking that would be north of "Colter's Hell." It was close, but when the park was created in 1872 thin pieces of it overlapped into Montana and Idaho. Unexplained in the Montana-Wyoming boundary is a fairly uniform southerly dip from the 45th parallel that the line takes in Yellowstone National Park. Correspondence with the park and county historical societies in which the anomaly occurs in both states failed to uncover an explanation.

The story explaining the north-south segment of the Montana-Wyoming border is that the intention again was to skirt Yellowstone and draw a line south to the Continental Divide. This nearly happened, but it still leaves a slice of the park in Montana and Idaho. Why it was deemed necessary to stop the east-west line at the 34th meridian west of Washington and then go south to the Continental Divide rather than continuing west along the 45th parallel to the divide is not explained.

Montana Territory memorialized Congress in May 1866 asking for its southern boundary to be moved 1 degree south to the 44th parallel between the 114th and 106th meridians. The reasoning behind this request was that Montanans felt they could better support and protect the miners who where moving into the area which was, at that time, a part of Dakota Territory. The area was effectively beyond the reach of the Dakota Territorial capital in Yankton, in present southeast South Dakota. The Montanans also felt the additional degree would add symmetry to Montana's western and southern boundaries, thereby placing the boundary on a more-natural and better-defined line than the current one. This proposal would have redefined a part of the western boundary which was then along the crest of the Rocky Mountains, but it is curious as to why the proposal didn't extend the line all the way to the 27th meridian west of Washington (104th meridian west of Greenwich). In any event, the proposal did not get anywhere in Congress, probably because it would have made a state that is already very large even larger.

With Idaho. The boundary between Montana and Idaho was decided in Washington, D.C., and seemed to make sense to politicians a couple of thousand miles away from the affected area. The Territory of Idaho was enormous in 1864, so when the territorial legislature petitioned Congress to form a new territory east of the Rocky Mountains, Congress was receptive. The process of locating the boundary required considerable negotiation. Sidney Edgerton, then an Idaho Territory justice and representing the interests on the east side of the Rocky Mountains (later governor of Montana from June 1864 to July 1866), managed to persuade Idaho's territorial delegate to Congress William Wallace that part of the boundary should be along the Bitterroot Mountains rather than the Rocky Mountains. (See map 10.7.) (Wallace was a busy politician. He had earlier been both governor and territorial delegate of Washington Territory.)

Edgerton's overt reasoning was that settlers, especially miners, between the two mountain ranges were denied access to the Idaho capital of Lewiston for about eight months of the year and that even in good weather it was a two-month trip. This placed a hardship on miners and others wanting to file claims. On the other hand, access to Bannack, which became Montana's first territorial capital, was available year-round. Wallace and other influential politicians bought into this idea. Wallace and Edgerton presented this boundary plan to the House Committee on Territories, which placed the boundary along the Bitterroots. This was passed by both the House and Senate and became law. A covert reason of Edgerton's was that he wanted to maintain for Montana the rich mines and farmland between the mountain ranges.

Idahoans expected the boundary with Montana to be along the Rocky Mountains, and the Bitterroots are considerably west of the Rockies, causing a considerable loss of land. (See map 10.7.) This loss so incensed the citizens of Idaho that Wallace was relieved of the duties of his office in the next election. Consequently, the boundary now runs considerably west of where most Idahoans intended it to be, creating the thin Idaho Panhandle which, for many years, was nearly inaccessible from the south because of the rugged Salmon River Mountains. Idaho petitioned Congress to return this "stolen" area, but it was unsuccessful. Various schemes were advanced later that would have formed a territory out of eastern Washington, northern Idaho, and western Montana, but these proposals got nowhere.

Since the boundary is following a mountain range, one might wonder why the Montana-Idaho border becomes a straight line in the north. The reason is that the Bitterroots become indistinct near the 48th parallel, so the last 70 miles is a line drawn due north to the 49th parallel.

New Mexico

Hostilities between the United States and Mexico heightened after the United States annexed Texas in 1845. The United States considered the boundary between the two countries as the Rio Grande, while Mexico considered the boundary the Nueces River northeast of the Rio Grande. (See map 8.15.) In a show of force the United States stationed troops west of the Nueces River. Responding to this, Mexico sent troops across the Rio Grande, which the United States considered an invasion of its territory, and the Mexican War of 1846–1848 began.

This war ended with the Treaty of Guadalupe Hidalgo establishing the boundary at the Rio Grande. In this treaty Mexico ceded to the United States territory which comprised the future states of California, Nevada and Utah; large parts of Arizona and New Mexico; and small sections of Colorado and Wyoming. (See map 1.1.) The international border was vaguely defined and based on a map that was latter discovered to be inaccurate. Generally, the boundary ascended the Rio Grande from the Gulf of Mexico to the southern boundary of the Department of New Mexico, as it was known under the Republic of Mexico. The boundary then proceeded west along the department's boundary to its western extremity, and then north along the department's western boundary to the Gila River, and then westward along the Gila to its confluence with the Colorado River. From this point it went in a straight line to a point on the Pacific Coast 1 marine league (3 miles) south of the southernmost part of the Port of San Diego. (See maps 1.1 and 9.7.)

Surveyors, interpreting treaty language as best they could, put the east-west line about 40 miles north of El Paso, which was about 32 miles further north than the U.S. treaty negotiators intended. A sharp dispute naturally arose between the two countries over this misunderstanding. In the treaty the United States had intended a boundary that would give it a route for a railroad to the west

Map 9.7. New Mexico Territory

and the potentially rich farming area in the Mesilla Valley in southern New Mexico. Since the boundary drawn from the provisions of the Treaty of Guadalupe Hidalgo didn't provide for a suitable railroad route to the west, the United States sent diplomat and railroad entrepreneur James Gadsden to Mexico to negotiate the purchase of additional land in 1853. He was successful in negotiating a block of land called the "Gadsden Purchase." (See map 9.7.)

By 1850 California, also a part of the Mexican Cession, had already formed a provisional government and had specified boundaries. Congress was willing to grant California the boundaries it asked for, so Congress wrestled with how to divide the remainder of the Mexican Cession. Some proposals were to divide the area along north-south axes and some east-west. They settled on an east-west axis and considered several parallels of latitude for dividing the area into Utah and New Mexico territories. Stephen A. Douglas, chairman of the Senate Committee on Territories, suggested the 38th parallel west of the Rocky Mountains but was willing to accept the 37th or even 36 degrees 30 minutes as the boundary between New Mexico and Utah territories. He wanted to include as many of the Mormon settlements as possible in the northern territory and still divide the area fairly equally. The placement of the boundary was also tied to the extension of slavery problem that was then gripping the country. A vote to put the boundary at 36° 30' failed by only one vote; the 37th parallel was accepted as a compromise between northerners and southerners. The boundary east of the Continental Divide was the 38th parallel because this area had traditionally been occupied by Hispanics who looked to Santa Fe for what government the area had.

New Mexico is bounded almost entirely by lines of latitude and longitude, the only exception being the 15 or so miles along the Rio Grande.

With Mexico. Mexico was in need of money in the 1850s and agreed to sell addi-

tional land to the United States. U.S. emissary James Gadsden had hoped to acquire enough land to get a U.S. port on the Gulf of California but was unable to do this. He did, however, acquire 29,640 square miles of land south of the Gila River that was suitable for the railroad. The purchase also included the rich farm lands the United States had expected to get in the Treaty of Guadalupe Hidalgo. The United States paid $10 million for land that is, with some exception, largely barren, deserted, and desolate. This purchase moved New Mexico's southern boundary to a line beginning where the parallel of 31 degrees 47 minutes crosses the Rio Grande, then west on this parallel for 100 miles, then south to the parallel of 31 degrees 20 minutes, and continuing west on that parallel to the Arizona border. (See map 9.7.)

With Arizona. Congress established the New Mexico boundary with Arizona when it divided New Mexico Territory and created Arizona Territory in 1863. The reasons for dividing the territory were familiar — remoteness of the westerners from the capital in Santa Fe, lack of governmental protection, and inadequate administration. Several proposals surfaced in Congress to divide New Mexico Territory. Southerners favored an east-west dividing line thinking that slavery would be more likely to extend to the area with such a division. Northerners favored a north-south dividing line because they did not want to see slavery extended in the west. The latter won out because southern states seceded from the Union in 1860–61 and Congress set the dividing line for Arizona Territory as an extension of the western Colorado boundary — the 32nd meridian west of Washington. This satisfied Congress's propensity for placing western boundaries along meridians and parallels and divided the territory nearly equally.

With Colorado. As originally constituted, the Colorado–New Mexico boundary was along the 37th parallel west of the Rocky Mountains and the 38th parallel east of them. Congress took New Mexico's land north of the 37th parallel in 1861 and added it to Colorado Territory. (See map 9.7.) The change was made to provide Colorado with a straight southern boundary, thus matching its other three borders. New Mexico's delegate in Congress protested this loss in 1865 but without positive effect. The change added symmetry to the region's boundaries, but the people living in the area had traditionally been aligned with New Mexico in culture and politics.

The 37th parallel is the longest continuous straight-line boundary in the United States (allowing for curvature of the earth). It stretches about 1,000 miles from the western Missouri border to the eastern border of Nevada. A slight jog in the boundary in the New Mexico county of Rio Arriba is due to errors in survey alignment and measurement.

With Oklahoma. When Congress hammered out an agreement in 1850 with Texas establishing its western boundary at the 103rd meridian, New Mexico's entire eastern boundary was set as an extension of that line, thereby establishing New Mexico's boundary with Oklahoma. However, the boundary with Oklahoma and Texas do not constitute a straight line. (See map 9.8.) The boundary with Oklahoma is about 2.1 miles east of the Texas boundary. The discrepancy is because the Oklahoma portion of the line was surveyed by a different crew from that of the Texas portion of the line. The Oklahoma portion is accurately placed, while the Texas portion is not.

With Texas. The struggle to establish the Texas–New Mexico boundary was protracted and hard fought. When Texas entered the Union in 1845, it considered its western boundary to be the Rio Grande all the way to its headwaters in Colorado and then due north to the 42nd parallel. (See map 8.15.) The federal government did not agree, as Texas had never established any control in the Santa Fe area. Texans were adamant

Map 9.8. New Mexico

about retaining control to the Rio Grande. The issue was tied to slavery politics, and so it pitted the South against the North. U.S. troops, leftover from the Mexican War, were in Santa Fe and aided the locals to set up a rudimentary government.

Notwithstanding Texas pride of not wanting to lose any precious soil, the state needed money to pay off its creditors from its days as a republic. Some of those creditors were influential easterners who were exerting pressure on Texans to pay up. Texas senators Sam Houston and Thomas J. Rusk were both willing to sell some Texas land, much of which they felt could never support slavery or much of anything else anyway, but they needed a plan that would protect Texas interests and their own political careers.

Congress considered several proposals for establishing the boundary. One was to run a straight line from the Rio Grande and 32nd parallel to the intersection of the 100th meridian and Red River. Another, by Maryland senator James A. Pearce, was strictly latitudinal and longitudinal lines that began at the 100th meridian and parallel of 36 degrees 30 minutes, ran west to the 102nd meridian, then south to the 33rd parallel, then west to the Rio Grande.

Pearce used the 102nd meridian to gain support of northerners knowing they wanted to limit the western expansion of slavery. The 33rd parallel was a compromise, as other groups proposed the 34th and 32nd parallels. Texans didn't like the 102nd meridian because it created an unsightly and thin northern panhandle. Northern senators opposed the 33rd parallel because it included within Texas some settlements traditionally seen as New Mexican.

To meet the objections to his proposal, Pearce moved the north-south boundary to the 103rd meridian and the east-west boundary to the 32nd parallel. (See map 8.15.) Rusk and Houston accepted this plan. It didn't satisfy everyone, but at least it was enough to pass Congress. Southern radicals didn't like it partly because they were hoping for a military confrontation in New Mexico that would lead to secession of southern states. Texas received $10 million for the land it ceded to the federal government.

The two states disputed their short boundary along the Rio Grande resulting in New Mexico bringing suit against Texas in the U.S. Supreme Court in 1920. New Mexico contended that the boundary should be where the Rio Grande channel was in 1850 before an 1864 avulsion; Texas agreed. They disagreed, however, on where the river was in that year. Both states presented maps supporting their case. The court appointed a special master, who, after reviewing all the pertinent data, ruled in favor of Texas. As a consequence, the current boundary varies from ½ to 2½ miles west of the river and is sinuous as one would expect from an old riverbed.

Utah

Fleeing persecution in the United States, Mormons entered the unorganized area of the Salt Lake Valley of Utah in 1847 and decided this was the place for them to settle. They wanted the federal government to establish a government, but that request was denied. Church leaders then decided in 1849 to set up their own government called "Deseret."

Although Deseret had indefinite boundaries, it was nonetheless huge. It covered all of Utah, most of Nevada and Arizona, and parts of Oregon, California, New Mexico, Colorado, Wyoming, and Idaho. (See map 9.9.) The area encompassed in Deseret had little rainfall, little arable land, and a good deal of it was an area of internal drainage called the "Great Basin." To indicate what a lot of people thought of the area, Senator James A. Seddon of Virginia, a man who would be a secretary of war in the Confederate States of America, said during congressional debates that the Utah Territory had been given to the Mormons because it was mostly worthless. A notable aspect of Deseret was that it included access to the Pacific Ocean near the present city of San Diego. Although the federal government never recognized Deseret, the idea of establishing temporary governments, not sanctioned by Congress, had previously been done in Oregon, Tennessee, Vermont, and California.

Map 9.9. Deseret

Owing to the massive migration of Mormon settlers into Utah, the federal government recognized that a government needed to be formed for the area, although some U.S. congressmen considered the Mormons unfit for self government. The impetus behind the establishment of government in the area was the U.S. acquisition of the Mexican Cession stemming from the 1848 Treaty of Guadalupe Hidalgo. The cession consisted essentially of all land south of the 42nd parallel and north of the Gila River, from the Pacific Ocean to the Rio Grande. (See map 1.1.) The United States divided this huge area into three jurisdictions in 1850 — California, New Mexico Territory, and Utah Territory. Utah Territory was bounded on the west by California, on the east by the Rocky Mountains, by the 42nd parallel in the north, and by the 37th parallel in the south. (See map 9.10.)

The territory, created in 1850, was only a temporary arrangement and later lost land to the territories of Colorado, Nebraska, Idaho, Nevada, and Wyoming and the state of Nevada before it was pared to its final size. The reasons for the loss of land were because Congress never intended for Utah to remain so large when it originally created the territory and other regional interests had to be satisfied in the form of additional territories and the needs of miners. Another important factor was that the polygamous Mormons were despised in the Congress and by U.S. citizens generally and so never had much political clout. Additionally, the Mormons were frequently involved in serious confrontations with federally appointed territorial officials. The Mormons were also suspected and accused of being robbers and murderers. Congress demanded the complete denouncement of polygamy in 1870 before statehood would be granted; the Mormons did so in 1890, and Utah entered the Union in 1896 as the forty-fifth state. Utah is the smallest of the states formed from the Mexican Cession.

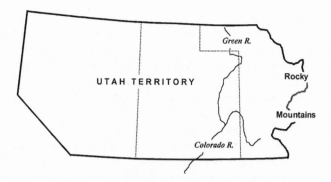

Map 9.10. Utah Territory

The southeast corner of Utah is where four states intersect at a common point called "Four Corners," the only place in the United States where this occurs. Utah is one of three states with boundaries consisting entirely of lines of latitude and longitude — the other two are Colorado and Wyoming.

With Nevada. Miners discovered silver east of the Sierra Nevada Mountains in the extreme western part of Utah Territory in the mid 1850s. As the word got around, more miners entered the area, and they soon outnumbered the Mormons who had settled there. In an effort to regain control of the area, the Mormons sent additional members to the town of Genoa (near Virginia City), but still they did not outnumber the miners. (See map 10.8.)

The miners did not want to be a part of predominantly agricultural and Mormon Utah and petitioned California to annex western Utah. California asked Congress to extend the upper part of its eastern border to the 118th meridian, an additional 2 degrees to the east. Congress ignored the request but took note of the needs of miners in western Utah Territory. Then in 1857 the residents of Genoa petitioned Congress to form a territory separate from Utah. This petition passed the House but died in the Senate. A similar request died in 1859. Later that year the Comstock Lode (just northeast of the bend in the west boundary of Nevada) was discovered, and miners flocked to the area, swelling the population enough to make territorial status a possibility. Southern states opposed the creation of another territory because they feared it would be a nonslave area. When southern states seceded in 1860–61 the main opposition to territorial status for Nevada no longer existed, and Nevada became a territory in 1861.

The first eastern boundary for Nevada Territory was the 39th meridian west of Washington (approximately 116 degrees west of Greenwich). (See map 10.8.) The next year Congress sliced an additional degree of longitude from Utah Territory and added it to the eastern boundary of Nevada Territory. Nevada became a state in 1864 and then in 1866 received another degree of longitude on its eastern border at the expense of Utah Territory, placing its boundary at the 37th degree west of Washington (approximately 114 degrees west of Greenwich). The reasons Nevada received this additional land at the expense of Utah Territory was because Nevada wanted the rich mining area of Pahranagat and had the political clout to get it. Other factors were to compensate Nevada for land it did not get in its negotiations with California in 1862 and the strained relations between the federal government and the Mormons.

Map 9.11. Utah

With Idaho. The northern limit of Mexican lands was the 42nd parallel, and this established the boundary with Idaho. Congress expanded Nebraska Territory in 1861 and took part of Utah's northeastern corner, creating a "notch." No explanation has been uncovered as to why Congress expanded Nebraska Territory to the 33rd meridian west of Washington that created the notch. This was the first instance whereby Utah got a "notch" in the northeast part of the territory. When Congress created Idaho Territory in 1863, it was given this area as well as a great deal of other land.

With Wyoming. The east-west part of the Utah-Wyoming border is the result of the protrusion of Nebraska Territory in 1861 and the extension of the northern Colorado boundary when Congress reduced the size of Nebraska Territory in 1861. (See map 9.11.) Why Congress placed the western boundary of Nebraska Territory at the 33rd meridian west of Washington rather than the 32nd meridian, the western edge of Colorado, is not known.

When Congress created Wyoming Territory in 1868, it took 1 more degree of the "notch" from Utah and added it to Wyoming. For unexplained reasons Congress wanted to make Wyoming a rectangular state and was willing to take more land from Utah to do that. Congress also took 1 degree from eastern Idaho to add to Wyoming. (See maps 10.6 and 10.7.) Part of the argument in Congress was that extending the notch would place it along a mountain range, and the area was not populated. Some justification exists in this reasoning because the current boundary is only about 3 miles east of the Crawford Mountains. These mountains, however, do not run continuously along this border, so the rationale is somewhat specious.

With Colorado. Utah Territory's eastern boundary was the Rocky Mountains, east of the Rockies was Kansas Territory. Miners in western Kansas Territory didn't fit in well with the farmers in the eastern part of that territory and asked Congress for their own territory in 1859. This request went unheeded, but in 1861 Congress created Colorado Territory partly from western Kansas and partly from eastern Utah Territory. The thinking of Congress in taking land from Utah was that miners were dominant not only on the eastern slopes of the mountains but also on the western slopes, and they should all be in one jurisdiction. The Congressional repugnance toward Mormons was another factor. The boundary between the two territories was placed at 32 degrees west of Washington (approximately 109 degrees west of Greenwich) in a desolate area about halfway between the growing cities of Denver and Salt Lake City. A slight jog exists in the Colorado-Utah boundary in the Utah county of San Juan that is due to faulty surveying.

With Arizona. The United States acquired a lot of land from Mexico as spoils of the war between that country and the United States in 1846–1848. The boundaries of the cession were delineated in the 1848 Treaty of Guadalupe Hidalgo. Congress divided the cession into the state of California and the territories of New Mexico and Utah in 1850.

The ultimate boundary between the states of Utah and Arizona came from the deliberations in Congress as it considered the boundary between the territories of Utah and New Mexico. Stephen Douglas, chairman of the Senate Committee on Territories and senator from Illinois, first suggested that the 38th parallel as the boundary, or even the 37th parallel, so as to include most of the Mormon settlements within Utah. Southern congressmen, however, were in favor of the 36th parallel or perhaps 36 degrees 30 minutes. Their thinking was that such a line would extend the Missouri Compromise line further west and thus extend the area in which slavery would be permitted. A vote to put the line at 36° 30' failed by only one vote. What the southern senators failed to adequately recognize was that the arid land of the West was not conducive to support the plantation slave culture of the South, so their energies would never bear fruit in the West under any circumstances. Northern senators wanted the boundary put at the 38th parallel as they wanted to limit Mormon influence. After the failure to place the line at 36° 30', the Senate settled on the 37th parallel in July 1850 as a political compromise without much consideration either for geography nor the people who lived in the area. The House later concurred in the placement of the line.

The issue was not entirely settled, however, as far as the Mormons were concerned. In 1865 the Utah territorial legislature asked Congress to move its southwestern boundary to the Colorado River, an area called the "Arizona Strip" (areas *A* and *B* on map 9.3). The Utahns seemed to think that having control over this part of the Colorado River would given them access to a navigable part of the river and thus an outlet to the Gulf of California and then to the Pacific Ocean. This proposal never made it out of congressional committee.

Utah was nonetheless persistent in trying to get the area in Arizona north of the Colorado River. Between the years of 1897 and 1910, after Utah became a state and Arizona was still a territory, Utah made further attempts to acquire land north of the Colorado River (area *B* on map 9.3). First Utah tried to persuade the Arizona Territory legislature to cede it the area. Arizona was understandably opposed to such an idea. Then Utah tried to convince Congress to give it the area. Utah was hoping that its status as a state would have a positive impact on Congress at the expense of the lesser status of a territory. This proposal didn't get out of committee. Utah made an additional attempt to get the "Strip" in 1919, but Congress turned this proposal down as it had the previous ones. Utah's requests, while not very realistic, were not without merit. It claimed that the sparsely settled area was cut off from Arizona and that what settlements existed there were mostly Mormon and had strong ties to Utah. All this was true, but it had no effect on Congress.

Map 9.12.
Dakota Territory

Wyoming

The area that became Wyoming fell into several different jurisdictions during its history. In 1861 the northern part was in Dakota Territory that Congress created from Nebraska Territory. (See map 7.14.) Then in 1863 it came within the aegis of Idaho Territory. (See map 10.6.) In 1864 Idaho Territory was pared down as Congress created Montana Territory and returned most of what would become Wyoming back to Dakota Territory. (See map 9.12)

The boundaries of Wyoming were not an important consideration in the early 1860s because that area was just a place to go through on the way to greener pastures farther west. All that changed when the Union Pacific Railroad tracks reached Wyoming in 1867 and the population began to boom.

At that time Wyoming was a part of Dakota Territory and territorial officials in Yankton, in the eastern part of the territory, were small-town shopkeepers, merchants, and farmers. Most of them were willing to get rid of their western area because their interests and pursuits differed from those in that part of the territory. They also feared the population boom in the western part of the territory would grow so fast that the rough-and-tumble miners of South Pass and hell-on-wheels railroaders would come to dominate territorial politics. Other reasons were that travel and communication be-

tween the two discrete areas was very difficult.

Another factor was that the creation of Montana Territory in 1864 had divided Dakota Territory into two easily identifiable areas, further suggesting division. (See map 9.12.) As a consequence, the westerners, in collusion with lobbyists for the Union Pacific Railroad, petitioned Congress in 1865 to create a separate territory in the western part of Dakota Territory with the name "Lincoln," although other names were also suggested. Congress did not heed the request nor similar requests for a new territory over the next two years. By 1868, however, Congress could no longer ignore the requests of officials in Yankton and the growing city of Cheyenne in the western part of Dakota Territory, and territorial status was granted to the western area, calling it "Wyoming Territory." Congress balked at the name Lincoln because it didn't want to name the territory for a president. However, Congress had no such qualms in naming Washington Territory in 1853 to honor the first president.

The boundaries for Wyoming territory, which also became state boundaries in 1890, were the 27th and 34th meridians west of Washington and the 41st and 45th parallels. Wyoming is one of only three states with boundaries formed entirely by lines of latitude and longitude, the others are Colorado and Utah. New Mexico is also almost entirely bounded by lines of latitude and longitude, the exception being about 15 miles of border with Texas along an old Rio Grande riverbed west of the current river.

The area included in Wyoming came from parts of the Louisiana Purchase, the Oregon Country, and the Mexican Cession. (See map 1.1.) At various times it had also been included in the Territory and District of Louisiana, Indian Country, Republic of Texas, and the territories of Missouri, Nebraska, Idaho, Dakota, Oregon, Washington, and Utah.

With Utah. When Congress created Wyoming Territory in 1868 it seemed bent, due to the prodding of influential members, on the idea of making the new territory rectangular, and so they took a piece of the northeastern Utah Territory notch and added it to the new territory. Congress felt that the Mormons had abandoned the area and thus had no misgivings about adding it to Wyoming. Advocates for taking this land from Utah advanced the argument that extending the notch would place it along a range of mountains. The current boundary does in fact come within about 3 miles of the Crawford Mountains. These mountains are not continuous, however, so the argument was a little weak. Keep in mind that Congressional knowledge of western geography was sparse. Since a part of the notch had already been given to Nebraska Territory in 1861, taking more of it apparently didn't pose a problem for Congress.

The east-west part of the Wyoming-Utah boundary stems from when Congress reduced the size of Nebraska Territory and made this border an extension of the northern border of Colorado Territory, which they created in 1861.

With Idaho. When Congress severed the western part of Dakota Territory and formed Wyoming Territory in 1868, Wyoming had an irregular western border. (See map 9.12.) It was the will of Congress, or at least of some of its influential members, to make Wyoming rectangular. To do this they sliced off 1 degree of longitude from Idaho and added it to Wyoming. It was also the intent of Congress to make Wyoming a large territory because they considered it a part of the Great American Desert and felt it would take a lot of land to sustain a population necessary to form a future state. Also, congressional members maintained that the area to be removed from Idaho Territory had no inhabitants and thus would generate no opposition.

The Idaho delegate to Congress, perhaps remembering what happened to previous Idaho territorial delegate William Wallace after his part in the determination of the

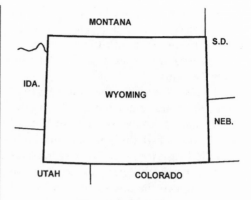

Map 9.13. Wyoming

Idaho-Montana boundary, spoke sharply against the loss of a slice of eastern Idaho to the proposed Wyoming Territory. The editor of the *Cheyenne Leader*, however, made the unfounded claim that the 1-degree-wide area was intended by nature to be a part of Wyoming. The delegate's protestation notwithstanding, Congress gave the Idaho area and a piece of Utah to Wyoming to make it a rectangular territory. (See map 9.13.)

With Montana. When Congress formed Montana Territory out of Dakota Territory in 1864 they placed the new territory's southern boundary along the 45th parallel. They chose this parallel with the intent of keeping the boiling cauldron called "Colter's Hell," now Yellowstone National Park, out of Montana. Montanans were interested in gold and not interested in a desolate area of geysers and sulfur springs. When the park was created in 1872, it extended slightly across the Wyoming boundary into Montana.

The same rationale was used in the north-south boundary between Wyoming and Montana, i.e., an attempt to keep Yellowstone in Dakota Territory and not in Montana Territory. Congress chose the 34th meridian west of Washington as the point to go south from the 45th parallel. Again, a thin piece of the park is west of the Wyoming boundary in Montana and Idaho. In drawing this north-south line Congress wanted to extend the boundary to the Continental Divide, which it did. However, it is not clear why Congress felt it needed to head south rather than continuing along the 45th parallel west to intersect with the divide other than the idea of creating a rectangular Wyoming Territory.

The Montana-Wyoming boundary line, like most others, is not precisely along the 45th parallel. Near the west end of Yellowstone National Park the boundary line takes a 21-mile-long, ¾-mile-wide jog to the south then back north that seems too regular to be a correction in the line or mere surveyor error. The author communicated with officials at the park, county historical societies encompassing the area, and the states of Montana and Wyoming, but no one knows the reason for the jog.

With South Dakota. In January 1867 the Dakota Legislative Assembly created Laramie County consisting of that part of the territory west of the 104th meridian. This county boundary, an extension of the eastern boundary of Montana, became the future eastern boundary of the territory and state of Wyoming. This meridian had been established as a boundary in 1863 when Congress originally created the huge Idaho Territory. (Congress chose the 27th meridian west of Washington rather than the 104th west of Greenwich.) Why Congress chose this meridian is not known, but it may have been looking to the future when Dakota Territory would be divided into two states that would have nearly equal areas to other states in the central Plains area.

With Nebraska. The Nebraska-Wyoming boundary is an extension of the South Dakota–Wyoming boundary and results from the formation of Laramie County in 1867 and the 1868 congressional act when Congress placed the eastern boundary of Wyoming at the 27th meridian west of Washington. This meridian had previously been the eastern boundary of Idaho Territory created by Congress in 1863. Congress wanted to make Wyoming rectangular, and this boundary helped maintain the symmetry.

With Colorado. Congress didn't know much about the west when it formed Colorado Territory boundaries in 1861 and placed them without regard to natural features. The territory's northern boundary was put at the 41st parallel. The territory was content with this until it became apparent that a transcontinental railroad was going to run north of the territory. In 1867 Colorado officials petitioned Congress to have their northern border raised 1 degree into what was then Dakota Territory. Congress was not receptive, and the proposal died.

The reasons for the choice of the 41st parallel are not explicitly stated, but in dividing the West Congress was always looking at how the area could be parceled into individual states. It knew much of the West was very arid, and it believed that the area would not sustain a large population. It followed, therefore, that in order for a potential territory to have a large enough population for admittance as a state into the Union, Congress needed to create large areas. Colorado's claim for an additional degree would have created a state larger than apparently deemed necessary to sustain such a population. Furthermore, Congress probably felt that 1 degree would be needed by a state to the north. This is speculation on the part of the author, but it makes sense from what is known about western boundary decisions.

10

WEST REGION

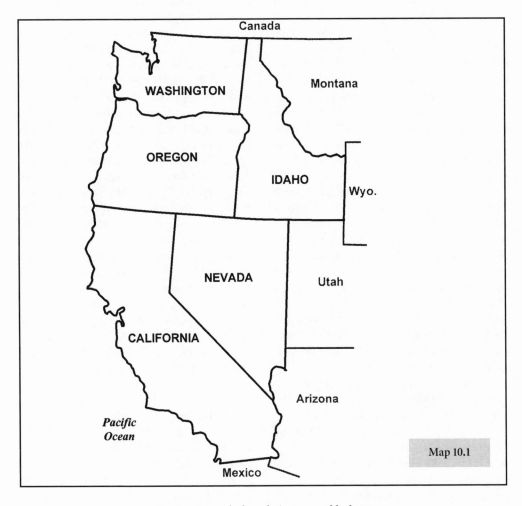

Canada

WASHINGTON

Montana

OREGON

IDAHO

Wyo.

NEVADA

Utah

CALIFORNIA

Arizona

Pacific
Ocean

Map 10.1

Mexico

Map is not to scale; boundaries are roughly drawn.

California

Although California is the most populous state in the Union and the third largest in size behind Alaska and Texas, 450 years ago it was sparsely settled by Native Americans and only in the incipient stages of being explored by the Spaniards. California became part of Spanish America and later passed into Mexican control when Mexico won its independence from Spain in 1821.

California came under the aegis of the United States in 1848 as part of the Mexican Cession in the Treaty of Guadalupe Hidalgo negotiated after the 1846–1848 Mexican War. Californians wanted to enter the Union without going through the territorial stage that was so popular with Congress. California delegates met in 1849 to form a government, draw boundaries, and petition Congress for admittance to the Union as a state. The eastern boundary posed the only real challenge; the northern and southern boundaries were already recognized, and the western boundary was the Pacific Ocean coastline.

While the California delegates were wrestling with the problem of creating a state, Congress grappled with the bigger question of how to divide the Mexican Cession, a chunk of land extending from the international boundary with Mexico to the 42nd parallel and from the Rocky Mountains to the Pacific Ocean. (See map 1.1.) The Congressional act that created the state of California also created the territories of Utah and New Mexico thus bringing U.S. government to all the Mexican Cession.

The boundaries proposed by California delegates created a very large and geographically diverse area. Congress approved these boundaries in large part because it thought the area consisted of a large portion of desert and mountains and did not contain a disproportionate amount of arable land. Nonetheless, the fact that California is so large gave rise to proposals beginning in 1861 and lasting into modern times to divide California along an east-west axis into two states. None of the proposals has won widespread favor.

With Oregon. When France sold the Louisiana Purchase to the growing United States in 1803, this new nation became an unwelcome neighbor to Spain's lands in the New World. The boundaries of the purchase were vague, and this caused a very uneasy situation between the two countries that demanded a resolution. When Charles Maurice de Talleyrand-Périgord, the French minister of foreign affairs, was asked by U.S. statesman James Monroe and American minister to France Robert R. Livingston about the boundaries, he said only, "You have made a noble bargain, I expect you will make the most of it."*

U.S. secretary of state John Quincy Adams and Don Luis de Onís, Spanish minister to Washington, met in 1819 to resolve the common border placement. Their negotiations resulted in the Adams-Onís Treaty that defined the boundary from the Gulf of Mexico all the way to the Pacific Ocean. (See map 8.14.) From the Rocky Mountains to the ocean they placed the border along the 42nd parallel. This parallel was then the boundary between Oregon Country and Spanish land. This treaty ultimately established the boundary between California and Oregon because it was an established boundary when the two jurisdictions were created. The actual line wanders back and forth across the true parallel by a small amount due to surveying inaccuracies. (See map 10.2.)

With Nevada. When the California delegates met in 1849, the location of the eastern boundary of California was a major concern. They discussed many different schemes for boundaries; some advocated an eastern boundary of the Rocky Mountains

*Quoted in Edward S. Barnard, ed., Story of the Great American West (Pleasantville, New York: The Reader's Digest Association, Inc.), p. 34.

to provide a large tax base. Opponents of this idea said such a large area could not effectively be governed and Congress would not allow it anyway. Another group advocated the crest of the Sierra Nevada in an attempt to avoid conflict with Mormon settlements. They also felt a smaller jurisdiction would have a better chance of congressional approval. Some delegates felt this created too small a state.

After considerable debate the delegates compromised on the two extremes and chose a boundary beginning at the 42nd parallel along the 120th meridian extending south to the 39th parallel, a point that is in Lake Tahoe. From this point the boundary is an oblique line to the junction of the 35th parallel and Colorado River, then down this river to the international boundary with Mexico. This boundary included both sides of the Sierra Nevada and placed the boundary somewhat parallel to the Pacific Ocean coastline. (See map 10.2.) The delegates felt this was a governable jurisdiction and one that Congress would approve. This proved to be the case when Congress admitted California as the thirty-first state in 1850.

California's eastern border was nonetheless the subject of later attempted revisions. When Congress created Nevada Territory in 1861, it set the western boundary of that territory at the crest of the Sierra Nevada, creating a very serious conflict with the state of California. This problem is dealt with more fully in the Nevada section in this chapter.

With Arizona. The 1849 California delegates set the boundary between California and Arizona as the middle of the channel of the Colorado River from the 35th parallel to the international boundary with Mexico. This seems straightforward enough except that the Colorado River floods and meanders and thus changes its course from time to time. This caused many boundary disputes between the two states. To settle the matter, both states appointed commissioners to meet and work out the conflicts. The com-

Map 10.2. California

missioners made an attempt to determine the channel when California became a state, but this was impossible, so the commission attempted to place the boundary so as to effect an equitable distribution of disputed land and fixed it so that future changes in the course of the river will not affect the boundary. The 1963 agreement effected by the commissioners placed the boundary mostly in the center of the channel according to 1962 aerial photographs, an exception is shown in map 10.3 where the dashed line is the boundary.

With Mexico. The 1848 Treaty of Guadalupe Hidalgo specified a line drawn from the confluence of the Gila and Colorado rivers to a point one marine league (about 3½ miles) south of the southernmost part of the Port of San Diego according to the plan of the port made in 1782.

With Pacific Ocean. The U.S. Geological Survey says that generally speaking the individual states recognize an offshore boundary of 3 nautical miles. The United States territorial sea limit contiguous zone has been set at 12 nautical miles but is expected to be extended to 24 nautical miles. The exclusive

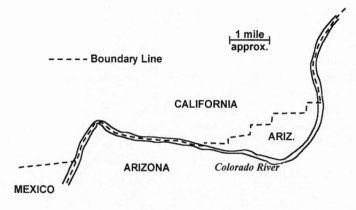

Map 10.3. Lower California-Arizona Boundary

economic zone boundary is 200 nautical miles. (A nautical mile equals 1.15 land miles.)

Idaho

When Congress established the boundary for the state of Oregon in 1859 and added the remainder of Oregon Territory to Washington Territory, it felt that the population of the forests and deserts east of the Cascade Mountains would proceed so slowly that no new territories would be needed for the remainder of the century. (See map 10.9C.) The 1860s gold rush to the Salmon and Clearwater River areas of Idaho changed that notion as population in the mining area soon exceeded that of the area west of the Cas-

cades. A movement began to create a territory exclusively for the mining interests along those two rivers in what would eventually become the state of Idaho. Part of the reason behind the movement to create a new territory was that administration of the mining area was almost impossible from the Washington territorial capital of Olympia on Puget Sound.

The territory that was to be created was Idaho. It was originally part of the Oregon Country, then the Oregon Territory, and then Washington Territory before becoming a territory of its own in 1863. Congress formed Idaho Territory from parts of the territories of Washington, Nebraska, and Dakota. (See maps 10.4 and 10.6.)

Idaho Territory as first created in 1863 was huge — larger than Texas. As with all large territories, this was only a temporary creation, and forces were quickly working to reduce it. Two of the early plans to divide Idaho Territory are shown on map 10.4. One plan would have divided it with an east-west axis (shown with dashed line on map 10.4) and named the northern part "Idaho Territory" and the southern portion "Montana Territory." Another plan would have divided the territory mostly along the crest of the Rocky Mountains with a short portion of the 113th meridian also used (shown with a dotted line on map 10.4) and named the territories "Idaho" and "Jefferson." These proposals did not carry the day when Congress created Montana Territory a little more than a year later in 1864. (See map 10.6.) At this time Congress also added the area that would become most of the territory and state of Wyoming to Dakota Territory, leaving Idaho Territory with the boundaries shown on map 10.6.

The shape of modern Idaho did not come about easily. The area was originally divided between Oregon and Washington

Map 10.4. Two Plans to Divide Idaho Territory

territories when Congress created Washington Territory in 1853. (See map 10.9*B*.) The area was united again in 1859 as part of Washington Territory when Oregon became a state. (See map 10.9*C*.) However, Idaho had a long history of north-south division because the two areas were separated by nearly impassable mountains. The northern Idahoans generally saw themselves as naturally aligned with eastern Washington and western Montana.

In 1886 Senator William M. Stewart of Nevada devised a plan that would have divided Idaho, annexing the Panhandle to Washington and the southern part to Nevada. Nevadans were in favor of this plan, and Stewart managed to get a bill passed in the U.S. Congress in 1887. The division so aroused the indignation of Idahoans that the territorial legislature approved a memorial denouncing the division. President Grover Cleveland vetoed the bill, and Idaho officials began to work out their differences.

The forces of division were only dormant and not dead. In 1907, seventeen years after statehood, certain interest groups proposed creating the Territory of Lincoln that would include not only the Idaho Panhandle but also a piece of western Washington and some of the northeast corner of Oregon. (See map 10.5*A*.) Southern Idaho would also have become larger under this proposal. This idea didn't get anywhere because state boundaries were already well established for all three states, and no one in Oregon nor Washington wanted to see them changed.

Again the matter of possible division of Idaho was revisited. In 1917 state legislators in both the northern and southern portions of Idaho suggested splitting the state. (See map 10.5*B*.) This plan actually passed the Idaho House of Representatives but failed in the senate.

With Montana. Idaho's boundary problems with Montana undoubtedly caused the most bitter taste to Idahoans of any of the border issues. Idaho had barely been formed into a territory when agitation began in

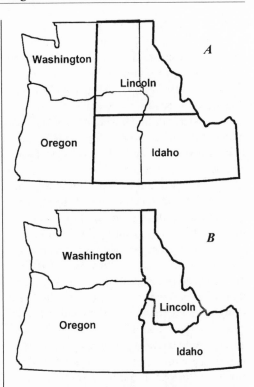

Map 10.5 A, B. Post-Statehood
Idaho Boundary Proposals

Montana to create another territory there. A plan presented in the U.S. Congress in late 1863 would have divided the huge Idaho Territory along an east-west axis with the northern part retaining the name Idaho and the southern part becoming Montana Territory. (See map 10.4.) James M. Ashley, chairman of the House Committee on Territories, strongly favored this plan.

This scheme did not get far as people pointed out that the natural division of the area was along a north-south axis, not east-west. Two north-south mountain ranges offered natural boundaries—the Bitterroots and the Rockies. A memorial from the Territory of Idaho to Congress suggested a boundary that generally followed the crest of the Rocky Mountains.

Early discussion, and certainly the goal of most Idahoans, was to put the eastern boundary along the crest of the Rocky Mountains, providing for a very sizeable state. The residents of Lewiston were especially in favor of this boundary; it was the territorial capital in 1863, and a boundary at the Rocky Mountains would enhance that city's chances of retaining its status. When Congress created Montana Territory in 1864, it ignored the requests of Gem State officials for a Rocky Mountain boundary and shifted much of the border to the Bitterroot Mountains, thus depriving Idaho of a very large chunk of land. (See map 10.7.)

The story about how the boundary got shifted from the Rockies to the Bitterroots is an interesting bit of politics. Sidney Edgerton, who had financial and political interests east of the Rockies and who was representing citizens from the eastern part of Idaho Territory, persuaded William H. Wallace, then Idaho's territorial delegate to the U.S. Congress and previously Idaho's territorial governor (who had also previously been a governor and territorial delegate from Washington Territory), to move the boundary from the Rockies to the Bitterroots. Edgerton's argument hinged on the idea that the Bitterroots created an impassable barrier for about two-thirds of the year and that people, mostly miners, living between the Bitterroots and Rockies faced a two-month journey even in good weather to the territorial capital of Lewiston to file claims. On the other hand, the Rocky Mountains were a much less formidable barrier, and citizens could travel easily from one mining camp to another between the two mountain chains. Wallace endorsed this idea, and the two men presented this boundary change to the House Committee on Territories. Congress enacted the boundary. Edgerton, who recognized not only the mining wealth of the area between the mountain ranges but also its richness as agricultural land, had considerable influence in Washington because he was a personal friend of Abraham Lincoln and other political shakers and movers.

Governor Wallace greatly misjudged the thinking of Idahoans, who were incensed when they discovered the boundary was not along the Rockies; they responded by voting Wallace out of office at the next election.

That the boundary was not along the Rockies is notable also because that had been a natural boundary between the Oregon Country and territories to the east. President Lincoln later appointed Edgerton as the first territorial governor of Montana.

The northern 70-or-so miles of the Idaho-Montana border does not follow the Bitterroot Mountains because the range becomes indistinct at about the 48th parallel. Therefore, at that point the decision was made to simply draw the boundary due north. The boundary description says that it should follow the Bitterroots to the 39th meridian west of Washington then due north to the 49th parallel.

With Wyoming. When Congress created Wyoming Territory in 1868, it set its western boundary at the 34th parallel west of Washington. This shaved 1 degree from Idaho's eastern boundary. (Compare maps 10.6 and 10.7.) Since Idaho and Utah, which also lost some land to Wyoming, were both territories at the time, Congress could make any shifts in boundaries it pleased, and it was the apparent goal of Congress to make Wyoming symmetrical, with straight-line boundaries, allowing, of course, for earth curvature.

The tendency of Congress to occasionally use meridians west of Washington rather than west of Greenwich caused some unforeseen problems. The 34th meridian runs through a rugged area of the Teton Mountains, putting a part of some valleys in Idaho and part of them in Wyoming and creating some local foment among the citizenry to change the boundary. An attempt was made in 1897 to get Congress to move the boundary, but it rejected the idea. Congress finally granted permission in 1931 to Idaho and Wyoming to adjust their common boundary in this area. After meetings held two years later with the seventy-four people who would be affected by a potential change, the citizens voted unanimously to leave the boundary as it was. The problem would not have occurred at all if Congress had used a Greenwich meridian as the boundary. The 111th meridian west of Greenwich is 2.29 miles east of the 34th meridian west of Washington. Such a boundary description would have placed the valleys almost entirely within Idaho.

With Utah and Nevada. The United States and Spain agreed to make the 42nd parallel their international boundary in 1819 from the Rocky Mountains to the Pacific Ocean under provisions of the Adams-Onís Treaty. (See map 8.14.) This parallel was thus an established boundary when Congress created the Northwest territories and states. Congress could have changed this boundary but chose not to do so.

Nevada made an attempt to move the boundary north in 1886. That state was suffering an economic downturn and was casting eyes on southern Idaho to augment its economic base. Some southern Idahoans favored this idea. The majority, however, including Idaho's governor and territorial delegate, did not. This annexation plan gave rise to a movement that Idaho must not be divided. This was quite a change in mindset for Idahoans, especially considering previous agitation to divide the territory. Nonetheless, Congress approved a bill to annex northern Idaho to Washington and southern Idaho to Nevada in 1887. President Grover Cleveland, however, refused to sign the bill. Now that Idahoans began to see themselves as a political unit even the northerners were happy the bill was not enacted. Astute politicians in Boise appeased the northerners by locating the state university in Lewiston.

With Oregon. The Idaho boundary with Oregon was set by

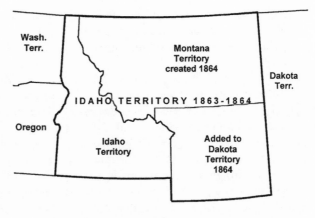

Map 10.6. Idaho Territory

Congress when it created the state of Oregon in 1859. The boundary runs south along the Snake River from the 46th parallel to the confluence of the Snake and Owyhee rivers where the boundary then goes due south to the 42nd parallel. (See map 10.7.) The reason Congress chose this boundary is not disclosed, but it likely had to do with ensuring that Oregon would have enough land to support a population suitable for a state. (This topic is covered in greater detail in the Oregon section of this chapter.) The Snake River does form a formidable boundary especially in the Snake River Canyon portion, and this fact may have been known to Congress at the time it created the state of Oregon. The

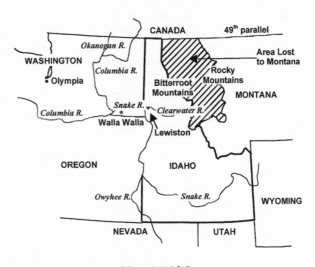

Map 10.7. Idaho

Snake River turns to the east at its confluence with the Owyhee River, so this made a natural point from which to continue the border south.

With Washington. Idaho was a part of Washington Territory when miners discovered gold along Idaho's Salmon and Clearwater rivers in the early 1860s. Their distance from the territorial capital of Olympia in western Washington Territory made governing impractical, and agitation began to split the huge territory. The Idaho-Washington boundary resulted from a lot of politics, principally among three towns that wanted to be the territorial capital. Olympia, on Puget Sound, wanted to continue its status as a territorial capital, whereas Lewiston, on the Snake River near the center of the territory, and Walla Walla, in the south-central part of the territory, wanted to become territorial capitals of the new territory to be created out of Washington Territory.

Olympia officials favored a boundary that was essentially an extension of the eastern Oregon border, that is, along the Snake River then due north at the confluence of the Snake and Clearwater rivers near Lewiston where the Snake River turns sharply west. Olympia liked this idea because it preserved as much land as possible for Washington Territory and still cut off the growing population of miners that threatened to move the capital to a city eastward. Lewiston didn't like this idea because it figured that it would not be the capital of anything if a border were placed near it. Lewiston did, however, become the first capital of Idaho Territory in 1863 when Congress created the territory. It lost this status in 1864 when Boise became the capital.

Lewiston officials favored a western boundary along the Cascade Mountains and preserving for the new territory the eastern Washington Territory boundary of the Rocky Mountains. The Portland *Oregonian* also promoted a boundary along the Cascades, some said at the insistence of the Oregon Steam Navigation Company which monop-

olized shipping on the Columbia River who felt their economic interests would best be served by a boundary along the Cascade Mountains.

Walla Walla, on the other hand, figured its chances for becoming a territorial capital were enhanced if the boundary were placed along the Columbia and Okanogan rivers. (See map 10.7.) In 1863 the U.S. House passed a bill to place the boundary along these rivers. Strong lobbying by officials from Olympia and the influence of William H. Wallace, former governor of Washington Territory and current delegate to Congress from that territory, convinced the Senate to change the boundary to that wanted by Olympia politicians, which is the present boundary.

Although Congress had placed the boundary, it was not settled in the minds of many politicians outside the national capital. A range of mountains in the central part of modern Idaho created a nearly impassable barrier and a division of its people into northern and southern factions who didn't want to be bound together. After Boise became the capital of Idaho Territory in 1864, Lewiston began advocating a plan to create a new territory out of northern Idaho, eastern Washington, and western Montana, which had become a territory by this time. This plan had the support of southern Idahoans because Idaho Territory then included the area that eventually became the state of Wyoming, so they felt they could jettison the northern area and still be very large. This idea did not get anywhere due to objections from eastern Washington and western Montana.

Officials in northern Idaho did not give up as they advocated a plan to attach the northern panhandle to eastern Washington. Northern and southern Idahoans really did not want to have anything to do with each other.

Annexation of the Idaho Panhandle would have augmented the population of Washington Territory and thereby enhanced the territory's chances for statehood. This was an attractive idea to the politicians in Olympia, but they were still afraid of losing their capital status and so opposed the plan to annex the northern Idaho counties. By 1886, however, sentiment in southern Idaho changed concerning the loss of the northern counties, and the southerners began to court the northerners.

With Canada. The short 45-mile boundary with Canada in the northern part of Idaho's Panhandle was established at the 49th parallel as the international boundary between the United States and Great Britain in the 1846 Oregon Treaty.

Nevada

Like all the states formed from land south of the 42nd parallel and west of the Rocky Mountains, Nevada was previously a part of a Spanish colony and, after Mexico achieved independence in 1821, a part of that country. It became a part of the United States in the Mexican Cession after the war of 1846–1848 and signing of the Treaty of Guadalupe Hidalgo.

Nevada was first organized as a part of the Mormon territory of Deseret in 1848. Deseret encompassed a huge area partly because the Mormons felt they needed a large area since most of it was arid and rocky and unsuitable for cultivation. (See map 9.9.)

In 1850 the U.S. Congress wrestled with the problem of how to divide the Mexican Cession. (See map 1.1.) The result was to create the state of California, giving California the boundaries its constitutional convention asked for, and divide the remainder of the area into two territories—New Mexico and Utah. Utah Territory encompassed the area be-

tween the 42nd and 37th parallels and from the Rocky Mountains to the California border. (See map 9.10.) Congress organized the remainder of the cession as New Mexico Territory. (See map 9.7.)

Miners discovered silver in the extreme western part of Utah Territory near Virginia City, and others flocked to the area. Mormons had also settled in the area, but soon miners outnumbered the Mormons and wanted either a separate government or to be attached to California. The miners did not want to have anything to do with the Mormons, and, besides, the territorial capital, Salt Lake City in the eastern part of the territory, was just too far away.

The Mormons sent more settlers to the area to bolster their influence, but it was not enough. In 1857 the citizens of Genoa, near Virginia City, petitioned Congress for a separate territory to be called "Columbus." Congress was never quick to act on petitions to divide territories, and they didn't rush this one either. One reason was the slavery issue in Congress. Southerners blocked efforts to create the new territory until they had assurance that slavery would be allowed in it.

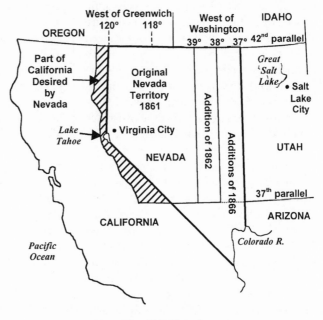

Map 10.8. Nevada

After southern states seceded from the Union in late 1860 and early 1861, slavery was no longer such a divisive issue in Congress, and it created Nevada Territory in March 1861 with boundaries as shown on map 10.8. The boundaries of Nevada Territory were to change during the next few years as shown on that same map.

Nevada has the singular distinction of having a western boundary defined as a meridian west of Greenwich, the 120th, and an eastern boundary defined as a meridian west of Washington, the 37th.

With Oregon and Idaho. Nevada's boundaries with Oregon and Idaho are easy to understand. The Adams-Onís Treaty of 1819 established the 42nd parallel as an international boundary between the United States and Spain between the Rocky Mountains and the Pacific Ocean; therefore, it had been a boundary for thirty-one years when Congress formed Utah Territory in 1850. (See map 8.14.) A part of this boundary was firmly fixed in 1859 when Oregon entered the Union with its southern boundary at the 42nd parallel.

This historical boundary notwithstanding, Nevada was suffering an economic downturn in the 1880s, and the legislature asked Congress to give it an area in southern Idaho that contained some silver mines to augment its economic base. Congress approved a bill to annex southern Idaho to Nevada in 1887, but President Grover Cleveland refused to sign the bill at the insistence of politicians in southern Idaho.

With Utah. The boundary with Utah is a complicated matter. When Congress created Nevada Territory in 1861, it set the territory's eastern boundary at the 39th meridian west of Washington with the expectation that Nevada was going to gain some land on its western boundary from California, the shaded area on map 10.8. This unlikely event is detailed in the following paragraphs discussing California, which was unwilling to cede any land. Nonetheless, Congress de-

cided that Nevada deserved more area, so they sliced off a 1-degree chunk of Utah Territory and added it to Nevada Territory in 1862. (See map 10.8.)

The boundary issue was not yet resolved because in 1866 Nevada desired more land on its eastern border to ensure jurisdiction over the rich mining area of Pahranagat, then in western Utah Territory. Both Utah Territory and the state of Nevada (which had been granted statehood in 1864) wanted control of the area. Nevada as a state had two senators and one representative in Congress who could argue that Nevada was a dry and desolate area that needed more land; Utah Territory had but one territorial delegate. This, coupled with the reality that the polygamous Mormons were looked down upon, not only by the Congress but also by the population in general, cost Utah more area. Congress granted Nevada's request by slicing another degree from Utah to establish the 37th meridian west of Washington as Nevada's final eastern border with Utah. (See map 10.8.)

With Arizona. Congress must have been really favorably disposed toward the Silver State in 1866. In addition to the land it gave Nevada at Utah Territory's expense, it also gave Nevada land south of the 37th parallel. (See the lower part of the "additions of 1866" on map 10.8.) The Nevada congressional delegation lobbied for this area as it was thought to contain valuable mining land, and access to the Colorado River would give the land-locked state access to the Gulf of California. The 31,850 square miles Congress added was between the 37th meridian west of Washington and the California border from the 37th parallel south to where the California border met the Colorado River. Nevada has not used the river for navigation in any significant way.

This triangle of land was a desolate area of desert, volcanic rock, and sagebrush, and it was thought by some Nevadans to be worthless. In the early stages of discussion some of them were not even sure they wanted the area. Nevadans did not formally accept the area until 1867. This triangle of land now holds the sprawling and rich gambling and resort mecca of Las Vegas.

With California. Miners discovered gold and silver in the area near Virginia City and wanted to be annexed to California in 1860 rather than being a part of Utah Territory. The proposal was to move California's eastern boundary from the 120th meridian west of Greenwich to the 118th from the 42nd parallel to where it would intersect the existing diagonal line forming California's eastern boundary. Instead, Congress decided to form the original Nevada Territory as shown on map 10.8.

Nevadans still had the idea that their western boundary should be the crest of the Sierra Nevada, and some members of Congress thought California might grant such a request. Since California was already a state (in 1850), Congress could not arbitrarily change its borders as it could for territories. Nevada sent representatives to California in 1862 to convince that state to cede to Nevada its land east of the crest of the Sierra Nevadas. What rarefied thinking might have led the Nevadans to think Californians would actually cede some land one can only guess. The representatives were, of course, unsuccessful — California was not about to give away any of its land. Logically, the plan of the Nevadans made sense, the crest of the mountains was a natural dividing line, and California was a very large state. Logic, however, usually plays little part in the formation of boundaries, especially in the West, where parallels of latitude and meridians of longitude dominate state boundary lines. Since Nevada was denied land to its west, Congress added to Nevada land from Utah in 1862 and 1866 and from Arizona Territory in 1866.

Still, Nevada did not give up on the idea of moving its western boundary to the crest of the Sierras. In 1871 officials memorialized the California assembly to set their common boundary at the crest of the mountains. This request was once again turned down, and Nevada's western boundary remains today where it was initially — the 120th meridian and the diagonal line formed by California's eastern boundary.

Oregon

Explorers from several nations plied the sea adjacent to the Northwest — Great Britain, Russia, Spain, France, and the United States. France never claimed any land, but the other four contested strongly for dominance of the area. By the early 1800s this region became known as Oregon Country as the United States and Great Britain established hegemony over the area, and Russia and Spain concentrated on lands to the north and south respectively. The boundaries of the Oregon Country were vague but generally stretched from the Rocky Mountains to the Pacific Ocean, south of Russia, approximately the 54th parallel (the southern tip of the Alaskan Panhandle), and north of Spain, approximately the 42nd parallel (the current California-Oregon border). (See map 10.12.)

Eventually the boundaries of the Oregon Country became more definite. In 1819 with the signing of the Adams-Onís Treaty, the southern boundary was placed between U.S.–claimed land and Spanish land at the 42nd parallel from the Rocky Mountains to the Pacific Ocean. (See map 8.14.) The United States and Great Britain made treaties with Russia in 1824 and 1825 to establish the southern limits of Russian Alaska at the parallel of 54 degrees 40 minutes. The western and eastern limits remained unchanged.

The United States and Great Britain agreed in 1818 that neither country should exercise governmental jurisdiction in the Oregon Country, in essence a joint occupation. This agreement was renewed in 1828 and continued until 1846 when the two nations agreed to establish their international boundary in the northwest at the 49th parallel. (More detail on this boundary is in the Washington section later in this chapter.)

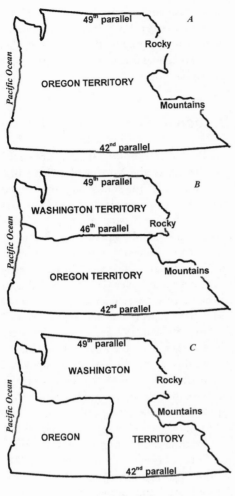

Map 10.9 A, B, C. Evolving Oregon

Map 10.10. Oregon Proposed
Boundary above 46th Parallel

Historian Clinton Snowden has said the Oregon Territory "is the only territory the United States has ever acquired by discovery, exploration and settlement; the only territory that cost us nothing in cash by way of purchase, or by use of military or naval force."*

Now that the United States had control over the northwest to the 49th parallel, Congress moved to set up a government in the area and in 1848 established the Oregon Territory. This territory was huge, as it extended from the 42nd to 49th parallels and from the Rocky Mountains to the Pacific Ocean. (See map 10.9A.) Five years later, in 1853, Congress created Washington Territory by dividing Oregon Territory along an east-west axis. (See map 10.9B.) When Congress admitted Oregon as a state in 1859 it trimmed off the eastern portion of Oregon Territory and added it temporarily to Washington Territory. (See map 10.9C.)

With Washington. One proposal to divide the original Oregon Territory was to run the boundary along the crest of the Cascade Mountains. (See map 10.11.) This certainly would have made sense in combining like geographical areas. Western Washington and Western Oregon are alike geographically, whereas the western and eastern parts of the two states are not. This common-sense proposal did not get anywhere. The boundary adopted by Congress was along the Columbia River from the Pacific Ocean to the 46th parallel, then along this parallel to the Rocky Mountains. (See map 10.9B.) This divided the territory fairly equally.

When Oregonians made plans to join the Union, the state constitution placed the boundary with Washington along the Columbia and Snake rivers rather than along the Columbia to the 46th parallel where Congress had placed the division of the two territories in 1853 when it created Washington Territory. (See map 10.10.) This same document said that Congress could change

*Clinton A. Snowden, History of Washington, vol. I (New York: The Century History Company, 1909), p. 4.

the boundary to that delineated when Congress created Washington Territory, i.e., the 46th parallel. This is just what Congress did when it admitted Oregon as a state in 1859.

This did not entirely settle the boundary in the minds of some Oregonians because in 1866 the Oregon legislature petitioned Congress to change the boundary to that specified in the original Oregon constitution. Similar petitions were made in 1873 and 1876. The House Committee on Territories in July 1876 recommended the change saying that the rivers constituted a natural boundary that was difficult to cross; that the citizens of the affected area (north of the 46th parallel and south of the Columbia and Snake rivers) were economically tied to Portland, and thus to Oregon; that it was much easier for citizens in the affected area to get to Oregon's capital, Salem, in the Willamette Valley, than to the Washington territorial capital of Olympia on Puget Sound; and that the citizens in the area wanted the change.

G. L. Fort, a member of the House committee, filed a minority report arguing against the proposal. He said that the reasons Congress settled upon the 46th parallel in 1853 were "compactness and regularity of form," balancing the sizes of the two territories, and "some regard for latitude and longitude."* Additional points of his argument were that Congress felt that the 46th parallel was appropriate because at the 46th parallel the Columbia River turns sharply to the north, and a river boundary would be some 50 miles, at the furthermost point, from the 46th parallel. Also, the two counties proposed to be brought into Oregon consisted of about 34,000 square miles of very fertile land. He argued that Oregon was already quite large and didn't need the land nor its tax base, whereas Washington Territory did need it. He claimed that about one-fourth of the territory's population lived in the affected area and that to remove them from Washington Territory would postpone indefinitely the

admission of Washington into the Union as a state. Congress accepted his argument and denied the boundary change.

The boundary in the Columbia River is in the middle of the channel and follows the middle of the widest channel around islands. The shifting of the channel in the Columbia gave rise to boundary disputes, so in 1910 Congress gave Washington and Oregon the authority to fix their boundary and settle disputes concerning island jurisdiction. The result was a series of tangents defined by 191 geodetic points. The two states agreed to this arrangement in 1958. These points approximate the river's channel but will not change over time.

With Idaho. In the 1857 Oregon Constitutional Convention the delegate from Wasco proposed the meridian of 121 degrees 30 minutes west of Greenwich, slightly east of the Cascade Mountains, as the eastern boundary of the proposed state of Oregon. (See map 10.11.) The convention delegates rejected this, claiming it would make the state too small.

Map 10.11. Oregon

*U.S. House, 44 Cong, 2 sess. Boundaries of the State of Oregon *(H. Rpt. 764), Washington: Government Printing Office), p. 3.*

A bill in the U.S. House of Representatives in 1857 proposed an eastern boundary at the 120th meridian, thereby making it the same as the eastern boundary of California. However, Oregon territorial delegate Joseph Lane asked that the eastern boundary be moved to the 118th meridian, saying the 120th limited the state too much. Nonetheless, the bill that went to the Senate still contained the 120th meridian for the eastern boundary. Stephen A. Douglas of the Senate Committee on Territories reported a boundary amendment from that committee setting the eastern boundary from the 46th parallel along the Snake River to its confluence with the Owyhee River (close to the 117th meridian), then due south to the 42nd parallel.

Discussion pointed out that this created a very large state of about 97,000 square miles, but since it consisted of considerable mountains and deserts, it contained only about the same amount of arable soil as Ohio. Due to the considerable influence of Douglas in territorial affairs, this is the line adopted by Congress as the boundary between Oregon and Idaho. In this case Congress abandoned its tendency to choose even parallels even when it could have. The non-river part of the boundary as established is only slightly west of the 117th meridian west of Greenwich and about where the 40th parallel west of Washington would be.

Map 10.12. Oregon Country

With Nevada and California. Oregon's boundary with Nevada and California was effectively set in 1819 with the signing of the Adams-Onís Treaty. This boundary was reaffirmed in 1828 between the United States and Mexico after this nation achieved independence from Spain in 1821. These agreements established an international boundary that Congress simply transferred into a boundary between states. Congress admitted California as a state in 1850 with its northern boundary as the 42nd parallel. This established a part of Oregon's southern boundary, and Congress chose to extend the parallel as a boundary as far east as the eastern Idaho boundary.

With Pacific Ocean. The act admitting Oregon into the Union in 1859 defined its boundary in the Pacific as 1 marine league into the sea, about 3½ land miles. The U.S. Geological Survey says that generally speaking the individual states recognize an offshore boundary of 3 nautical miles. The United States territorial sea limit contiguous zone has been set at 12 nautical miles but is expected to be extended to 24 nautical miles. The exclusive economic zone boundary is 200 nautical miles. (A nautical mile equals 1.15 land miles.)

Washington

The Pacific Northwest was initially called the Oregon Country and generally encompassed the area from the Pacific Ocean to the Rocky Mountains and from the 42nd to 54th parallels. (See map 10.12.) Several countries were acutely interested in the Pacific Northwest and competed keenly for possession of that land. Some explorers were in the area as early as the mid-sixteenth century, but activity became most acute during the last quarter of the eighteenth century. The most important players in this quest for domination were Spain, Russia, Great Britain, and the United States. The latter two countries were the only ones to send people into the area in any quantity, and those were mostly trappers and others associated with the fur trade. The British established a major fur trading center at Vancouver, just north of the Columbia River. The generosity and sense of fair play of the chief factor of this center, John McLoughlin, was crucial to the survival of American settlers who streamed into the Pacific Northwest along the Oregon Trail in the 1840s.

In 1818 Great Britain and the United States agreed to a joint occupation of the area whereby neither would exercise governmental jurisdiction. The two countries renewed this agreement in 1828, and it was in effect until 1846 when they settled the international boundary issue at the 49th parallel.

In the early 1850s the leaders of Oregon Territory realized that the territory was much too large to be governed and proposed to Congress that the territory be split. (See map 10.9A.) Reasons for dividing it were the usual ones: The territorial capital, in this case Oregon City south of the Columbia River, was too far from people in the northern part of the territory who were clustered around Puget Sound, and the river posed a formidable obstacle to those northerners needing to travel to the territorial capital.

Washington leaders wanted to name their new territory "Columbia" and initially wanted an area only as far east as the Columbia River. (See map 10.14.) Instead, when Congress created Washington Territory in 1853 for the approximately 4,000 settlers north of the river, it divided Oregon Territory at the Columbia River and then extended the line along the 46th parallel from the point where that parallel intersects the river as it turns sharply to the north. Washington Territory got all the area above this line all the way to the Rocky Mountains. (See map 10.9B.) Washington Territory received additional land when Oregon Territory was reduced to form the state of Oregon. (See map 10.9C.) In addition to denying the requested boundaries, Congress also denied the requested name and substituted Washington, to honor the first U.S. president.

Congress would later deny naming territories after presidents Jefferson and Lincoln.

Congress reduced Washington Territory in 1863 when it created Idaho Territory, placing the eastern boundary where it is today. (See map 10.14.) Congress admitted Washington to the Union in 1889.

With Canada. The United States and Great Britain were beset by boundary problems all along their vast border soon after the end of the War for American Independence. Great strides were made in resolving the problem in 1842 with the Webster-Ashburton Treaty. This treaty, however, extended only as far west as the crest of the Rocky Mountains, and the two countries could not agree on the boundary beyond that point.

Citizens in the Oregon Country wanted the boundary west of the Rockies placed at the parallel of 54 degrees 40 minutes, hence the slogan of "Fifty-four Forty or Fight" that was part of the Democratic platform in the presidential election of 1844. The British, however, wanted a boundary running along the 49th parallel to the Columbia River and down that river to the Pacific Ocean. (See map 10.14.)

Democrat James Polk was elected president and took office in 1845. Even though the official Democratic stance was for 54° 40', Polk offered to the British minister to settle on the 49th parallel all the way to the Pacific. The minister refused the offer, angering Polk to such an extent that he gave notice that the United States was giving the necessary one-year notice to terminate the joint occupation agreement and would insist on 54° 40' as the boundary from the Rockies to the Pacific.

Neither Britain nor the United States was eager to go to war over this boundary. In 1846 the two countries negotiated the Oregon Treaty, setting the boundary from the Rocky Mountains along the 49th parallel to the Strait of Georgia, then circling south around Vancouver Island to the Pacific Ocean. The British had come to realize that the land between the 49th parallel and the Columbia River was probably lost to them anyway be-

Map 10.13. Strait of Georgia

finally decided to give the matter to the William I, Emperor of Germany, for adjudication. Each nation was allowed one representative to present its case. After hearing all arguments the emperor referred the question to three judges. They gave separate decisions in writing. Using these decisions, the emperor made his determination in 1872. The United States prevailed, and Haro Strait became the international boundary in the Strait of Georgia when the two nations agreed to the emperor's decision in 1873. This was quite an important determination for the United States as it included the San Juan Islands.

The 49th parallel created an interesting anomaly in the north part of the Strait of Georgia. The tip of a small peninsula extends below the parallel, creating a 5-square-mile area of U.S. land called Point Roberts. (See map 10.13.) Children of citizens living here are bused to school in Blaine, Washington, just south of the United States–Canada border.

cause Americans had settled in the area in large numbers. McLoughlin had repeatedly asked the British government to send settlers, but his requests were ignored. The United States also wanted the part of Vancouver Island below the 49th parallel, but it gave this up to the British, who considered it of great importance to possess the entire island.

The 1846 treaty between the United States and Great Britain defined the boundary in the Strait of Georgia as "...the middle of the channel which separates the continent from Vancouver Island; and thence southerly through the middle of the said channel, and of Fuca's Straits, to the Pacific Ocean." This imprecise description quite naturally caused a disagreement about the exact location in the channel.

The British interpreted the treaty as referring to Rosario Strait, in the eastern part of the Strait of Georgia (the dotted line on map 10.13 east of the San Juan Islands). The United States, on the other hand, interpreted the treaty as referring to Haro Strait (the dashed line on map 10.13 west of the San Juan Islands), which was closer to Vancouver Island. The two countries could not agree and

With Idaho. The eastern boundary of Washington was effectively settled when Congress created Idaho Territory in 1863, but since both Washington and Idaho were territories, Congress could still change the boundary if it chose. Before statehood, the Washington territorial legislature tried in 1869, 1871, 1873, and 1878 to include the northern counties of Idaho. The legislatures of both territories had memorialized Congress for inclusion of three northern Idaho counties in Washington Territory.

The Idaho Panhandle counties were in favor of annexation to Washington, but politicians in Olympia, the territorial capital, became fearful that if Washington extended too far east, the capital would be moved, and they began to earnestly fight the annexation. This movement was successful, and the boundary remained where Congress had originally placed it in 1863. Notwithstanding the wishes of western Washingtonians, Congress passed legislation to annex the three counties to Washington in 1887 and sent it to President Grover Cleveland. He did not sign it, apparently at the request of Idahoans who by this time did not want to be annexed to Washington.

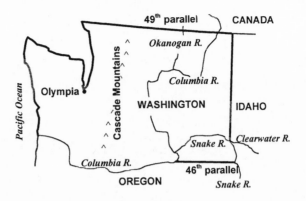

Map 10.14. Washington

With Oregon. When Congress created Washington Territory out of Oregon Territory in 1853, it put the boundary between the two territories along the Columbia River, one of the dominant natural features of the region. Then, in an attempt to divide the territory nearly equally north and south, and considering regularity of form and a regard for latitude, Congress extended the boundary along the 46th parallel to the eastern terminus of Oregon Territory, the Rocky Mountains. (See map 10.9*B*.) The 46th parallel was a good choice as the river takes a sharp turn to the north near the parallel and tends to create a natural extension of the east-west part of the river. This boundary also divided the territory into somewhat equal parts, although the southern part was larger. (See map 10.14.)

Oregonians were not totally content with this boundary along the 46th parallel, however. The constitution they adopted in 1857 prior to joining the Union placed the boundary along the Columbia and Snake rivers rather than along the 46th parallel. (See map 10.10.) However, when Congress admitted Oregon to the Union, it retained the 46th parallel boundary. Nonetheless, in 1866, 1873, and 1876 the Oregon legislature petitioned Congress to change the boundary to the Columbia and Snake rivers. The reasons being that the people in the area wanted the change because access to Salem, Oregon's new capital in the Willamette Valley, was easier than to the Washington capital of Olympia on Puget Sound, and they were economically tied to the major Oregon city of Portland via transportation along the Columbia River. Congress rejected these petitions partly because Washington Territory needed that area for its economic base and its population if the territory was going to qualify for admittance to the Union. (Additional discussion is in the Washington paragraphs of the Oregon section.)

With Pacific Ocean. The boundary in the ocean is one marine league from land, approximately three and one-half land miles. The U.S. Geological Survey says that generally speaking the individual states recognize an offshore boundary of 3 nautical miles. The United States territorial sea limit contiguous zone has been set at 12 nautical miles but is expected to be extended to 24 nautical miles. The exclusive economic zone boundary is 200 nautical miles. (A nautical mile equals 1.15 land miles.)

11

NONCONTIGUOUS REGION

Map 11.1

Map is not to scale; boundaries are roughly drawn.

Alaska

Alexander I of Russia decreed in 1821 that Russia claimed ownership of the Pacific Northwest as far south as the 51st degree of latitude (approximately the northern tip of Vancouver Island, Canada) and barred all foreigners from either trading or fishing within 100 miles of the coast. This edict alarmed both Britain and the United States, who also had meager, but important interests in the area. These two countries then entered into negotiations with Russia to curb that country's grandiose plan in the area, resulting in boundary agreements with the United States in 1824 and Great Britain in 1825. The 1824 agreement between Russia and the United States limited Russia to the parallel of 54 degrees 40 minutes, the southern tip of the current Alaskan Panhandle. At that time the United States had some small pretensions of claiming land in the Pacific Northwest as far north as that parallel encapsulated in the slogan "Fifty-four Forty or Fight" that was later a part of the Democratic Party platform during the presidential election of 1844.

Great Britain, on the other hand, already claimed land in the area now called Canada and so was interested in limiting the southern and eastern Russian boundaries. Consequently, the agreement Great Britain negotiated with Russia in 1825 also defined a north-south boundary between the two countries. The boundary agreed to began at the southern tip of Prince of Wales Island, which is at 54° 40', then running up the Portland Canal to the 56th parallel, then following the summit of the mountains parallel to the coast as far as the 141st meridian west of Greenwich. This agreement further provided that if the range of mountains exceeded 10 marine leagues from the coast (about 34.5 miles) that the boundary was to follow the windings of the coast, but in any event was never to exceed 10 marine leagues from the coastline. After reaching the 141st meridian

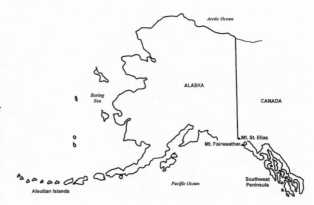

Map 11.2. Alaska

(Mount St. Elias) the boundary followed that meridian to the Arctic Ocean.

An obvious question arises as to why Alaska includes the thin strip of land in the southeast, called the Panhandle. Russian negotiators argued for this area based on the idea that their settlements on the adjacent islands would be unsupported without Russian settlements on the mainland and, thus, at the mercy of whoever was settled there. Great Britain conceded the point and negotiated the agreement with Russia that included the Panhandle.

The above-described line was an international boundary when the United States bought Alaska from Russia in 1867 for $7,200,000. The boundary description was general, and it took many years for Canada and the United States to work out the specifics.

With Canada. Canada received its independence from Great Britain in 1867, the same year the United States bought Alaska from the Russians. The exact location of the boundary between the United States and Canada was not then an issue as the area was mountainous and sparsely inhabited. When British Columbia entered the Canadian Confederation in 1871, it pressed the Canadian government to negotiate with the United States to precisely locate the boundary. Neither country was eager to undertake such an arduous task and its concomitant expense, but finally in 1892 representatives of both countries met to consider the problem.

The representatives surveyed the area and determined that no range of mountains parallel to the coast was identifiable because the interior is a sea of mountains rather than a range of mountains, so this provision of the 1825 Russia–Great Britain agreement was impossible to implement. The representatives decided the boundary would have to be drawn using the 10-marine-league limit from the coast. Implementing this idea would have been a surveyor's nightmare considering the sharply indented coastline, the ruggedness of the inland area, and the fact that it is about 1,200 miles from the Portland Canal to Mount St. Elias where the boundary then follows the 141st meridian north to the Beaufort Sea.

The question then became from where this 10-marine-league line should be drawn. Should it be from the general trend of the coast, the option favored by the Canadians as this would give them claim to the heads of the many of the inlets, or should it be drawn including the deeply indented inlets, thereby giving the Americans a continuous coast?

The boundary issue was further complicated when gold was discovered in the Klondike River area in 1896, an event that underscored the need to settle the boundary question. The Canadians wanted a deep-water port of entry through the Panhandle to the gold fields, and they interpreted the 1825 agreement as being a line from the general trend of the coastline. They also advocated a boundary along the mountains facing the coast. Either interpretation would have given them access through at least one of the northern inlets. The United States, however, kept arguing for a boundary that would give it control of the heads of all inlets.

The Canadians didn't have much of a case for any of their proposals. All maps, even those created by the British, gave an unbroken coastline to the United States. Canada had never challenged this until the gold rush gave added value to the heads of the inlets, especially to the land at the head of the Lynn Canal which leads to Skagway. (See map 11.3.) Further damaging the Canadian case was the fact that Native Americans living at the head of Lynn Canal gave sworn testimony that they had considered themselves under Russian protection before 1867 and American protection after that.

To adjudicate this boundary issue, a tribunal of six commissioners, three from the United States, two from Canada, and one from Great Britain, met in 1903 to resolve the problem. Their decision was a compromise of the two country's proposals and provided for a continuous strip of land 15 to 30 miles wide from the Portland Canal to Mt. St. Elias, thus generally upholding the American contention for an unbroken coastline including the heads of all inlets. The only point in which Canada won a major concession was that the tribunal awarded two of four disputed islands at the head of Portland

Map 11.3. Alaska Panhandle Boundary

Canal (southern part of the boundary) to the Canadians. During negotiations the British representative frequently voted with the Americans.

The intent of the agreement was to give the United States an unbroken coastline, but the tribunal didn't give enough consideration to the ebb and flow of glaciers. The boundary in Glacier Bay was originally 12 miles inland from the east front of the glacier as it was in 1894, then a direct line to Mt. Fairweather. By 1912, however, the glacier had retreated so that Canada actually had a harbor, although it was not a very viable area because it could be accessed only by U.S. waters and it could be covered by ice again at any time. A United States Geological Survey map of 1987 indicates that the glacier front and the boundary are identical, suggesting that Canadian land is either very meager or nonexistent.

With Oceans. Russia included the islands in the Bering Sea and the Aleutians in the 1867 sale of Alaska to the United States. The Alaska boundary in its seas and oceans is 3 nautical miles from the mean high-water mark, about 3.45 land miles.

Hawaii

Boundary location is not really an issue in the case of Hawaii, so a brief look into the how and why the islands came into U.S. possession and why the state consists of certain islands and not others constitutes the discussion for this state.

The reasons Hawaii is a state are due mostly to economics and military usefulness. Some of the first Americans to inhabit the islands in the early 1800s were missionaries, many of whose sons grew up and entered the sugar business. These families became very wealthy and influential by the 1880s, with a vested interest in the success of the sugar industry.

The United States removed a tariff on raw sugar imported from foreign countries in 1890. Before the tariff was removed, Hawaiian sugar producers had an advantage selling in the U.S. market. The tariff removal caused a drastic drop in sugar production and, thus, caused an economic depression in Hawaii. The group of producers concluded that the answer to the economic depression, and other problems, was annexation to the United States. A Committee of Safety formed consisting of white nonnative (American) sugar producers, all in favor of annexation.

With the help of the American minister to Hawaii and some troops from a U.S. warship, the committee took possession of the government office building, abrogated the monarchy, set up a provisional government, and applied for annexation to the United States in early 1893. They expected annexation to happen quickly. The United States, however, was not interested in annexing Hawaii, partly because mainland sugar producers were against it and many citizens didn't want to annex a land as ethnically diverse as Hawaii. The sugar producers in Hawaii had imported many Asians, mostly Chinese and Japanese but also others, as laborers in the sugar industry.

Deeply disappointed, the Hawaiian provisional government realized that a more permanent form of government was needed until the United States would annex the islands. They called a constitutional convention in 1894 which adopted a new constitution that summer and established the Republic of Hawaii. The officials of the provisional government controlled the process of forming the republic, which was not a republic at all, as power was not distributed. Even though sentiment was in favor of annexation, some Hawaiian sugar producers were unsure about annexation, as they feared what that might do to the supply of cheap labor from Asia.

While discussions were taking place concerning annexation, the United States sent emissaries to Hawaii in the early 1890s to clandestinely scout the islands for military purposes. Their report demonstrated that the islands had considerable potential as a military base. Nonetheless, the United States did not become acutely interested in annexing the islands until the 1898 Spanish-American War demonstrated the critical need for a U.S. base in the Pacific. Resolutions for annexation were introduced in the House and Senate in 1898. President William McKinley signed the annexation bill in July of that year. Although Hawaii came under U.S. control, it continued to operate under the laws of the republic until 1900, when Congress passed the act creating the Territory of Hawaii.

The state consists of eight inhabited is-

lands, the smallest of which has a land mass of only 45 square miles. (See map 11.4.) It also includes an additional 124 islets, reefs, and shoals, some of which are shown on map 11.5. These islands extend for about 1,700 miles in a general northwest to southeast direction in the Pacific Ocean approximately 2,800 miles east-southeast of California. The total land mass of the islands is about 6,425 square miles, with nearly two-thirds of that in the single island of Hawaii, called appropriately the "Big Island." The Big Island is still growing due to lava flows that run down the shield volcanoes and solidify when they reach the sea.

All the islands are on the edge a fault line called the Pacific Plate, and all are close enough to each other to form an island group. The nearest other island group is about 500 miles from any of the Hawaiian islands. The two Midway Islands, near the western edge of the group, are part of the Hawaiian island group but are not part of the state of Hawaii. (See map 11.5.) They were annexed to the United States in 1867 and put under the jurisdiction of the U.S. Navy in 1903.

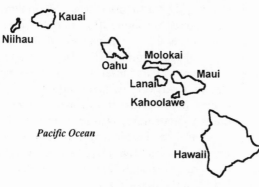

Map 11.4. Populated Hawaii

Map 11.5. Greater Hawaii

Johnston Island, Sand Island, Palmyra Island, and Kingman Reef were traditionally under the jurisdiction of Hawaii but were excluded from the 1958 statehood bill because of their distance from the main island group and, thus, the difficulty of governing them from Honolulu. They all remain under federal jurisdiction as territories. They are very small and uninhabited except for one.

Johnston Island was reserved for military use and is now administered by the U.S. Defense Nuclear Agency. Johnston and nearby Sand Island (sometimes called atolls) were annexed to the United States in 1858 and are about 800 miles west-southwest of Honolulu, about one-third of the way from Hawaii to the Marshall Islands. These islands have no native population but about 1,200 military personnel live there. Palmyra Island (also called an atoll) was annexed in 1862 and incorporated into the Hawaiian Islands by congressional act in 1898; it is 1,100 miles south-southeast of Honolulu, about halfway from Hawaii to American Samoa. Kingman Reef, near Palmyra Island, was annexed to the United States in 1922. It is currently under the control of the navy and the responsibility of the Department of Defense. Both Palmyra Island and Kingman Reef are uninhabited.

Appendix A

Citizen and State Nicknames

	Citizen Nickname	State Nickname
Alabama	Alabamans	Cotton State, Heart of Dixie
Alaska	Alaskans	Last Frontier, Land of the Midnight Sun
Arizona	Arizonans	Grand Canyon State
Arkansas	Arkansans	Land of Opportunity, Razorback State
California	Californians	Golden State
Colorado	Coloradans	Centennial State
Connecticut	Connecticuters	Constitution State, Nutmeg State
Delaware	Delawareans	Diamond State, First State, Blue Hen State
Florida	Floridians	Sunshine State
Georgia	Georgians	Empire State of the South, Peach State
Hawaii	Hawaiians	Aloha State
Idaho	Idahoans	Gem State
Illinois	Illinoisans	Prairie State, Land of Lincoln
Indiana	Hoosiers or Indianians	Hoosier State
Iowa	Iowans	Hawkeye State
Kansas	Kansans	Sunflower State, Jayhawk State
Kentucky	Kentuckians	Bluegrass State
Louisiana	Louisianians	Pelican State
Maine	Mainers	Pine Tree State
Maryland	Marylanders	Old Line State, Free State, Pine Tree State
Massachusetts	Massachusettsans	Bay State, Old Colony State
Michigan	Michiganders	Wolverine State, Great Lakes State, Water Wonderland
Minnesota	Minnesotans	North Star State, Gopher State, Land of 10,000 Lakes
Mississippi	Mississippians	Magnolia State
Missouri	Missourians	Show Me State
Montana	Montanans	Treasure State
Nebraska	Nebraskans	Cornhusker State, Tree Planters State
Nevada	Nevadans	Silver State, Sagebrush State, Battle Born State

	Citizen Nickname	*State Nickname*
New Hampshire	New Hampshirites	Granite State
New Jersey	New Jerseyans or New Jerseyites	Garden State
New Mexico	New Mexicans	Land of Enchantment
New York	New Yorkers	Empire State
North Carolina	North Carolinians	Tar Heel State, Old North State
North Dakota	North Dakotans	Peach Garden State, Sioux State
Ohio	Ohioans	Buckeye State
Oklahoma	Oklahomans	Sooner State
Oregon	Oregonians	Beaver State
Pennsylvania	Pennsylvanians	Keystone State
Rhode Island	Rhode Islanders	Little Rhody, Ocean State
South Carolina	South Carolinians	Palmetto State
South Dakota	South Dakotans	Coyote State, Mount Rushmore State
Tennessee	Tennesseans	Volunteer State
Texas	Texans	Lone Star State
Utah	Utahns	Beehive State
Vermont	Vermonters	Green Mountain State
Virginia	Virginians	Old Dominion, Mother of Presidents
Washington	Washingtonians	Evergreen State
West Virginia	West Virginians	Mountain State
Wisconsin	Wisconsinites	Badger State
Wyoming	Wyomingites	Equality State

Appendix B

Principal Boundary Dates

1606   Virginia Company receives grant

1607   Virginia Company establishes Jamestown

1609   London Company receives grant for Virginia

1620   Pilgrims settle Plymouth Colony

1622   Ferdinando Gorges and John Mason receive grant between Merrimack and Kennebec Rivers

1629   Georges and Mason divide their grant
        Massachusetts Bay Colony receives charter
        Plymouth Colony receives charter
        Robert Heath receives grant for Carolana

1632   Cecil Calvert receives grant for Maryland

1634   Puritans leave Massachusetts for Connecticut

1635   William Stirling receives grant for Long Island

1638   Puritans settle New Haven

1641   New Hampshire comes under Massachusetts jurisdiction

1642   Nathaniel Woodward and Solomon Saffery survey Connecticut-Massachusetts boundary

1644   Commission confirms Duke of York's claim to Long Island
        Roger Williams receives patent for Rhode Island

1662   Connecticut receives charter

1663   Charles II grants Carolina to eight Englishmen
        Rhode Island receives charter

1664   Duke of York receives charter for New York, New Jersey, Maine, and islands
        Duke of York grants New Jersey to John Berkeley and George Carteret

1665   Charles II increases size of Carolina grant
        New Haven combines with Connecticut

1667   New York acknowledges Connecticut's rights to land west of Connecticut River

1670   Commission surveys Maryland-Virginia boundary on Eastern Shore

1681   William Penn receives charter for Pennsylvania
        Charles II decrees 12-mile arc around New Castle as Pennsylvania-Delaware boundary

1683   Connecticut and New York agree on boundary

1685   Charles II divides Delmarva Peninsula
        Lords of Trade rule Delaware belongs to Duke of York

1691   Maine becomes a part of Massachusetts jurisdiction
        Massachusetts absorbs Plymouth Colony
        Nantucket Island and Martha's Vineyard become part of Massachusetts
        William and Mary decree New Hampshire a royal colony

1703   Connecticut and Rhode Island agree on boundary

1710   Rhode Island and Massachusetts settle east-west boundary

1713   Connecticut and Massachusetts agree on resurveyed boundary

1728   Surveyors mark North Carolina–Virginia boundary

1729   George II buys Carolina from proprietors
        George II divides Carolina

1730   Board of Trade determines South Carolina-North Carolina boundary
        George II decrees Maine–New Hampshire boundary

1731   New York receives the Oblong

1732   James Oglethorpe receives grant for Georgia

1735   Beginning of North Carolina-South Carolina boundary surveys; completed in 1815

1739   George II determines boundary between New Hampshire and Maine

1740   George II settles boundary between New Hampshire and Massachusetts

1741   Richard Hazen surveys New Hampshire–Massachusetts boundary
        Royal commission confirms Rhode Island's right to east side of Narragansett Bay

1750   James Oglethorpe and associates surrender Georgia charter
        New Hampshire governor begins making land grants in southwest Vermont
        New York and Massachusetts agree on boundary
        Surveyors mark southern Delaware boundary

1757   Board of Trade establishes "line of peace" 20 miles east of Hudson River

1760   Penns and Calverts agree on Pennsylvania-Maryland boundary

1763   France cedes land west of Mississippi River to Spain and east of the river to Great
           Britain
        Spain cedes land east of Mississippi River to Great Britain except Isle of Orleans
        George III extends Georgia's southern boundary

1764   Board of Trade decrees New Hampshire's western boundary
        Board of Trade increases West Florida
        Charles Mason and Jeremiah Dixon survey Maryland-Pennsylvania boundary

1771   New York and New Jersey (1772) agree on boundary
        Valentine and Collins survey 45th parallel boundary between United States and Great
           Britain

1776   Virginia establishes Kentucky District

1777   Vermont citizens declare themselves an independent republic

1779   Pennsylvania and Virginia agree to extend Mason-Dixon Line
        Thomas Walker and Richard Henderson begin survey of Tennessee-Kentucky bound-
            ary

1780   New York releases claim to western lands

1781   New York agrees to limit western boundary to a meridian drawn from western end
            of Lake Ontario

1782   United States and Great Britain establish boundary at 31st parallel
        Federal commission determines Connecticut Valley belongs to Pennsylvania

1783   Great Britain retrocedes Florida to Spain
        Treaty establishes independence of the United States and the U.S.–Great Britain
            boundary

1784   Tennesseans establish State of Franklin
        Virginia releases claim to western territory

1785   Massachusetts releases claim to western territory

1786   Connecticut releases claim to western territory
        Surveyors mark New York–Pennsylvania boundary

1787   Delaware adopts Constitution
        Pennsylvania adopts Constitution
        New Jersey adopts Constitution
        Beaufort Convention puts Georgia's northern boundary at 35th parallel and clarifies
            Georgia–South Carolina boundary
        New York and Massachusetts settle boundary location
        Northwest Ordinance establishes framework for territorial creation
        Supreme Court determines northern branch as headwaters of Potomac River

1788   Georgia adopts Constitution
        Connecticut adopts Constitution
        Massachusetts adopts Constitution
        Maryland adopts Constitution
        South Carolina adopts Constitution
        New Hampshire adopts Constitution
        Virginia adopts Constitution
        New York adopts Constitution
        Francis Deakins surveys north-south portion of Maryland-Virginia (now West Vir-
            ginia) boundary

1789   North Carolina adopts Constitution
        North Carolina releases claim to western lands

1790   Rhode Island adopts Constitution
        Commission resolves New York–Vermont boundary
        Congress organizes Territory of the United States South of the Ohio River

1791   President George Washington determines boundaries for national capital
        Vermont joins Union

1792   Kentucky joins Union
        Pennsylvania buys Erie Triangle

1795   Pinckney's Treaty establishes 31st parallel as U.S.–Spain boundary

1796   Tennessee joins Union

U.S. and British delegates decide on Schoodic River as boundary between Maine and Great Britain

1797   Andrew Ellicott and Esteban Minor begin survey of 31st parallel

1798   Congress creates Mississippi Territory
First survey of Ohio-Indiana boundary

1799   Commission marks North Carolina–Tennessee boundary

1800   Congress creates Indiana Territory
Spain retrocedes Louisiana to France in Treaty of San Ildefonso
Supreme Court affirms Kentucky-Ohio boundary in Ohio River

1802   Federal government increases size of Mississippi Territory
Surveyors mark Virginia-Tennessee boundary

1803   Georgia creates Walton County beginning the Walton War between Georgia and North Carolina
Louisiana Purchase doubles size of United States
Ohio joins Union

1804   Congress divides Louisiana Purchase into two districts
Connecticut and Massachusetts agree to boundary in Congamond Lakes area

1805   Congress creates Michigan Territory

1807   Thomas Freeman surveys Alabama-Tennessee boundary

1809   Congress creates Illinois Territory

1811   Earthquake creates New Madrid Bend

1812   Congress adds part of West Florida to Mississippi Territory
Congress creates Missouri Territory
Louisiana joins Union

1814   Treaty of Ghent makes adjustments to northern international boundary

1816   Indiana joins Union
John Sullivan surveys Indian Boundary Line (between Iowa and Missouri)

1817   Congress creates Alabama Territory
Mississippi joins Union
Nathaniel Pope changes congressional bill to extend northern Illinois boundary
William Harris surveys Ordinance Line (Illinois/Indiana/Ohio)

1818   Illinois joins Union
James Camack and James Gaines determine northwest corner of Georgia on 35th parallel
John Fulton surveys Ordinance Line
United States acquires parcel north of Louisiana Purchase
United States and Great Britain agree to joint occupation of Oregon Country; continued until 1846
United States buys land from Chickasaw Indians (Kentucky)

1819   Adams-Onís Treaty establishes U.S.–Spain boundary in West
Alabama joins Union
Congress creates Arkansas Territory
Georgia and North Carolina agree on boundary
Spain abandons claim to Oregon Country

	Spain cedes Florida to United States Surveyors mark North Carolina–Georgia boundary
1820	John Coffee and Thomas Freeman survey Alabama-Mississippi boundary Maine joins Union Supreme Court rules on Kentucky-Ohio boundary; ruling later extended to Ohio's boundary with Indiana and Illinois
1821	Missouri joins Union Surveyors complete southern part of North Carolina–Tennessee boundary
1822	Congress creates Florida Territory
1824	Russia abandons claim to Oregon Country
1825	Treaty with Choctaws ultimately establishes part of Arkansas-Oklahoma boundary
1826	Georgia marks Georgia-Alabama boundary; Alabama acknowledges it in 1840
1828	Mexico and United States affirm Adams-Onís boundary after Mexico achieves independence from Spain in 1821 Treaty with Cherokees ultimately establishes part of Arkansas-Oklahoma boundary
1831	Congress establishes 31st parallel as Alabama-Florida Territory boundary
1834	Congress increases size of Michigan Territory New York and New Jersey make agreement concerning Ellis Island
1835	Toledo War over the Toledo Strip begins New Hampshire takes control of Indian Stream Territory
1836	Arkansas joins Union Congress creates Wisconsin Territory Missouri authorizes Joseph Brown to survey Iowa-Missouri boundary United States recognizes Republic of Texas
1837	Commissioners mark Mississippi-Tennessee boundary Congress adds Platte Purchase to Missouri Michigan joins Union Tennessee and Mississippi settle on boundary
1838	Congress creates Iowa Territory
1840	Thomas Cram surveys Michigan-Wisconsin boundary
1842	Webster-Ashburton Treaty finalizes much of northern U.S. international boundary
1845	Florida joins Union Republic of Texas joins Union
1846	Congress establishes boundary between Iowa and Minnesota Territories Congress returns to Virginia that part of Washington, D.C., south of Potomac River Iowa joins Union Oregon Treaty establishes U.S.–Great Britain boundary west of Rocky Mountains
1847	Supreme Court rules on Iowa-Missouri boundary
1848	Congress consents to change in Texas-Louisiana boundary Congress creates Oregon Territory Treaty of Guadalupe Hidalgo ends U.S.–Mexico war and establishes boundary Wisconsin joins Union
1849	Congress creates Minnesota Territory Supreme Court rules on Iowa-Missouri boundary

1850   California joins Union
        Congress creates New Mexico Territory
        Congress creates Utah Territory
        Congress establishes Washington Meridian
        Texas agrees to sell land to federal government

1852   First survey of 100th meridian between Texas and Oklahoma; additional surveys
        occur in 1857–59, 1860, 1892, and 1902

1853   Boston Corners separates from Massachusetts and becomes part of New York
        Congress creates Washington Territory
        Gadsden Purchase extends boundary of New Mexico Territory

1854   Congress creates Kansas Territory
        Congress creates Nebraska Territory

1857   Congress determines Minnesota Territory boundaries
        House bill proposes eastern Oregon boundary at 120th meridian; Stephen Douglas
        amends bill to modern boundary
        Oregon constitution includes area between 46th parallel and Snake River

1858   Minnesota joins Union
        United States annexes Johnston and Sand Islands

1859   Commissioners from Rhode Island and Massachusetts agree to exchange land
        John Clark surveys 103rd meridian and 32nd parallel between New Mexico Territory
        and Texas
        Oregon joins Union with northern boundary along Columbia River and 46th paral-
        lel
        Supreme Court rules on Georgia-Alabama boundary in Chattahoochee River
        Surveyors mark straight-line segment of Georgia-Florida boundary

1861   Congress alters Nebraska Territory boundaries
        Congress creates Colorado Territory
        Congress creates Dakota Territory
        Congress creates Nevada Territory
        Congress takes land from New Mexico Territory and gives it to Colorado Territory
        Kansas joins Union
        Massachusetts and Rhode Island agree on north-south boundary

1862   James Ashley proposes boundary between Arizona and New Mexico Territories as
        extension of Utah Territory-Colorado Territory boundary
        Nevada Territory lobbies California to put boundary at crest of Sierra Nevada; an-
        other attempt made in 1871
        Nevada Territory gains additional land from Utah Territory

1863   Congress creates Arizona Territory
        Congress creates Idaho Territory
        Congress creates Washington Territory
        West Virginia separates from Virginia and joins Union

1864   Congress creates Montana Territory
        Congress returns Wyoming area to Dakota Territory
        Nevada joins Union

1865   Utah Territory asks Congress to move southern boundary to Colorado River; addi-
        tional attempts made in 1897, 1920, and 1919

1866	Congress attaches part of Arizona and Utah Territories to Nevada
	Oregon petitions Congress to move part of Oregon-Washington boundary to Snake River rather than 46th parallel; similar petitions made in 1873 and 1876
1867	Colorado Territory asks to extend northern boundary
	Dakota Territory petitions Congress to create a new territory from its western lands
	High water creates McKissick's Island (Nebraska/Missouri)
	Nebraska joins Union
	United States annexes Midway Islands
	United States purchases Alaska
1868	Congress creates Wyoming Territory
	E.N. Darling surveys boundary between Colorado and New Mexico Territories
	Discussions between Florida and Alabama concerning Panhandle
1869	Washington Territory tries to add Idaho Territory Panhandle counties; further attempts made in 1871, 1873, and 1878
1870	Nebraska acquires exclave from Dakota Territory
	Supreme Court rules Wolf Island belongs to Kentucky
1873	Congress adds Lost Dakota Territory to Montana Territory
	United States and Canada resolve boundary in Strait of Georgia
1874	Maryland and Virginia resolve boundary in Chesapeake Bay
1876	Colorado joins Union
1877	Avulsion creates Carter Lake (Nebraska/Iowa)
1880	Connecticut acknowledges New York's claim to Fishers Island
1882	Congress redefines Nebraska-Dakota Territory boundary
1885	Constitutional convention proposes dividing Dakota Territory along 7th standard parallel
1886	Nevada tries to extend northern boundary
1889	North Dakota joins Union
	South Dakota joins Union
	Montana joins Union
	Washington joins Union
1890	Congress creates Oklahoma Territory
	Idaho joins Union
	Supreme Court rules that Green River Island belongs to Kentucky
	Wyoming joins Union
1896	Supreme Court rules Prairie Dog Town Fork of Red River is Texas-Oklahoma Territory boundary
	Utah joins Union
1898	United States annexes Hawaiian Islands
1900	Congress creates Hawaii Territory
1902	H.B. Carpenter resurveys Colorado–New Mexico Territory boundary
1903	Commissioners meet to resolve Alaska Panhandle boundary between United States and Canada
1905	Congress changes boundary between Arkansas and Oklahoma Territory
	Supreme Court rules McKissick's Island is part of Nebraska

	Supreme Court rules on gulf boundary between Mississippi and Louisiana
1907	Oklahoma joins Union
1909	Congress grants authority to Louisiana and Mississippi to exchange exclaves along Mississippi River
1910	Congress gives Oregon and Washington authority to settle their Columbia River boundary; finally settled in 1958
1911	Congress affirms Texas–New Mexico Territory boundaries as surveyed by John Clark
1912	New Mexico joins Union
	Arizona joins Union
	Congress creates Alaska Territory (it had been governed as if it were a territory since 1884)
	Congress repeals Washington Meridian Act
	Joint commission recommends exchange of land between United States and Mexico along Rio Grande
1920	Supreme Court rules on New Mexico–Texas boundary in Rio Grande
1921	Pennsylvania formally cedes Delaware Wedge to Delaware
	Supreme Court rules on location of Texas-Oklahoma boundary in Red River
1922	Supreme Court rules on northern part of South Carolina–Georgia boundary
1925	Supreme Court rules on southern Colorado boundary
	Supreme Court upholds 1868 survey of Colorado–New Mexico boundary
1926	Supreme Court rules on 100th meridian boundary between Oklahoma and Texas
1930	Commissioners from Maryland and Virginia agree on boundary in Potomac River
1935	Supreme Court rules on Delaware–New Jersey boundary in Delaware River
1939	Iowa and Missouri agree on boundary in Des Moines River
1943	Nebraska and Iowa agree to a boundary as main channel in Missouri River except for Carter Lake
1949	Kansas and Missouri agree to swap exclaves along Missouri River
1950	Kansas and Missouri agree on boundary in Missouri River
1959	Alaska joins Union
	Hawaii joins Union
1961	Congress consents to a transfer of land from Minnesota to North Dakota
1963	California and Arizona agree on Colorado River boundary
1977	Georgia brings suit in Supreme Court to settle lower Savannah River boundary
1996	Texas-Oklahoma commission settles boundary in Red River
1998	Supreme Court awards land-filled part of Ellis Island to New Jersey
1999	Congress approves Nebraska-Missouri Boundary Compact
2001	Supreme Court determines island in Piscataqua River belongs to Maine

BIBLIOGRAPHY

General Reference

Note: The first seven sources were consulted to such an extent, or were so generally useful, they deserve special mention rather than mere inclusion in one of the subsequent sections.

Atlas and Gazetteer (various states). Yarmouth, Maine: DeLorme (various years).

Carpenter, Allan, and Carl Provorse. *The World Almanac of the U.S.A.* Mahwah, N.J.: World Almanac Books, 1996.

Douglas, Edward M. *Boundaries, Areas, Geographic Centers and Altitudes of the United States and the Several States.* 2nd ed. Washington: U.S. Government Printing Office, 1939. Geological Survey Bulletin 817.

Encarta. CD–ROM encyclopedia. Microsoft Corporation, 1994, 2000.

Kagan, Hilde Heun, ed. *The American Heritage Pictorial Atlas of United States History.* New York: American Heritage Publishing Co., Inc., 1966.

Van Zandt, Franklin K. *Boundaries of the United States and the Several States.* Washington, D.C.: U.S. Government Printing Office, 1966. Geological Survey Bulletin 1212.

_____. *Boundaries of the United States and the Several States*, Washington, D.C.: U.S. Government Printing Office, 1976. Geological Survey Professional Paper 909. ("The first Geological Survey record setting forth the history of the boundaries of the United States and the several States and Territories was prepared by Henry Gannett, assisted by Franklin G. Butterfield, and was published as Bulletin 13 of the Geological Survey in 1885. The second edition, revised and enlarged by Henry Gannett, was published as Bulletin 171 in 1900. The third edition, also revised by Gannett, was published as Bulletin 226 in 1904. A revision and enlargement of Bulletin 226, which included additional matter incidentally connected with boundaries, was prepared by Edward M. Douglas and issued in 1923 as Bulletin 689. It was again revised by Douglas in 1930 as Bulletin 817. Bulletin 1212, prepared in 1964 by Franklin K. Van Zandt, is a revision of Bulletin 817. This professional paper, prepared in 1974-75, is a revision of Bulletin 1212." p. v).

Introduction

Armstrong, John M., and Peter C. Ryner. *Ocean Management: A New Perspective.* Ann Arbor, Mich.: Ann Arbor Science Publishers Inc., 1981.

Baldwin, P.M. "A Historical Note on the Boundaries of New Mexico." *New Mexico Historical Review*, V, no. 2 (1930): 117–37.

Barnard, Edward S., ed. *Story of the Great American West.* Pleasantville, New York: The Reader's Digest Association, Inc., 1977.

Beals, Carleton. *Colonial Rhode Island.* Camden, N.J.: Thomas Nelson Inc., 1970.

Bergeson, Nancy. *History of the Forty-Second Parallel as a Political Boundary Between Utah and Idaho.* Logan, Utah: Utah State University, 1983.

Berkhofer, Robert F., Jr. "The Northwest Ordinance and the Principle of Territorial Evolution." In *The American Territorial System*, ed. John Porter Bloom. Athens, Ohio: Ohio University Press, 1973, 45–55.

Capps, Clifford Sheats, and Eugenia Burney. *Colonial Georgia.* Camden, N.J.: Thomas Nelson Inc., 1972.

Carter, Hodding. *Man and the River, the Missis-sippi*. Chicago: Rand McNally & Company, 1970.

Christensen, Gardell Dano, and Eugenia Burney. *Colonial Delaware*. Camden, N.J.: Thomas Nelson Inc., 1974.

Clark, Joseph Stanley. "The Northern Boundary of Oklahoma." *Chronicles of Oklahoma* 15, no. 3 (1937): 271–90.

Clark, Thomas D. *Historic Maps of Kentucky*. Lexington: The University Press of Kentucky, 1979.

Cushing, Sumner W. "The Boundaries of the New England States." *Annals of the Association of American Geographers* X (1920): 17–40.

Daniels, George G., ed. *The Spanish West*. New York: Time-Life Books, 1976.

DenBoer, Gordon, compiler, with George E. Goodridge Jr. *Atlas of Historical County Boundaries: New Hampshire, Vermont*, John H. Long, ed. New York: Simon and Schuster, 1993.

De Vorsey, Louis, Jr. *The Georgia–South Carolina Boundary*. Athens, Ga.: The University of Georgia Press, 1982.

Ehrlich, Daniel Henry. "Problems Arising from Shifts of the Missouri River on the Eastern Border of Nebraska." *Nebraska History* 54, no. 3 (Fall 1973): 341–63.

Ellis, Erl H. *Colorado Mapology*. Frederick, Colo.: Jende-Hagen Book Corporation, 1983.

_____. *International Boundary Lines Across Colorado and Wyoming*. Boulder, Colo.: Johnson Publishing Company, 1966.

Ernst, Joseph W. *With Compass and Chain: Federal Land Surveyors in the Old Northwest, 1785–1816*. New York: Arno Press, 1979.

Faris, John T. *The Romance of the Boundaries*. New York: Harper & Brothers Publishers, 1926.

Fritz, Percy Stanley. *Colorado: The Centennial State*. New York: Prentice-Hall, Inc., 1941.

Goodwyn, Lawrence. *The South Central States*. New York: Time Incorporated, 1967.

Green, D. Brooks. "The Idaho-Wyoming Boundary: A Problem in Location." *Idaho Yesterdays* 23, no. 1 (Spring 1979): 10–14.

Harrell, Clifford Leslie. *Boundaries of Alabama*. Auburn, Ala.: Master's Thesis, Alabama Polytechnic Institute, 1939.

Hart, Albert Bushnell, ed. *Commonwealth History of Massachusetts*. Vols. 1, 3. New York: The States History Company, 1927, 1929.

Haywood, John. *Civil and Political History of the State of Tennessee*. Knoxville: Heiskell & Brown, 1823.

Hemperley, Marion R., and Edwin L. Jackson. *Georgia's Boundaries: The Shaping of a State*. Athens, Ga.: Carl Vinson Institute of Government, 1993.

Homsher, Lola. "History of Albany County to 1880." *Annals of Wyoming* 21, nos. 2–3 (July–Oct. 1959): 181–213.

Howes, Charles C. *This Place Called Kansas*. Norman: University of Oklahoma Press, 1952.

Hughes, Sarah S. *Surveyors and Statesmen: Land Measuring in Colonial Virginia*. Richmond: The Virginia Surveyors Foundation, Ltd., and The Virginia Association of Surveyors, Inc., 1979.

Johannsen, Robert W. "Stephen A. Douglas and the Territories in the Senate." In *The American Territorial System*, ed. John Porter Bloom. Athens, Ohio: Ohio University Press, 1973, 77–92.

Johnson, Cecil. *British West Florida, 1763–1783*. New Haven: Yale University Press, 1943.

Kenney, Bruce Ericksen. *The Historical Development of the Boundaries of Utah*. Master's Thesis, Chico State University, 1991.

Kleber, John E., ed. *The Kentucky Encyclopedia*. Lexington: The University Press of Kentucky, 1992.

Klein, Philip Shriver. *President James Buchanan: A Biography*. University Park: The Pennsylvania State University Press, 1962.

Labaree, Benjamin W. *Colonial Massachusetts: A History*. Millwood, N.Y.: KTO Press, 1979.

Landrum, Francis S. "A Major Monument: Oregon-California Boundary." *Oregon Historical Quarterly* 72, no. 1 (1971): 5–53.

Malone, Michael P., Richard B. Roeder, and William L. Lang. *Montana: A History of Two Centuries*. Seattle: University of Washington Press, 1976.

McCormack, Jack C. *Surveying Fundamentals*. Englewood Cliffs, N.J.: Prentice-Hall, Inc., 1983.

Metraux, Daniel A. "Was Vermont Ever a Republic?" *Vermont History* 55, no. 3 (Summer 1987): 167–73.

Milton, John R. *South Dakota: A Bicentennial History*. New York: W.W. Norton & Company, Inc., 1977.

Morris, Richard B. *The Peacemakers*. New York: Harper & Row, Publishers, 1965.

Morrison, Charles. *The Fairfax Line: A Profile in History and Geography*. Parsons, W.Va.: McClain Printing Company, 1970.

_____. *An Outline of Maryland Boundary Disputes*. Parsons, W.Va.: McClain Printing Company, 1974.

Olson, James C., and Ronald C. Naugle. *History of Nebraska*. 3rd ed. Lincoln: University of Nebraska Press, 1997.

Onuf, Peter S. *The Origins of the Federal Republic*. Philadelphia: University of Pennsylvania Press, 1983.

_____. *Statehood and Union: A History of the Northwest Ordinance*. Bloomington and Indianapolis: Indiana University Press, 1987.

Patrick, Rembert W. *Florida Under Five Flags*. Gainesville: University of Florida Press, 1945.

Paullin, Charles O. *Atlas of the Historical Geogra-*

phy of the United States. Baltimore: A. Hoen & Co., Inc., 1932.

Paxson, Frederic L. *The Boundaries of Colorado*. Boulder, Colo., 1904. Reprint *University of Colorado Studies* II, no. 2 (July 1904).

Pomeroy, Earl S. *The Territories and the United States: 1861–1890*. Philadelphia: University of Pennsylvania Press, 1947.

Powell, John Wesley. *Down the Colorado*. New York: E.P. Dutton & Co., Inc., 1969.

Prow, Wolf. *Virginia's Boundaries*. Hampton, Va.: Thomas Nelson Community College, 1977, reprinted 1988.

Quaife, M.M., and Sidney Glazer. *Michigan: From Primitive Wilderness to Industrial Commonwealth*. New York: Prentice-Hall, Inc., 1948.

Richeson, A.W. *English Land Measuring to 1800: Instruments and Practices*. Cambridge, Mass.: The Society for the History of Technology and The M.I.T. Press, 1966.

Robinson, Elwyn B. *History of North Dakota*. Lincoln: University of Nebraska Press, 1966.

Robinson, Will Grow. "South Dakota Boundaries." *Report and Historical Collections* XXXII (1964): 232–59.

Rogers, William Warren, Robert David Ward, Leah Rawls Atkins, and Wayne Flynt. *Alabama: The History of a Deep South State*. Tuscaloosa: The University of Alabama Press, 1994.

Sage, Leland L. *A History of Iowa*. Ames: The Iowa State University Press, 1974.

Skaggs, Marvin Lucian. *North Carolina Boundary Disputes Involving Her Southern Line*. Chapel Hill: The University of North Carolina Press, 1941.

State of New Mexico vs. the State of Colorado, a brief in behalf of the State of Colorado, in the Supreme Court of the United States October term, 1924, no. 12. Denver, Colo.: Clark Quick-Printing Co., 1924.

Stephens, Elizabeth Pearl. *The Historical Geography of the Boundaries of Oklahoma*. Norman, Okla.: University of Oklahoma. Master of Arts thesis, 1964.

Stevens, Frank E. *Life of Stephen Arnold Douglas*. Springfield, Ill.: Illinois State Historical Society. Reprint *Journal of the Illinois State Historical Society* XVI, nos. 3 and 4 (Oct. 1923–Jan. 1924).

Stewart, Lowell O. *Public Land Surveys*. Ames, Iowa: Collegiate Press, Inc., 1935.

Summers, Lewis Preston. *History of Southwest Virginia, 1746–1786, Washington County, 1777–1870*. Johnson City, Tenn.: The Overmountain Press, 1989; original copyright by L.P. Summers, 1903.

Taylor, Robert J. *Colonial Connecticut: A History*. Millwood, N.Y.: KTO Press, 1979.

Tebeau, Charlton W. *A History of Florida*. Coral Gables, Fla.: University of Miami Press, 1971.

Thwaites, Reuben G. "The Boundaries of Wisconsin." Collections of the State Historical Society of Wisconsin XI (1888): 451–501.

Tolles, Frederick B. *James Logan and the Culture of Provincial America*. Boston: Little, Brown, & Co., 1957.

Trewartha, Glen T., Arthur H. Robinson, and Edwin H. Hammond. *Physical Elements of Geography*. New York: McGraw-Hill Book Company, 1967.

U.S. House. 23 Cong., 1 sess. *Southern Boundary of Tennessee*. (H. Rpt. 445). Washington: Government Printing Office, 1834. (Serial Set 262).

U.S. House. 32 Cong., 1 sess. *Reports of Surveyors General of Illinois, Missouri, and Oregon*. (H. Ex. Doc. 52). [No place or publisher] 1851–52. (Serial Set 640)

Uzes, Francois D. *Chaining the Land: A History of Surveying in California*. Sacramento: Landmark Enterprises, 1977.

Weir, Robert M. *Colonial South Carolina: A History*. Millwood, N.Y.: KTO Press, 1983.

White, C. Albert. *A History of the Rectangular Survey System*. Washington: Government Printing Office, n.d.

Williams, Frederick D. *The Northwest Ordinance: Essays on Its Formulation, Provisions, and Legacy*. East Lansing, Mich.: Michigan State University Press, 1989.

Williams, John Alexander. *West Virginia: A Bicentennial History*. New York: W.W. Norton & Company, Inc., 1976.

Williams, Samuel. *The Natural and Civil History of Vermont*. Walpole, N.H., 1794 (microcard).

Wissler, Clark. *Indians of the United States*. Garden City, N.Y.: Doubleday & Company, Inc., 1966.

Wood, James Playsted. *Colonial New Hampshire*. Camden, N.J.: Thomas Nelson, Inc., 1973.

Wunder, John R. "Tampering with the Northwest Frontier: The Accidental Design of the Washington/Idaho Boundary." *Pacific Northwest Quarterly* 68, no. 1 (Jan. 1977): 1–12.

New England Region

CONNECTICUT

Bowen, Clarence Winthrop. *The Boundary Disputes of Connecticut*. Boston: James R. Osgood and Company, 1882.

Calder, Isabel M. *The New Haven Colony*. New Haven: Yale University Press, 1934.

Faris, John T. *The Romance of the Boundaries*. New York: Harper & Brothers Publishers, 1926.

Hart, Albert Bushnell, ed. *Commonwealth History of Massachusetts*. Vols. 1, 3. New York: The States History Company, 1927, 1929.

Hooker, Roland Mather. *Boundaries of Connecticut*. Published for the Tercentenary Commission of the State of Connecticut. New Haven: Yale University Press, 1933.

Morgan, Forrest, ed. *Connecticut as a Colony and as a State*. Vols. 1, 2, 4. Hartford: The Publishing Society of Connecticut, 1904.

Roth, David M. *Connecticut: A Bicentennial History*. New York: W.W. Norton & Company, Inc., 1979.

MAINE

Chase, Suzi Forbes. *New England*. New York: Prentice Hall Travel, 1994.

Clark, Charles E. *Maine: A Bicentennial History*. New York: W.W. Norton & Company, Inc., 1977.

Corey, Albert B. *The Crisis of 1830–1842 in Canadian-American Relations*. New Haven: Yale University Press, 1941.

Cushing, Sumner W. "The Boundaries of the New England States." *Annals of the Association of American Geographers* X (1920): 17–40.

Eliot, Thomas H. *Governing America: The Politics of a Free People*. New York: Dodd, Mead, & Company, 1964.

Engelman, Fred L. *The Peace of Christmas Eve*. New York: Harcourt, Brace & World, Inc., 1962.

Federal Writers' Project. *Maine: A Guide Down East*. Boston: Houghton Mifflin Company, 1937.

Jones, Howard. *To the Webster-Ashburton Treaty*. Chapel Hill: The University of North Carolina Press, 1977.

White, James. *Boundary Disputes and Treaties*. Toronto: Glasgow, Brook & Company, 1914.

MASSACHUSETTS

Cushing, Sumner W. "The Boundaries of the New England States." *Annals of the Association of American Geographers* X (1920): 17–40.

Fox, Dixon R. *Yankees and Yorkers*. Port Washington, N.Y.: Ira J. Friedman, Inc., 1940.

Gill, Crispin. *Mayflower Remembered: A History of the Plymouth Pilgrims*. New York: Taplinger Publishing Company, 1970.

Hart, Albert Bushnell, ed. *Commonwealth History of Massachusetts*. Vols. 1, 3. New York: The States History Company, 1927, 1929.

Jones, Matt Bushnell. *Vermont in the Making, 1750–1777*. Hamden, Conn.: Archon Books, 1968.

NEW HAMPSHIRE

Daniell, Jere R. *Colonial New Hampshire: A History*. Millwood, N.Y.: KTO Press, 1981.

DenBoer, Gordon, compiler, with George E. Goodridge Jr. *Atlas of Historical County Boundaries: New Hampshire, Vermont*. John H. Long, ed. New York: Simon and Schuster, 1993.

Faris, John T. *The Romance of the Boundaries*. New York: Harper & Brothers Publishers, 1926.

Jones, Matt Bushnell. *Vermont in the Making, 1750–1777*. Hamden, Conn.: Archon Books, 1968.

Morison, Elizabeth Forbes, and Elting E. Morison. *New Hampshire: A Bicentennial History*. New York: W.W. Norton & Company, Inc., 1976.

Suzzalo, Henry, ed. *National Encyclopedia*. Vol. 7. New York: P.F. Collier & Son Corporation, 1944.

RHODE ISLAND

Federal Writers' Project. *Rhode Island: A Guide to the Smallest State*. Boston: Houghton Mifflin Company, 1937.

Hart, Albert Bushnell, ed. *Commonwealth History of Massachusetts*. Vols. 1, 3. New York: The States History Company, 1927, 1929.

James, Sydney V. *Colonial Rhode Island*. New York: Charles Scribner's Sons, 1975.

Lippincott, Bertram. *Indians, Privateers, and High Society*. Philadelphia and New York: J.B. Lippincott, 1961.

McLoughlin, William G. *Rhode Island: A Bicentennial History*. New York: W.W. Norton & Company, Inc., 1978.

Richman, Irving Berdine. *Rhode Island: Its Making and Its Meaning*. 2nd ed. New York: G.P. Putnam's Sons, 1908.

Ullman, Edward L. "The Eastern Rhode Island–Massachusetts Boundary Zone." *The Geographical Review* XXIX, no. 1 (Apr. 1939): 291–302.

_____. "The Historical Geography of the Eastern Boundary of Rhode Island." *Research Studies of the State College of Washington* IV, no. 1 (1936): 67–87.

VERMONT

Chase, Suzi Forbes. *New England*. New York: Prentice Hall Travel, 1994.

Crane, Charles Edward. *Let Me Show You Vermont*. New York: Alfred A. Knopf, 1937.

DenBoer, Gordon, compiler, with George E. Goodridge Jr. *Atlas of Historical County Boundaries: New Hampshire, Vermont,* John H. Long, ed. New York: Simon and Schuster, 1993.

Eliot, Thomas H. *Governing America: The Politics of a Free People*. New York: Dodd, Mead, & Company, 1964.

Faris, John T. *The Romance of the Boundaries*. New York: Harper & Brothers Publishers, 1926.

Hill, Ralph Nading. *Contrary Country*. Brattle-boro, Vt.: The Stephen Greene Press, 1961.

Jones, Howard. *To the Webster-Ashburton Treaty*. Chapel Hill: The University of North Carolina Press, 1977.

Jones, Matt Bushnell. *Vermont in the Making, 1750–1777*. Hamden, Conn.: Archon Books, 1968.

Lates, Richard, and Harold Meeks. "The Line Which Separates Vermonters from Canadians: A Short History of Vermont's Northern Border with Quebec." *Vermont History* 44, no. 2 (Spring 1976): 71–77.

Mahler, Susan. "Vermont: Land of Debatable Boundaries." *Vermont History* 34, no. 4 (Oct. 1966): 241–45.

Morrissey, Charles T. *Vermont: A Bicentennial History*. New York: W.W. Norton & Company, Inc., 1981.

Williams, Samuel. *The Natural and Civil History of Vermont*. Walpole, N.H., 1794. (microcard)

Mid-Atlantic Region

DELAWARE

Faris, John T. *The Romance of the Boundaries*. New York: Harper & Brothers Publishers, 1926.

Hoffecker, Carol E. *Delaware: A Bicentennial History*. New York: W.W. Norton & Company, Inc., 1977.

Munroe, John A. *Colonial Delaware: A History*. Millwood, N.Y.: KTO Press, 1978.

_____. *Federalist Delaware, 1775–1815*. New Brunswick, N.J.: Rutgers University Press, 1954.

_____. *History of Delaware*. 3rd ed. Newark: University of Delaware Press, 1993.

MARYLAND

Bailey, Kenneth A. *Thomas Cresap: Maryland Frontiersman*. Boston: The Christopher Publishing House, 1944.

Beverley, Robert. *The History and Present State of Virginia*. Williamsburg, Va.: The University of North Carolina Press, 1974.

Brugger, Robert J. *Maryland: A Middle Temperament*. Baltimore: The John Hopkins University Press, 1988.

DiLisio, James E. *Maryland: A Geography*. Boulder, Colo.: Westview Press, 1983.

Finlayson, Ann. *Colonial Maryland*. Nashville, Tenn.: Thomas Nelson Inc., 1974.

Land, Aubrey C. *Colonial Maryland: A History*. Millwood, N.Y.: KTO Press, 1981.

McSherry, James. *History of Maryland*. Baltimore: The Baltimore Book Co., 1904.

Morton, Richard L. "The Reverend Hugh Jones: Lord Baltimore's Mathematician." *William and Mary Quarterly*, third series, VII, no. 1 (Jan. 1950): 107–15.

Papenfuse, Edward C., and Joseph M. Coale III. *The Hammond-Harwood House Atlas of Historical Maps of Maryland, 1608–1908*. Baltimore: The Johns Hopkins University Press, 1982.

_____, and Richard H. Richardson. *Where Is Watkins Point?: In Search of Maryland's Boundaries*. No publisher nor date indicated.

Prow, Wolf. *Virginia's Boundaries*. Hampton, Va.: Thomas Nelson Community College, 1977, reprinted 1988.

Squires, W.H.T. *Through Centuries Three: A Short History of the People of Virginia*. Portsmouth, Va.: Printcraft Press, Inc., 1929.

Stanard, Mary Newton. *The Story of Virginia's First Century*. Philadelphia: J.B. Lippincott Company, 1928.

State of New Mexico vs. the State of Colorado, a brief in behalf of the State of Colorado, in the Supreme Court of the United States October term, 1924, no. 12. Denver, Colo.: Clark Quick-Printing Co., 1924.

Watson, Bud. "Border Wars." *Southern Exposure* 10, no. 3 (May/June 1982): 77.

Writers' Program. *Virginia: A Guide to the Old Dominion*. New York: Oxford University Press, 1940.

DISTRICT OF COLUMBIA

Bryan, Wilhelmus Bogart. *A History of the National Capital*. Vol. 1. New York: The Macmillan Company, 1914.

Green, Constance McLaughlin. *Washington: Village and Capital, 1800–1878*. Princeton: Princeton University Press, 1962.

Lewis, David L. *District of Columbia: A Bicentennial History*. New York: W.W. Norton & Company, Inc., 1976.

NEW JERSEY

Cunningham, John T. *Colonial New Jersey*. Camden, N.J.: Thomas Nelson Inc., 1971.

_____. *This Is New Jersey*. New Brunswick, N.J.: Rutgers University Press, 1994.

Fleming, Thomas. *New Jersey: A Bicentennial History*. New York: W.W. Norton & Company, Inc., 1977.

McCormick, Richard P. *New Jersey from Colony to State*. Princeton: D. Van Nostrand Co., Inc., 1964.

Pomfret, John E. *Colonial New Jersey*. New York: Charles Scribner's Sons, 1973.

_____. *The Province of East New Jersey, 1609–1702*. Princeton: Princeton University Press, 1962.

_____. *The Province of West New Jersey, 1609–1702.* Princeton: Princeton University Press, 1956.

Stansfield, Charles A., Jr. *New Jersey: A Geography.* Boulder, Colo.: Westview Press, 1983.

Suzzalo, Henry, ed. *National Encyclopedia.* Vol. 7. New York: P.F. Collier & Son Corporation, 1944.

New York

Bliven, Bruce, Jr. *New York: A Bicentennial History.* New York: W.W. Norton & Company, Inc., 1981.

Christensen, Gardell Dano. *Colonial New York.* Camden, N.J.: Thomas Nelson Inc., 1969.

Colden, Cadwallader. "Answers and Proposals from the New York Commissioners to the Connecticut Commissioners on the Boundary Question." *New York Historical Society Collections* 50 (1917): 161–64.

Cushing, Sumner W. "The Boundaries of the New England States." *Annals of the Association of American Geographers* X (1920): 17–40.

Faris, John T. *The Romance of the Boundaries.* New York: Harper & Brothers Publishers, 1926.

Flick, Alexander C. "How New York Won and Lost An Empire." *Proceedings of the New York State Historical Association* XXXV (1937): 370–77.

_____, ed. *History of the State of New York.* Vols. II, III, V, VI. New York: Columbia University Press, 1933, 1934.

Fox, Dixon R. *Yankees and Yorkers.* Port Washington, N.Y.: Ira J. Friedman, Inc., 1940.

Hart, Albert Bushnell, ed. *Commonwealth History of Massachusetts.* Vols. 1, 3. New York: The States History Company, 1927, 1929.

Jones, Howard. *To the Webster-Ashburton Treaty.* Chapel Hill: University of North Carolina Press, 1977.

Kammen, Michael. *Colonial New York: A History.* New York: Charles Scribner's Sons, 1975.

Lossing, Benson J. *The Empire State.* Hartford, Conn.: American Publishing Co., 1888.

Report of the Regents of the University on the Boundaries of the State of New York. Documents of the Senate of the State of New York, Ninety-sixth Session, 1873, vol. 5, nos. 108 and 109. Albany: The Argus Company, Printers, 1874.

Schwarz, Philip J. *The Jarring Interests.* Albany, N.Y.: University of New York Press, 1979.

_____. "To Conciliate the Jarring Interests." *New York Historical Society Quarterly* 59, no. 4 (Oct. 1975): 299–319.

Stansfield, Charles A., Jr. *New Jersey: A Geography.* Boulder, Colo.: Westview Press, 1983.

White, James. *Boundary Disputes and Treaties.* Toronto: Glasgow, Brook & Company, 1914.

Pennsylvania

Cochran, Thomas C. *Pennsylvania: A Bicentennial History.* New York: W.W. Norton & Company, Inc., 1978.

Cumming, John. "George Burges and the Erie Triangle." *Western Pennsylvania Historical Magazine* 49, no. 3 (1966):231–50.

Day, Sherman. *Historical Collections of the State of Pennsylvania.* Port Washington, N.Y.: Ira J. Friedman, Inc. First published 1843; reissued 1969.

Faris, John T. *The Romance of the Boundaries.* New York: Harper & Brothers Publishers, 1926.

Hudson, Patricia. "Penning a Legacy." *American History* (February, 1998).

Illick, Joseph E. *Colonial Pennsylvania: A History.* New York: Charles Scribner's Sons, 1976.

Jenkins, Howard M., ed. *Pennsylvania, Colonial and Federal: A History.* Vol. 2. Philadelphia: Pennsylvania Historical Publishing Association, 1906.

Klein, Philip S., and Ari Hoogenboom. *A History of Pennsylvania.* 2nd ed. University Park: The Pennsylvania State University Press, 1980.

Lechner, Carl B. "The Erie Triangle: The Final Link Between Philadelphia and the Great Lakes." *Pennsylvania Magazine of History and Biography* 116, no. 1 (1992): 33–58.

Shimmell, L.S. *A History of Pennsylvania.* New York: Charles E. Merrill Co., 1900.

Stevens, Sylvester K. *Pennsylvania: Birthplace of a Nation.* New York: Random House, 1964.

Tolles, Frederick B. *James Logan and the Culture of Provincial America.* Boston: Little, Brown, & Co., 1957.

White, James. *Boundary Disputes and Treaties.* Toronto: Glasgow, Brook & Company, 1914.

Upper South Region

Kentucky

Channing, Steven A. *Kentucky: A Bicentennial History.* New York: W.W. Norton & Company, Inc., 1977.

Clark, Thomas D. *Historic Maps of Kentucky.* Lexington: The University Press of Kentucky, 1979.

_____. *Kentucky: Land of Contrast.* New York: Harper & Row, Publishers, 1968.

Faris, John T. *The Romance of the Boundaries.* New York: Harper & Brothers Publishers, 1926.

Harrison, Lowell H., and James C. Klotter. *A New History of Kentucky.* Lexington: The University Press of Kentucky, 1997.

Kleber, John E., ed. *The Kentucky Encyclopedia.* Lexington: The University Press of Kentucky, 1992.

Smith, Z.F. *The History of Kentucky*. Louisville: The Prentice Press, 1895.

U.S. Congress. *American State Papers*. 15 Cong., 1 sess. "Boundary Between Kentucky and Tennessee," 451. Washington: Gales and Seaton, 1834. (Serial Set ASP038).

_____. *American State Papers*. 16 Cong., 1 sess. "Adjustment of the Boundary Between Kentucky and Tennessee." 490. Washington: Gales and Seaton, 1834. (Serial Set ASP038)

NORTH CAROLINA

Boyd, William K. *History of North Carolina: Volume 2, The Federal Period 1783–1860*. Spartanburg, S.C.: The Reprint Company, 1973.

Cappon, Lester J., editor-in-chief. *Atlas of Early American History*. Princeton: Princeton University Press, 1976.

Connor, R.D.W. *History of North Carolina: Volume 1, The Colonial and Revolutionary Periods 1584–1783*. Spartanburg, S.C.: The Reprint Company, 1973.

Haywood, John. *Civil and Political History of the State of Tennessee*. Knoxville: Heiskell & Brown, 1823.

Hemperley, Marion R., and Edwin L. Jackson. *Georgia's Boundaries: The Shaping of a State*. Athens, Ga.: Carl Vinson Institute of Government, 1993.

Lefler, Hugh Talmage, and Albert Ray Newsome. *North Carolina*. Chapel Hill: The University of North Carolina Press, 1954.

_____, and William S. Powell. *Colonial North Carolina*. New York: Charles Scribner's Sons, 1973.

Merrens, Harry Roy. *Colonial North Carolina in the Eighteenth Century*. Chapel Hill: The University of North Carolina Press, 1964.

Powell, William S. *North Carolina: A Bicentennial History*. New York: W.W. Norton & Company, Inc., 1977.

_____. *North Carolina Through Four Centuries*. Chapel Hill: The University of North Carolina Press, 1989.

State and County Boundaries of Mississippi. Prelim. ed. Jackson, Miss.: The Mississippi Historical Records Survey, 1942.

TENNESSEE

Corlew, Robert E. *Tennessee: A Short History*. 2nd ed., updated through 1989. Knoxville: The University of Tennessee Press, 1981.

Durham, Walter T. "The Southwest and Northwest Territories, a Comparison, 1787–1796." *Tennessee Historical Quarterly* XLIX, no. 3 (Fall 1990): 188–96.

Dykeman, Wilma. *Tennessee: A Bicentennial History*. New York: W.W. Norton & Company, Inc., 1975.

Folmsbee, Stanley J., Robert E. Corlew, and Enoch L. Mitchell. *Tennessee: A Short History*. Knoxville: The University of Tennessee Press, 1969.

Garrett, William R. "Northern Boundary of Tennessee." *The American Historical Magazine* 6, no. 1 (Jan. 1901): 18–39.

Haywood, John. *Civil and Political History of the State of Tennessee*. Knoxville: Heiskell & Brown, 1823.

Henry, Robert S. "The Extension of the Northern Line of Tennessee to the West of Cumberland Gap — Matthews Line." *Tennessee Historical Magazine* 6, no. 3 (Oct. 1920): 177–84.

Sioussat, St. George L. "Document." *Tennessee Historical Magazine* 1, no. 1 (1915): 40–65.

U.S. House. 23 Cong., 1 sess. *Southern Boundary of Tennessee*. (H. Rpt. 445). Washington: Government Printing Office, 1834. (Serial Set 262).

VIRGINIA

Billings, Warren M., John E. Selby, and Thad W. Tate. *Colonial Virginia: A History*. White Plains, N.Y.: KTO Press, 1986.

Boyd, William K. *William Byrd's Histories of the Dividing Line Betwixt Virginia and North Carolina*. Raleigh: The North Carolina Historical Commission, 1929.

Cappon, Lester J., editor-in-chief. *Atlas of Early American History*. Princeton: Princeton University Press, 1976.

Clark, Thomas D. *Historic Maps of Kentucky*. Lexington: The University Press of Kentucky, 1979.

Faris, John T. *The Romance of the Boundaries*. New York: Harper & Brothers Publishers, 1926.

Finlayson, Ann. *Colonial Maryland*. Nashville, Tenn.: Thomas Nelson Inc., 1974.

Haywood, John. *Civil and Political History of the State of Tennessee*. Knoxville, Tenn.: Heiskell & Brown, 1823.

Hemperley, Marion R., and Edwin L. Jackson. *Georgia's Boundaries: The Shaping of a State*. Athens, Ga.: Carl Vinson Institute of Government, 1993.

Morton, Richard L. *Colonial Virginia*. Vol. II. Chapel Hill: The University of North Carolina Press, 1960.

Powell, William S. *North Carolina: A Bicentennial History*. New York: W.W. Norton & Company, Inc., 1977.

Prow, Wolf. *Virginia's Boundaries*. Hampton, Va.: Thomas Nelson Community College, 1977, reprinted 1988.

Rubin, Louis D., Jr. *Virginia: A Bicentennial History*. New York: W.W. Norton & Company, Inc., 1977.

Summers, Lewis Preston. *History of Southwest Virginia, 1746–1786, Washington County, 1777–1870*. Johnson City, Tenn.: The Overmountain Press, 1989; original copyright by L.P. Summers, 1903.

Writers' Program. *West Virginia: A Guide to the Mountain State*. New York: Oxford University Press, 1941.

West Virginia

Ambler, Charles H., and Festus P. Summers. *West Virginia: The Mountain State*. 2nd ed. Englewood Cliffs, N.J.: Prentice-Hall, Inc., 1958.

Faris, John T. *The Romance of the Boundaries*. New York: Harper & Brothers Publishers, 1926.

Williams, John Alexander. *West Virginia: A Bicentennial History*. New York: W.W. Norton & Company, Inc., 1976.

Winberry, John J. "Formation of the West Virginia–Virginia Boundary." *Southeastern Geographer* XVII, no. 2 (Nov. 1977): 108–24.

Wright, Louis B. *South Carolina: A Bicentennial History*. New York: W.W. Norton & Company, Inc., 1976.

Writers' Program. *West Virginia: A Guide to the Mountain State*. New York: Oxford University Press, 1941.

Lower South Region

Alabama

Abernethy, Thomas Perkins. *The Formative Period in Alabama, 1815–1828*. Tuscaloosa: The University of Alabama Press, 1965.

Carter, Hodding. *Man and the River, the Mississippi*. Chicago: Rand McNally & Company, 1970.

Cushing, Sumner W. "The Boundaries of the New England States." *Annals of the Association of American Geographers* X (1920): 17–40.

Hamilton, Virginia Van der Veer. *Alabama: A Bicentennial History*. New York: W.W. Norton & Company, Inc., 1977.

Harrell, Clifford Leslie. *Boundaries of Alabama*. Auburn, Ala.: Master's Thesis for Alabama Polytechnic Institute, 1939.

Johnson, Cecil. *British West Florida, 1763–1783*. New Haven: Yale University Press, 1943.

Roberts, Francis C. "Thomas Freeman — Surveyor of the Old Southwest." *The Alabama Review* XL, no. 3 (July 1987): 216–30.

Rogers, William Warren, Robert David Ward, Leah Rawls Atkins, and Wayne Flynt. *Alabama: The History of a Deep South State*. Tuscaloosa: The University of Alabama Press, 1994.

Writers' Program. *Alabama: A Guide to the Deep South*. New York: Richard R. Smith, 1941.

Florida

Cappon, Lester J., editor-in-chief. *Atlas of Early American History*. Princeton: Princeton University Press, 1976.

Hanna, Kathryn Abbey. *Florida: Land of Change*. 2nd ed. Chapel Hill: The University of North Carolina Press, 1948.

Hemperley, Marion R., and Edwin L. Jackson. *Georgia's Boundaries: The Shaping of a State*. Athens, Ga.: Carl Vinson Institute of Government, 1993.

Jahoda, Gloria. *Florida: A Bicentennial History*. New York: W.W. Norton & Company, Inc., 1976.

Morris, Richard B. *The Peacemakers*. New York: Harper & Row, Publishers, 1965.

Patrick, Rembert W. *Florida Under Five Flags*. Gainesville: University of Florida Press, 1945.

State and County Boundaries of Mississippi. Prelim. ed. Jackson, Miss.: The Mississippi Historical Records Survey, 1942.

Tebeau, Charlton W. *A History of Florida*. Coral Gables: University of Miami Press, 1971.

Georgia

Cappon, Lester J., editor-in-chief. *Atlas of Early American History*. Princeton: Princeton University Press, 1976.

Coleman, Kenneth. *Colonial Georgia: A History*. New York: Charles Scribner's Sons, 1976.

Cooper, William J., Jr., and Thomas E. Terrill. *The American South*. New York: Alfred A. Knopf, 1990.

Coulter, E. Merton. "The Georgia-Tennessee Boundary Line." *Georgia Historical Quarterly* XXXV, no. 4 (Dec. 1951): 269–306.

De Vorsey, Louis, Jr. *The Georgia–South Carolina Boundary*. Athens, Ga.: The University of Georgia Press, 1982.

Hemperley, Marion R., and Edwin L. Jackson. *Georgia's Boundaries: The Shaping of a State*. Athens, Ga.: Carl Vinson Institute of Government, 1993.

Martin, Harold H. *Georgia: A Bicentennial History*. New York: W.W. Norton & Company, Inc., 1977.

Reidinger, Martin. *The Walton War and the Georgia–North Carolina Boundary Dispute*. Self-published, 1981.

Skaggs, Marvin Lucian. *North Carolina Boundary Disputes Involving Her Southern Line*. Chapel Hill: The University of North Carolina Press, 1941.

Wallace, David Duncan. *South Carolina: A Short History*. Columbia: University of South Carolina Press, 1951.

MISSISSIPPI

McLemore, Richard Aubrey, ed. *A History of Mississippi*. Vol. I. Jackson: University and College Press of Mississippi, 1973.

Riley, Franklin L. "Location of the Boundaries of Mississippi." *Publications of the Mississippi Historical Society* 3 (1898, 1914): 167–84.

Skates, John Ray. *Mississippi: A Bicentennial History*. New York: W.W. Norton & Company, Inc., 1979.

State and County Boundaries of Mississippi. Prelim. ed. Jackson, Miss.: The Mississippi Historical Records Survey, 1942.

Writers' Program. *Alabama: A Guide to the Deep South*. New York: Richard R. Smith, 1941.

SOUTH CAROLINA

Brown, Douglas Summers. *The Catawba Indians*. Columbia: The University of South Carolina Press, 1966.

De Vorsey, Louis, Jr. *The Georgia–South Carolina Boundary*. Athens, Ga.: The University of Georgia Press, 1982.

Hemperley, Marion R., and Edwin L. Jackson. *Georgia's Boundaries: The Shaping of a State*. Athens, Ga.: Carl Vinson Institute of Government, 1993.

Kovacik, Charles F., and John J. Winberry. *South Carolina: A Geography*. Boulder, Colo.: Westview Press, 1987.

Merrell, James H. *The Indians' New World*. Chapel Hill: University of North Carolina Press, 1989.

Wallace, David Duncan. *South Carolina: A Short History*. Columbia: University of South Carolina Press, 1951.

Wright, Louis B. *South Carolina: A Bicentennial History*. New York: W.W. Norton & Company, Inc., 1976.

Great Lakes Region

ILLINOIS

Carr, Clark E. "An Address Delivered before the Faculty and Students of the University of Illinois, Illinois Day, December 3, 1911." *Illinois State Historical Society Journal* 5, no. 1 (1912): 5–24.

Davis, Charles G. "The Indian Boundary Line Under the Treaty of August 24, 1816." *Illinois State Historical Society Journal* 28, no. 1 (Apr. 1935): 26–48.

Horsley, A. Doyne. *Illinois: A Geography*. Boulder, Colo.: Westview Press, 1986.

INDIANA

Peckham, Howard H. *Indiana: A Bicentennial History*. New York: W.W. Norton & Company, Inc., 1978.

Pence, George, and Nellie C. Armstrong. *Indiana Boundaries: Territory, State, and County*. Indianapolis: Indiana Historical Bureau, 1933.

Sheehan, Mrs. Frank J. "The Northern Boundary of Indiana." *Indiana Historical Society Publications* 8, no. 6 (1928): 289–321.

Thwaites, Reuben G. "The Boundaries of Wisconsin." Collections of the State Historical Society of Wisconsin XI (1888): 451–501.

U.S. Senate. 23 Cong., 2 sess. *Boundary Line Between Indiana and Michigan*. (S. Doc. 134.) Washington: Duff Green, 1834. (Serial Set 268).

MICHIGAN

Catton, Bruce. *Michigan: A Bicentennial History*. New York: W.W. Norton & Company, Inc., 1976.

Cutcheon, Byron M., and Henry M. Utley. *Michigan as a Province, Territory and State*. Vol. 2. The Publishing Society of Michigan, 1906.

Ellis, William Donohue. *Land of the Inland Seas*. New York: Weathervane Books, 1974.

Faris, John T. *The Romance of the Boundaries*. New York: Harper & Brothers Publishers, 1926.

Gilpin, Alec R. *The Territory of Michigan*. East Lansing: Michigan State University Press, 1970.

Jones, Howard. *To the Webster-Ashburton Treaty*. Chapel Hill: The University of North Carolina Press, 1977.

Morris, Richard B. *The Peacemakers*. New York: Harper & Row, Publishers, 1965.

Quaife, M.M., and Sidney Glazer. *Michigan: From Primitive Wilderness to Industrial Commonwealth*. New York: Prentice-Hall, Inc., 1948.

Sheehan, Mrs. Frank J. "The Northern Boundary of Indiana." *Indiana Historical Society Publications* 8, no. 6 (1928): 289–321.

Smith, Alice E. *The History of Wisconsin*. Vol. 1. Madison: State Historical Society of Wisconsin, 1973.

Thwaites, Reuben G. "The Boundaries of Wisconsin." Collections of the State Historical Society of Wisconsin XI (1888): 451–501.

White, James. *Boundary Disputes and Treaties*. Toronto: Glasgow, Brook & Company, 1914.

OHIO

Cappon, Lester J., editor-in-chief. *Atlas of Early American History*. Princeton: Princeton University Press, 1976.

Faris, John T. *The Romance of the Boundaries.* New York: Harper & Brothers Publishers, 1926.

Peckham, Howard H. *Indiana: A Bicentennial History.* New York: W.W. Norton & Company, Inc., 1978.

Thwaites, Reuben G. "The Boundaries of Wisconsin." Collections of the State Historical Society of Wisconsin XI (1888): 451–501.

Weisenburger, Francis P. *The Passing of the Frontier: 1825–1850.* Vol. III of *The History of the State of Ohio.* Carl Wittke, ed. Columbus: Ohio State Archaeological and Historical Society, 1941.

White, James. *Boundary Disputes and Treaties.* Toronto: Glasgow, Brook & Company, 1914.

WISCONSIN

Austin, H. Russell. *The Wisconsin Story.* Milwaukee: The Milwaukee Journal, 1957.

Current, Richard Nelson. *Wisconsin: A Bicentennial History.* New York: W.W. Norton & Company, Inc., 1977.

Ellis, William Donohue. *Land of the Inland Seas.* New York: Weathervane Books, 1974.

Faris, John T. *The Romance of the Boundaries.* New York: Harper & Brothers Publishers, 1926.

Smith, Alice E. *The History of Wisconsin.* Vol. 1. Madison: State Historical Society of Wisconsin, 1973.

Thwaites, Reuben G. "The Boundaries of Wisconsin." Collections of the State Historical Society of Wisconsin XI (1888): 451–501.

North Central Region

IOWA

Christianson, Theodore. *Minnesota: The Land of Sky-Tinted Waters.* Chicago: The American Historical Society, Inc., 1935.

Faris, John T. *The Romance of the Boundaries.* New York: Harper & Brothers Publishers, 1926.

Landers, Frank E. "The Southern Boundary of Iowa." *Annals of Iowa* 1, no. 8 (Jan. 1895): 641–51.

Sage, Leland L. *A History of Iowa.* Ames: The Iowa State University Press, 1974.

Shambaugh, Benjamin F. "Maps Illustrative of the Boundary History of Iowa." *Iowa Journal of History and Politics* 2, no. 3 (July 1904): 369–80.

Wall, Joseph Frazier. *Iowa: A Bicentennial History.* New York: W.W. Norton & Company, Inc., 1978.

MINNESOTA

Anderson, William. "Minnesota Frames a Constitution." *Minnesota History* 36, no. 1 (March 1958): 1–12.

Blegen, Theodore C. *Minnesota: A History of the State.* Minneapolis: University of Minnesota Press, 1975.

Christianson, Theodore. *Minnesota: The Land of Sky-Tinted Waters.* Chicago: The American Historical Society, Inc., 1935.

Corey, Albert B. *The Crisis of 1830–1842 in Canadian-American Relations.* New Haven: Yale University Press, 1941.

Folwell, William Watts. *A History of Minnesota.* Vol. I. Saint Paul: Minnesota Historical Society, 1921.

Jones, Howard. *To the Webster-Ashburton Treaty.* Chapel Hill: The University of North Carolina Press, 1977.

Lass, William E. *Minnesota: A Bicentennial History.* New York: W.W. Norton & Company, Inc., 1977.

_____. "Minnesota's Separation from Wisconsin: Boundary Making on the Upper Mississippi Frontier." *Minnesota History* 50, no. 8 (1987): 309–20.

White, James. *Boundary Disputes and Treaties.* Toronto: Glasgow, Brook & Company, 1914.

NEBRASKA

Creigh, Dorothy Weyer. *Nebraska: A Bicentennial History.* New York: W.W. Norton & Company, Inc., 1977.

Ehrlich, Daniel Henry. "Problems Arising from Shifts of the Missouri River on the Eastern Border of Nebraska." *Nebraska History* 54, no. 3 (Fall 1973): 341–63.

Olson, James C., and Ronald C. Naugle. *History of Nebraska.* 3rd ed. Lincoln: University of Nebraska Press, 1997.

Watkins, Albert. "Nebraska, Mother of States." *Collections of the Nebraska State Historical Society* 17 (1913): 48–52.

NORTH DAKOTA

Anderson, Grant K. "The First Movement to Divide Dakota Territory, 1871–77." *North Dakota History* 49, no. 1 (Winter 1982): 20–28.

Jones, Howard. *To the Webster-Ashburton Treaty.* Chapel Hill: The University of North Carolina Press, 1977.

Robinson, Elwyn B. *History of North Dakota.* Lincoln: University of Nebraska Press, 1966.

Spalding, Burleigh. "Constitutional Convention, 1889." *North Dakota History* 31, no. 3 (July 1964): 151–64.

Wilkins, Robert P., and Wynona Huchette Wilkins. *North Dakota: A Bicentennial History.* New York: W.W. Norton & Company, Inc., 1977.

South Dakota

Congressional Globe, 36 Cong., 2 sess., pts. 1 and 2, Feb. 18, 1861. Washington: Government Printing Office, 1861.

Jones, Charlotte Foltz. *Mistakes That Worked.* New York: Delacorte Press, 1991.

Kingsbury, George W. *History of Dakota Territory.* Vol. II. Chicago: The S.J. Clarke Publishing Company, 1915.

Robinson, Will Grow. "South Dakota Boundaries." *Report and Historical Collections* XXXII (1964): 232–59.

Schell, Herbert S. *History of South Dakota.* Lincoln: University of Nebraska Press, 1968.

Visher, Stephen Sargent. "The Boundaries of South Dakota." *South Dakota Historical Collections* 9 (1918): 380–85.

South Central Region

Arkansas

Ashmore, Harry S. *Arkansas: A Bicentennial History.* New York: W.W. Norton & Company, Inc., 1978.

Morris, John W., Charles R. Goins, and Edwin C. McReynolds. *Historical Atlas of Oklahoma.* Norman: University of Oklahoma Press, 1976.

Writers' Program. *Arkansas: A Guide to the State.* New York: Hastings House, 1941.

Kansas

Creigh, Dorothy Weyer. *Nebraska: A Bicentennial History.* New York: W.W. Norton & Company, Inc., 1977.

Davis, Kenneth S. *Kansas: A Bicentennial History.* New York: W.W. Norton & Company, Inc., 1976.

Gower, Calvin W. "Kansas Territory and Its Boundary Question: 'Big Kansas' or 'Little Kansas'." *Kansas Historical Quarterly* XXXIII, no. 1 (Spring 1967): 1–12.

Holloway, John N. *History of Kansas.* Lafayette, Ind.: James, Emmons & Co., 1868.

Howes, Charles C. *This Place Called Kansas.* Norman: University of Oklahoma Press, 1952.

Johnston, Joseph E. "Surveying the Southern Boundary Line of Kansas." Edited by Nyle H. Miller. *Kansas Historical Quarterly* 1, no. 2 (Feb. 1932): 104–39.

Stephens, Elizabeth Pearl. *The Historical Geography of the Boundaries of Oklahoma.* Norman, Okla.: Master of Arts Thesis, 1964.

Stevens, Frank E. *Life of Stephen Arnold Douglas.* Springfield, Ill.: Illinois State Historical Society. Reprint of *Journal of the Illinois State Historical Society* XVI, no. 3 (Oct. 1923–Jan. 1924).

Louisiana

Ashmore, Harry S. *Arkansas: A Bicentennial History.* New York: W.W. Norton & Company, Inc., 1978.

Creigh, Dorothy Weyer. *Nebraska: A Bicentennial History.* New York: W.W. Norton & Company, Inc., 1977.

Frantz, Joe B. *Texas: A Bicentennial History.* New York: W.W. Norton & Company, Inc., 1976.

Kniffen, Fred B., and Sam Bowers Hilliard. *Louisiana: Its Land and People.* Rev. ed. Baton Rouge: Louisiana State University Press, 1988.

Morris, John W., Charles R. Goins, and Edwin C. McReynolds. *Historical Atlas of Oklahoma.* Norman: University of Oklahoma Press, 1976.

Stephens, Elizabeth Pearl. *The Historical Geography of the Boundaries of Oklahoma.* Norman, Okla.: University of Oklahoma. Master of Arts thesis, 1964.

Taylor, Joe Gray. *Louisiana: A Bicentennial History.* New York: W.W. Norton & Company, Inc., 1976.

White, C. Albert. *A History of the Rectangular Survey System.* Washington: Government Printing Office, n.d.

Missouri

Houck, Louis. *A History of Missouri.* Vol. I. Chicago: R.R. Donnelley & Sons Company, 1908.

Kelley, Max L. "John Hardeman Walker — Cattle King." Jefferson City, Missouri, Sept. 1930. Reprinted in "Missouri History Not Found in Textbooks." *Missouri Historical Review* XXV, no. 2 (Jan. 1931): 383–85.

McCandless, Perry. *A History of Missouri: 1820 to 1860.* Vol. II. Columbia: University of Missouri Press, 1972.

Nagel, Paul C. *Missouri: A Bicentennial History.* New York: W.W. Norton & Company, Inc., 1977.

Rafferty, Milton D. *Missouri: A Geography.* Boulder, Colo.: Westview Press, 1980.

U.S. House. 27 Cong., 2 sess. *Northern Boundary of Missouri.* No place or publisher, 1841-42. (Serial Set 402).

Oklahoma

Clark, Joseph Stanley. "The Northern Boundary of Oklahoma." *Chronicles of Oklahoma* 15, no. 3 (1937): 271–90.

Harbour, Emma Estill. "A Brief History of the Red River Country Since 1803." *Chronicles of Oklahoma* 16, no. 1 (1938): 86–87.

Morgan, H. Wayne, and Anne Hodges Morgan. *Oklahoma: A Bicentennial History.* New York: W.W. Norton & Company, Inc., 1977.

Morris, John W., Charles R. Goins, and Edwin C. McReynolds. *Historical Atlas of Oklahoma*. Norman: University of Oklahoma Press, 1976.

"Notes on the Boundary Dispute Between the State of Texas and the State of Oklahoma." *Chronicles of Oklahoma* 36, no. 4 (1958–59): 483–85. [This document is a letter written by George I. Shannon to Henry B. Bass.]

Parker, Mary Ann. "The Elusive Meridian." *Chronicles of Oklahoma* 51, no. 2 (1973): 150–58.

Stephens, Elizabeth Pearl. *The Historical Geography of the Boundaries of Oklahoma*. Norman, Okla.: University of Oklahoma. Master of Arts thesis, 1964.

TEXAS

Brinkley, Alan. *The Unfinished Nation: A Concise History of the American People*. Boston: McGraw-Hill, 1993.

Calvert, Robert A., and Arnoldo De León. *The History of Texas*. Arlington Heights, Ill.: Harlan Davidson, Inc., 1990.

Faris, John T. *The Romance of the Boundaries*. New York: Harper & Brothers Publishers, 1926.

Fehrenbach, T. R. *Lone Star: A History of Texas and the Texans*. New York: The Macmillan Company, 1968.

Frantz, Joe B. *Texas: A Bicentennial History*. New York: W.W. Norton & Company, Inc., 1976.

John, George O'Brien. *Texas History: An Outline*. New York: Henry Holt and Company, 1935.

Webb, Walter Prescott, editor-in-chief. *The Handbook of Texas*. Vol. I. Austin: The Texas State Historical Association, 1952.

Whisenhunt, Donald W. *Texas: A Sesquicentennial Celebration*. Austin: Eakin Press, 1984.

Rocky Mountain Region

ARIZONA

Bancroft, Hubert Howe. *History of Arizona and New Mexico*. San Francisco: The History Company, 1889.

Comeaux, Malcolm L. "Attempts to Establish and Change a Western Boundary." *Annals of the Association of American Geographers* 72, no. 2 (1982): 254–71.

Powell, John Wesley. *Down the Colorado*. New York: E.P. Dutton & Co., Inc., 1969.

Powell, Lawrence Clark. *Arizona: A Bicentennial History*. New York: W.W. Norton & Company, Inc., 1976.

Sacks, B. *Be It Enacted: The Creation of the Territory of Arizona*. Phoenix: Arizona Historical Foundation, 1964.

COLORADO

Abbott, Carl, Stephen J. Leonard, and David McComb. *Colorado: A History of the Centennial State*. Boulder, Colo.: Colorado Associated University Press, 1982.

Bancroft, Hubert Howe. *History of Nevada, Colorado, and Wyoming*. San Francisco: The History Company, 1890.

Clark, Joseph Stanley. "The Northern Boundary of Oklahoma." *Chronicles of Oklahoma* 15, no. 3 (1937): 271–90.

Congressional Globe, 36 Cong., 1 sess., pt. 3, May 11, 1860. Washington: John C. Rives, 1860.

Congressional Globe, 36 Cong., 2 sess., pts. 1 and 2, Feb. 18, 1861. Washington: Government Printing Office, 1861.

Frazier, J.L. "Prologue To Colorado Territory." *Colorado Magazine* 38, no. 3 (July 1961): 161–73.

Fritz, Percy Stanley. *Colorado: The Centennial State*. New York: Prentice-Hall, Inc., 1941.

Hafen, LeRoy R. *Colorado: The Story of A Western Commonwealth*. Denver: The Peerless Publishing Company, 1933.

Hafen, L.R. "Steps to Statehood in Colorado." *The Colorado Magazine* III, no. 3 (March 1926): 97–110.

Johnson, Frank Minitree. "The Colorado–New Mexico Boundary." *The Colorado Magazine* IV, no. 3 (May 1927): 112–15.

Lamar, Howard R. *The Far Southwest 1846–1912: A Territorial History*. Rev. ed. Albuquerque: University of New Mexico Press, 2000.

Noel, Thomas J., Paul F. Mahoney, and Richard E. Stevens. *Historical Atlas of Colorado*. Norman, Okla.: University of Oklahoma Press, 1994.

Paxson, Frederic. "The Territory of Colorado." *American Historical Review* 12, no. 1 (Oct. 1906): 53–65.

Rocky Mountain News, various issues Apr. 1859–Mar. 1861.

Sprague, Marshall. *Colorado: A Bicentennial History*. New York: W.W. Norton & Company, Inc., 1976.

MONTANA

Congressional Globe, 36 Cong., 2 sess., pts. 1 and 2, Feb. 18, 1861. Washington: Government Printing Office, 1861.

Jones, Howard. *To the Webster-Ashburton Treaty*. Chapel Hill: The University of North Carolina Press, 1977.

Malone, Michael P., Richard B. Roeder, and William L. Lang. *Montana: A History of Two Centuries*. Seattle: University of Washington Press, 1976.

Murray, Genevieve. "The 'Lost' Dakota Territory." *North Dakota History* 35, no. 1 (Winter 1968): 63–67.

Palmer, Edith. "The Shape of Montana." *The Dillon Examiner*, Dec. 25, 1946. [On file at Montana Historical Society Library.]

U.S. Senate, 39 Cong., 1 sess. *Memorial of the Legislative Assembly of Montana.* (S. Misc. Doc. 111). Washington: Government Printing Office, 1866. (Serial Set 1239).

Walter, Dave. Letter written to a fourth-grade class by the Montana Historical Society reference librarian concerning Montana's boundaries. [On file at Montana Historical Society Library.]

Wheeler, W.F. *An Historical Fact.* [Typewritten notes in MC 65, Box 2, Montana Historical Society Library.]

White, James. *Boundary Disputes and Treaties.* Toronto: Glasgow, Brook & Company, 1914.

NEW MEXICO

Baldwin, P.M. "A Historical Note on the Boundaries of New Mexico." *New Mexico Historical Review* V, no. 2 (1930): 117–37.

Bancroft, Hubert Howe. *History of Arizona and New Mexico.* San Francisco: The History Company, 1889.

Comeaux, Malcolm L. "Attempts to Establish and Change a Western Boundary." *Annals of the Association of American Geographers* 72, no. 2 (1982): 254–71.

Keleher, William A. *Turmoil in New Mexico, 1846–1868.* Albuquerque: University of New Mexico Press, 1952.

Larson, Robert W. *New Mexico's Quest for Statehood, 1846–1912.* Albuquerque: The University of New Mexico Press, 1968.

Simmons, Marc. *New Mexico: A Bicentennial History.* New York: W.W. Norton & Company, Inc., 1977.

Stegmaier, Mark J. *Texas, New Mexico, and the Compromise of 1850.* Kent, Ohio: The Kent State University Press, 1996.

UTAH

Bancroft, Hubert Howe. *History of Arizona and New Mexico.* San Francisco: The History Company, 1889.

Bergeson, Nancy. *History of the Forty-Second Parallel as a Political Boundary Between Utah and Idaho.* Logan, Utah: Utah State University, 1983.

Kenney, Bruce Ericksen. *The Historical Development of the Boundaries of Utah.* Chico State University. Master's thesis, 1991.

Peterson, Charles S. *Utah: A Bicentennial History.* New York: W.W. Norton & Company, Inc., 1977.

Poll, Richard D, general editor. *Utah's History.* Provo: Brigham Young University Press, 1978.

Pomeroy, Earl. *The Pacific Slope: A History of California, Oregon, Washington, Idaho, Utah, and Nevada.* Seattle: University of Washington Press, 1965.

Whitney, Orson F. *History of Utah.* Salt Lake City: George Q. Cannon & Sons Co., Publishers, 1892.

WYOMING

Bancroft, Hubert Howe. *History of Nevada, Colorado, and Wyoming.* San Francisco: The History Company, 1890.

Brown, Robert Harold. *Wyoming: A Geography.* Boulder, Colo.: Westview Press, 1980.

Cheyenne Leader. Various issues Oct. 22, 1867–July 27 1868.

Congressional Globe, 40 Cong. 2 sess., pt. 3, June 3, 1868. Washington: Government Printing Office, 1868.

Congressional Globe, 40 Cong. 2 sess., pt. 5, July 7, 1868. Washington: Government Printing Office, 1868.

Coutant, C.G. "History of Wyoming." *Annals of Wyoming* 13, no. 1 (Jan. 1941): 74–80.

Erwin, Marie H. "Maps of Early Wyoming Tell Fascinating Story." *Annals of Wyoming* 11, no. 1 (Oct. 1939): 281–92.

_____. *Wyoming Historical Blue Book.* Denver: Bradford-Robinson Printing Co., 1946.

Gould, Lewis L. *Wyoming: A Political History, 1868–1896.* New Haven: Yale University Press, 1968.

Kenney, Bruce Ericksen. *The Historical Development of the Boundaries of Utah.* Chico State University. Master's thesis, 1991.

Larson, T.A. *History of Wyoming.* 2nd ed., rev. Lincoln: University of Nebraska Press, 1978.

_____. *Wyoming: A Bicentennial History.* New York: W.W. Norton & Company, Inc., 1977.

West Region

CALIFORNIA

Baldwin, P.M. "A Historical Note on the Boundaries of New Mexico." *New Mexico Historical Review,* V, no. 2 (1930): 117–37.

Bancroft, Hubert Howe. *History of Arizona and New Mexico.* San Francisco: The History Company, 1889.

Bergeson, Nancy. *History of the Forty-Second Parallel as a Political Boundary Between Utah and Idaho.* Logan, Utah: Utah State University, 1983.

Cleland, Robert Glass. *A History of California: The American Period.* New York: The Macmillan Company, 1923.

Daniels, George G., ed. *The Spanish West*. New York: Time-Life Books, 1976.

Hunt, Rockwell D., and Nellie van de Grift Sánchez. *A Short History of California*. New York: Thomas Y. Crowell Company Publishers, 1929.

John, George O'Brien. *Texas History: An Outline*. New York: Henry Holt and Company, 1935.

Kenney, Bruce Ericksen. *The Historical Development of the Boundaries of Utah*. Chico State University. Master's thesis, 1991.

Lavender, David. *California: A Bicentennial History*. New York: W.W. Norton & Company, Inc., 1976.

Stegmaier, Mark J. *Texas, New Mexico, and the Compromise of 1850*. Kent, Ohio: The Kent State University Press, 1996.

Thomas, Benjamin E. "The California-Nevada Boundary." *Annals of the Association of American Geographers* 42, no. 1 (1952): 51–68.

Uzes, Francois D. *Chaining the Land: A History of Surveying in California*. Sacramento: Landmark Enterprises, 1977.

IDAHO

Arrington, Leonard J. *History of Idaho*. Vol. 1. Moscow: University of Idaho Press, 1994.

Bergeson, Nancy. *History of the Forty-Second Parallel as a Political Boundary Between Utah and Idaho*. Logan, Utah: Utah State University, 1983.

Collins, E. Harry. "Why the Idaho Panhandle." *Pacific Northwesterner* 18, no. 3 (1974): 41–46.

Deutsch, Herman J. "The Evolution of Territorial and State Boundaries in the Inland Empire of the Pacific Northwest." *Pacific Northwest Quarterly* 51, no. 2 (April 1960): 115–31.

Green, D. Brooks. "The Idaho-Wyoming Boundary: A Problem in Location." *Idaho Yesterdays* 23, no. 1 (Spring 1979): 10–14.

Hailey, John. *The History of Idaho*. Boise: Syms-York Company, Inc., 1910.

Hulse, James W. "Idaho Versus Nevada: The 1887 Struggle Between Nevada's Senator and Idaho's Governor." *Idaho Yesterdays* 29, no. 3 (Fall 1985): 26–31.

"Idaho's Centennial: How Idaho Was Created in 1863." *Idaho Yesterdays* 7, no. 1 (Spring 1963): 44–58.

Peterson, F. Ross. *Idaho: A Bicentennial History*. New York: W.W. Norton & Company, Inc., 1976.

Pomeroy, Earl. *The Pacific Slope: A History of California, Oregon, Washington, Idaho, Utah, and Nevada*. Seattle: University of Washington Press, 1965.

"Territorial Governors of Idaho." *Idaho Yesterdays* 7, no. 1 (Spring 1963): 14–23.

Thomas, Benjamin E. "Boundaries and Internal Problems of Idaho." *The Geographical Review* 39 (1949): 99–109.

Wells, Merle W. "Idaho's Season of Political Distress." *Montana: The Magazine of Western History* 37, no. 4 (Autumn 1987): 58–67.

_____. "The Idaho-Montana Boundary." *Idaho Yesterdays* 12, no. 4 (Winter 1968): 6–9.

_____. "Walla Walla's Vision of a Greater Washington." *Idaho Yesterdays* 10, no. 3 (Fall 1966): 20–31.

White, James. *Boundary Disputes and Treaties*. Toronto: Glasgow, Brook & Company, 1914.

NEVADA

Bancroft, Hubert Howe. *History of Nevada, Colorado, and Wyoming*. San Francisco: The History Company, 1890.

Hulse, James W. "The California-Nevada Boundary: The History of a Conflict." *Nevada Historical Society Quarterly* XXIII, no. 2 (Summer 1980): 97–109.

_____. *The Silver State*. Reno: University of Nevada Press, 1991.

Laxalt, Robert. *Nevada: A Bicentennial History*. New York: W.W. Norton & Company, Inc., 1977.

Pomeroy, Earl. *The Pacific Slope: A History of California, Oregon, Washington, Idaho, Utah, and Nevada*. Seattle: University of Washington Press, 1965.

Shamberger, Hugh A. "The Evolution of Nevada by Boundaries." In *Nevada: The Silver State*. Vol. I. Carson City: Western States Historical Publishers, Inc., 1970: 145–49.

OREGON

Barry, J. Neilson. "Oregon Boundaries." *Oregon Historical Quarterly* 33 (1932): 259–67.

Congressional Globe, 34 Cong., 1 sess., June 24, 1856. Washington: John C. Rives, 1856.

Congressional Globe, 34 Cong., 3 sess., Jan. 31, 1857. Washington: John C. Rives, 1857.

Creigh, Dorothy Weyer. *Nebraska: A Bicentennial History*. New York: W.W. Norton & Company, Inc., 1977.

Deutsch, Herman J. "The Evolution of Territorial and State Boundaries in the Inland Empire of the Pacific Northwest." *Pacific Northwest Quarterly* 51, no. 2 (April 1960): 115–31.

Dodds, Gordon B. *Oregon: A Bicentennial History*. New York: W.W. Norton & Company, Inc., 1977.

Dryden, Cecil. *Dryden's History of Washington*. Portland: Binfords & Mort, Publishers, 1968.

Faris, John T. *The Romance of the Boundaries*. New York: Harper & Brothers Publishers, 1926.

"Idaho's Centennial: How Idaho Was Created in 1863." *Idaho Yesterdays* 7, no. 1 (Spring 1963): 44–58.

Johannsen, Robert W. *The Frontier, the Union, and Stephen A. Douglas.* Chicago: University of Illinois Press, 1989.

Jones, Howard. *To the Webster-Ashburton Treaty.* Chapel Hill: The University of North Carolina Press, 1977.

Landrum, Francis S. "A Major Monument: Oregon-California Boundary." *Oregon Historical Quarterly* 72, no. 1 (1971): 5–53.

McArthur, Lewis A. "The Oregon State Boundary." *Oregon Historical Quarterly* 37, no. 4 (Dec. 1936): 301–07.

Pollard, Lancaster. *Oregon and the Pacific Northwest.* Portland: Binfords & Mort, Publishers, 1946.

Snowden, Clinton A. *History of Washington.* Vols. I and III. New York: The Century History Company, 1909.

U.S. House. 35 Cong., 1 sess. *The Preamble, Constitution, and Schedule, adopted by the People of the Territory of Oregon, preparatory to admission into the Union of the States.* (H. Misc. Doc 38.) Washington: James B. Steedman, Printer, 1858. (Serial Set 961).

U.S. House. 44 Cong., 2 sess. *Boundaries of the State of Oregon.* (H. Rpt. 764). Washington: Government Printing Office, 1876. (Serial Set 1712).

WASHINGTON

Clark, Norman H. *Washington: A Bicentennial History.* New York: W.W. Norton & Company, Inc., 1976.

Deutsch, Herman J. "The Evolution of Territorial and State Boundaries in the Inland Empire of the Pacific Northwest." *Pacific Northwest Quarterly* 51, no. 3 (July 1960): 115–31.

Dryden, Cecil. *Dryden's History of Washington.* Portland: Binfords & Mort, Publishers, 1968.

Faris, John T. *The Romance of the Boundaries.* New York: Harper & Brothers Publishers, 1926.

Kingston, C.S. "The North Idaho Annexation Issue." *Washington Historical Quarterly* XXI, no. 2 (April 1930): 133–37.

Painter, Harry M. "The Birth of a State." In *Building a State: Washington.* Vol. III. Edited by Charles Miles and O. B. Sperlin. Tacoma, Wash.: Washington State Historical Society, 1940.

Snowden, Clinton A. *History of Washington.* Vols. I and III. New York: The Century History Company, 1909.

White, James. *Boundary Disputes and Treaties.* Toronto: Glasgow, Brook & Company, 1914.

Wunder, John R. "Tampering with the Northwest Frontier: The Accidental Design of the Washington/Idaho Boundary." *Pacific Northwest Quarterly* 68, no. 1 (Jan. 1977): 1–12.

Noncontiguous Region

ALASKA

Bailey, Thomas A. "Theodore Roosevelt and the Alaska Boundary Settlement." In *Alaska and Its History.* Morgan B. Sherwood, ed. Seattle: University of Washington Press, 1967.

Clark, Henry W. *History of Alaska.* New York: The Macmillan Company, 1930.

Faris, John T. *The Romance of the Boundaries.* New York: Harper & Brothers Publishers, 1926.

Hulley, Clarence C. *Alaska 1741–1953.* Portland: Binfords & Mort, Publishers, 1953.

Hunt, William R. *Alaska: A Bicentennial History.* New York: W.W. Norton & Company, Inc., 1976.

Mazour, Anatole G. "The Prelude to Russia's Departure from America." In *Alaska and Its History.* Morgan B. Sherwood, ed. Seattle: University of Washington Press, 1967.

Tompkins, Stuart R. "Drawing the Alaskan Boundary." *Canadian Historical Review* 26, no. 1 (1945): 1–24.

White, James. *Boundary Disputes and Treaties.* Toronto: Glasgow, Brook & Company, 1914.

HAWAII

Armstrong, R. Warwick, ed. *Atlas of Hawaii.* Honolulu: University Press of Hawaii, 1973.

Kuykendall, Ralph S., and A. Grove Day. *Hawaii: A History.* New York: Prentice-Hall, Inc., 1948.

Lueras, Leonard, ed. *Hawaii.* Hong Kong: Apa Productions, Ltd., 1980.

Rayson, Ann. *Modern Hawaiian History.* Rev. ed. Honolulu: The Bess Press, 1994.

Tabrah, Ruth M. *Hawaii: A Bicentennial History.* New York: W.W. Norton & Company, Inc., 1980.

Map Sources

*Note: The author has recreated all maps to include only such information as was deemed necessary to illustrate the text. Map designations are in **boldface** type; the page number of the source immediately follows.*

AAA Road Atlas. Chicago: American Automobile Association, 1993: **3.7**, 50; **3.9**, 76; **3.14**, 102; **4.4**, 44.

Abernethy, Thomas Perkins. *The Formative Period in Alabama, 1815–1828.* Tuscaloosa: The University of Alabama Press, 1965: **5.2**, 92.

Arrington, Leonard J. *History of Idaho.* Vol. I. Moscow: University of Idaho Press, 1994: **10.9**, 212.

Bailey, Thomas A. "Theodore Roosevelt and the Alaska Boundary Settlement." In *Alaska and Its History.* Morgan B. Sherwood, ed. Seattle: University of Washington Press, 1967: **11.3**, 392.

Blegen, Theodore C. *Minnesota: A History of the State.* Minneapolis: University of Minnesota Press, 1975: **7.6**, 218.

Brown, Douglas Summers. *The Catawba Indians.* Columbia: The University of South Carolina Press, 1966: **5.12**, **5.13**, 32.

Calendar Creator Clip Art, SoftKey International Inc., 1996: **2.2**; **2.8**; **2.9**; **2.10**; **2.11**; **3.4**; **3.8**; **3.10**; **3.13**; **4.2**; **4.8**; **4.10**; **4.11**; **5.4**; **6.13**; **10.2**; **11.1**; **11.2**; **11.4**.

Comeaux, Malcolm L. "Attempts to Establish and Change a Western Boundary." *Annals of the Association of American Geographers* 72, no. 2 (1982). Washington, D.C.: Association of American Geographers: **9.3**, 264.

Connecticut/Rhode Island Atlas & Gazetteer. Yarmouth, Maine: DeLorme, 1999: **2.3**, 53.

Corey, Albert B. *The Crisis of 1830–1842 in Canadian-American Relations.* New Haven: Yale University Press, 1941: **2.12**, 163.

DiLisio, James E. *Maryland: A Geography.* Boulder, Colo.: Westview Press, 1983: **3.3**, 17; **3.5**, 86.

Ehrlich, Daniel Henry. "Problems Arising from Shifts of the Missouri River on the Eastern Border of Nebraska." *Nebraska History* 54, no. 3 (Fall 1973). Nebraska State Historical Society: **7.12**, 351.

Flick, Alexander C., ed. *History of the State of New York.* Vol. V. New York: Columbia University Press, 1934: **3.12**, 86.

Gill, Crispin. *Mayflower Remembered: A History of the Plymouth Pilgrims.* New York: Taplinger Publishing Company, 1970: **2.7**, 62–63.

Hanna, Kathryn Abbey. *Florida: Land of Change.* 2nd ed. Chapel Hill: The University of North Carolina Press, 1948: **5.5**, 155.

Harrison, Lowell H., and James C. Klotter. *A New History of Kentucky.* Lexington: The University Press of Kentucky, 1997: **4.7**, 22.

Hemperley, Marion R., and Edwin L. Jackson. *Georgia's Boundaries: The Shaping of a State.* Athens, Ga.: Carl Vinson Institute of Government, 1993: **5.8**, 32; **5.9**, 97.

Hooker, Roland Mather. *Boundaries of Connecticut.* Published for the Tercentenary Commission of the State of Connecticut. New Haven: Yale University Press, 1933: **2.4**, 25.

"Idaho's Centennial: How Idaho Was Created in 1863." *Idaho Yesterdays* 7, no. 1 (Spring 1963): **10.4**, 57; **10.7**, 55.

Kagan, Hilde Heun, editor in charge. *The American Heritage Pictorial Atlas of United States History.* New York: American Heritage Publishing Co., Inc., 1966: **7.5**, **7.8**, **8.7**, **8.12**, 200–01; **7.7**, **10.12**, 158; **8.5**, 188–89; **9.4**, **9.5**, **9.12**, **9.13**, 244.

Kenney, Bruce Ericksen. *The Historical Development of the Boundaries of Utah.* Chico State University. Master's thesis, 1991: **9.9**, 60.

Kentucky Atlas & Gazetteer. Yarmouth, Maine: DeLorme, 1997: **4.3**, 32; **4.6**, 81.

Kniffen, Fred B., and Sam Bowers Hilliard. *Louisiana: Its Land and People.* Rev. ed. Baton Rouge: Louisiana State University Press, 1988: **8.8**, 138.

Missouri Atlas & Gazetteer. Yarmouth, Maine: DeLorme, 1998: **8.6**, 19; **8.11**, 69.

Morris, John W., Charles R. Goins, and Edwin C. McReynolds. *Historical Atlas of Oklahoma.* Norman: University of Oklahoma Press, 1976: **8.4**, 61.

Murray, Genevieve. "The 'Lost' Dakota Territory." *North Dakota History* 35, no. 1 (Winter 1968). State Historical Society of North Dakota: **9.6**, 62.

North Carolina Atlas & Gazetteer. Freeport, Maine: DeLorme Mapping, 1992: **4.9**, 24.

Patrick, Rembert W. *Florida Under Five Flags.* Gainesville: University of Florida Press, 1945: **5.3**, 27.

Peckham, Howard H. *Indiana: A Bicentennial History.* New York: W.W. Norton & Company, Inc., 1978: **6.6**, **6.11**, 37.

Premier World Atlas. Chicago: Rand McNally and Company, 1997: **2.5**, 132; **3.2**, 100; **3.6**, 14; **10.13**, 140; **11.5**, 104.

Quaife, M.M., and Sidney Glazer. *Michigan: From Primitive Wilderness to Industrial Commonwealth.* New York: Prentice-Hall, Inc., 1948: **6.2**, 160.

Rafferty, Milton D. *Missouri: A Geography.* Boulder, Colo.: Westview Press, 1980: **4.5**, 43; **7.13**, 42; **8.10**, 41.

Runquist, Phillip. *Outline Maps of U.S. States and Regions.* New York: Dover Publications, 1994: **2.1**, **3.1**, **4.1**, **5.1**, **6.1**, **7.1**, **8.1**, **9.1**, **10.1**, plates 16 and 17.

Sage, Leland L. *A History of Iowa.* Ames: The Iowa State University Press, 1974: **6.14**, 53; **7.3**, 85; **7.4**, 66.

Shambaugh, Benjamin F. "Maps Illustrative of the Boundary History of Iowa." *Iowa Journal of History and Politics* 2, no. 3 (July 1904). State Historical Society of Iowa: **7.2**, 377.

Sheehan, Mrs. Frank J. "The Northern Boundary of Indiana." *Indiana Historical Society Publications* 8, no. 6 (1928). Printed for the Society: **6.8**, 290.

Thomas, Benjamin E. "Boundaries and Internal Problems of Idaho." *The Geographical Review* 39 (1949). American Geographical Society, **10.5**, 104.

_____. "The California-Nevada Boundary." *Annals of the Association of American Geographers* 42, no. 1 (1952). Washington, D.C.: Association of American Geographers: **10.8**, 57.

Trewartha, Glen T., Arthur H. Robinson, and Edwin H. Hammond. *Physical Elements of Geography.* New York: McGraw-Hill Book Company, 1967: **1.2**, 15.

Weisenburger, Francis P. *The Passing of the Frontier: 1825–1850.* Vol. III of *The History of the State of Ohio.* Carl Wittke, ed. Columbus: Ohio State Archaeological and Historical Society, 1941: **6.12**, 307.

Wells, Merle W. "The Idaho-Montana Boundary." *Idaho Yesterdays* 12, no. 4 (Winter 1968). Idaho Historical Society: **10.4**, 6.

Williams, John Alexander. *West Virginia: A Bicentennial History.* New York: W.W. Norton & Company, Inc., 1976: **4.12**, 79.

Van Zandt, Franklin K. *Boundaries of the United States and the Several States.* Washington, D.C.: U.S. Government Printing Office (Geological Survey Professional Paper 909), 1976: **1.1**, **8.14**, 11; **2.6**, 16; **3.11**, 76; **5.6**, **5.7**, 101; **5.10**, **5.11**, 106; **6.3**, **6.4**, **6.5**, **6.7**, 114; **6.9**, **6.10**, 128; **6.15**, **6.16**, 132; **7.9**, **7.10**, **7.11**, 137; **7.14**, **7.15**, **7.16**, 136; **8.2**, **8.3**, 119; **8.9**, 108; **8.13**, 140; **8.15**, **8.16**, 121; **9.2**, **9.7**, **9.8**, 162; **9.10**, **9.11**, 160; **10.3**, 154; **10.6**, 157; **10.10**, **10.11**, **10.14**, 156.

INDEX